The Diplomat

The Diplomat

**LESTER PEARSON and
the SUEZ CRISIS**

Antony Anderson

For my parents

Edited by Judy Phillips.
Cover and page design by Julie Scriver.
Cover photo detail: United Nations.
Printed in Canada.
10 9 8 7 6 5 4 3 2 1

We acknowledge the generous support of the Government of Canada, the Canada Council for the Arts, and the Government of New Brunswick.

Nous reconnaissons l'appui généreux du gouvernement du Canada, du Conseil des arts du Canada, et du gouvernement du Nouveau-Brunswick.

Goose Lane Editions
500 Beaverbrook Court, Suite 330
Fredericton, New Brunswick
CANADA E3B 5X4
www.gooselane.com

Library and Archives Canada Cataloguing in Publication

Anderson, Antony, author
    The diplomat : Lester Pearson and the Suez Crisis / Antony Anderson.

Includes bibliographical references and index.
Issued in print and electronic formats.
ISBN 978-0-86492-874-0 (bound). --
ISBN 978-0-86492-803-0 (epub). --
ISBN 978-0-86492-843-6 (mobi)

1. Pearson, Lester B., 1897-1972.
2. Egypt--History--Intervention, 1956.
3. United Nations Emergency Force--History.
4. United Nations--Peacekeeping forces--History.
5. Canada--Foreign relations--1945-.
6. Egypt--Foreign relations--1952-1970.
7. Suez Canal (Egypt)--History. I. Title.

FC623.S84A53 2015   971.063'3
C2015-901866-8   C2015-901867-6

Contents

Preface

Born Canadian overseas, visiting only during summer holidays, and finally moving here for good at age eighteen, I found myself in an unknown country which I set out to explore in very conscious fashion. As I mapped my way through the interweaving narratives that make up our collective story, Lester Pearson's name surfaced again and again. As a civil servant and foreign minister, he played an extraordinary role in shaping how we act in the world and his wise, pragmatic diplomacy during the 1940s and 1950s culminated in him receiving the Nobel Prize for Peace. That legacy alone would mark him out as an exceptional citizen. Then as prime minister during the 1960s, he presided over the country's most creative post-war government. Heading an embattled minority, he introduced social legislation that still defines us (medicare, the national pension plan, the trial abolition of capital punishment), laid the foundations for official bilingualism and a more meaningful partnership between French and English Canada, brought in our own system of national honours, and raised the symbol that flies above all our regional and linguistic divisions, the Maple Leaf flag. This modest son of a Methodist minister, born in the nineteenth century, helped to create the twentieth-century Canada that I admire and treasure so much, a country where more and more of us could bring out the best in ourselves in a more generous and inclusive society. In the 1990s, I decided to make a documentary about Pearson, something that even then hadn't been done in two decades.

In that bewildering season of constitutional angst that seemed to imperil Confederation itself, I managed to raise enough funds to film interviews with many of Pearson's former colleagues in politics and diplomacy. Unfortunately, I got stranded on the brink of editing, twice securing broadcast licences and twice seeing them fall apart. Even when I worked at the Dominion Institute producing historical television programmes, I could not raise the interest and the post-production funds to finish my epic-in-waiting—and wait it did. I was encouraged not to abandon the project entirely when the Donner Canadian Foundation provided a grant to create a website on Pearson and Suez, www.suezcrisis. ca.

Eventually, two people whom I find very hard to deflect, my wife, Litsa Sourtzis, and my comrade-in-arms at the Dominion Institute, Rudyard Griffiths, simultaneously began to suggest and then insist that I turn my interviews and research into a book. I resisted, relented, and decided to focus on Suez and how Pearson convinced the UN to create the first peacekeeping force. Here I gladly acknowledge the milestones in my wandering through the labyrinth to understand the man and his actions.

Like anyone who writes about Lester Pearson, I owe a huge intellectual debt to John English and his excellent two-volume biography, *Shadow of Heaven: The Life of Lester Pearson, Volume One, 1897–1948* and *The Worldly Years: The Life of Lester Pearson, Volume Two, 1949–1972*. As I wrote over the years, these books were constantly at hand for guidance and inspiration. From the first time I interviewed him in 1993, Professor English graciously fielded all my numerous queries. If he had written a full account of Suez, there would have been no need for mine. During my initial filming and on subsequent documentaries, I also interviewed two of Canada's most accomplished historians, Robert Bothwell and Jack Granatstein, and was influenced and enlightened by their insights. Along with Professor English, they often felt like my unofficial thesis advisers.

When I began the book, I soon realized there was no really full account of Pearson's diplomatic wizardry at Suez. I of course turned to Michael G. Fry's landmark essay, "Canada, the North Atlantic and the U.N.," published in *Suez 1956: The Crisis and Its Consequences* in 1989, still the best single article and starting point for any scholar on this topic. The indispensable source of official documents is the twenty-second volume of *Documents on Canadian External Relations*, edited by Greg Donaghy, head of the historical section at the Department of Foreign Affairs, Trade and Development. Dr. Donaghy has also been incredibly helpful with my queries over the years.

For a quarter century after its publication in 1964, the key text on Pearson's role remained journalist Terence Robertson's *Crisis: The Inside Story of the Suez Conspiracy*. A historian himself, and keen to shape the version of history he wanted to prevail, then-Prime Minister Pearson gave Robertson unprecedented access to numerous highly sensitive cables from External Affairs, which Robertson paraphrased as narrative or dialogue. Pearson also asked senior officials to talk with Robertson off the record—privileged access allowed no one else. As well, Pearson himself met with Robertson for an interview. Unfortunately, I could not locate a copy of the interview, nor indeed any of Robertson's research, in his papers at McMaster University. Mrs. Robertson told me that after her husband's death, people dispatched by the publisher showed up and wheeled away a huge filing cabinet, possibly with the research in it. I checked the McClelland & Stewart papers, also at McMaster, and searched Pearson's papers at Library and Archives Canada, all to no avail. Aside from not being allowed to quote directly from the External Affairs memos and cables, my major qualm with Robertson's book stems from the great deal of dialogue he recreated seven to eight years after the fact. There are also various errors in his timeline of events. One of Pearson's key officials during the crisis, Geoff Murray, told me that he found some of the scenes overly dramatized to the point of distortion. Robertson apparently admitted to Murray that he hoped his book would be turned into a Hollywood film. Still, both Murray and another key player, John Holmes, praised the book, saying the essentials were solid, as indeed they are.

Aside from talking with Robertson, Pearson gave only one other lengthy on-the-record interview on Suez, and that was to the CBC for his television memoirs. His editors used this to complete the draft chapter he had sketched out for his written memoirs shortly before he died. Pearson's account in his memoirs is at once frank and restrained, limited by the fact that he didn't complete it himself, and what he did write was done while many of the central actors were still alive and thus he could not help but be ever diplomatic.

In 2009, Michael K. Carroll produced a good account of the actual peacekeeping mission Pearson helped to set up, *Pearson's Peacekeepers*.

Canada and the United Nations Emergency Force, 1956–67, and this concentrates on the story where I leave off. In 2006, John Melady published *Pearson's Prize: Canada and the Suez Crisis*, a short, solid summary that did not break any new ground. Since Robertson's 1964 book and Professor Fry's 1989 article, no one has produced a major work on how and why Pearson convinced the United Nations to take a chance on sending a peacekeeping force to Egypt.

Given that my book began as a documentary, I inevitably spent a great deal of time simply trying to raise money just to get started. I was lucky to receive support from some of Pearson's former colleagues and friends, most of whom, alas, are no longer with us. Nonetheless, I would feel remiss if I did not express thanks for their support and also to those others who helped make this odyssey possible. The Hon. Keith Davey met with me several times to offer tactical advice and open up his formidable list of contacts, yielding contributions from Hon. David Collenette, Hon. J. Trevor Eyton, Hon. Jon Gerrard, Hon. Daniel Lang, and Hamilton Southam, as well as Onex Corporation and Power Corporation. The Massey Foundation, William B. Harris, and Hon. Hartland de Molson were especially generous. These funds enabled me to capture the interviews that provide some of the most original material in the book.

As the work progressed, the following historians kindly agreed to read specific chapters: Robert Craig Brown, Phillip Buckner, Greg Donaghy, Jack Granatstein, John Hilliker, Wm. Roger Louis, Stuart Macdonald, Timothy J. Paris, Neil Semple, Charles D. Smith, and Michael T. Thornhill. They all offered invaluable comments and suggestions and thankfully caught some factual errors. I am especially grateful to John English, who read my first draft, and Robert Bothwell, who read the final draft.

Through the years of research, I received excellent assistance from the following staff at Library and Archives Canada, even as budgets were cut: Michel Brideau, Maureen Hoogenraad, Cédric Lafontaine, Alix McEwen, Ilene McKenna, Rebecca Murray, Sylvie Robitaille, Dominique Taylor, and especially Paulette Dozois.

My thanks also extend to Kevin M. Bailey, Dwight D. Eisenhower Library; Marilyn Bentley, Association for Diplomatic Studies and Training; Samantha Blake, BBC Written Archives Centre; Deirdre Bryden,

Queen's University Archives; Remi Dubuisson, United Nations archives; Clark Davey, formerly with the *Globe and Mail*; Patti Harper and Lloyd Keane, Carleton University Archives; Colin Harris, Bodleian Libraries, University of Oxford; Mary Ellen Worgan Houde, McGill University Archives; Shannon Hodge, Jewish Public Library Archives; Susan Lee Kurtas, Dag Hammarskjöld Library, United Nations; Jennifer Lambert, for so much patient advice; Sylvia Lassam, Trinity College Archives; Loryl MacDonald, University of Toronto archives; Ken Puley, CBC Radio archives; Michael Riordan, St. John's College archives, Oxford; Professor Ryan Touhey, University of Waterloo; Gregory J. Viola, Canada's permanent mission to UN; and Toby Zanin who assisted with additional research in Toronto. Judith Robertson kindly shared her memories of her father, Norman, and was a wonderful source of information about who was who in 1950s Ottawa. From the very start, Pearson's children, Geoffrey and Patricia, were very welcoming, opening up their family papers and photographs and, more importantly, their personal impressions of their father. I must also thank Hon. Landon Pearson for her support over the years.

I was lucky to find three indefatigable researchers who never gave up until they had tracked down the necessary documents. Roger E. Nixon tackled Britain's National Archives at Kew, Richmond, and Susan Strange worked the American National Archives and Library of Congress in Washington, DC. In Ottawa, I relied on Beryl Corber, who knows more about the quirks and terrain of our national archives than I could have imagined. Over the years we worked together, I knew Beryl was trying to retire from freelance researching, but she still cheerily took on my requests and told me she would not stop until I had reached the last page. I am eternally grateful.

Rudyard Griffiths not only pushed me to write this book but introduced me to Linda Pruessen, then at Key Porter, and she, as the daughter of a history professor, appreciated right away the story I wanted to tell. Linda offered me a contract and re-launched the dormant project. All went well until Key Porter went under in 2010. A good and persistent friend, Griffin Ondaatje, encouraged me to contact Goose Lane, where Colleen Kitts-Goguen read my pitch and successfully championed it. The team at Goose Lane has been a pleasure to deal with, especially publisher

Susanne Alexander, creative director Julie Scriver, and production editor Martin Ainsley. I am grateful they paired me with editor Judy Phillips and copy editor Jill Ainsley, who shepherded me through my first book with grace and patience.

Writing may be a solitary process, but my family and friends ensured it was never a lonely one. Over many years, they encouraged me onwards and rallied my spirits when I flagged. It's impossible to express how much their support means to me. Above all, my wife, Litsa, and daughters, Sofia and Julia, kept me grounded, sustained, and committed. From time to time, Sofia would ask, "Dad, when will you ever finish this book? You've been writing it almost as long as I've been alive!" How incredible that I could finally answer her question.

Prologue

Saturday November 3, 1956
The United Nations, New York City

For the past three days he has not stopped moving. There's too much at stake. Israel has invaded Egypt. France and Britain are threatening to land their forces to impose a ceasefire. The United States and the Soviet Union are demanding that everyone stand down. Now, at about ten in the evening, the diplomat is at last standing still, facing the world assembly, about to read from a piece of paper that contains a proposal made up of seventy-eight words. These words have been shaped by caution and hope, put to paper after a ruthless appraisal of power, painstakingly crafted for overlapping objectives: to stop the conflict in Egypt from becoming a world war fought throughout the Middle East, to heal the Western alliance, and to prevent the Commonwealth from falling apart.

The man standing at the rostrum has served on the international stage for so long that he has no illusions about the feeble reach of world bodies, but he is here nonetheless because no matter what the faults and limitations of the United Nations, it remains the only global forum that includes the planet's democracies, the Communist prison states, and the non-aligned.

After days of failing to make peace, all eyes in the General Assembly lock on Canada's secretary of state for External Affairs, Lester B. Pearson. He is probably the most famous Canadian in the world, and in this emergency, the pivotal player. Few of his counterparts can match his experience, his web of contacts, his sublime mastery of the game, and his phenomenal capacity to mediate. On the surface he is charming, unpretentious, even boyish, but the winning smile, the lisp, and the infectious sense of humour conceal a ruthlessly pragmatic professional committed to the diplomacy of the possible.

While his personal powers are considerable, he does not forget where he lives. Lester Pearson represents a country blessed with vast geography but only moderate economic, political, and military muscle. He cannot threaten or enforce or intimidate. He can only suggest, inspire, and perhaps persuade. So here he stands in front of angry, tired delegates looking for an answer to the madness unfolding around them. He has done everything he can to dream one up.

The Suez Crisis has erupted from a fog of grand illusions, firm convictions, and good intentions. In July, Egypt nationalized the French- and British-owned Suez Canal Company, which operated the hundred-mile waterway connecting the Mediterranean and Red Seas. Convinced this was a prelude to communist contagion, London and Paris secretly persuaded Israel to invade Egypt. This aggression would provide them with the needed excuse to intervene and remain to rule once again. Once Israel played its part and attacked, the two permanent members of the United Nations Security Council ignored calls for an immediate ceasefire and instead threatened to impose peace themselves, even if this required dropping bombs on a country already defending itself from a military assault. In this piece of theatre, the risks are chilling. The crisis could trigger a larger war that might spread throughout the Middle East. The Russians just might enter the conflict on the Arab side.

In this surreal week, too many of Pearson's worst nightmares have come true. The unity of the Western alliance, critical to Canada's survival, appears to be disintegrating in public. In stark contrast, Russia and America have joined in harassing Britain and France at the Security Council. The Commonwealth mosaic has ruptured into black and white factions: India, Pakistan, and Ceylon howl for British blood, while New Zealand and Australia stand firm by the Mother Country. In the corridors of the UN, diplomats speculate about branding France and Britain as aggressors and hitting them with economic sanctions. From the very first hours of the crisis, Pearson has held back and stood apart. He has expressed concern and doubt but not explicitly condemned the British and French intention to land their troops in Egypt. This restraint has placed him and his country in a precarious position. For daring to stake out the middle ground instead of fully supporting Great Britain, many Canadians consider him a traitor; others regard him as a hero for acting in an independent manner. Like other diplomats caught up in the storm, Pearson is deeply suspicious of his allies' motives but anxious to craft an escape route for them. Grasping for any practical solution, he has seized on an old idea that has been floating around in a vague fashion for some time, and amplified it. For the last three days and nights, he has dedicated his energy to persuading the doubtful and encouraging the like-minded to create the world's first United Nations police and peacekeeping force. The odds against him are formidable.

Given the mood in this hall of peace, how can he persuade the General Assembly to put aside the craving to punish? Given the bitter split in the Western alliance, how can he cajole allies who now distrust each other to reconverge and sign on? And even if the assembly votes for his proposal, then what? The UN needs time to organize a force that can function effectively in a war zone. At this late hour, nothing but questions and doubt loom over the Canadian diplomat. But as Pearson has said during various eruption points in his long career, "We'll jump off that bridge when we get to it."

And so he does.

ONE

Where Is Here?

The Dutch may have their Holland, the Spaniard have his Spain.
The Yankee to the south of us, must south of us remain.
For not a man dare lift a hand, against the men who brag,
That they were born in Canada, beneath the British flag.
   —E. Pauline Johnson, "Canadian Born"

The map may have seemed like something out of a fairy tale or perhaps the young boy simply took it for granted. Whether treasured or ignored, it wove through the daily fabric of his world, materializing in an atlas at home, hanging on a wall in his schoolroom or a post office, or proudly displayed in a relative's parlour. In some versions, illustrations of exotic peoples never seen in his parish decorated the map's borders: near naked, dark-skinned, carrying spears and shields; riding camels beneath palm trees; or dressed in animal fur, moving through a land of ice. The map sometimes showed pale-skinned soldiers on horseback wearing familiar uniforms and wielding swords. He could not doubt which of these people were entitled to rule and which of them were compelled to submit. It is easy to imagine the boy's father or teacher guiding him through the obvious and essential pattern in the map, a pattern he absorbed without question, a pattern laden with tremendous assumptions and implications. For here laid out before Lester Pearson was an inheritance that transcended geography. Here was a view of the political construction he belonged to, infinitely greater than his home and native land. Here was an invitation to possibilities and horizons unfolding far beyond the narrow confines of his sheltered childhood. Here was a map of his potential.

Growing up, he would see different versions of the interlocking maze of countries, but in each one a recurring colour inexorably imprinted itself on his imagination — the red-pink glow of the omnipresent British empire: a disjointed collage of skin tones, mother tongues, household gods, and incompatible manners which covered, at its greatest reach, roughly one-quarter of the world's land surface containing, with varying degrees of consent and coercion, some 450 million subjects, one-fifth of the planet's population.

This creeping haphazard construct was accumulated over three centuries by religious fundamentalists seeking virgin ground to live as devoutly as they desired, pirates sanctioned by the state to plunder foreign rivals, dreamers reckless enough to escape a suffocating class system, and merchant adventurers willing to sell anything — human beings from Africa, narcotics from India, tobacco from the Americas, sugar from the West Indies, or fur, fish, and lumber from Canada. Unleashing and feeding consumer cravings inadvertently created a global network of trade routes, supply chains, investment flows, and local infrastructures, which at times required unflinching protection. What was largely informal and commercial became increasingly defended and governed, reinforced by and playing into a techno-financial revolution that remade a primarily agricultural economy into the world's first industrial nation. For much of an imperial century, the tiny portion of humanity living in Great Britain produced more steel and pig iron, exported more textiles, mined more coal, built more ships, manufactured and exported more goods, and commanded a greater share of world trade than any other society at the time.

Profit motives, political will, and naval supremacy converged so seamlessly that by Lester Pearson's childhood, the proud son of empire could trace his fingers across any map of the world to embark on a wondrous expedition of the British fact. Beginning at the remote depths of the southern Pacific hemisphere, he would see tiny pink fragments huddling around the self-governing islands of New Zealand. Moving north, the imperial hue enveloped a floating continent, Australia, then brushed over an Asian archipelago composed of Singapore, Malaya, and Borneo. Looking closely at the map revealed that even the middle kingdom of

The Pearsons ca. 1900: Anne, Lester standing on chair, Vaughan held by Edwin, Marmaduke (bottom right) (Library and Archives Canada/C-18704)

China had to endure the minuscule but defiant flake of pink called Hong Kong. Travelling west, he encountered India, a magical sub-universe of fabulous tales and opulence, the shining jewel in the imperial Crown, containing more subjects than anywhere else in the empire. Leaving India, the boy reached the claustrophobic web of armed camps making up Europe. The only imperial markers here perched on the southern edge of Spain and out in the Mediterranean, where Her Majesty's Government had claimed Gibraltar, Malta, and Cyprus.

Looking to the North Sea, the boy arrived at the most curious detail on the journey. The heart and centre of this worldwide dominion turned out to be nothing more than a knot of unimposing rain-drenched islands comprising several ancient nations, now unified under one crown. Without having ever visited them, Lester Pearson knew the culture, the history, and geography of the British Isles almost as intimately as those of his own country.

Gliding south, the imperial pink resurfaced in a landscape of pyramids and pharaohs, through African deserts, jungles, and grasslands down to windswept Cape Agulhas, the southernmost edge of the continent. The boy would have passed over a man-made passage, too small to pick out on the map, which cut through one hundred miles of Egyptian soil to join the Mediterranean with the Red Sea. Dreamed of for centuries, jealously guarded as the lifeline of empire, this was the Suez Canal, the greatest of all imperial waterways. Vital to Britain's economic and military traffic as well as to her prestige, this brilliant shortcut was considered absolutely untouchable. And still the young boy's journey continued.

Westwards across an ocean, glimmers of Britain sparkled in the southern Atlantic, leading on to the Falkland Islands at the bottom tip of South America. Here, British ambition disintegrated against the hard reality of Spanish and Portuguese conquest. The boy found only a few slivers of pink in Central and South America and the Caribbean. While connected to the metropolitan centre by informal economic tentacles, the new world stood almost devoid of the formal imperial presence.

One stunning exception prevailed, however — the largest expanse of pink on the entire map, unfolding across the northern half of North America from the Atlantic to the Pacific to the Arctic Oceans, encompassing five million souls, humbling geography, punishing weather, generous harvests, and mineral splendour. This was Canada: a spoil of war seized from France and the original Aboriginal populations, guarded from the Americans, and now one of the empire's most inventive improvisations. Acting with enlightened self-interest, the triumphant British minority sought to accommodate the conquered French majority, allowing them to keep their language, their religion, and their civil code of law. When francophone and anglophone subjects demanded more autonomy, a few even mounting a minor rebellion, London gave in to what it could not suppress and, in 1867, granted a kind of home rule, which evolved without bloodshed into a confederation of all the North American colonies. This became the empire's first self-governing entity, which the founding architects chose to call a dominion.

Lester Pearson was born into the imperial matrix a British subject; his flag, the Union Jack; his anthem, "God Save the Queen." British authors wrote the books he loved best in childhood. British history, proudly considered his own, shaped his view of the past, present, and future. Some of his schoolbooks featured a Union Jack fluttering over the exuberant and unremarkable declaration: "One Flag, One Fleet, One Throne." Despite the cringing this caused later historians and citizens eager to erase what they saw as a colonial purgatory, the trans-Atlantic, transnational connection—this dominion of duality and layered identity—was something most anglophones treasured, celebrated, and took for granted. It was not even paradox. "The idea that one could be both British and something else was easy to accept since they were already British and something else," historian Phillip Buckner has observed of these Canadians. "They were English, Irish, Scottish, or Welsh," he notes. "Britishness did not preclude multiple overlapping identities."[1]

Emotional and cultural synthesis was mirrored in political symbiosis. Pearson grew up in a Canada that boasted its own parliament, its own elected representatives, and its own courts but which could not amend the fundamental law of the land, the Canadian constitution, without London's approval. Canadian courts rendered the final word on criminal cases, but the court of final appeal for civil cases resided in London with the Judicial Committee of the Privy Council; in other words, Canadians could bypass their own government in search of a more satisfying verdict. The commanding officer of the modest Canadian militia was British, and it was the Royal Navy that defended Canada's Atlantic and Pacific coasts. If the dominion was largely sovereign at home, its voice on the world stage was faint and filtered.

In the year of Lester Pearson's birth, his country did not have a department of foreign affairs shaping a foreign policy and dispatching ambassadors to embassies in foreign capitals. On key international matters, Great Britain spoke for Canada, as for all parts of the empire. However, Ottawa was allowed to negotiate minor commercial treaties (which still needed to be sealed by a British signature), administer trade and immigration offices, and assign a High Commissioner to London and Paris to promote the dominion's interests—as long as these did not conflict with the wider imperial interest.

The Canadian experiment illustrated the British empire's creative incoherence where multitudes lived, willingly or otherwise, beneath the same flag by very different rules and lengths. Yet while the map of empire laid out before the young boy did not lie, it couldn't tell the entire story. Despite its imposing presence, this realm that dared to outrace the setting sun was an overextended, precarious structure exemplified by the imperial spectre in India, where an estimated three hundred million subjects were administered by some one thousand British civil servants and held in check by a garrison of seventy-five British troops, all dependent upon the 150,000 natives in the Indian Army. As historian William Roger Louis puts it: "Never, perhaps, had so few governed so many for the benefit of the British state."[2] This outrageous sleight of hand became more difficult as the British economy inexorably lost its fearsome primacy to various rivals. However, at the beginning of the twentieth century, the diminutive island kingdom remained the only truly global financial, military, and political presence.

The loyal subject who grew to know and admire this empire in the early 1900s had no sense of its fragility. When he looked at any map of the world, all he perceived was British glory effortlessly transcending the curving black lines of longitude and latitude, with his own country holding pride of place at its physical summit. For Lester Pearson, as for millions of other sons and daughters of the empire, it was impossible to conceive that one day the pink hues would fade and recede to the island centre and that much of his life and almost all of his diplomatic career would unfold within these retreating imperial shadows.

I had no awareness, no real awareness of the outside world nor did very many people of my generation. What was the outside world to us? The outside world was the next city.
—Lester Pearson discussing his childhood, February 3, 1970[3]

Lester Pearson was born April 23, 1897, in the tiny village of Newton-brook, now enveloped within modern-day north Toronto. The middle son of "fine and saintly" parents, homemaker Annie and Methodist minister Edwin, he and his two brothers, Vaughan and Marmaduke, enjoyed "an atmosphere of simplicity, security, obedience and discipline," according to Pearson. "We had the normal kind of trouble that families have but nothing comparable to what you read so much about." No angst or search for larger answers touched his teenage years, or so he claimed with disarming humour: "I must say, I must be a very superficial person because I didn't go through that thing at all."

The daily texture of Pearson's early years was homegrown and hand-made, not yet bathed in the glow and hum of electricity and all the devices that feed on it. People still wrote letters more often than they made phone calls. The home entertainment centre was most likely a piano. Public streets smelled of horse manure. The only skin seen in public appeared above the neck and below the wrist. Boredom did not exist for the young boy. "We did not need movies, radio, or television to help us pass the time, for we never had enough time for all the things we wished to do," he remembered. "We had little money, but our greatest pleasures cost us nothing."[4]

One of those pleasures was reading George Alfred Henty's roughly one hundred and twenty historical novels, many of them celebrating British heroes and their epic victories. The titles alone evoke a manly action-packed world immensely appealing to boys all over the empire: *The Dash for Khartoum: A Tale of the Nile Expedition, With Clive In India — Or, the Beginnings of an Empire, By Sheer Pluck: A Tale of the Ashanti War.* "Henty was, I must admit, the author whom I knew best among all English writers until I went to college." Later when Pearson travelled the world as foreign minister, Henty would rise occasionally to the surface of his memory. "There was hardly a place I visited," wrote Pearson, "which I had not known through that prolific but now almost forgotten writer."[5] Reverend Pearson and his wife, loving but strict, deemed Henty's books appropriate but shielded their three sons and themselves from the hydra heads of earthly vices, shunning alcohol, tobacco, cards, dancing and, for a while, even the novelty of moving pictures — until Pearson senior learned the theatre owner not only attended church but also contributed to the collection plate.

In the Pearson household, one purely secular passion was permitted, if not indulged — so much so that some of the more pious parishioners thought there was something curiously loose-jointed and sloppy in the good minister's mental makeup. His father's unapologetic love of sports "caused almost a revolution inside the Methodist Church," the equally casual son remembered approvingly. Parishioners "split into two factions.

Those who thought it was alright for the Methodist minister to play base-ball and those who thought it was really unbelievable that he should want to do it."[6]

Pearson shared this passion so deeply that it seems quite possible that he would have been as happy playing professional ball as conducting foreign policy. His love for sports endured through his adult life. In the 1930s, he escaped from League of Nations sessions in Geneva to play tennis. In the 1940s, in Washington, he organized baseball games between the Canadian legation and the US State Department. During the 1950s in New York City, he checked out from the General Assembly to watch baseball. In the 1960s, one of the defining images of his time as prime minister came in a CBC documentary that showed him in his office, reclining in a chair, distracted by a World Series game on television while one of his Cabinet ministers tried to engage his attention about an industrial dispute. Ultimately, the passion for service won out over the passion for play, but Pearson's athletic gifts and instincts infused his diplomatic moves and coloured the way his colleagues remembered him. During the Suez Crisis, Pearson's "role was that of quarterback," according to adviser John Holmes, "inventing plays and giving signals, shifting his ground to take advantage of openings." Pearson's officials, Holmes added, "were sometimes bewildered by the mobility of his tactics."[7]

Pearson had to learn very early to shift his ground because he spent his childhood in a state of semi-permanent flux. In a routine that neatly foreshadowed his son's later voyages as a foreign minister, Reverend Pearson uprooted the family every two or three years to serve in a dif-ferent station in the Methodist parish circuit. By the time he started university, Lester had moved through Newtonbrook, Davisville, Aurora, Toronto, Peterborough, and Hamilton.

At every new parsonage, the Pearson clan disembarked already sad-dled with expectations and assumptions, consigned to enjoy or endure a minor form of celebrity if not a low rung of aristocracy, for they arrived as the professional representatives of a worldly yet still divine mission. The middle son understood that even he and his brothers "had to set an ex-ample."[8] Inside the church walls, the family sat marked out and on display in a reserved pew, highlighting their social otherness. Being caught in and conscious of this constant social glare encouraged a perceptive child to carefully gauge what was spoken out loud, to be aware that one was on duty and on show, to always present the appropriate public face—ideal lessons for any future diplomat.

Looking back at his childhood upheavals, Pearson appeared unscathed. "There was hardly time to take root or become attached," he later wrote. "I made friends very quickly and could move easily from one town to another without feeling that I was homesick."[9] Perhaps the recurring transitions helped to reinforce a personal inclination towards detachment, for if the arrivals and departures came easily to him, making a deep emotional connection did not. Herein lies the most obvious contradiction in Pearson's emotional makeup.

Most in his circle recalled and delighted in his humour, his charm, his refreshing candour and lack of pretension, but they also acknowledged the sense of something withheld, the standing apart across a deep reserve. Arnold Heeney, Canada's ambassador to Washington during the Suez Crisis, confided to his diary in 1955 that "over the years although consistently friendly and satisfactory with me, he is increasingly impersonal—a deep one whose secret self very few if any can know." Tom Kent, one of his closest political advisers, concluded: "He was a man who could make an enormous range of, in a sense, easy friendships but found it very difficult to be really intimate, I think, with anybody." One aide saw that the outwardly gregarious diplomat "was a real loner. He preferred to have lunch alone, perfectly content to have a drink by himself or with one other person."[10]

Familiar with these observations, Pearson's son, Geoffrey, did not find anything unusual about the discrepancy between his father's open, engaging exterior and the reserved interior, and he cautioned against looking for any great mysteries lurking behind that reserve. "His public demeanour and his private life were much the same. What you saw was what you got," he recalled. "He wasn't all that private a person, in the sense like others I can think of—Dag Hammarskjöld, the great UN Secretary-General who was a mystic and wrote in his diary about his visions. My father was not a private person in that sense. He had no secret life. He wasn't Walter Mitty. So I don't remember ever wondering if he had a secret life. He didn't."[11]

I am neither Imperialist nor anti-Imperialist; I am Canadian first, afterwards
and forever.
> —Sir Wilfrid Laurier, campaigning in St. Jerome, Quebec,
> August 24, 1911[12]

There are those in this country and there are some whose views have been
expressed in this House who feel that we should have automatically supported
the United Kingdom and France...those who feel that way will be disappointed
at the action we have taken. We thought it was the right action for a Canadian
delegation to take. It was an objective attitude, it was a Canadian and independent attitude.
> —Lester Pearson, House of Commons, November 27, 1956[13]

This was one of his earliest memories. Around one o'clock in the afternoon on October 10, 1901, Lester Pearson, four-and-a-half years old,
perched on his father's shoulders, waiting with his mother, his two brothers, and their neighbours, at the Aurora, Ontario, train station, hoping
for a glimpse of two glittering beings from a far-off world — the Duke
and Duchess of Cornwall and York, or rather, the future King George V
and Queen Mary of Canada, Australia, New Zealand, India, and the rest
of their vast and scattered dominion. On that day, the British empire was
at war in southern Africa to impose decency, democracy, and imperial
rule upon the defiant Boer republics of Transvaal and the Orange Free
States, which preferred to worship their own faith in their own distinct
language, beneath their own flag.

An excited Pearson and his family, "still lingering on the euphoria
of Boer War patriotism," at last heard a distant whistle blow, but this just
signalled the unattached pilot engine roaring ahead to ensure the track
was clear. Seconds later, the royal coaches came into view, inciting the delighted subjects to applaud and cheer and flutter their Union Jacks. Alas,
for the faithful at the Aurora station, they discovered all too soon that
they were just another blur on a jammed itinerary. "The train didn't stop,"
Pearson recalled. "We were badly let down but it slowed down. They came
to the platform and I can remember it as if it were yesterday."[14] Despite
the momentary disappointment, the Pearsons' emotional attachment
to their empire undoubtedly remained undimmed, because, for over

three frenetic weeks from Quebec City to Vancouver and back, the Duke and Duchess of York had done everything in their power to intensify that connection, delivering and enduring heartfelt clichés, unveiling monuments and memorials, and presenting medals to veterans for their actions on the veldt. When they began their tour, the mayor of Quebec City declared that Canada's francophones and anglophones presented "to the world the spectacle of a free, united and happy people…attached to the King and country." Touching on Canadian deaths in the remote conflict, he accepted the losses as part of the price willingly paid for Canada's membership in a "mighty realm whose protection we enjoy and to which we rejoice to belong."[15] But war in Africa had not aroused any rejoicing between the two Canadas.

The francophone solitude, having themselves been conquered by the British, felt no desire to support the imperial drive to subdue a religious, linguistic minority. One of their most prominent MPs on the government benches, Henri Bourassa, had resigned his seat in protest. French and English students fought each other in Montreal and during the clash anglophones vandalized francophone newspaper offices. A brave few in Quebec voiced their support for the war but they were drowned out by the sweeping communal renunciation. English Canada was another world.

"A martial spirit seems to have descended upon this usually prosaic capital," a popular Ottawa columnist recorded. "It really is impossible to talk or think of anything but the war." Drowning out marginal voices of protest, the more rabid English newspapers inflamed that martial spirit with outrageous fantasies of Boer atrocities. Concerned anglophones judged it only proper that London should step in to protect British subjects living in such a violent, primitive society.[16] Not content to watch from the sidelines, thousands willingly sailed for the distant conflict to join their brothers-in-arms from across the empire.

Pearson's parents did not leave behind any papers indicating where they stood on the wide spectrum of opinion, but the genial Methodist minister and wife likely shared the moderate views of the *Christian Guardian*, their church's official newspaper, which declared its "confidence in the righteousness of Britain's cause" and condemned the Boer government as "a tyrannous plotting, self-serving and unjust oligarchy." However, editorials also agonized over the racial discord generated at home and encouraged its congregation not "to aggravate our French fellow-citizens by charges of disloyalty but rather to conciliate them, and to always keep in mind in our national policy the unalterable fact that we are a people of two races." The *Guardian* extended this tolerance to the Boers themselves, urging "there should be no feeling of revenge or animosity in our hearts toward those who are now our enemies."[17]

So even as the Pearsons waved the flag at the Aurora train station, theirs was most probably a reasonable patriotism, untainted by the darker undercurrents of imperial attachment, and even that attachment, while heartfelt, should probably be kept in a perspective framed by the 1904 satire *The Imperialist*. Affectionately mocking a fictional but emblematic Ontario town, author Sara Jeannette Duncan noted the obvious prevalence of a "sentiment of affection for the reigning house" but shrewdly perceived that "the fall of a British government would hardly fail to excite comment, and the retirement of a Prime Minister would induce [local newspapers] to publish a biographical sketch of him, considerably shorter than the leader embodying the editor's views as to who should get the electric light contract."[18]

In times of peace, those ties of affection could be managed without exacerbating Canada's religious and linguistic fault lines, but as Pearson would witness for so much of his life and career, imperial emergencies abroad would repeatedly inflame the connection and undermine the on-going accommodations at home. The townsfolk of *The Imperialist* perfectly captured this formula. Immersed in the minutiae of their own lives, they "recognized dimly" that England's foreign policy "was part of the huge unnecessary scheme of things for which she was responsible." But their self-absorption and indifference could be overthrown, "whenever, down the wind, across the Atlantic, came the faint far music of the call to arms. Then the old dog of war that has his kennel in every man rose and shook himself, and presently there would be a baying! The sense of kinship, lying too deep for the touch of ordinary circumstances, quickened to that; and in a moment 'we' were fighting, 'we' had won or lost."[19]

When the Mother Country went to war in southern Africa, Canada's prime minister, Wilfrid Laurier, publicly supported London's stated concern for the political rights of British immigrants in the Boer republics, but he could see no reason for Ottawa to get deeply involved. In

Parliament, he summed up his position with cool detachment. "While every Canadian admits that he would be ready to contribute our treasure and our blood, and the resources of Canada at the disposal of this country, for the rescue of England, were she engaged in a life and death struggle," Laurier declared, "there are many Canadians who are not ready to take part in the secondary wars of England." Steel beneath velvet, Laurier all through Pearson's childhood conducted a foreign policy that was simultaneously a domestic policy, summed up by one contemporary journalist as "fifteen years of saying 'No'" to the most powerful empire in the world, whether to its war in Africa or to the passionate crusade conducted by imperialists across the empire to fashion a grand economic and military federation.[20] His steadfast refusal was almost instinctual.

Three of Laurier's six predecessors weren't even born in Canada, but his ancestors had arrived in the New World some eight generations before, and unlike countless anglophones, he knew no other home. At the same time, however, Laurier's pride in his ancestry fused seamlessly with his admiration for British values and institutions. Even in his insistence on maintaining a sovereign space, he understood that Canada's fate remained inextricably bound up with the island kingdom. The "salvation of England is the salvation of our own country," he argued, noting: "therein lies the guaranty of our civil and religious freedom and everything we value in this life."[21] Pearson's attitudes in adulthood revealed he too shared these fundamental dualities. Well into his thirties he retained a strong desire born of affection, respect, and history to stay connected to the Mother Country, while fully supporting the national drive for more and more autonomy.

Confronted with a divided country and a divided Cabinet, Laurier, "perhaps the most perfect political leader" in Canadian history, strained his party's unity to fashion a translucent compromise barely tolerable to either side.[22] No Canadian would be compelled to fight in Africa, but Ottawa would pay to raise, train, and dispatch a volunteer contingent to serve under British command. Anything more was flirting with political disaster in Quebec. Anything less was equally toxic in English Canada. Forming the dominion's first overseas expeditionary force, approximately 7,300 Canadians choose to serve their country, sovereign, and empire in the African theatre. For all the grief this caused the government, the

Canadian contribution was a modest gesture compared to the roughly twenty thousand Australians and 6,500 New Zealanders sailing from their much smaller populations to join nearly half a million troops from all over the Empire.

At the war's outset, the Quebec newspaper *La Presse* captured the essence of the national divide. "We French Canadians belong to one country, Canada; Canada is for us the whole world," the paper observed, "but the English-Canadians have two countries, one here and one across the sea."[23] Given this schism, the British assault on African soil unleashed fundamental foreign policy challenges for any Canadian leader: how to hold together the two nations, already clashing within the bosom of their single federal state, when they disagreed about a remote conflict that did not directly affect any of Canada's primary interests; and, given the country's modest room for manoeuvre, how to satisfy the insistent demands of a self-centred superpower ally, remain a credible member of a transglobal alliance, and still preserve a measure of autonomy? Five decades later, Lester Pearson faced a similar dilemma when London appealed to the dominions to support the flag in Egypt over a canal that most Canadians had never seen or cared about. The anglophile nationalist would not operate in a vacuum. His actions and impulses were instructed and framed, to a large degree, by the example of a wise leader who struggled to hold a precarious balance between furious extremes.

And there was another empire that shaped the architecture of Pearson's mind, one he never acknowledged in public or perhaps ever to himself.

One would hesitate to put church matters either before or after politics among the preoccupations of Elgin. It would be safer and more indisputable to say that nothing compared with religion but politics, and nothing compared with politics but religion.

—Sara Jeannette Duncan, *The Imperialist*

The cameras rolled. The production crew waited. It was February 1970, almost two years after Lester Pearson stepped down as prime minister. At home in Ottawa, beginning a long series of interviews with the CBC for his television memoirs, the son, grandson, and nephew of Methodist ministers struggled to explain why he did not follow the religious path laid out for him by his ancestors, hardly an uncommon choice in his generation but one which evoked obvious discomfort for him. "Religion," he said, "meant very little to me as religion, but you could not help but be impressed by a kind of religion which gave you such wonderful parents and who seemed to get so much out of their religion."

Clearly not happy with his response, he started again, stumbling on-wards: "Religion…uh…didn't mean very much to me…even later in my teenage…it didn't mean very much to me…It was almost automatic. It wasn't something I came to believe in. It was automatic. I wasn't converted because," (and here he finally breaks into his infectious laughter), "I was immersed from the day I was born…my religious life having developed in that rather automatic way made it perhaps less fundamental than if I had acquired it of my own volition.…difficult to explain this."[24] Difficult to explain, perhaps, because of the cameras recording his every word and because, even at the age of seventy-two, the minister's son did not seem to have fully resolved for himself what he had, consciously and unconsciously, renounced and retained from his youthful immersion.

The movement that came to encompass multitudes began in 1729 at Oxford University with a handful of Anglican students who had pro-nounced themselves "the Holy Club." These fervent few endeavoured to live up to the name with stringent church attendance, Bible study, prayers, and visits to the poor, the sick, and the imprisoned. In their own version of group therapy, a relentless confessional accounting of inner struggles underpinned their good works in the world. Fellow students mocked the fervour and rigour of their "methodical" devotions but that insult became their banner. One member, John Wesley, an Anglican priest blessed with unyielding drive and discipline, became the catalyst innovator able to transplant these marginal, private methods into the larger world.

Wesley's years of anguished striving for a palpable state of divine communion culminated one evening in May 1738 at a religious meet-ing where, listening to a fellow seeker reading the Bible, he suddenly experienced his faith born-again. "I felt my heart strangely warmed," he later wrote. "I felt I did trust in Christ, Christ alone, for salvation." And then, in an outpouring that would characterize and set Methodism apart from more refined, restrained practices, Wesley immediately shared his epiphany with those gathered about him. This emotionally amplified connection to his god led the conservative Anglican priest literally outside the bounds of the established order. Overcoming his apprehensions ("I should have thought the saving of souls almost a sin if it were not done in church"), Wesley started preaching in the open air, in unconsecrated buildings, on roadsides, reaching out to the working class, the destitute, to all those hungry for a more vibrant relationship with their faith and creator. He found a revolution waiting to happen.[25]

Travelling thousands of miles through Great Britain, Wesley's passion and presence triggered an upheaval that grew far beyond his scope to define and contain, spreading by word of mouth, by pamphlets, by intense personal communion in new holy clubs which appalled more reserved, well-fed Anglicans, and at times, Wesley himself. Like a living art form, the Methodist enthusiasm did not solidify into one coherent doctrine but unfolded into smaller variants which in turn broke off into even smaller clusters of faith and practice, eventually flowing from the British Isles into the New World colonies.

By the time young Lester Pearson was following his itinerant minister father around Southern Ontario, Methodism had become a "formidable empire of the spirit," the largest Protestant denomination in Canada, embraced by all classes. In the 1901 census, approximately 917,000 Canadians called themselves Methodists, making up seventeen percent of the total population. They were followed by 842,000 Presbyterians and just over 680,000 Anglicans. The largest denomination remained Roman Catholic, numbering 2.2 million believers, slightly over half of them in Quebec. The Methodist fact was especially concentrated in Pearson's home province, where his spiritual brethren made up thirty percent of the provincial population.[26]

Even in an era marked by religious devotion, the two streams of Pearson's family did not just believe; they served on the front lines. His father, paternal grandfather, and maternal uncle were ordained ministers, while his maternal grandfather and two great-uncles took up the calling as lay preachers—those church members deemed by others and themselves to have "the gift of public speech and a fervent spirit" and who, after some doctrinal direction, volunteered to fill the pulpits when their regular work was done. "I cannot recall ever hearing them discussing how to feed hogs or fatten cattle or fertilize soils," Pearson's uncle, Reverend Bowles, wrote of those great-uncles. "Never did I hear them debating the feed value of different kinds of fodder. The Preacher and his last Sunday's sermon was a frequent topic," he noted, and "their minds gravitated always to religion and Church affairs."[27]

In marked contrast, Pearson confessed in his memoirs that he found the proximity of church and home "almost oppressive," especially on the holiest seventh day of the week, when he had to attend a morning and evening service, and Sunday school. At intense revival meetings, where the true believer might feel the Holy Presence and cry out in ecstasy, he merely felt a "mild guilt" that he did not express any wish to be saved. "Frankly," he asserted, "I was aware of no condition from which saving was required." Under his parents' roof, he performed the rituals faithfully, but once ensconced at Victoria College in the University of Toronto, the usually well-behaved son quietly defied their expectations and did not study to become a minister.[28]

Later, he and his Methodist-raised wife, Maryon, did not raise their two children as Methodists (then merged into the United Church) or in any other denomination. "They made a stab at it," daughter Patricia recalled. "They tried to send us to Sunday school a few times, but we kept moving so much that we didn't have an established community church ever. We tried in Ottawa once or twice, but it didn't really take." While the surface manifestations of Pearson's faith faded away, his son, Geoffrey, felt his father remained "a person who had a spiritual life but who was unable to demonstrate it in any outward way. He didn't go to church, and that must be explained by the fact that he lost his belief in the sort of formal trappings of the Church. He was not an atheist."[29] And it seemed, as the son suggests, the father did retain a spiritual core. Towards the very end of his CBC interviews, Pearson felt compelled to make his most consciously articulated statement on what he believed. His language is non-denominational but clearly reflects his intense youthful immersion.

> I would put at the front of my fundamental beliefs a belief in the inherent good of the individual person...my belief in the perfect-ibility of human nature under the influence of, what you might call,

a divine being; that there's more of that in human beings than there is of the opposite, more God than anti-Christ. And when I get depressed...about the state of the world, I can take encouragement from that belief that there are more good people in the world than there are bad, and that somehow, the good will overcome the evil.[30]

Beyond this personal sense of an underlying goodness, Methodism served to infuse Pearson's world view with two distinct elements, universalism and pragmatism. Rather than obsessing about an ethereal afterlife, the Methodist gaze had been brought down to earth by a grim industrial landscape scarred by a spectrum of sin or, as it came to be viewed, social injustice. The Christ of Pearson's childhood was more activist than gentle preacher. Like the original members of the Holy Club, political missionaries ventured far from their pews into Canadian slums, poor houses, and brothels, and onto street corners, bringing the promise of individual and social salvation. Their mission was not just local but global; indeed it was universal. John Wesley and his followers had rejected the doctrine of predestination in which even believers were divided into "the elect" (the chosen) and the damned. Accepting the essential equality of all and the essential unity of all, Methodists proclaimed that heaven was potentially open to all because any person could, through his or her own faith and God's grace, achieve salvation.[31]

As Pearson biographer John English has pointed out, "In Methodist churches there was [always] a picture of Jesus with children of all colours surrounding Him, all the children of the world coming together around Him. And it's that kind of thing that at its simplest level created Pearson's sense of the world and sense of its purpose." That elemental influence pervades a revealing line in Pearson's memoirs. He later recalled that during his years as foreign minister, "[My colleagues and I] always asked ourselves not only 'What kind of a Canada do we want?' but 'What kind of a world do we want?'" His ancestors would, of course, have wanted a Methodist world. He strove for universal peace, order, and good governments.[32]

The universalist spirit shone through in Pearson's clear-eyed commitment to the United Nations; in his determined but failed struggle to make NATO more than a one-dimensional military alliance and turn it into a social and economic federation; in his work to make the Commonwealth more multiracial by accommodating the newly independent and republican India; and in small diplomatic gestures. He briefly ignored Cold War politics and dared to chat informally with Chinese foreign minister Zhou Enlai at the 1954 Indochina Conference, whereas American secretary of state John Foster Dulles refused to even shake the Communist's hand. Pearson recalled looking past a Soviet diplomat's "unscrupulous" and "bitter" verbal assaults to recognize this enemy off-duty as "a cultivated, amusing and agreeable person," as he wrote in his memoirs, "all smiles, and lively with engaging conversation about literature and life."[33]

In a neat parallel, even the physical contours of Pearson's secular work echo back two centuries to Methodism's genesis. There is a continuity from John Wesley following his circuits through the British Isles with his message of inclusion and universal salvation to Lester Pearson travelling his own circuits through international councils, preaching universal cooperation and peace. Indeed, Pearson's expansive, inclusive sense of the world where there could be no salvation, or as he would put it, no international peace, without involving all members of the parish reflects one of Wesley's most famous lines: "I look upon all the world as my parish." While Pearson understood the bitter divisions of ideology and borderlines, and properly viewed the Soviet Union as an evil empire, he perceived the greater unity of interests lying underneath. He reasoned that, as there were no local or even national solutions to international problems, only a universal response could solve universal dilemmas, hence he worked for collective or universal security through universal assemblies. When those efforts failed, as they so often did, he settled for temporary compromises, however unsatisfying and frustrating. But he always kept his eye on the ever-distant goal. "It was not a waste of time to talk about and advocate world peace and world federation or, on a less exalted level, an Atlantic Community or a permanent United Nations Peace Force—even when existing circumstances seemed to make a mockery of such idealism," he wrote in his autobiography. "I knew that peace was a policy as well as a prayer."[34]

Undoubtedly, the innately tolerant diplomat was personally disposed to Methodism's universalism, but it was also able to flourish in his practice and not just in his preaching because this universalism could mesh seamlessly with the demands and restraints of middle-power diplomacy. If superpowers preferred to act single-mindedly, without consulting even their friends, oblivious to the havoc they could wreak on their surroundings, middle powers were acutely aware of the ties that bound one and all. They had no choice. Sensitive to and affected by minute tremors rippling through the interconnected landscape, sensible middle powers understood their relative position in the community and accepted that there could be only security and solutions in numbers. If Pearson had failed to inherit a universalist streak from his buried faith, he would probably have been forced to acquire it in the trenches of middle-power diplomacy.

In an age of peace, Pearson might have endured a diplomacy of banality, but he lived through or alongside some of the darkest nightmares of the twentieth century: two world wars where he lost close friends; the creation of horrific technologies that could turn all life to ash; the rise of vicious tyrants; the enslavement of innocents. Given the stakes, his diplomatic mission resonated with a deep Methodist promise that, as historian David Hempton notes, "spoke of the possibility of salvation and a new start" and "dared hope for a transformed life." Pearson dreamed of transforming his damaged world and felt Canada had no real option but to be directly involved, observing: "Everything that happens in the world affects us, and to a degree greater than most countries. Consequently, it is always foolish to assume that we can safely leave global matters of war and peace to the Great Powers while we modestly concentrate our energies on protecting our sovereignty and increasing our gross national product. Economic growth as a first objective of foreign policy is an uncertain trumpet sound to Canadians, scarcely stirring the blood or inspiring hope for a better country and a more secure world."[35] Unwittingly evoking the evangelist tradition, he clearly intended his work to sound a powerful trumpet and stir the blood, just as John Wesley had done two centuries before. And even if he didn't consciously connect his mission with that earlier crusade, he was sometimes bluntly reminded.

In September 1948, after twenty years in the civil service, Pearson was sworn in as His Majesty's Canadian secretary of state for External Affairs. The appointment made headlines across the country, and the new minister dutifully called his widowed mother with the impressive news. "I told her that I was now in the Cabinet and she expressed a reasonable satisfaction over this promotion and this honour," he recalled. But seeing her son attain this stellar position in the political stratosphere was not where Mrs. Pearson and her husband had hoped their son would end up. That night in 1948, decades after seeing her hopes dashed, she employed a characteristic Pearson touch, coating hard edges with humour. "Well, I always wanted you to be a minister, and I'm glad you've become a minister, if only a second-class one," she said.[36]

TWO

Growing Up Canadian

A Nation spoke to a Nation,
A Throne sent word to a Throne:
"Daughter am I in my mother's house,
But mistress in my own.
The gates are mine to open,
As the gates are mine to close,
And I abide by my Mother's house"
Said our Lady of the Snows.
—Rudyard Kipling, "Our Lady of the Snows"

The rebels are outnumbered but willing to fight to the death. Dreaming of independence from Ottoman rulers and European puppet masters, their rallying cry is "Egypt for the Egyptians." Her Majesty's Government in London prefers to keep Egypt for itself and refuses to cede its economic stake in and informal political control over the country that contains the hundred-mile-long Suez Canal, the essential imperial waterway that joins the Mediterranean with the Red Sea out to the far East. When diplomatic postures fail to restore sense and order in the restless natives, London dispatches the world's most terrifying force on the fighting seas.

Watching from the sidelines, a dashing British expatriate talks with his noble wife about the crisis in their adopted home, where two bitter rivals circle each other for dominance over this gateway to India. "Supremacy in Egypt has always been the dream of the French," he tells her. "Had it not been for our command of the sea, they would have obtained possession of the country in Napoleon's time. Their intrigues here have, for years, been incessant. Their newspapers in Egypt have continually maligned us, and they believe that the time has come when they will be the real, if not the nominal, rulers of Egypt. The making of the Suez Canal was quite as much a political as a commercial move."[1]

Who knows what the young Lester Pearson, safely in Canada, made of these observations as he lost himself in another epic by his favourite author, George Alfred Henty, but he was probably riveted by the ironclads and gunboats shelling Alexandria into submission while the Egyptians fought gallantly, though they proved no match for the overwhelming British firepower that turned their battlements into ruins.

It is highly unlikely that in his childhood Pearson ever doubted Britain's God-given right to bomb a foreign country in order to reimpose its rule on so many ungrateful natives, not when raised in the unshakeable faiths of Methodism and imperialism. Dimly aware of the world beyond his parish, what he knew was refracted through the prism of empire. The idea of "British and Canadian soldiers charging the Boers and driving them headlong" impressed him. He accepted that London had properly undertaken the duty of "looking after the 'lesser breeds' and keeping the French and Germans under control." He later recalled "faint stirrings of interest as a boy over the threat from the Kaiser to Britain's naval supremacy and what Canada should do to help meet that threat."[2] And perhaps he even imagined himself playing a part in bravely confronting surly challenges to his empire.

Anecdotes from his childhood certainly highlight an attraction to the pomp and circumstance of military spectacles. "The militia used to parade in Peterborough," he recalled. "They had a very good regiment and I wanted to join the militia there as soon as I was old enough, but because of the uniforms. They were very smart."[3] Pearson's parents, however, expected their second son to become a minister and live a wandering life, just like his father, preaching and serving God's Word.

In the fall of 1913, the sixteen-year-old enrolled at the University of Toronto's Victoria College, established by Methodists to establish future Methodists. Preferring baseball diamonds and hockey rinks to pews and study halls, the minister-in-training religiously devoted himself to sports, although he did manage to score a first in his modern history course.

Lester Pearson, age 20, in Royal Flying Corps, England, 1917
(Library and Archives Canada/PA-110824)

"That's what I was interested in and where that would lead me to I never worried about," he recalled. "I would meet that problem when it arose."[4]

Then, on June 28, 1914, bullets fired on the other side of the world tore apart all the preordained paths lying before Pearson. On that day, a Serbian nationalist assassinated the archduke of Austria-Hungary and heir to the throne, Franz Ferdinand, and his wife, Sophie, as they sat in the back of an open car. Demanding revenge, Austria threatened Serbia, which brought in Russia to defend Serbia, which brought in Germany to support Austria. The vortex of alliances sucked in the French and the British, who, on the fourth of August, declared war against their economic and military rival, Germany.

In that same instant, the faraway Dominion of Canada was immediately at war. Seventeen-year-old Lester Pearson was playing baseball on the night London telegraphed the declaration across the Atlantic. "It never occurred to us that this was something that was constitutionally, politically or morally arguable. We just took it for granted. The King, the British were at war, we were at war," Pearson said. About to return to his second year at Victoria College, he expected to see a G.A. Henty novel come to life, but not close up. "The war was far away, and would be over soon with a Charge of the Light Brigade and a Battle of Trafalgar," he wrote. "It could not affect me or my family."[5]

From a total population hovering just over seven million people, close to 620,000 Canadians, predominantly anglophones, eventually crossed the sea to fight, in varying degrees, for their King, their Empire, their notion of democracy, their personal sense of destiny, and in some cases, a steady job. Most were volunteers, comprising an astonishing number returning to defend home ground. Nearly 230,000, or thirty-seven percent, of the Canadian troops were born in Great Britain. Only fifty-one percent had been born in Canada. On foreign fields soaked in mud and filth and human remains, these British subjects would kill and be killed, some face to face, watching eyelids close, hearing last breaths go silent. They would also experience and deliver impersonal, industrial death made possible by brutally efficient guns and chemicals. Roughly sixty thousand were killed. Close to 173,000 were wounded, mostly in action, surviving to endure an appalling spectrum of anguish: losing their limbs, their sight, their hearing, and some, their minds.

The unworldly student became intoxicated by the lies governments tell their citizens in order to arouse the collective hate and selfless action necessary for war. "I thought the Germans were devils," he later admitted, "because I believed everything that was written about them and that we were saving the world for democracy. Also it was going to be a great adventure. I don't know which got priority." On April 27, 1915, four days after his eighteenth birthday, Pearson signed up with the Canadian Army Medical Corps to do his bit in what he called, "the greatest and most glorious cause in history." He was anxious "to not be in the rear when the rest were marching forward."[6] The young lad's time in uniform, however, would prove to be a dreary descent through tedium and banality, culminating in profound disillusionment.

Within three weeks of signing up, Private 1059 shipped off for England and found himself crammed like cannon fodder in the hold of a ship, hopelessly seasick, desperately homesick, and unable to eat the wretched food. He would say later that the first week on board was the single worst experience of the entire war for him: "If the Captain had said, 'Men, the ship is sinking,' I would have shouted 'Three cheers for the Captain.'" After close to a fortnight at sea, he finally set eyes for the first time on the almost mythical Mother Country.[7]

Sighting Plymouth just after dawn, his British-framed mind imagined the Elizabethan hero and privateer Sir Francis Drake preparing to fight the Spanish Armada. "From this port the dauntless old sea-dogs of England had set forth to search for new lands; to this port the inhabitants of those new realms were now returning to help the Motherland in her hour of need," he noted in the diary he kept. In stark contrast to his later public image as a mild-mannered "man of peace," the eighteen-year-old Pearson hungered for military adventure from the very start. When he watched Canadian troops parade before their visiting prime minister, Robert Borden, he lamented, "How I admired those stalwart chaps as they snapped their bayonetted rifles to the 'present.' I longed to be carrying one instead of wearing the Red Cross on my sleeve."[8]

The earnest son of empire found himself stationed near Dover. "I expected to be sent quickly to the trenches, rescuing the wounded in no man's land with that calm courage that warranted, even if it did not receive, a Victoria Cross," he recalled. "The reality was very different."[9] As a night orderly at the camp hospital, Private Pearson learned to change bedpans, wash floors, and tend the patients who mocked or cursed his fumbling attempts to soothe them. Through long insomniac nights, he listened to their tales from hell.

A low long ward, eighteen cots on either side, in each cot a soldier. Darkness enshrouds all, save at one end where a light flickers. I am perched at one end of a bed listening to a story of blood and carnage, the low monotone of the raconteur broken now and then by a cry from one of the wounded, dreaming of the nightmare nights of Ypres or the senseless sleep babbling of another fighting his battles over and over again."[10]

If his lowly duties dismayed him, Pearson's love affair with Great Britain deepened when he finally encountered what he called "the true heart of a world Empire." His visits to Westminster Abbey, Buckingham Palace, and the Tower of London took on the aura of a pilgrimage. At the British Museum, he gazed in awe at revered explorer Robert F. Scott's final words, scrawled while starving and freezing to death in the Antarctic. "It was the spirit of Trafalgar, of the Light Brigade," he recorded in his diary.[11]

Five months after landing in England, Pearson and his comrades finally set sail, so they presumed, for the trenches in France. They soon learned they would not be making the brief passage across the Channel. Instead their troop ship headed south and began navigating an imperial matrix flowing from the English coast down through the Atlantic into a distant body of water that, despite being bordered by European countries and Ottoman provinces, London still deemed almost a British lake. The Canadians would land on a stretch of northern Africa, also considered British, and where the long, twisting chain of events and motives leading towards the Suez Crisis was being hammered into place.

We do not want Egypt or wish it for ourselves any more than any rational man with an estate in the north of England and a residence in the south, would have wished to possess the inns on the north road. All he could want would have been that the inns should be well kept, always accessible and furnishing him, when he came, with mutton-chops and post-horses.
   —Prime Minister Lord Palmerston, 1859[12]

In 1869, a canal cut through the Isthmus of Suez formally opened for business to join the Mediterranean and the Red Sea in a seamless mesh of politics and profit. Dreamed of for centuries, remapping ancient trading routes, the hundred-mile waterway had been willed into reality by a retired and disgraced French diplomat, Ferdinand de Lesseps. Almost forty years before, during a posting to Egypt, he was taken with a far-fetched scheme to excavate a canal between two seas and reroute the world's shipping traffic. That might not have happened had Lesseps not, with shrewd calculation, befriended an unhappy, overweight member of the Egyptian royal family, secretly feeding him his favourite and forbidden dish, macaroni. Although not directly in line to the succession, that boy, Mohammed Said, eventually became the pasha (governor) of Egypt. Handed the potential for redemption and glory, Lesseps rushed to present himself before the new ruler of Egypt, and with nothing more than spin and charm inspired Said into granting him a concession to build the canal and, upon completion, operate it for ninety-nine years. This improbable victory was merely the starting point.

A relentless Lesseps beguiled investors with visions of lucrative canal dues, slashed travel times between European and Asian markets, and when necessary, shimmering visions of a more unified and peaceful world. Having spent much of the nineteenth century fighting to shield Egypt from rival incursions, the alarmed British government lashed out at the suspicious French plan to dig through a treasured sphere of influence. Lesseps persisted with almost freakish confidence and resolve and raised the capital needed to begin the work, sustained by waves of affordable, virtually enslaved labour. The Suez Canal reduced the voyage between Plymouth and Bombay (present-day Mumbai) from roughly ten thousand miles to six thousand.[13] More than any other country, British merchants embraced the shortcut that allowed them to escape the punishing marathon down the African coast, around the Cape of Good Hope, to the lush plunder in the East. The British government saw its far-flung empire suddenly come within closer reach. Very quickly, economic dependence fused with and fuelled imperial imperatives.

In 1875, stratospheric national debt compelled Egypt's ruler, the khedive Ismail Pasha, to pawn off his forty-four percent stake in La Compagnie Universelle du Canal Maritime de Suez, the French company that managed and operated the waterway. Fearing another contender moving in first, Prime Minister Benjamin Disraeli bought up the entire share. His people cheered his pluck and forgave his lack of consultation with Cabinet or Parliament. Disraeli boasted to his admirer and sovereign,

Queen Victoria, "It is just settled; you have it, Madam"—but Her Imperial Majesty did not actually "have" the Suez Canal.[14]

With Disraeli's coup, the British government became the largest single shareholder in the French company granted the concession to run the canal until 1968. London did not own any physical part of the Suez Canal and, other than appointing board members, did not participate in the day-to-day operations or play any role in administering the company, which was headquartered in Paris. Nonetheless, in the imperial game, perception could be tantamount to reality, and the waters running through Egyptian soil reflected (at least in British eyes) only the proud red, white, and blue of the Union Jack.

An economic catalyst and engineering marvel shape-shifted into a multiplicity of metaphors—umbilical cord, lifeline, jugular vein—connecting the Mother Country to the most essential jewel in the imperial crown. Soon after the purchase, one of Disraeli's colleagues underlined this geographic link. "It is now the *Canal and India*," he wrote; "there is no such thing now to us as India alone."[15] For the architects and defenders of the world's largest empire, Egypt, in a sense, had almost always been about India—a distant labyrinthine trading venture conducted at first by company men, which had evolved into an imperial necessity eventually controlled by the home government. India fed Britain's insatiable consumer and industrial cravings (teas, spices, textiles, narcotics), offered a captive market for British products and, arguably most important, provided the diminutive island kingdom in the North Atlantic with its greatest weapon on land, the so-called native Indian army, comprising a quarter-million soldiers.[16] The viceroy of India, Lord Curzon, did not exaggerate when he addressed a London audience in 1904:

> If you want to save your Colony of Natal from being overrun by a formidable enemy, you ask India for help, and she gives it; if you want to rescue the white men's legations from massacre at Peking, and the need is urgent, you request the Government of India to despatch an expedition, and they despatch it; if you are fighting the Mad Mullah in Somaliland, you soon discover that Indian troops and an Indian general are best qualified for the task, and you ask the Government of India to send them; if you desire to defend any of your

extreme outposts or coaling stations of the Empire: Aden, Mauritius, Singapore, Hong Kong, even Tien-tsin or Shan-hai-kwan, it is to the Indian Army that you turn; if you want to build a railway to Uganda or in the Soudan, you apply for Indian labour....It is with India coolie labour that you exploit the plantations equally of Demerara and Natal; with Indian trained officers that you irrigate Egypt and dam the Nile; with Indian forest officers that you tap the resources of Central Africa and Siam.[17]

In a private letter, Curzon acknowledged the stakes more pithily: "As long as we rule India, we are the greatest power in the world. If we lose it, we shall drop straight away to a third rate power."[18] If London deemed India essential to the Empire's prosperity, authority, and survival, then it followed that the geography connecting the subcontinent to the Mother Country remained hallowed ground. Thus when the nominal ruler of Egypt, the Ottoman Empire, sided with Germany and Austria-Hungary against Britain in 1914, threatening to place the Suez Canal in enemy hands, London declared Ottoman Egypt a British protectorate—whether the locals liked it or not.

Landing in Alexandria in 1915, eighteen-year-old Lester Pearson marvelled at the coexisting contrasts of languages and races; recoiled at the disorder, the poverty, and the pungent odours, and yet still romanticized this exotic land of Biblical customs. Stationed for a few weeks in a desert camp, he remembered the "heat, sand, flies and date jam. The heat got under our cork helmets and made us weak and lazy; the flies got into our tents; the sand got into our eyes, hairs and blankets; they all managed to get into the jam." The well-raised minister's son was also put out when Australian soldiers "treated the natives with scant respect and in some cases with unpardonable roughness," noting: "I doubt very much if their presence did anything to make British rule more popular."[19] Pearson may have been able to acknowledge that the Egyptians might resent being protected against their will, but he did not explore this line of thought and what it might portend.

In November, he and his comrades set sail for the northeastern Greek town of Salonika, where the British were lending support to their ally, Serbia. Wearing summer uniforms, the Canadians set up a field hospital in a sea of mud and prepared to take in retreating Allied soldiers. Pearson wrote in his war memoir of "ceaseless rain and fierce wind; of horse ambulances coming down the road with their loads of human agony." He documented "nightmare days when we all worked till we dropped, when we ate as we worked; but the chance for real service, the goal of all our weary months of training."[20] The wave of frantic activity subsided, and this front congealed into a stalemate guarded by small patrols. Pearson's medical unit waged a war against malaria, pneumonia, dysentery, fever, typhus, grinding weather, and boredom. When possible, he escaped into soccer and hockey. After he fainted in the operating tent when a surgeon cut into a patient, he was assigned to the quartermaster stores. His two brothers addressed him in their letters as "Dear Fighting Grocer."

Languishing on a dormant front, keenly aware that many friends were waging a far more heroic war, the grocer yearned to do his duty, and so not for the first or the last time in his life, Pearson took advantage of impressive family connections. In the autumn of 1916, he wrote his father, then living in Chatham, Ontario, and asked him to persuade an old Methodist acquaintance, now the minister of the militia, Sam Hughes, to get him transferred to an infantry unit so he could start fighting. Methodist strings pulled from Greece to Chatham to Ottawa to London to Salonika, transferred Pearson in March 1917, back to England. After sixteen months in purgatory, he seemed set at last to star in a G.A. Henty epic of his own.

> The heavens are their battlefield; they are the Calvary of the clouds. High above the squalor and the mud, so high in the firmament that they are not visible from earth, they fight out the eternal issues of right and wrong....Every flight is a romance, every record is an epic. They are the knighthood of this War.
>   —Prime Minister David Lloyd George, House of Commons,
>   October 29, 1917[21]

Through the spring and early summer of 1917, Lester Pearson savoured a short time in heaven when he attended an officer training camp at Oxford University—a dreamlike refuge compared to the dismal field hospital in Salonika. But he knew full well he was preparing to join the legions slaughtered without ceremony on chaotic battlefields by unseen phantoms launching shells or squeezing machine-gun triggers. Perhaps this was why, in the autumn, he abruptly switched destinies and volunteered for the only glamorous arena of the war, the fledgling Royal Flying Corps. Here, gallant knights in flying machines soared above the muddy carnage, engaging the enemy one-on-one in a thrilling duel of pluck and skill, "celebrated as popular heroes, honoured as demigods, objects of an unparalleled secular holy cult." The price for this glamour and honour: a chilling life expectancy that measured, depending on the battlefield, from months to hours. The public read about a jaunty indifference to danger and death, but the pilots endured nightmares, ulcers, and insomnia.[22]

In a fitting symbol of rebirth, Lester was rechristened when he joined the aerial knighthood. Apparently the Canadian squadron commander blanched when he heard Pearson's name: "He looked up and said: 'This is meant to be a fighting squadron. There'll be no Lesters around here. I'll call ya 'Mike.'" For the rest of his life, as a returning student, teacher, civil servant, diplomat, and Cabinet minister, Pearson always introduced himself as Mike. "It stuck," he later wrote, "and I was glad to lose Lester."[23]

Starting at aeronautics school in October 1917, Pearson was rushed through a rudimentary curriculum that covered flight theory, navigation, operating the wireless, and engines. In November, at Hendon aerodrome, just north of London, the novice took his first flight with an instructor in a Grahame-White biplane, a skeletal arrangement of fabric, wire, metal, and wood. Through a grey misty sky, Pearson flew exposed in the open cockpit, cold wind rushing into his face, engine vibrations rattling through the frame, propeller noise drowning out all sounds, with very little protection between his flesh and bones and the solid ground below—and he loved it. In a letter home he noted: "I think I took to it like a duck to water."[24]

Often grounded by rain, he accumulated a paltry one hundred minutes' flying time with his instructor, and they almost did not return from one of their sessions. Flying at about seven hundred feet, the engine cut out, and they were forced to make a crash landing: "We smashed the machine all up but beyond a good shaking up, a scare and some cuts, I was okay." And he was far luckier than some of his fellow cadets, who discovered the randomness of survival even before they reached the front. "We were being pushed too fast," Pearson recalled, "and two of the cadets in our training squadron were killed because they weren't ready to do the things they were asked to do." In his memoirs, he mentioned only in passing that one of the casualties was his roommate. Given what future friends and colleagues said about the deep reserve lying beneath his affable surface, it is possible to see in Pearson hints of the coping responses experienced by another fighter pilot who, to endure the punishing emotional strain, "cultivated an impersonal detachment," declining to share "his most intimate thoughts with others."[25]

While Pearson learned to fly without killing himself, the Canadian government tried to wage war without tearing the country apart. The cataclysm that was supposed to last weeks had dragged on for over three years, with still no end in sight. Plagued by falling enlistment and a rising death toll, Prime Minister Robert Borden decided that only conscription could fill the ravenous gap. He understood with stark clarity the political nightmare his decision would unleash, but anything less than complete devotion to the cause was, for him and the majority of his fellow anglophones, sacrilege. For francophones, the prospect of being compelled into service rather than being allowed to volunteer was equally profane especially as Borden had publicly promised early in the war and again in 1916 that there would be no conscription. So they protested and rioted in the streets of Montreal, preached civil disobedience, and dynamited the summer home of a pro-conscription newspaper publisher.

A despairing Borden could find no middle ground between the furious solitudes howling at one other in two languages, each faithful to its own vision of Canada. Putting his principles above partisan politics, the Conservative leader painstakingly crafted a coalition Union government that attracted anglophone Liberal defectors serving their conscience rather than their party's anti-conscription platform, and repelled Conservative francophones for parallel reasons. Seeking a mandate, however poisoned, Borden called an election in which he blatantly manipulated the voting rules. For the first time, certain women — those married or directly related to a soldier — received the right to vote in a federal election, while those likely to vote against the government—specific religious minorities, conscientious objectors, and relatively recent immigrants from the enemy countries—were not allowed to cast a ballot. To mollify rural constituents concerned about losing their labour force, farmers and their sons would not face conscription. Borden's methods were ruthless, but he was not a cynical operator. He had sat at the bedside of wounded soldiers in France, heard their tales of sacrifice, and openly wept. He would never betray them.

After two-and-a-half years in uniform, Pearson knew exactly where he stood. "Those detestable anti-conscriptionists are doing their best to give Canada a bad name," he declared in a letter home written just two weeks before the election. "The feeling here is very bitter against Quebec." Pearson would cast his vote, as he put it, "on the right side, with those who are trying to keep Canada in the proud position in which her army has placed her, and against those traitors who would drag them from that position, and have her dishonoured for all time."[26] It would have been unusual for a twenty-year-old soldier from deepest Protestant Ontario to feel otherwise.

On December 17, Borden's electoral manipulations helped him secure a decisive majority with the seat count: 153 pro-conscription Union MPs versus eighty-two anti-conscription Liberals. On the surface, the breakdown reflected the racial divide, with Quebec delivering sixty-two of its sixty-five seats to the Liberals, who also made a respectable showing in the Maritimes. In counterpoint, anglophones from Ontario to British Columbia, elected a crushing majority of pro-conscription MPs. However, the seat count was deceptive. Actual votes revealed a Canada much more resistant to the enforced call of duty. Of the approximately 1.6 million civilians who voted in the election, the pro-conscriptionists outnumbered their opponents by a mere 97,065 ballots, less than one percent. Civilian Canada split almost evenly on the issue. The 215,849 soldiers who supported conscription saved the government's plan. "Weren't the election results fine," a delighted Pearson wrote to his parents. "I sure am proud of Canada."[27]

Anxious to reinforce his nation's honour, Pearson continued to train for the ever-approaching adventure in France, racking up just over eight hours of flying time, although his first solo flight almost proved to be his last. "Everything seemed easy until they signalled me to come down," he recalled. "I wasn't sure I knew how to get down. I felt I was safe as long as I was up there." He made a rough landing, bounced the plane, and instinctively took off again, which apparently was the safe thing to do. "If I had bounced down again, I would have crashed. There's a very slim undercarriage so I flew around again and landed alright. That was the beginning of my short and inglorious flying career." Within the next forty-eight hours, on another solo flight, Pearson crashed again but not seriously, doing more damage to the plane than to himself. He was given leave and on the evening of December 18 headed into London to enjoy himself in appropriate Methodist fashion with lively conversation and good food, rather than sinning with cigarettes and alcohol.[28]

At approximately 6:15 p.m. that evening, lumbering Gothas, twin-engined long-range biplanes, crossed the English coast carrying a deadly payload. In the middle of Pearson's dinner, an air raid siren sounded, and he immediately caught a bus heading back to Hendon aerodrome. In the wartime blackout, street lamps were doused and motor vehicles drove without headlights turned on. Bombs falling within earshot, the alarmed bus driver came to a stop and ordered everyone off. As Pearson ran across the darkened street, he stepped into the path of an oncoming bus: "He hit me flat on and how I ever survived that, God knows." He regained consciousness to find two policemen pushing him on a cart to a doctor's house, where gashes in his leg and on his head were sewn up. The police returned him to Hendon but not into his bed, and he spent the night on the floor, too injured to call for help.[29]

An officer found him the next morning, barely able to talk, his head still splattered with mud, and his leg becoming infected. He was finally taken to a hospital. "It was a very inglorious finish to my military career, but it was a very lucky finish for me," he later acknowledged. Pearson's luck was underscored in the bombing's aftermath: during the raid, ten people were killed and seventy were injured. In a sardonic coda, which Pearson would recount with self-mocking amusement, he found himself in a ward, flanked on one side by a soldier who had been kicked by a mule and on the other by a pilot suffering from asthma—hardly the stuff of G.A. Henty. Unlike millions of other soldiers, he was supremely fortunate just to be present and accounted for, and he knew it: "I got hurt before I got a chance to get killed—that's about what it amounts to. Looking back now, there seems to be something that was protecting me. I didn't realise it. I never expected to come back from that war."[30]

Given leave to recover, Pearson dared to hope he might be sent home, but then, in early January 1918, he learned he was probably heading to the front. Ever the considerate son, he tried to downplay the setback. "Please don't be too disappointed," he wrote to his parents. "I am really perfect physically so I think after all it's my duty to go to France."[31] After that, his letters began to focus on a looming appointment with an army medical board, which would seem somewhat unnecessary for someone in perfect physical condition.

On the path to likely death, Pearson allowed himself a profound soul searching. "It was a time I shall never forget," he later wrote in his autobiography. "It was then that I became an adult. I began to think of things beyond the pleasures and excitements, the troubles and fears of the moment. I began to think, for the first time, about the war in its deeper significance and to realize its full horrors and gruesome stupidities." He recalled how he "would meet friends in London on leave from France and learn a few weeks later that they had gone for good." Pearson spent much of this interlude with another Canadian pilot in training, Clifford Hames, also the son of a minister, also a University of Toronto student, also someone whose brothers had signed up. The two young men assumed that their generation was lost to a war that would never end, and that they too would be consumed in the sacrifice. "We spent hours trying to get some understanding of what we were being asked to do; to bring some reason to the senseless slaughter," Pearson wrote. "For what? King and country? Freedom and democracy? These words sounded hollow in 1918 and we increasingly rebelled against their hypocrisy."[32]

What was being questioned, discarded, retained, and remade in the personal realm reflected a parallel quest in the political sphere, forged by Canadian blood and Robert Borden's inner steel. The dominion had raised a citizen's army that fought with manifest distinction, but from the first declaration of war, Britain issued orders and Canadians followed them. Compounding the insult, in the first two years, the prime minister of this fearsome army received most of his information about the conflict from the daily press. Even the ever-patient Borden got fed up with such maternal contempt. "It can hardly be expected that we shall put 400,000 or 500,000 men in the field and willingly accept the position of having no more voice and receiving no more consideration than if we were toy automata," he wrote. "Any person cherishing such an expectation harbours an unfortunate and even dangerous delusion."[33]

Yet British officials tenaciously harboured that delusion, inciting Borden to hammer away at centuries-old habits of mind. As was so often the case with Canadian foreign policy objectives, external circumstances beyond the government's control made all the difference. Borden found his opening only when David Lloyd George became British prime minister in December 1916. The dynamic new war leader needed more soldiers and knew they would have to come from the dominions. Bowing to the unavoidable linkage between military might and diplomatic influence, Lloyd George established an Imperial War Cabinet in which the dominion leaders were informed, consulted, and, at times, even heeded.

Given the size of Canada's involvement and his own formidable skills, Borden emerged as a senior voice at these gatherings. True to his intentions, he presented his fellow prime ministers with the radical Resolution IX, which in dry, moderate language proposed the recognition of the dominions as fully autonomous and equal nations with a right to conduct their own external affairs. Resolution IX began to remake, with British acquiescence, a hierarchical empire into a commonwealth of equals. The goal was clear; the process was muddled.

As the great powers eventually prepared for a world after war, Borden learned that the dominions were expected to participate at the peace conference subsumed within an imperial delegation. Writing to his wife, he bemoaned Canada's vague state of being. "The difficulty arises from an anomalous position; a nation that is not a nation," he wrote. "It is about time to alter it." And alter it he did. Borden's unyielding temper compelled a reluctant London to accept that, however anomalous, Canada would send forth a Canadian delegation composed of Canadian delegates speaking for Canada. And in the proposed League of Nations, the dominion would hold its own separate seat. The war to save democracy in Europe ended up becoming, in the judgment of some historians, Canada's war of independence. But the greater independence attained, while undeniable, was still partial; Borden was no separatist. Even as he achieved more autonomy for his anomaly, the British subject still envisioned an enduring and intimate embrace between mother and daughter. Most Canadians remained comfortable with the fusion and indeed expected it. Perpetuating the tradition of duality, Borden agreed to have Canadians serve at the Versailles peace conference on the British Empire delegation. At some sessions, therefore, delegates heard some Canadians speaking for Canada and other Canadians speaking for the empire. As Borden's biographer, Robert Craig Brown, has written, complete or absolute independence was "revolutionary and far beyond the most advanced thinking about Canada's future entertained by either party in Parliament."[34]

Far from the exalted councils of power and the vast reworking of Canada's place in the imperial scheme, two novice pilots, Mike Pearson and Clifford Hames, reached the end of their brief, intense time together. Hames returned to his squadron, and Pearson returned to Canada, landing at Saint John, New Brunswick, on April 6, 1918, before taking a train to Toronto's Union Station for a joyous reunion with his parents. Home was now Guelph, Ontario, where his family had moved while he was overseas.

Pearson never told the whole story about the circumstances surrounding his return to Canada. In his memoirs, he wrote simply that he received a telegram ordering him home for an unspecified length of time. What actually unfolded was far more complicated than he ever wanted to reveal. In an outtake from his CBC television memoirs, Pearson let slip that he was "marked unfit and sent back" with other "wounded and discharged soldiers" but insisted he was "fit for further service." Only someone who had read a small notice in the April 8, 1918, edition of the *Guelph Mercury* would know that Pearson had returned from the war "largely owing to an injury received which has largely shattered his nerves." This was another way of saying shell shock, or nervous breakdown.[35]

In Toronto, Pearson reported to a medical board, where a doctor he knew from Salonika examined him. He too marked the returning soldier unfit to serve. "I was fit for further service," Pearson maintained, "but he thought I had had enough" and recommended a complete discharge on medical grounds. Then a Royal Air Force officer, suspecting Pearson of trying to shirk his duty, probed the young man before him, saying,

"You're marked 'unfit for further service.' Do you feel that you have no further service to give?" Pearson responded, "Well I can't feel that physically." Seeking to serve in some capacity, he offered to become a flight instructor. The RAF granted his request, and so the pilot who could barely fly spent the last months of the war in Toronto teaching what little he knew to unsuspecting cadets. When the war ended a few months later, Pearson's only problem, as he put it, "was merely to start again where I had left off in the spring of 1915 and to finish my university course."[36] But again, this was nothing close to the full story.

A report in Pearson's medical records dated May 6, just one month after returning home, described him as fidgety, pale, and very nervous. His lips and facial muscles trembled when he spoke, and he suffered from insomnia. His condition may have deteriorated when tragic news arrived from England. During a morning flight on April 25, his friend Clifford Hames stalled his engine, didn't have enough height to recover from the resulting dive, and crashed to his death. In his memoirs, Pearson did not discuss the emotional impact beyond allowing that "Cliff Hames and I came closer together in that short time than I have ever been with any person since, outside my family."[37] Losing Hames may have devastated Pearson. Perhaps he was already too numbed, after coming so close to death in his own plane crashes and bus accident, to take in any more grief. Either way, by the spring of 1918, Pearson had fallen apart. In the next medical report, dated September 10, he still appeared nervous and easily excited, still suffered nightmares about flying and crashing, and he stuttered in conversation.

During this period, he lived at the University of Toronto, which housed the aeronautics school where he was teaching and, ever the obsessive athlete, found time to play rugby for the Royal Air Force team, shining as a quarterback—fast, slippery, smart. "I was well enough to play football," he later commented, "but not well enough to fly." Family scrapbooks filled with press clippings boast of Pearson's wizardry on the field, and biographer John English concludes that these games were "Mike Pearson's sanatoria; the crowd's cheers the sedatives for his jangled nerves. The medical boards had told him that he needed rest, and he found it, paradoxically in physical exertion."[38]

On November 11, 1918, peace broke out. Grief-stricken nations celebrated in the gloom cast by millions of hovering ghosts. Pearson could
finally accept that he would not die in France. "That was the most dramatic and exciting moment of my life up till that time," he said. "This was
a reprieve. I didn't know what was going to happen. None of us did. We
might have had to go back again. I might have got fit."[39]

After the patriotic anthems and thanksgiving ceremonies ceased,
the survivors returned home, to endure yet more tragedy. An influenza
pandemic reached into every continent and faith, ignoring prayers and
good behaviour, and devoured far more souls than had died in the war.
Unemployment, inflation, falling standards of living and widespread
strikes that smacked of open class warfare blighted the Canadian economy. Veterans couldn't get jobs or decent benefits from the government
that had vowed to take care of them. Farmers and workers started or-
ganizing themselves into political parties. The English and the French
would not easily forget or forgive the trespasses committed during the
bitter battle to bring in conscription.

With the guns silenced in Europe, Africa, and the Middle East,
Pearson returned to the University of Toronto in January 1919. In a
hurried single term that made allowances for time spent overseas, he
completed his history degree while, of course, squeezing in as much
hockey as possible. By April, a year after his return to Canada, Pearson's
medical report indicated signs of his recovery. He was now described as
only "slightly nervous," exhibiting a "slight impediment in speech." His fingers no longer shook, and he could get a full night's sleep. A few shadows
lingered: he was easily agitated by sudden noises, troubled by nightmares,
and "unable to concentrate on work or sit still during lectures."[40] Despite
this, he managed to pass his exams. His charm and social skills clearly
remained intact, as he was voted class president.

Pearson's reticence about this episode in his life is not surprising. In a
society just beginning to delve into psychological depths, still intolerant of
something as unmanly as a nervous collapse, shame undoubtedly sealed
his lips on this matter forever. His daughter, Patricia, only learned what
her father had gone through when John English unearthed his medical
records. "I was very surprised because he always seemed to be able to
rise to every occasion, and his career was always straight ahead," she

said. "He never seemed to have any emotional problems that we were aware of. So it was a great surprise, but then on the other hand, he never talked about feelings or emotions, so maybe that was just something he wanted to bury and forget." In interviews with English, former colleagues recalled Pearson's foot, "which would constantly jiggle while he was talking, nervous habits that he had with his fingers, and that type of thing. He couldn't rest in the way a more relaxed person could," English concluded. "I also think it affected him deeply in the way that he confronted things. He was a person who could not get terribly involved emotionally." Looking beyond the breakdown to his father's overall war experience, Pearson's son, Geoffrey, observed: "I think it gave him a sense of the darker side of life and, in a way, added a strain to his personality which you see all through his life, which was a kind of pessimism about the future of mankind."[41]

For Pearson and his generation of diplomats, war could never be an abstraction; the Glorious Dead would never be faceless. When he later taught at the University of Toronto, he would walk by a large memorial for the fallen, and when he cared to look up at the wall, he could see amongst the long list of names carved in stone that of Clifford Hames. The century's first universal war remained the emotional backdrop for a diplomatic career conducted through so many other wars.

In the summer of 1919, Pearson left the University of Toronto to seek a living in the fractious postwar landscape. "I didn't know what to do," he recalled. "I was restless. I had lost four years."[42] The twenty-two-year-old felt no inclination to mount any political barricades. Neither did he burn with furious earthly ambition. Having renounced his pre-ordained path into the Methodist ministry, he ended up meandering through periods of drift punctuated by abrupt decisions to start anew. He would need close to a decade to find his true calling. It took Canada that long to create the kind of work he was born to do.

THREE

Sovereignty and Association

Whether we like to admit it or not, and I for one quite frankly admit it, Canadians are North Americans. We have a divided interest. While sentimentally and patriotically, we are bound closely to Great Britain, economically and geographically, we are bound to the North American continent.... I find myself irritated by the continued animosities of Europeans. I find myself remote from these continual quarrels and I believe we all do—which is only another way of saying that we live on the North American continent.

> —Agnes Macphail, MP for Grey-Bruce, House of
> Commons, March 2, 1936[1]

He won first place. Now everything would change.

As the news seeped through the University of Toronto in the summer of 1928, no doubt some eyebrows were raised in surprise. How exactly did the easygoing, boyish assistant history professor do so well on the entrance examinations for the Department of External Affairs? It was not an unreasonable question. While the thirty-one-year-old Lester Pearson, better known as Mike, toiled dutifully, if sometimes all too casually, in the classroom, his more obvious passion lay with coaching the university's hockey, rugby, lacrosse, and basketball teams. Even in retirement, reminiscing about writing the exams, Pearson encouraged the bewilderment. "I thought [diplomacy] would be a very interesting profession, but I never made any move to join. I was very happy where I was," he later said. "I didn't have any particular intention of taking the job, but I thought it would be interesting to write it. And I never can resist a competition."[2] That last throwaway line revealed his true hand: the joy in play, the willingness to risk, the desire to win.

Yet his high score on the External Affairs exam was hardly inevitable. In the decade after graduating from the University of Toronto, a sense of drift disrupted by sudden lunging to a greater destiny marked Pearson's path. He endured one excruciating week at a Toronto law firm, then spent the summer of 1919 playing semi-professional baseball in Guelph and working at a tire company. Then he decided to become rich.

An uncle in America wangled him a job at a vast meat-packing corporation. Imbued with great expectations, the would-be captain of industry expected his climb up the corporate ladder to start off with his being appointed an executive assistant, but instead he was posted to a subsidiary in Hamilton, Ontario, where he learned to stuff sausages with an air hose. He also worked briefly in the meatloaf kitchen. Not content with this, Pearson contrived a transfer in 1920 to the head office in Chicago.

After a year of clerking in the fertilizer department, the twenty-two-year-old realized he had walked into another dead end. "I was not exactly thrilled but tried to be a competent clerk," he remembered. "I was forging ahead, doing my best to think that the world revolved around our Big Crop brands, and that I was a benefactor to humanity in trying to get them into the hands of farmers."[3] Twelve months after emigrating, he decided to become a scholar and conduct his graduate work at one of the greatest academies in the empire, where he had lived for a few months during the war.

Oxford was an expensive dream, so Pearson applied for a Massey Foundation fellowship. Vincent Massey had taught Pearson at the University of Toronto and was an Oxford man himself. As someone who also abandoned a corporate destiny for public service, Massey was apparently impressed by Pearson's "desire to forsake the fleshpots of Chicago for the educational opportunities of Oxford" and approved his application. In the fall of 1921, Pearson returned to the Mother Country. He found student life at St. John's College entrancing, perhaps because he devoted his days to hockey, lacrosse, tennis, rugby, and, when his schedule permitted, attending to his degree.[4] The irrepressible athlete graduated in 1923 with a respectable if unimpressive second in history and managed

Undersecretary of State for External Affairs Oscar Douglas Skelton (left)
and Lester Pearson, 1930s (Library and Archives Canada/PA-110825)

to secure a teaching position at his Canadian alma mater. In all this
meandering, he had, twice, decided to renounce a life abroad. He had,
twice, decided to remain Canadian.

The twenty-six-year-old lecturer, not much older than his students,
preferred face-to-face interaction in seminars to researching in seclu-
sion, and in his new role followed old habits, ensuring that teaching
did not interfere with multiple coaching duties. He later conceded with
a decent measure of self-knowledge that he was never cut out to be "a
cloistered scholar," and during five years at the University of Toronto,
Coach Pearson did not produce a single major or even minor piece of
scholarship.[5]

Indeed, his most significant achievement was to marry one of his students, Maryon Moody, a bright, stylish, lapsing Methodist from Winnipeg.
Only a few years apart in age, they delighted in each other's sense of
humour, and were engaged by early 1924, just months after first meeting.

At some point Pearson would learn that his witty wife could be acidic, intimidating to lesser beings and children, and unafraid to say things in public that he would never dare. For better and for worse, she was his opposite and complement. Daughter Patricia recalled: "He was very, very affable, genial, good-tempered, good-natured, nearly always in a good mood. And my mother tended to be a bit moody, and he could always sort of jolly her out of her moods. So it really worked well that way." In her twenties, the well-raised doctor's daughter mused vaguely about some kind of adventure or career beyond marriage, yet however much she talked about doing her own thing—no easy task in such a constrictive time and place—Maryon was ultimately too conservative to escape the predictable. Her rebellion came in later years, when she refused to play in full the role of the politician's doting wife. She smoked in public without apology, swore within earshot of reporters and party officials, and felt few qualms about expressing her displeasure. Party executive Keith Davey recalled one of the faithful making a glowing but interminable introduction before Pearson was to speak. Maryon Pearson leaned over and snapped all too loudly, "When will that woman shut up?" In the 1960s, she broke protocol and refused to curtsy to the wife of the governor general. "She was much more outspoken than he was," her observant son, Geoffrey, noted. "She wasn't running for office. She was able to say what she thought and did. She was shrewd and I think saw through people better than he did."[6]

If Maryon Pearson found tedious the duties and rituals of her husband's public life, she had only herself to blame, because she dreamed of it, perhaps before he did. Very early in their relationship, she gushed to a friend about her new fiancé. "We don't want to stay in Toronto all our lives—and I think shall take the odd chance in foreign climes," she wrote. "He is full of brains and could get university work almost anywhere. He is going to write a bit too. I should love him to get into the diplomatic service one day—and be Ambassador somewhere. After all, why not dream?" She ended on a confident note: "I am quite sure he will do something big in the world some day."[7]

Dreaming of joining the diplomatic service was not so farfetched in a dominion still shifting from something far more than a colony into something less than a fully sovereign country. However, those dreams had to materialize in a Canada bound by the deadweight of the thousands devoured in an imperial war. When Pearson came to represent his country, he would have to conduct a diplomacy of, as he later described it, "timidity and isolation and withdrawal" — and all for very sensible, even defensible, reasons that he at times fully supported.[8]

Canada desires no special privilege. We believe that the decision of Great Britain on any important public issue, domestic or foreign, should be made by the people of Britain....so the decision of Canada on any important issue, domestic or foreign, we believe should be made by the people of Canada.
— William Lyon Mackenzie King, October 8, 1923, Imperial Conference in London[9]

On a Saturday afternoon in September 1922, the man who would define Canadian foreign policy for a quarter of a century and who would, by extension, preside over Lester Pearson's career during that time, was interrupted just as he was about to walk into a packed hall in Sharon, Ontario, a short drive north of Toronto. Inside, a huge crowd waited to see Prime Minister William Lyon Mackenzie King, who had only been in office for nine months. Long-time observer and journalist Bruce Hutchison wrote of that early period: "One thing was said everywhere with assurance — he would not last long. All Conservative politicians...and not a few Liberals, agreed that King's arrival had been an accident from which a sensible country would soon recover."[10] Capable of great charm in private, the permanent bachelor was purposefully dull in his well-crafted speeches, maddeningly evasive in his machinations. Cautious to the bone, King preferred to govern as much as possible within the bosom of majority opinion. Few contemporaries could fathom that behind his immaculate, unremarkable facade, he consulted with mediums to talk with dead relatives, beheld signs from the Almighty in the everyday around him, and obsessively analyzed his dreams for messages from his deepest psyche and beyond.

Fortunately for the Liberal Party, its leader's lifelong quest through the spirit realm did not hamper his political mission on Earth. This dedicated Soldier of God, fervent mystic, and emotional journeyman remained a shrewd, occasionally ruthless, gladiator equipped with hypersensitive antennae that could gauge the fluctuating shadings of the collective Canadian consciousness with fine precision. He seemed to know exactly what was possible in his party and in his country. Confounding current and future detractors, King would become Canada's longest-serving prime minister and, at the time of his death, the longest-serving prime minister in Commonwealth history. But in September 1922, a crisis erupting on the other side of the ocean suddenly threatened his tenuous hold on power.

On that September afternoon, a reporter from the *Toronto Daily Star* handed the neophyte leader a news despatch announcing that His Majesty's Government in Great Britain had requested his government in Canada to consider sending military and moral aid in a potential clash with Turkey, which was seemingly poised to attack a British garrison guarding the port of Chanak on the strategic Dardanelles straits. Gazing at those words, King confronted his political nightmare: the Mother Country summoning her oldest dominion without any advance warning to some foreign battle meaningless to Canada but poisonous to her unity.

King contained his undoubted anger and made a bland statement to the reporter, saying he would discuss the matter with Cabinet. The obvious omission was telling. He had declined to offer any support to the imperial emergency. After he delivered his prepared speech to the waiting crowd, he returned to Ottawa to formulate his response to the imperialists in London and the imperialists in Canada. He knew what he wanted to say. He needed to work out how and when to say it.

The September 18 Toronto *Globe* framed the issue with the blunt headline "British Lion Calls Cubs to Face the Beast of Asia." The prime minister lamented in his diary, "Everyone seemingly is ready for war —nurses, soldiers, churches…There is no attempt to consider the issue, just that Britain has issued a call, therefore we should respond." Speaking for widespread anglophone desire to face the foreign beast, Leader of the Opposition Arthur Meighen declared in typically unambiguous tones: "Let there be no dispute as to where I stand. When Britain's message came then Canada should have said: 'Ready, aye ready; we stand by you.' I hope the time has not gone by when that declaration can yet be made."[11]

King turned to his predecessors for guidance. John A. Macdonald had rejected an imperial summons to send troops to the Sudan—"almost a complete parallel," King noted in his diary—and Laurier had resisted and reframed the call to South Africa.[12] Following in these footsteps, the man so often accused of having no principles or spine informed the world's only global superpower that Canada would not automatically jump when beckoned. His mantra was straightforward—"Parliament will decide"—and he meant it. He was naturally accused of betraying the Mother Country, but, happily for him, luck crowned his unheroic, evasive method. The momentarily all-consuming crisis abruptly evaporated without war between Britain and Turkey. King emerged triumphant on several domestic fronts: his response did not inflame lingering tensions between anglophones and francophones, he reasserted Macdonald and Laurier's position, and he stayed faithful to his core constituencies.

The prime minister's stance arose from an inevitable fusion of conviction and circumstance. He never forgot that the Liberal Party's success was anchored in Quebec, a fortress of isolationism with no interest in fighting any British wars anywhere. He knew isolationist currents also flowed beyond that province, through a war-weary nation still mourning sons, brothers, husbands, and fathers, all the glorious dead who reached into the waking moments of those who once cheered the giddy rush to oblivion. And King had personally experienced the domestic shockwaves generated by overseas emergencies.

In the 1917 election, he remained loyal to the anti-conscriptionist Laurier when most Liberal anglophone MPs defected to the pro-conscription Conservatives. King lost his bid for a seat in Ontario but earned the respect of Liberals in Quebec, who en masse had rejected conscription. What could have ended his political career forever became his saving grace at the 1919 convention when francophone delegates remembered his loyalty and made him the new Liberal leader. To his last days in office, King would remain obsessed with the spectre of Canadian discord, acutely aware that his country was a patchwork of two dominant nations with multiple and highly flammable notions of loyalty. To achieve his essential objective—keeping Canada united—he would strive for a difficult balance. "Our policy is not one of unconditional isolation nor is it one of unconditional intervention. It depends upon the specific situation in Europe and also in our country," he stated at the 1923 Imperial Conference. "It would be worse than useless for the representatives of Canada here to pledge themselves to policies which may have no effective backing in the country."[13] The equally pragmatic Lester Pearson would follow that approach throughout his career.

While King resisted the imperial summons to Chanak, Pearson was chasing pucks and rugby balls at Oxford. He did not leave behind any opinions about the crisis, but a very general attitude to foreign affairs can be gleaned from articles he wrote during that period for a Methodist newspaper, the *Christian Guardian*. They display his lifelong sense of irony and absurdity, his mocking skepticism about great power fumbling, the acid awareness that his generation's sacrifice had not raised up a better world. In an article written in 1922, about holidaying through German territory still occupied by Allied troops, the veteran's gloomy words mirrored his country's recoil from the darkening continent and, by implication, international entanglements:

> The Germans nourish a bitter hatred for France and the French, and view with ill concealed animosity, the presence of French soldiers. ... To any one who is a sincere lover of peace and who marched off to the great struggle full of the noble ideal that this was a "war to end war," this hatred of whole nations for each other, causes more than discouragement; it brings something akin to despair. France, with a devastated region and a million and half dead ever before her eyes, can only see her salvation in a crushed and cowed Germany. The latter only feels that the heel of the conqueror is on her neck. A German lady told me the other day that the hatred of France being implanted in the minds of the school children is something appalling. ... Newspapers talk about the "lost lands," and their fellow Germans in the "unredeemed provinces." Amiable old gentlemen who never slept in the mud themselves or crawled in the filth and slime of a no-man's land, are ... predicting the time when they will be able to send forth other millions of young Germans to a glorious war of revenge.

Seemingly free of any resentment against his recent enemy, the future internationalist continued, posing questions that would run through his entire diplomatic career: "Why is it impossible to tear out the spirit of international hate from the minds of millions of human beings who boast of their modern civilization, and who glory in being followers of Him Who said 'Peace on earth, good will towards men'?" Pearson asked. "Canada may well be thankful that she can contemplate the future without her vision being blurred by the story of a blood stained past. It is her strength."[14]

Mackenzie King shared those same apprehensions, and feared that Britain's imperial needs would draw Canada back to another cataclysm. And so Pearson lived in an age when the prime minister conducted a sustained, calculated mission to realign the imperial construct so that Canada could conduct its own foreign policy without having to ask permission. This would be a civilized, constitutional grappling of words and relationships between people who shared the same language, the same religion, the same culture and skin tone. Bearing in mind the exceptions in South Africa against the Boers and in Ireland against the Catholics, the imperial government treated subjects in the "white" dominions rather differently from subjects in Africa and Asia.

King knew full well that the British were not going to send gunboats up the St. Lawrence, or use chemical warfare on Canadian villages like they did in Iraq, or fire into unarmed crowds in Canada as they did in India. However, for an empire keen to maintain the semblance of unity in the face of foreign threats and local uprisings, appearances mattered, and the Foreign Office viewed Canada's sovereignist impulses as an alarming declaration of disunity. Thus, London blanched and resisted when King pushed for more sovereignty and countered with intense pressure to have Canada join a vague imperial foreign and defence scheme. This was a tantalizing prospect for those Canadians who believed their country would derive greater influence in the world working through an international assembly of nations. Relentless, exasperating, and principled, King rejected this strategic hope and instead pursued a policy that amplified the economic and political forces already at work dissolving and reducing the British Empire to a more modest commonwealth.

The Canadian prevailed, in part, because London implicitly agreed with him. King wanted for Canada exactly what the British wanted for their own government: complete freedom of action in foreign affairs. Accustomed to ruling in splendid isolation, no British government would ever countenance sharing that treasured rule with former colonies in any kind of formal framework. Despite all the rhetoric about a policy by and for the entire empire, London never introduced concrete proposals on how to construct such an unwieldy network of conflicting opinions and interests. In their own time, the other dominions would come to share Canada's insistence on a decentralized empire.

Yet typically for an anglophone Canadian of his generation, King remained, even in his moment of supreme resistance, a British subject willing to rally to the Mother Country in time of real emergency. At the 1923 Imperial Conference, he assured the British government: "If a great and clear call of duty comes, Canada will respond, whether or not the United States responds, as she did in 1914." He added a crucial caveat, however, stating that Canada and America's isolationist streaks were "a most important consideration against intervention in lesser issues."[15] Mackenzie King would spend much of his time in office arguing with London about what exactly constituted a "lesser issue," for even as he won significant battles at the conference table through the 1920s, he could not easily purge absent-minded assumptions forged over centuries. His triumphant resistance over Chanak, celebrated in the historical literature to come, was followed by his own, scarcely known, version of the Suez Crisis, to which he responded in a fashion similar to Lester Pearson's thirty years later.

In November 1924, the newly appointed British foreign secretary Austen Chamberlain unintentionally set the stage when he declared at London's Guildhall that he must be ever mindful that he spoke not just for Great Britain but for all the dominions, and that it was, he underlined, his "imperative duty to preserve in word and act" the empire's diplomatic unity. "Our interests are one," he said, "and we must speak with one voice in the Councils of the world."[16] Just nine days later, Mackenzie King did his best to try to puncture that delusion.

In Cairo, assassins unfazed by the aura of imperial power gunned down Britain's commander of the Egyptian army and the governor general of the Sudan, Major-General Lee Stack. His assassination turned Egypt into yet another potential imperial battleground. Chamberlain informed Canada's High Commissioner in London, Peter Larkin, and his dominion counterparts that His Majesty's Government would never acquiesce to Cairo's demand that Great Britain withdraw from the Sudan and relinquish its stake in the Suez Canal. The waterway, asserted Chamberlain, remained absolutely vital to the security of the empire.

Trying to defuse the situation by internationalizing it, as Pearson would during his Suez crisis, Larkin suggested that London take the dispute to the League of Nations. Foreshadowing the same attitudes the British government would express in 1956, the British foreign minister of 1924 replied that "anything that concerned territory already held, would not be permitted to be adjudicated on by anybody—even by the League of Nations." Unimpressed by this argument, Larkin raised the matter once more, but Chamberlain insisted that he "could not submit a question of that kind to any Council for decision."[17]

Within days of Stack's assassination, Royal Marines landed in Alexandria to reinforce the imperial hold. King wrote in his diary: "the conflict between England's determination to 'govern' & Egyptian desire for independence, & all that it involves of the control of the Suez makes a very unpleasant situation."[18]

When Mackenzie King met with Canada's governor general, His Excellency Lord Byng of Vimy, they circled each other in an old game. Byng tried to elicit from King some expression of support regarding the Suez Canal. The unyielding defender of Canadian sovereignty remained consistent in his resistance. In another foreshadow of Pearson's later stance, King told Byng with blunt insight that Canadians "favoured [the Suez Canal] being internationalized & matter being dealt with by the League of Nations & I did not imagine Grt. Br. would thank us for that expression of view."[19] Indeed, that would be the last thing Britain wanted to hear from a dominion.

Fortunately for King, this crisis did not generate anything like the momentary bloodlust ignited by Chanak, and soon enough the episode subsided without Canada being pressured for military or diplomatic support. But the British remained deeply obsessed with protecting the Suez Canal. In December, addressing the House of Commons but also beyond to the Middle East, Chamberlain stated that Egypt would "always be maintained as an essential British interest" because Egyptian stability was necessary for the empire's peace and security. "In Egypt all that we desire is that the Egyptian government should do their duty," Chamberlain declared, "and if they are willing to do that they will find no better, no firmer, and no more loyal friends than the Government and the people of this country."[20] Egyptians, however, displayed no desire to fulfill a duty to foreigners that entailed collective submission. In three decades, the matter would be settled for good with an outburst of violence and deception.

For the lucky few, the ongoing tension between the Mother Country and another set of subjects culminated peacefully and creatively in the landmark 1926 Balfour Report, which stated that Great Britain and its former colonies—Australia, Canada, the Irish Free State, Newfoundland, New Zealand, and South Africa—were "equal in status, in no way subordinate one to another in any aspect of their domestic or external affairs, though united by a common allegiance to the Crown." One of the empire's many death knells, this report was converted into legal and constitutional reality as the 1931 Statute of Westminster, and applied in slightly different fashion within each dominion. Canada characteristically held back from going all the way. "Full independence was there to be grasped if Canadians wanted it, but it is clear they did not," argue historians J.L. Granatstein and Norman Hillmer. "Certainly very few politicians did."[21]

His Majesty's Government in Ottawa decided that His Majesty's Government in London would retain the power to amend the Canadian constitution, continue to appoint the governor general, and provide Canadians with their final court of appeal on civil cases. The Canadian government freely decided that Canadians would remain British subjects represented overseas, overwhelmingly, by British diplomats. In this ongoing transition, most Canadians, like Pearson, accepted that they were both sovereign and associated, subject and free, and continued to infuse and blend their national identity with British overtones. Looking back at the 1920s, Pearson recalled: "I wanted Canada to have an independent position but always inside a British Commonwealth of Nations. Never in my wildest dreams would I have considered an independent Canada outside the British association. I was still a sentimentalist about the Throne and the British connection and the heritage going back to Magna Carta and beyond."[22]

Pearson's sense of connection at the time can be glimpsed in surviving lecture notes from a current affairs course he taught in 1927 called "Institutions of the Modern British Empire." Perhaps the single most telling word in the entire lecture comes when the thirty-year-old assistant professor refers to the British Empire as "ours." He felt utterly at home with the historic duality, stating: "We are British as well as Canadian citizens." He acknowledged failings—the empire, he said, "is not an idyllic creation. It has had in the past and has in the present certain ugly features that its well-wishers would like to see obliterated"—but he never questioned the empire's right to exist and rule. "One need not be accused of boastful flag-waving, in saying that, on the whole, the good from the Empire has far exceeded its evils," he told his students.[23]

Even as he said this, Pearson recognized that not all British subjects felt this way. As he surveyed the fragmented quarter of the world map that was then still coloured pink, he would turn at one point to Egypt, outlining without criticism the imperial rationale for not withdrawing after the occupation in 1882. This would have allowed, he said, "the restoration of the inept regime of the Khedive, the subjugation of the country by the Turk, the re-entry of the French." According to Pearson, the British had "remained to the great benefit of the peasant and the worker who had never before experienced any form of decent and orderly administration." He also sympathized with Egyptian grievances about limited freedoms granted in 1922. "These limitations have not been recognised as just by the Egyptian nationalists," he noted. "It is this refusal to recognise the settlement of 1922 that keeps alive the 'Egyptian Question.'"[24]

While Pearson taught his students in Toronto about an empire he assumed would endure into the foreseeable future, the cautious master architect at the centre of the national odyssey continued to move towards a more sovereignist state of affairs. In April 1926, Mackenzie King asked Vincent Massey, one of his former Cabinet ministers, to become the first fully accredited Canadian representative on the world stage. The intended posting was the United States, which King considered, as he wrote in private to Massey, "the most important country of all." At first

Massey declined because, as he later wrote, "I frankly did not think then that the Washington post offered an adequate opportunity for useful work." He promptly changed his mind, however, and accepted the groundbreaking position. While some Canadians applauded this step, others were outraged that a Canadian, and not a British, diplomat would speak for Canada. The appointment signalled a "parting of the ways and split up of Empire too serious to contemplate," one anonymous extremist warned Massey in writing. "If you are appointed to the position I will personally finish your course with a knife in your belly; shooting is too good for you."[25]

Less violent but still heartfelt anguish was expressed in the House of Commons during debate on the purchase of a building for the new legation. Leader of the Opposition R.B. Bennett foresaw "the last great adventure in our relation to Great Britain," declaring: "It is but the doctrine of separation, it is but the evidence in many minds of the end of our connection with the empire."[26] And the end of the old relationship was indeed nigh. In 1928, Britain broke centuries of speaking patterns and replaced the traditional one-man conduit between Ottawa and London, the British-appointed governor general, with a distinctly separate British representative, the High Commissioner. The position of governor general now became a ceremonial figurehead, the Crown's representative in residence. Canada was once more leading the rest of the dominions towards more autonomy. Britain did not open a High Commission in South Africa until 1931, and not in Australia until 1936.

The evolution of Canada's status in the world required diplomats to embody that status. Prime Minister King charged the undersecretary of state for External Affairs, Oscar Douglas Skelton, to seek out the brightest members of the postwar generation. In the summer of 1926, Pearson had been staying in Ottawa while conducting research at the Dominion Archives for a potential book (which he never wrote), and he was invited to a dinner honouring the chief archivist. In what seems like a phenomenal stroke of luck, Pearson found himself sitting next to Skelton, who talked about his plans to build a Canadian foreign service. The lecturer did not, however, appear to have been enticed or make any impression on his future boss. Both men parted that evening with no recorded follow-up.

In that phase of his life, not even married a full year, not yet a father, Pearson still enjoyed his tranquil days teaching and coaching. "It was a most rewarding and satisfying life," he said, "not in terms of money, but in terms of everything else." Although the Methodist minister's son typically downplayed what later unfolded as all luck and no sweat, John English has unravelled Pearson's entry into diplomacy, showing that it had everything to do with his well-honed skill in rallying supporters backstage while quietly and deliberately chasing the prize. Through the winter of 1926, Pearson presumably talked about joining External Affairs with at least one of his most senior colleagues at the history department, W.P.M. Kennedy, and possibly even asked him to write a reference letter. In January 1927, Kennedy, perhaps feeling that Pearson not true professor material, wrote to Skelton promoting Pearson as "a first class fellow with an engaging personality, wide interests, and sound judgement." Only then did Pearson follow up with his own letter. In May, Kennedy wrote to Skelton again to praise Pearson. "He is equitable in temperament and is not in the least likely to go off the handle," he wrote. "I am sure Pearson is full of the greatest promise."[27]

It took some time for a position to come open and Pearson did not sit for the exams until June 1928. Over four days, he wrote papers on international affairs and law, modern history, an essay on the rise of fascism, and crafted a précis. A Civil Service Commission board also grilled the candidate, one member picking up on a point made in a reference letter from the over-enthusiastic Kennedy, who declared that Pearson's war record glittered not only on the battlefield but also in camp back in England. Pearson explained that the "brilliant" record at camp involved his skill with a pointed stick picking up garbage to prepare the parade ground and hitting a home run for the 4th Reserve Battalion team. This self-deprecation went over very well. The oral exam factored into the written exams, and Pearson ended up taking first place. In his memoirs, he attributes his success to the preference given to veterans but again, as John English has shown, Pearson scored an impressive 85 percent average on the written exams, beating out tough competition, including several future colleagues. Pearson's "jaunty amiability and sporting tastes, his manner and personality," writes English, "led others to underestimate his considerable intellectual abilities."[28] Despite his win, Pearson still had to clear one more hurdle before being granted entry into Ottawa's prized sanctum.

Canada's envoy extraordinary and minister plenipotentiary in Washington, Vincent Massey, who had known Pearson since the assistant professor was an undergraduate and made possible his time at Oxford with a Massey fellowship, voiced doubts. In the summer of 1928, the very proper Massey raised pointed questions with Skelton about the candidate from Toronto, who clearly did not strike him as a refined diplomat in the making. "There is something curiously loose-jointed and sloppy about his mental makeup which, as a matter of fact, is reflected in some measure in his physical bearing," he wrote. "It is possible, however, that his other qualities offset this defect." Himself a transplant from academia, and perhaps not so put off by casual bearings, Skelton concurred in part. "I have just had an interview with Pearson," he replied. "You have exactly hit the nail on the head. There is something curiously loose-jointed in his physical bearing and perhaps to a lesser extent in his mental makeup. At the same time he has a very distinct capacity and attractive personal qualifications." Pearson's most obvious qualification for the new position was one essential in diplomacy; as Kennedy observed, he possessed an "extraordinary capacity for getting on with" people.[29]

The loose-jointed professor prevailed over these doubts and was invited to join Canada's fledgling diplomatic service as a first secretary. Then the University of Toronto threw him a very tempting curve ball, offering him the position of athletics director. His salary would be higher than his civil service pay, but—and this may have stung his pride—he would retain the rank of assistant professor, albeit with reduced teaching duties. Pearson claimed he considered taking it but for once dethroned his love of sports for a much more serious game that would allow him to unleash his full potential and exceed even his wildest dreams.

They were very unpompous people. They had a great dislike of pretension and particularly diplomatic pretension. Ours was to be a very different kind of service—more ordinary Canadian without fuss and protocol. . . . I remember Norman [Robertson] saying to me at the very beginning, "Never enter in your

passport 'Diplomat'; always put 'Civil Servant.' We are not trying to be anything
special." That was the tone...rather academic. They were all academics.
—Charles Ritchie, Department of External Affairs, 1934–1971[30]

Echoing his teenaged departure for war in Europe and his departure
for vast wealth in the United States, Pearson embarked on his new life
in Ottawa with great expectations. "I had rather a kind of exalted idea
of foreign offices and diplomacy from reading books and I considered
I had achieved a position of pretty high professional distinction," he
recalled. "I was now almost a diplomat. And perhaps I was a little too
impressed by my transition." When he followed Skelton into Parliament's
East Block, which housed External Affairs, Pearson noticed that the
guard saluted Skelton and ignored him. "I thought, 'Well, obviously
he doesn't know who I am,'" he remembered. "I was given this little
office away up in the attic. That was a bit of a disappointment. I thought
I might have a large office with an outer office, you know, and press
buttons and people would run, but this wasn't exactly where men who
made foreign policy worked."[31]

In those embryonic days, External Affairs' entire staff could fit into a
pair of double-decker buses. Aside from those dealing with administrative, accounting, and secretarial duties, only fourteen conducted actual
policy or diplomatic work. By 1930, they would still number only twenty-
one, serving in Ottawa, Washington, London, Paris, Geneva, and Tokyo.
External Affairs was so small that the new first secretary was actually
taken to meet Mackenzie King, then also the foreign minister, who possessed his own measure of charm. Pearson recalled, "Mr. King could be
a very warm human being, to younger people especially. I didn't see him
for a long time afterwards, but at that time he made me feel that he'd be
wanting to see me about every half an hour, I was so important." Starting
out, Pearson handled assignments all over the map: "Lighthouses in the
Red Sea, international tariffs on cement, the nationality of Anglo-Chinese
children living in Canada, aviation licences in Canada and Switzerland,
and the protection of young female artists travelling abroad."[32] Working
his way up from the ground floor, or rather downwards from his attic
office, the wandering war veteran, indifferent fertilizer clerk, second class

graduate student, and casual university lecturer realized he had, at last, discovered his true calling—and his timing was superb.

In this apprenticeship, Pearson found himself working in an intimate setting with people very much like himself. When Mackenzie King set out to create a foreign service, he decided to make it a meritocracy and, with Skelton as deputy, assembled the most celebrated group of public servants in Canada's history. This is the generation that served in the Great War and saw friends and family lost in its mayhem. When few Canadians either travelled outside the country or attended university, they earned post-graduate degrees abroad. While their parents knew Canada only as a quasi-colony, they saw their country become increasingly sovereign. Likely not any brighter or more capable than their successors, they were supremely fortunate in joining a skeletal infrastructure where they could pioneer and originate rather than pedal small wheels in anonymity. "They recognized that Canada had a place to play in the world, that government had a role to play in shaping the lives of people," J.L. Granatstein says of them, "These were the men—they were all men—who between 1935 and 1957 really made Canada over. They created the social policies that the government implemented in that period. They created the international persona that Canada developed in that period, and Pearson was one of the absolutely critical ones in that group."[33]

Except for a summer in Washington, the future world-roving diplomat spent his first seven years at External Affairs largely landlocked in Canada. In January 1930, Pearson attended his first international conference, where powers great and small gathered in London to contain the arms race at sea. He kept a diary during his three months abroad and his words show him already imbued with a useful skepticism about impractical acts of diplomacy. His lack of illusions about Canada's stature matched his lack of illusions about legislating peace on earth. Representing a country that sailed a minuscule navy, he accepted Canada's place on the sidelines. His main wrangles at the conference had nothing to do with battleships and everything to do with imperial relations, which exasperated him at times. "Navies might be reduced or navies might be increased, war and peace in the world might hang in the balance," Pearson wrote, "but Dominion status must be preserved at all cost."[34]

In 1930, dominion status remained a blurred state of being—even the empire, or Commonwealth, delegates themselves were not quite sure how the Mother Country and her ill-defined offspring should interact with each other and the rest of the world. When the dominion delegations were presented to their shared King, Pearson noted with a mocking tone, "A constitutional issue of infinite magnitude arose." Would British Prime Minister Ramsay Macdonald introduce all the Commonwealth delegates, or simply those from the United Kingdom? London wanted the honour all to itself. The Canadians wanted the separate delegations to introduce themselves. The Canadians prevailed. "Our national autonomy was saved," Pearson wrote.[35]

Throughout the remainder of the conference, that autonomy would have to be saved again and again because the British, however well intentioned, couldn't seem to break old habits. The instinctive compromiser sought the elusive middle ground where he could legitimately "safeguard the principle of separate Dominion representation while refraining from embarrassing the Br. govt. by unduly pressing its exercise." But the battles proved so numerous that even Pearson felt occasionally compelled to mount the ramparts to defend semantics and optics. When in one meeting, a British committee chairman used the term "British Empire" in a way that seemed to include all the self-governing dominions, Pearson moved behind the scenes to repair the damage, urging the British delegation refer to itself solely as the delegation of Great Britain. He also made sure the confounding phrase was changed in the meeting's minutes to "Great Britain." Afterwards he noted in his diary: "I hate this sort of thing but apparently it has to be done. I think the British were also rather peeved at my sensitiveness. They were chaffing me about it afterwards."[36]

The challenges underlying Pearson's modest attempt to clarify a hazy constitutional status were highlighted when the conference reconvened in The Hague after a short recess. "Australia and N.Z. unfortunately are not here," he fumed, "the former having adopted the deplorable course of sending full powers to act for her to the [British]. No wonder foreigners get a bit fed up with the Br. Dominions."[37]

Pearson remained for the entire conference, enduring the inevitable tedium of diplomacy: numbing speeches, glacial committees, self-reproducing sub-committees, pointless points of order—all failing to produce any kind of meaningful naval disarmament, largely because, as Pearson judged, "subjects could *not* be discussed merely as legal problems. They were political ones and this made any attempt at a solution at this time bound to fail."[38] His first experience of international diplomacy also allowed Pearson to witness superpowers so obsessed with their own fears and interests, they imperilled the very peace they professed to protect. As he would for the rest of his diplomatic career, he had no patience with nationalist obsessions that undermined universal cooperation.

Summing up, he advocated something Mackenzie King would have completely agreed with: the fine and necessary art of avoidance. "A pessimist might even insist and I'm not sure he would not be right that the Conference actually did more harm than good by bringing to light and emphasizing essential differences," he noted in his diary, concluding: "an international conference which actually does not succeed does more damage than if it had never been held." After observing the limits of diplomacy in Europe, Pearson returned to behold the hazards of political life in Ottawa. In July 1930, a majority of voters removed Mackenzie King from his nine years of mostly uninterrupted rule and transferred power to Richard B. Bennett, a Methodist-raised, devout believer in the bonds of empire who was given to fiery outbursts of temper. Even though Pearson occasionally felt Bennett's wrath at point-blank range, he seemed to prefer the directness to King's more passive aggression. The professional civil servant worked for the new prime minister with all the discipline and focus he gave to King.

In turn, Bennett recognized Pearson's talent and appointed him secretary on two major royal commissions, the first examining grain futures, the other probing corporate concentration and price fixing. The jobs required subtle manoeuvring through political minefields, and with his endless tact, administrative finesse, and drafting skills, Pearson shone, and to such an extent on the latter commission that he burnt out. The commissioners wrote Bennett praising Pearson for devoting "all his time" to the job. "By 'all' we mean on an average from 9 o'clock in the morning until midnight, Saturdays and Sundays included." They asked the prime minister to reward Pearson, and Bennett complied with a sizeable bonus, which he justified to the House, perhaps with a touch of hyperbole, saying, "Mr. Pearson is on the verge of a complete nervous breakdown."[39]

Bennett also decided his ambitious official should receive another sign of official favour. In the late spring of 1935, on board a ship bound for the Silver Jubilee celebrations in London, Bennett summoned Pearson to his cabin. Struggling with seasickness, Pearson was aghast to find his name on the honours list being compiled by the prime minister, who wanted him awarded the Order of the British Empire. Knowing Skelton, his immediate superior, nurtured a profound anti-imperial ire, Pearson asked Bennett whether he could get an increase in pay instead, adding with cheek, "You can't raise a family on an OBE." Despite his legendary temper, Bennett calmly advised Pearson to accept the order or forget about ever being promoted. Pearson wisely took the advice and honour, earned on the domestic front far from any external affairs.[40]

A few months later, Bennett would send Pearson back to the empire's capital, to serve in the High Commission. After seven years in Ottawa, Pearson had finally secured a diplomatic posting. The timing, however, was marked by dismal irony. Pearson made his entry onto the diplomatic stage when diplomacy failed to contain an appalling nightmare enveloping Europe. Democratically elected tyrants fuelled by homicidal ambitions ruled in Germany and Italy; a military clique held sway in Japan. Decent, thoughtful, well-intentioned people struggled to restrain these demons using decent, thoughtful methods, hoping against plain facts that Europe still held a chance for peace at an ethical price.

In this fog of delusion and good intentions, Pearson, the unknown novice, watched from the sidelines as a tenuous alliance of nations tried to stop a European power from invading a weak African country in defiance of world opinion and international good manners, risking a wider war in the process. He even witnessed a Canadian proposal, one that might have brought peace, create headlines around the world until Canada itself disavowed it. He was about to experience a dark mirror of his triumph at Suez.

FOUR

A Sense of Proportion

I later became very impatient of the idea that Canada was going to be sucked into another European war to defend the Treaty of Versailles and the boundaries of France....I thought it was intolerable as a Canadian that we should be involved in a European war every twenty years and if this was the price to pay for association with Great Britain, France, other countries then perhaps it was too high a price to pay.

—Lester Pearson, remembering the 1930s[1]

The idea that every twenty years this country should automatically and as a matter of course take part in a war overseas for democracy or self-determination of other small nations...risk the lives of its people, risk bankruptcy and political disunion, seems to many a nightmare and sheer madness.

—William Lyon Mackenzie King, House of Commons, March 30, 1939[2]

On the eleventh day of September, 1935, Lester Pearson joined an assembly of delegates, secretaries, bureaucrats, translators, journalists, and bystanders as the League of Nations agonized over how to prevent Italy, one of its most powerful members, from attacking Ethiopia, one of its most vulnerable. He had come to Geneva full of professional skepticism, uncertain whether he was about to witness another betrayal of the weak by the many. The chattering hum subsided when the British foreign secretary, Samuel Hoare, mounted the rostrum. The assembled still dared to hope they would hear the words desperately needed to tip the scales hovering between deliverance and havoc. But as with so many issues confronting this association of fifty-seven disparate members, few could agree on which words needed to be spoken. Some members thought deliverance would come only if the league forced Italy to back down and leave Ethiopia in one piece. Others argued that deliverance could be achieved only if the league itself backed down and allowed Rome to take all it desired.

Having attended only a few international conferences and representing a largely irrelevant power, Pearson was invisible, but he was not alone. Geneva was littered with dozens of equally faceless diplomats hoping to transcend the lowly stratum of their career. However, while the thirty-eight-year-old diplomat may have lacked experience and influence, he was infused with all the necessary personal qualities that would eventually enable him to emerge from the crowd.

The outwardly modest Canadian's delightful charm and self-mocking humour made him excellent company in a very communal profession. He understood the necessity of patience, and could listen to the egotistical and the plodding, the influential and the superfluous with focus and tact. Largely resistant to dogma, he was intelligent without being intimidating, intuitive rather than linear. He understood that behind the facade of diplomatic protocol, an undeniable hierarchy of power framed the world stage. He accepted the simple but ruthless equation that international influence was inextricably tied to economic clout and military might. Whether by training or inclination, he was willing to settle for what was feasible rather than hold out for the best, keenly aware of how little was possible at any given time. In his view, there were no end points in diplomacy, only continuous transitions. Even if he was disposed otherwise, he had little credible alternative as a Canadian diplomat but to practise this diplomacy of pragmatism.

Pearson's attitude towards the League of Nations spanned varying degrees of doubt and hope. As a war veteran, he was glad it existed. As a sovereignist, he took it as given that Canada should hold a seat separate from the Mother Country. As a professional diplomat, he understood that a constrained institution, unable to enforce the collective peace, reflected

Lester Pearson, ambassador to the US, at San Francisco Conference
to establish United Nations, 15 June 1945 (UN Photo 190914)

exactly what the members would tolerate. In a diary entry he wrote: "It's
too often forgotten that the League is only the aggregation of states
which compose it; that it can do nothing apart from the governments of
those states, and that this, in large measure means the governments of
[Great Britain] and France."[3]

By its very design, Pearson reasoned, the league could not confront
aggression, whether by economic sanctions or military force, because it
would be "virtually impossible at any time," for the members "to agree on
an aggressor." Even if a majority could agree, the decision to impose any
strong measures would require a unanimous vote, and this, Pearson con-

cluded, would be "almost inconceivable." Lowering his sights to achieve the modest rather than nothing at all, he judged the league would be most effective serving as a meeting place to express "the international spirit," whether outrage or approval: "The League, with only moral force behind it, is far more likely to use that moral force to the full extent of its powers."[4] His thinking displayed a sensible pragmatism, but Pearson accepted the reality of a constrained league that could only utter sermons for other, very Canadian reasons.

There was little possibility, he observed in a 1933 departmental memo, that Canada would ever need military assistance from other countries, thus Canada had little incentive to pledge any in return, especially when "their policies are so dangerous, their armaments so swollen, their boundaries so unstable and their national animosities so intense that there is every possibility of us being used at some time to redeem our promise." While still recommending Canada's membership in the league, he concluded, "The League must remain consultative and not executive. The teeth must be kept out of Articles X and XVI," the sections of the covenant dealing with collective defence and sanctions.[5] In this desire for a toothless league, Pearson was simply stating conventional wisdom in both External Affairs and a country anxious to avoid being dragged into another foreign bloodbath.

In December 1920, at the very first assembly, Canadian representative Newton Rowell had delivered the emblematic indictment. "It was European policy, European statesmanship, European ambition that drenched the world with blood and from which we are still suffering and will suffer for generations," he declared. "Fifty thousand Canadians under the soil of France and Flanders is what Canada has paid for European statesmanship trying to settle European problems." From their first moments on the world stage, Canadian delegates did everything they could to shield their country from European diplomacy and pushed hard to eviscerate any chance that the league might commit an act of collective security. Canada repeatedly called for the elimination of the covenant's ill-defined commitment to defend fellow members. Some resisted the Canadian campaign, but Ottawa refused to let the issue drop and in subsequent assemblies came close to securing the necessary majority to cripple Article X. A league official, F.P. Walters, judged that even while failing to win majority approval, "the Canadian proposal had nonetheless received such authoritative support that its essential purpose had been in practice achieved."[6] And so Canada's first independent actions in the world assembly served to enfeeble and undermine the league, all in the name of championing security and sovereignty.

In keeping with this dominant faith, sustained through the 1920s into the 1930s, Ottawa sent Pearson to the League of Nations, not to uphold the covenant but to subdue any internationalist impulses in the Canadian delegation. Arriving in Geneva in the fall of 1935, he was initially underwhelmed by his marginal duties, which reflected Canada's marginal place in the league. "There were days," he recalled, "when I had little work to do and solaced myself acting as golf gigolo to British wives whose husbands *were* busy."[7] He may have grumbled, but the astute civil servant no doubt understood his true assignment: keeping Canada on the sidelines, especially as the league was confronting perhaps its greatest crisis.

In 1935, a former newspaper editor who used postwar chaos and economic collapse to intimidate his way into power ruled Italy. Across Europe, many smart people hailed Benito Mussolini as a national saviour, who, as the cliché goes, made the trains run on time. But his country did not provide enough of a canvas for his fascist ego, so he looked to foreign fields for glory—and distractions from intractable domestic dilemmas.

Italy already presided over a sphere of exploitation in east Africa that encompassed Eritrea, Italian Somaliland, and Libya. One lingering piece of geography beckoned to be conquered—Ethiopia. Financially battered by the Great Depression, emotionally ravaged by the Great War, the league's principal powers, Britain and France, opposed Italy's imperial intentions, but their own economies feasted daily on African colonies seized from Germany after the last war. They also felt constrained in lecturing Italy too severely because they sensed a potentially larger threat embodied by a failed painter and decorated war veteran in Germany, already working to inflame his country's resentments and anxieties. Appointed chancellor in 1933, Adolf Hitler vowed to restore national honour, no matter what the neighbours thought. Transfixed by this spectre of resurgent German ambition, France did not want to offend Il Ducc lest he embrace the ultra-patriot in Berlin. Through 1935, months of properly conducted private discussions, earnest public proclamations, and meticulously crafted telegrams killed time, but not Mussolini's imperial ardour.

Then, on September 11, the chief diplomat for the most powerful member of the League of Nations stunned his listeners in Geneva and beyond and called for the defence of Ethiopia and, by extension, the principles of the covenant. For a glorious instant, Samuel Hoare made the improbable seem possible, but he also laid down a caveat: "If the burden is to be borne, it must be borne collectively. If risks for peace are to be run, they must be run by all." Even with this qualification, some delegates got caught up in the sudden wave of hope, including the usually skeptical Pearson. "That speech of his was one of the most moving and emotional statements I've ever listened to," he later commented. "We felt that the League of Nations had become an instrument for security, and not only [for] maintaining peace but defeating an aggressor."[8] But not everyone was as impressed as the junior diplomat.

Thousands of miles away, but still finding Geneva far too close for comfort, two Canadian politicians staked out a different approach to maintaining world peace. On a rainy Saturday evening in Quebec City, just four days before Hoare's stirring speech, two high priests of Canadian sovereignty, William Lyon Mackenzie King and his Quebec lieutenant, Ernest Lapointe, addressed a vast election rally. Lapointe said in the most quoted lines of the night: "No interest in Ethiopia is worth the life of a single Canadian citizen. No consideration could justify Canada's participation in such a war."[9] In an age before constant polling and focus groups, Lapointe was King's connection to Quebec. If he wanted to become prime minister again, King could not afford to ignore this voice. Not that this was an issue; the francophone and anglophone shared the unshakeable conviction that Canada must have the final say about being sucked into any European machinations.

When it came King's turn to speak to the thousands filling the market-place, he invoked the Chanak crisis from thirteen years before, when he had faced down a British summons for military and moral support against Turkey. "I made it clear," he said, "that no action would be taken involving Canada without parliamentary sanction." Drawing a direct line from that threat, King stated no imperial economic interests could justify another

Canadian sacrifice or another potential assault on Canadian sovereignty.[10] A few weeks after this declaration, King's potential nightmare in Africa and Europe became all too real.

Expecting the league to back down as it did over Japan's invasion of Manchuria in 1931, and confident that he had a gentlemen's agreement with France for a "free hand" in Ethiopia, Mussolini unleashed his mechanized divisions in early October. Rallying to protect a member but still observing diplomatic niceties, the league called a vote to determine whether Italy's murderous assault constituted an act of aggression. Even an agnostic could be caught up with new-found fervour. "For a few weeks," Pearson remembered, "we did think we could stop aggression for the first time in modern history by international action, international force behind international law. And I was as excited as anybody could be at that."[11]

But that excitement had not carried over to Ottawa, where Undersecretary of State Skelton fretted that Prime Minister Bennett, while opposed to military measures, might actually support the imposition of economic sanctions.[12] Also complicating matters, Parliament remained suspended in the midst of a federal election, which might bring in a new government. On the morning of the league's vote, the Canadian delegation in Geneva received its instructions from External Affairs: abstain.

Pearson was appalled. "Canada," he said, "would have been almost alone in the League of Nations refusing to do what should be done, and we could sense what a humiliating position that would have been."[13] Likewise appalled, the delegation's boisterous chief, Howard Ferguson, threatened to go golfing rather than endure such a public embarrassment.

Stepping beyond the bounds of cautious civil service, Pearson encouraged his chief to take advantage of a technology apparently never used by the delegation, the trans-Atlantic telephone, and call the prime minister directly to get the instructions changed. Connecting with the campaigning Bennett at a railway station in southern Ontario, Ferguson made his case for Canada voting with the majority. Pearson recorded the encounter in his diary, writing: "It was breakfast time there; lunch in Geneva. I knew RB well enough to feel sure that the result of this conversation, so important to Canada, would depend entirely on how the PM had enjoyed his breakfast. It must have been a good one, for the PM was off-hand and jovial about it all."[14] Inclined to support Britain in the world, not dependent on Quebec for political power, Bennett overruled the previous instructions and allowed Ferguson to brand Italy an aggressor.

And so, at the last minute, on October 9, 1935, Canada voted to condemn Mussolini's invasion. Pearson was delighted: "The League of Nations, for the first time in its history, formally voted one of the big powers to be an aggressor. It was very exciting to see collective action to come to life, it's what it meant to me, after the hesitations and the doubts and the efforts to weaken the covenant in the twenties and thirties."[15] In recalling his excitement, Pearson did not mention his hesitations and doubts, or Canada's lead role in the efforts to weaken the covenant.

Having collectively voted Italy an aggressor, the league of emboldened nations had to debate whether to fit on an actual muzzle. Pushing well beyond his instructions, not to mention the prevailing mindset in External Affairs, Ferguson made gallant declarations supporting the covenant and — even more subversively — approved Canada's place on the two committees established to deal with sanctions.[16] This free reign ended on October 14, when Canadian voters granted Mackenzie King what was then the largest majority in the country's history. As always, his primary objective was to keep Canada united, no matter what his tactics signalled to those countries anxious for peace and others hungry for war.

A change in political parties shifted the diplomatic scenery. The very Tory Ferguson departed from his position as High Commissioner in London and delegation head in Geneva to make way for the very Liberal Vincent Massey. In his aristocratic style and lukewarm support for the league, Massey was no Ferguson. The ever-wary King sent him to the empire's centre with very clear instructions "not to be drawn into 'imperial' councils, commitments or policies, to avoid becoming a member of any conference of the Dominions and Br. Govt."[17]

This mirrored the parameters laid down for Pearson's own posting to London, in which he essentially promised not to commit any acts of diplomacy. He clearly understood the "intense suspicion" so intimately intertwined with the "intense nationalism" permeating the prime minister's office. He shrewdly assured his superiors: "I do not think I shall be tempted to stray beyond the concept of my duties which would be quite satisfactory to you."[18] This proved a career-saving attitude, given what happened after a colleague in Geneva did just the opposite.

On November 2, just days back in office, Mackenzie King, the country, and the world learned that the Canadian advisory officer in Geneva, Walter Riddell had, without approval from Ottawa, proposed that oil, steel, coal, and iron be added to the list of materials denied to Italy. The world press immediately dubbed this escalation "the Canadian proposal." Mussolini needed these imports to keep his mechanized forces in motion, and he threatened out loud that oil sanctions meant war. King had approved banning the sale of armaments and munitions and cutting off trade, loans, and credits to Italy, but now he beheld his country simultaneously celebrated for confronting a dictator and condemned for leading the way to Armageddon. The newly elected King found himself thrust into a position that Quebec overwhelmingly opposed and that English Canada, at best, only tolerated.[19]

By now back in London at the High Commission and thus far removed from the intoxicating Geneva spirit, Pearson, in effect, sobered up. While he accepted "the principle of Italian aggression," he wrote to Ottawa in November, "we should not be dragged into unwise actions by any other state or states." He continued: "I also feel that we should not take any lead at Geneva in the application of sanctions." In a policy memorandum written at the same time, he worried about the effect of sanctions on Mussolini and mused whether it might be better to live with the devil they knew. Successful sanctions would force Mussolini to submit, and "Submission means for Signor Mussolini, humiliation. Humiliation would probably mean the end of the fascist regime. That would result in chaos for Italy.... One cannot, therefore, contemplate the crushing of Mussolini with equanimity no matter what opinion of him or his system of government may be held."[20] Pearson and his superiors and the country seemed in complete sync.

The hovering sense of apocalypse alarmed the prime minister, and in early December, he put an unceremonious end to Canada's place in the spotlight. Speaking on King's behalf, Ernest Lapointe informed the world that the Canadian government had not, in fact, proposed the extension of sanctions; rather the Canadian representative in Geneva had expressed his own personal opinion as a member of the sanctions committee. Muddying the position, Lapointe added that Ottawa still supported existing economic sanctions as well as other peaceful measures supported by the majority of league members.[21] As Riddell's proposal made headlines around the world, so too did his public decapitation. Conveniently, he left Geneva for a previous engagement in Chile.

Mussolini and his fascists delighted at the first crack in the enemy wall. To officials in the British Foreign Office, King's abrupt disavowal looked "like dirty work at the crossroads." In their judgment, "the Canadian government have very easily—and without much dignity—lost their nerve." But however clumsy the reversal, King acted consistent and true to deeply held principles. His new officer in London seemed to agree. At the time, Pearson wrote in his diary about "the unfortunate initiative," which he termed "a horrible mess," noting: "Riddell made a mistake in speaking without explicit instructions." He criticized External Affairs for its tardiness in sending instructions and the subsequent delay in repudiating the initiative, and he went on to argue, unconvincingly, that Ottawa "could have explained the position without causing any disturbance and without humiliating Riddell," but nowhere did he criticize Mackenzie King on the substance of the repudiation. "King unquestionably acted as the Canadian people wanted him to act," journalist Bruce Hutchison later wrote. "They were in no mood to save Ethiopia or the League."[22] Clearly, neither was Lester Pearson.

Despite the minor political earthquake generated in Canada, and the retrospective condemnations dumped on King, the whole episode was largely a distraction from the real battle against fascism. Even in the immediate aftermath, the British Cabinet did not discuss King's retreat. In his detailed history on the League of Nations, a former deputy secretary-general only briefly mentioned the incident. In their memoirs, British foreign ministers Samuel Hoare and Anthony Eden barely noted Riddell. In such a high stakes crisis, the modest dominion simply did not factor into the larger political equations.

As if to underscore the unforgiving hierarchy of power, just days later a far more blatant reversal completely overshadowed Riddell's repudiation. On December 9, the press revealed the infamous Hoare-Laval agreement. Negotiated in haste and in secret, and accepting that Italy had already devoured much of Ethiopia and was still not sated, the two most powerful representatives in the league, Britain's Samuel Hoare and France's Pierre Laval, proposed not to bury Mussolini but to appease him outright with even more Ethiopian territory, complemented by an exclusive economic zone in other parts of the country. A dismembered Ethiopia would be allowed to keep the leftovers.

This compromise offered less than Mussolini's demand for total evisceration, but coming from Hoare, the man who had stood before the league just three months before championing collective security, the proposal ignited a public outrage so intense that he was compelled to resign. Such naked surrender rang the death knell for any collective resistance and gave Mussolini the green light to complete his invasion. Thirty-five years later, Pearson claimed he was devastated: "I had got to the point where I had lost all faith in the League of Nations, collective security, which was like losing religion, almost, for me at the time, after the hope we had a few months before."[23] But his diary entries display a remarkable dispassion and, in parts, an almost amoral quality. In the aftermath, there was clearly no faith lost because there was so little to begin with.

In these private passages, Pearson does not cast Italy as a malevolent spirit, or Ethiopia as an innocent lamb. He stated matter-of-factly that the fascist dictator and his country held interests in the region and in Ethiopia that needed to be if not respected, then certainly accommodated: "The League should do everything it could to meet Italy's just claims...to a paramount place in any international control over [Ethiopia]."[24]

That Pearson considered Italy as having any credible claims might, at first glance, read like unrepentant imperialism or reflexive appeasement. More accurately, he was simply stating what he saw as the unavoidable in diplomacy. Italy was entitled to satisfaction in proportion to its influence and assets. The morals of the situation did not (perhaps because they could not) come into play.

Pearson's streak of amorality suffused his assessment of the widely loathed Hoare-Laval pact. He did not excoriate it for sacrificing Ethiopian territory to a dictator, but rather criticized it as a sloppy misreading of public opinion. The proposed pact was, in his word, "amazing" because he thought it unworkable, not because it was inherently appalling. The self-inflicted damage to Britain's reputation appeared to especially disturb Pearson. In first standing up to Mussolini, "England had placed herself in a position of prestige and moral leadership that she had not achieved for a long time. These [Hoare-Laval] proposals shattered that position overnight."[25] Other than calling the dictator a megalomaniac and a mad dog, nowhere in this lengthy diary entry did Pearson explicitly condemn Mussolini or express any kind of outrage over his aggression. This cool, hard thinking could not be readily seen in his sunny, charming exterior.

Sensing that Canadian diplomacy resided in safe hands, in December 1935, King and Skelton dispatched Pearson temporarily to Geneva. His status as a fully accredited delegate rather than a back-row adviser delighted him. In his sardonic fashion, he noted: "a few newspapermen congratulated me on having been chosen as the next Canadian victim for 'official repudiation.'" But the ambitious diplomat had no intention of repeating Riddell's alarming fumble. "My instructions, were the easiest instructions, in one sense, I ever had to carry out," he said. "Hear no evil, see no evil, certainly speak no evil." And he was faithful to those orders, however much he mocked them. "I made not a single speech; not even a 'hear-hear,'" he later recalled. "And you can't repudiate a man who won't even say 'hear-hear.'"[26]

Sometime after the Riddell debacle, the dutiful diplomat wrote Skelton an unrepentant declaration of independence and isolation from the darkness to come. "I would assume that war in Europe is certain within five years, that this country [Great Britain] . . . will slide into the mess, and that, in view of the bloody chaos which will result, our chief interest now is to avoid being involved in any circumstances," he wrote. "I admit we may not be able to avoid it, but I feel infinitely more strongly than I did six months ago that the keynote of our policy should be such avoidance."[27] If Europe had managed to muddle through the grey peace, Pearson would have ascended through the department's ranks in increasingly prestigious anonymity until he reached a senior resting place. But the larger currents around him were already shaping a different destiny for him and for Canada.

***

We beyond the seas must remember that each nation stands at the threshold of every other, that all frontiers touch one another throughout the world, that there can be no hermit nation and no hermit continent.

—Sir Robert Borden, 1926 Rhodes Memorial Lectures, Oxford University[28]

We achieved our political independence, our sovereignty, precisely at a time when, demonstrably, sovereignty and independence gave no assurance of security or of progress. We had to learn that the aspirations of independence often had to be reconciled with the necessities of interdependence.

—Lester Pearson[29]

The second world war of Lester Pearson's lifetime proved the futility of the paradigm shaped by the first: appeasement did not keep the peace, avoidance provided no lasting safety, and external alliances were lifelines, not quagmires. It took time for his generation to grasp what eventually seemed so obvious and construct a new paradigm to shape a global peace. The anguished evolution was captured in a moving letter Pearson wrote in November 1938, after yet another well-intentioned effort to placate Adolf Hitler. His confessional tone was all the more remarkable because he was addressing his devoutly isolationist boss, O.D. Skelton. All too familiar with his chief's suspicions about Britain's imperial intentions, Pearson, with his typical grasp of paradox, argued that this flawed, self-serving bastion of democracy still deserved Canada's support in the coming battle against the Nazis, because it was a Canadian battle as well:

My first emotional reaction to the events of the last two months is to become an out-and-out Canadian isolationist. Yet when I begin to reason it out it isn't as simple as that.... Would our complete isolation from European events (if such a thing were possible) save us from the effects of a British defeat; and, even if it did, could we stand by and watch the triumph of Nazidom, with all that it stands for, over a Great Britain which, with all her defects, is about the last abode of decency, reason and liberty on this side of the water?

If I am tempted to become completely cynical and isolationist, I think of Hitler screeching into the microphone, Jewish women and children in ditches on the Polish border...whatever the British side may represent, the other side does indeed stand for savagery and barbarism.[30]

In the final years of guilty peace, as Germany enveloped Austria and Czechoslovakia, Pearson renounced all traces of his isolationist temptations. By September 1939, when Hitler invaded Poland, compelling a reluctant, ill-equipped Britain and France to send another generation into battle, Pearson felt no doubts about the proper response to Nazi savagery. In Canada, faithful to his sense of autonomy and ever vigilant to maintain national unity, Mackenzie King did not automatically follow Britain over the top but instead summoned Parliament to debate what was largely a foregone conclusion. One week later the government issued Canada's first declaration of war.

In the deceptive lull after Hitler seized Poland, which came to be called the "Phony War," Pearson toiled on mundane negotiations about the price of Canadian wheat and other essential supplies that Britain needed at the lowest possible price. The haggling, he wrote, "was more fitting for a market-place than for two countries fighting and working together in a war for survival. The trouble...was that we did not know yet that it was a question of survival." Then, with devastating speed, Germany seized Denmark and Norway in April 1940, Holland and Belgium in May, and France in June, driving the British Army in retreat across the channel. "The whole thing still seems unbelievable," wrote Pearson in his diary. "[T]hat Germans could wander at will in parts of France which they couldn't reach in four years in the first war; that they could take towns without difficulty on which British communications depended; that they can now look across the Channel from Boulogne; well it just doesn't seem possible."[31]

That summer, the Luftwaffe surmounted Britain's geographic moat and tried to bomb the island kingdom into submission. One Sunday, the war veteran who had survived an air raid over London during the last war stood on the rooftop of Canada House in Trafalgar Square after the Germans had bombed nearby Whitehall. His colleague George Ignatieff stood by his side, and together they "watched the charred remains of civil service files fluttering in the wind as the fires were burning out of control all around." Pearson, Ignatieff later recalled, "said something to the effect that civilization could not stand much more of this kind of destruction and that we would have to try to stop it." This was, Ignatieff recalled, "about the only time I heard Pearson express personal feelings; he was not a communicative man."[32]

The war began for Canada as a closed family affair within the Commonwealth and empire. For many anglophone Canadians, the contours of imperial pink that circumnavigated all time zones and hemispheres remained resplendent proof of the Great in Britain and by extension in Canada. What they and Pearson, a former lecturer on imperial history, could not know was that in this desperate hour, with their country a critical ally, they were participating in a last intimate hurrah. The Second World War would effectively finish Britain as a global power. As the imperial fact faded from the map and as the island kingdom, despite vigorous denials, and enduring pretensions, became a more modest presence, the relationship forged across two centuries would begin to fade as well, eventually meaning less and less to Canada's place in the world and to the English-Canadian sense of self.

In 1941, after nearly six years in Britain, Pearson returned to Ottawa, still, as he noted, talking "Canadian." He had avoided the "unseemly example" of some who acquired a British accent during their stay. But pride in his home and native land co-existed with pride in his British inheritance. At a farewell dinner in London, he told his gathered friends: "God knows these people are not perfect. They have defects enough.... They often make me tear my hair. But, by and large, I feel that this country represents the furthest and finest stage mankind has yet reached in political and social development. As a Canadian, I am glad we still have our roots deep in its past."[33]

After a short spell in Ottawa, Pearson was posted to the American capital in early 1942, just months after the Japanese attack on Pearl Harbor roused the isolationist giant to join the British-led resistance. This proved a mixed blessing for London, since economic and military supremacy inevitably dictated that Washington would dominate the Western war effort, and incredibly lucky for Pearson, who found himself stationed in the true centre of Allied decision making. Here he encountered a diplomatic canvas far more demanding and creative than anything he had ever experienced. Pearson did not, however, delude himself that an essential Canadian dilemma had changed. In one memo to Ottawa, he admitted frankly that his country remained suspended "somewhat uneasily in the minds of so many Americans between the position of British colony and American dependency." Like Robert Borden during the Great War and Mackenzie King during the 1920s and 1930s, Pearson in the 1940s was consigned to penetrate a superpower's self-absorption and carve out a separate space for Canada. The US and Britain established boards to conduct the war effort, and Pearson learned over and over again that the US assumed that Britain's participation included Canada. "That should be enough for us—we were British," Pearson later said.[34]

Americans could be forgiven their confused image of Canada, a country where people were born British subjects: their official anthem "God Save the King," their official flag the Union Jack, though some also waved the Red Ensign and sang "O Canada." On one occasion, Pearson learned from the British consul in Detroit that the consulate routinely issued British passports to Canadians. "Nobody seems to care in Ottawa about this anomaly," Pearson noted in his diary. "It is humiliating in the extreme that Canada, which now bleats so much about its new status as a Middle Power, should continue to rely on United Kingdom Consuls for consular services in this country. It is about time we grew up." Even Pearson's boss in Washington, Leighton McCarthy, the man appointed to represent Canada, was liable to perpetuate the confusion in American minds. Going through the draft of one of McCarthy's speeches, Pearson flinched at the last sentence: "A British subject I was born and a British subject I will die." This could not stand. "I hope to save his reputation as a serious statesman by persuading him to eliminate it!" he wrote.[35] Pearson presumably won this skirmish, but the duality that defined being Canadian would endure for years to come.

As Pearson waged diplomatic battles in Washington, the Canadian people once again rallied to the industrial and military front lines. In a country of just over 11.5 million people, one in ten voluntarily enlisted; roughly 750,000 served in the army, 250,000 in the Royal Canadian Air Force, and 100,000 in the Royal Canadian Navy.[36] Even so, Pearson held no illusions about the discrepancy between rankings and hard figures. In sheer numbers, Canada's commitment could never measure up to that of the Americans or the British, let alone the Russians. The scale of national sacrifice remained so all encompassing, however, that Canadian officials refused to automatically take a back seat to the superpowers.

External Affairs' sharpest intellect, Hume Wrong, articulated a strategic approach that came to be called the "functional" principle or "functionalism." In essence, Canada's undeniable military and economic strength should yield an equal measure of diplomatic influence and inclusion.[37] This was hardly a new idea but, while sound on paper, nearly impossible to put into practice. While agreeing in principle with this linkage of responsibility and capability, immaculately conceived formulas held little appeal for Pearson. Soon after his arrival in Washington, he advocated a pragmatic approach to the frustrating British and American monopoly on decision making. "I do not think we will ever alter it merely by complaining about the way we are being treated," he wrote in a memo. "It might indeed be better frankly to accept the inevitability of 'two-power' war control in theory and see how we can protect our own interests in practice within this limitation.... Even when we are in the right, we won't win our case very often, if ever, by insisting on our full rights. It is, in a sense, humiliating to admit this, but, nevertheless, I think it is a fact."[38] Ottawa did not like what it was hearing from their man in Washington. One clash between allies would justify his appraisal of power and limits.

In 1942, China, the Soviet Union, Britain, and the United States (the Big Four) set out to establish the United Nations Relief and Rehabilitation Administration (UNRRA). Not surprisingly, they proposed to give themselves, and only themselves, seats on the central policy committee, which would make the key decisions. When informed about this after the fact, an insulted Ottawa pointed out that Canada was already producing enormous quantities of relief supplies—not to mention financially bailing out Britain with interest-free loans and outright gifts—and possessed the potential to deliver even more. Seeking only a proportional measure of respect and influence, the middle power asked for membership on the policy committee. Canada's current contribution was undeniable, the reasoning impeccable, its case entirely worthy—none of which mattered much when great powers defended their own interests.

Long accustomed to Canadian indignation, the British briefly promoted Canada's membership on the policy committee, but the Russians
refused to grant anyone else entry, even when Ottawa threatened not
to join UNRRA. Anxious to remain in step with the Soviet Union,
and worried that Canada might inspire other countries to demand
seats, Washington sided with Moscow. Pearson observed with chagrin
that the US "preferred a row with Canada to one with the USSR or
Latin America."[39] Not insensitive to Canadian pride and arguments,
Washington tried to placate the dominion, and in January 1943, offered
an alternative kind of representation suggesting that Canada take a seat
on a subcommittee dealing with supplies.

Pearson judged this a credible compromise, but Ottawa would not
yield. Meeting with Dean Acheson, US assistant secretary of state, he
dutifully conveyed Canada's official displeasure. But then, in familiar
fashion, Pearson strayed from his instructions and made his own move
to keep the door open, indicating to Acheson that he was personally
interested in the proposed American compromise for a Canadian seat
on the supplies committee. Confident in his judgment and abilities,
Pearson appeared to feel no hesitation in working backstage to strive
for what he saw as an entirely acceptable outcome. Some observers then
and now might consider this insubordinate. Others might appreciate his
independence of mind. And although he sensed that "he had widely been
accused in Ottawa of having 'gone American,'" working from Washington
provided him with a far more accurate read of what was possible in the
face of rigid superpower resistance.[40]

In late February, Washington improved upon the earlier compromise
and suggested that Canada actually chair the supplies committee, which
would also sit with the policy committee as needed. Pearson reasoned
that these committees would sit together more often than not and,
recognizing the value of substance over form, urged Ottawa to accept
the new offer. An intransigent External Affairs refused to retreat,
however. "It is felt here that this is a test case. . . . If we cannot go into the
[policy committee] by the front door we are unwilling to use a side or
back entrance." King instructed Pearson to convey yet another note of
intense displeasure to the State Department. He obeyed but "did not
use as strong and undiplomatic language as that of the telegram [from

External]," he confided to his diary. "I think we have been too stiff in this matter and that we might have accepted the compromise."[41]

In March, the British foreign secretary, Anthony Eden, arrived in Ottawa to extract a surrender. Making sure to return to the capital for this visit, Pearson met privately with Eden and was "disloyal enough to my Government," he frankly admitted, "to give [the British] some off-the-record advice as to the best way to approach Mackenzie King on the subject." Pearson also worked on the prime minister. After one chat on a chilly airport tarmac, where he stressed that Canada "should not turn down lightly the compromise," he noted to himself that King seemed "impressed." The prime minister even invited Pearson to a Cabinet meeting with Eden present, and when King asked his colleagues for comments on the UNRRA dilemma, Pearson saw an opening too important to miss. "I, being the junior person present, was the only one rash enough to say anything," he wrote afterwards." Later at a dinner, King discussed the issue once again with his rash underling. "He was good enough to tell me that my talk at the Cabinet had been 'most helpful,'" Pearson allowed, "which probably means that it did not embarrass him in any way."[42]

Greater forces ultimately overshadowed Pearson's maverick efforts. In one meeting, Eden told King that unless Ottawa accepted the compromise, "the whole business would have to fall through." A week after Eden's visit and Pearson's backstage manoeuvring, the master relented and followed the path that his accomplished apprentice had urged from the start. King conceded that this was "one of the cases where it is clearly impossible for a lesser power to really do other than be largely governed by the views of the greater powers. What we could gain by staying out of co-operation with them," he wrote in his diary, "I do not see." If he could have read this entry, Pearson would have agreed with every word. In his own journal, he allowed himself a slight pat on the back: "My arguments may have had some effect in Ottawa. In any event, I was a minority of one when I reached there."[43] Given Moscow's unwillingness to budge on granting Canada membership in the policy committee, and given the meaningful compromise offered by a true ally, the middle power probably achieved all that was possible. The diplomat, however, had only just begun.

In May 1943, Pearson journeyed to West Virginia for a disorganized, vaguely defined United Nations food conference that President Franklin Roosevelt had abruptly convened (although called the United Nations, the world organization did not yet exist, and this assembly was composed of those countries united in their declaration to defeat Japan, Italy, and Germany). Throughout the conference, Pearson witnessed allies locked in an unseemly rivalry. "The Americans are getting the feeling that the British are playing too big a part," he observed. "In contrast, the British feel they are really doing the hard work."[44] In almost reflex fashion, he mediated between the competing delegations and helped to draft the conference's declaration of purpose. In a signal show of admiration, he was elected chairman of the interim commission, which over two years laid the foundation for what would become the Food and Agriculture Organization. This marked his first official role serving a UN agency. So began his move into the media spotlight, the Canadian collective consciousness, and, quite probably, Mackenzie King's plans for the future.

In early November 1943, the prime minister reconfigured the Canadian delegation to UNRRA, demoting a Liberal MP and removing a Liberal senator. Deeming their political status too partisan for an international forum, King decided an untainted civil servant would be more appropriate. Pearson, as he was fond of saying, found himself appointed to head the delegation. Soon he found himself elected by the other delegations to chair the supplies committee. Colleague John Holmes wrote of this period that, despite Pearson's relatively "junior status," the diplomatic community was recognizing "his extraordinary capacity for reconciling contrary views in apt formulas, his geniality under stress, his tactical skill, and his inoffensive idealism." Pearson, Holmes concluded, "was exactly the person needed, and he came from the country best designed not only to propose compromises but to be a compromise."[45]

Still serving as minister-counsellor at the legation in Washington, a gruelling position on its own, Pearson delighted in taking on an even heavier workload. "In all my official career I have never been subjected to quite the pressure," he wrote to a friend, Lt. General Harry Crerar. "Instead of a seat in the back row, watching the performance, I have had to sit at the top of the table and try to keep the delegates from 44 so-called United Nations in order." Yet in typical fashion, no matter how immersed, he wanted more. "I became very restless around 1944," he later told an interviewer, "very restless."[46]

In March, he approached Crerar, commander of the First Canadian Army in Britain. "I have only one regret, and that is that I am not over there with you," Pearson wrote. "Your acute intelligence will probably have gathered the fact that I am trying to get overseas again; even that I am trying to get into your Army. This is an impulse that I simply cannot resist." Here was the lingering voice of the young lad who devoured G.A. Henty's grand imperial tales, who thrilled to the sight of the militia on parade in Peterborough, and who now longed, as he put it, to be "physically close to the actual war."[47]

Looking back, he mocked himself, but only just. "I saw myself in red tabs as a colonel and I'd be able to write my life later 'From Corporal to Colonel.' I got the most awful brush-off from him [Crerar] in a letter. It offended me for a long, long time." Pearson's ambition, at times all too obvious, brought a warning from the prime minister. "I had found," King reportedly told Pearson, "the greatest error was that when a man got one position he immediately wanted another and getting that he wanted another." While telling Pearson that a great future beckoned, the prime minister urged him "to concentrate on the task immediately at hand."[48] Despite this lecture, King propelled Pearson ever forward, appointing him, in January 1945, to the most critical post in the foreign service, ambassador to Washington. The legation was upgraded to an embassy.

Watching their diplomats perform on the world stage over the course of the war, Canadians began to believe they lived in a country with real influence and even greater potential. "Canada has undergone a far-reaching diplomatic revolution," one Canadian academic proclaimed. "Her relatively small population and lack of colonial possessions prevent her from being a major or super Power. But her natural wealth, the capacity of her people, the strength she has exerted and the potentialities she has displayed show that she is not a minor one. Henceforth in world politics she must figure as a Middle Power." This became the defining and enduring self-image for the victorious country, reflected and amplified through so much of the war's iconography. For instance, at the Quebec summit in 1943, Canadians could see for themselves their own prime minister sitting alongside Winston Churchill and

Franklin Roosevelt; perhaps not as their equal but present nonetheless. As J.L. Granatstein and Norman Hillmer point out, the truth was far more humbling. "Mackenzie King," they write, "provided the Scotch and the accommodations, and he was permitted to attend anodyne meetings. Whenever important matters were under discussion, however, there was no place for Canada."[49] This disconnection between mythic imagery and sobering fact endured for long afterwards. Perhaps too subtle to untangle at the time, what the country had legitimately earned was not so much influence as credibility—a factor essential to having any influence at all, but one which did not automatically or inevitably convert into real clout. The new Canadian ambassador to Washington had no illusions on this score.

Four months after his appointment, Pearson took a train to San Francisco, where some 850 delegates from forty-six victor and neutral states gathered to finalize the United Nations' founding document. Used to being a star in Washington, Pearson was not pleased to take a back seat to his old friends, now his superiors in Ottawa, Undersecretary Norman Robertson and Associate Undersecretary Hume Wrong. They had known each other since the 1920s, admired each other, and worked well together in general, but theirs was also a friendship with competitive edges and tensions. One of Pearson's juniors, Escott Reid, noticed his initial unhappiness. "Norman and Hume are doing all the work themselves," Reid wrote in his diary two days after the conference began. "They go to the meetings of the Steering Committee with the P.M. Mike feels very much left out of it and is sore. I doubt whether he will stay here for long."[50] The professional stayed for the duration.

However, while Pearson is typically remembered as helping to create the UN, John English points out rightly that even "his direct influence on Canadian policy and on Canada's work at the San Francisco conference was not great." Within the delegation, he toiled more as a messenger than a draftsman and at times served as a kind of roving firefighter dealing with flare-ups in various committees. Yet because he conducted the delegation's daily press conferences, his profile within and outside the delegation remained high. According to a *Vancouver Sun* columnist: "The reliability of these gatherings soon became so famous that it was impossible to restrict them to Canadians alone."[51]

At San Francisco, the hundreds representing millions had come to talk peace, but the tone was often hostile, suspicious, and, for Pearson, a headache. "We spend half our time on points of order," he complained, "and most of the remaining time on long, unnecessary speeches, from ambitious delegates of insignificant powers."[52] The sharpest clashes erupted over the veto, awarded by the Big Four to themselves alone, along with permanent seats on the UN's executive body, the Security Council. Put in their place, the smaller powers would have to fight elections to win a two-year term to this inner sanctum, but as non-permanent members they would not be allowed to wield a veto.

Preparing for the conference, Canada and other countries criticized the UN's autocratic composition, but the big four refused to dilute their privileges. Despite deep misgivings, Ottawa chose to tolerate the great-power veto so as not to destroy the great-power unity needed to establish the organization. Throughout the conference, by personal inclination and policy, the tactically mild-mannered Canadians deliberately played a restrained hand, "speaking only when we have to and keeping out of as many rows as possible." In stark contrast, the Australian foreign minister, Herbert Evatt, railed relentlessly and loudly against the offensive veto. The *New York Times* praised him "as the most brilliant and effective voice of the Small Powers, a leading statesman for the world's conscience." Pearson acknowledged Evatt's intelligence and passion but, in both his diary and later in his memoir, also recognized his vanity and arrogance. "Evatt thinks we are pretty cowardly," Pearson noted after one conflict where Canada held back yet again. "He, on the other hand, knows perfectly well that he can fight this battle to the very end without running the risk of suffering the consequences of a victory, e.g., no Charter at all, because certain more responsible States, like ourselves, will, by abstaining, save him from those consequences."[53]

As the union of nations argued itself into existence, the war's victors and vanquished were dividing and being divided, some against their will, into armed camps that genuflected to incompatible gods and visions. On one side of the chasm loomed the Soviet Union's totalitarian dictatorships. On the other stood imperfect democracies where citizens enjoyed rights and freedoms that would see them jailed in the Communist prison states. With these enemies about to be permanently stationed on the new

Security Council, each wielding a crippling veto, and with their allies and satellites aligned to vote in the General Assembly in predictable patterns, Pearson and his colleagues and counterparts could see all too clearly that the new world body would be incapable of dealing with the new world order.

While the diplomats argued the peace in San Francisco, allied soldiers ended the war in Europe, which seemed to make little emotional impression on Pearson. "The war for me in the last year or two became a blur of committees, conferences, and agencies," Pearson recalled in his TV memoirs. "I can't even remember the circumstances of the announcement of VE day in San Francisco. I knew the war had ended, but in contrast to November 11, 1918 — every hour of which I can remember — I'm very vague about the circumstances." In his diary he wrote, "Headlines such as 'Hitler Dead,' 'Mussolini Hanged by the Feet,' 'Berlin Captured,' 'Nazis Collapse Completely,' all leave me about as cold as the headline 'Yanks Win Two Games.'"[54]

Faced with strangling the UN at birth, Canada and the other delegations ultimately made the same galling calculation to take what they could get rather than end up with nothing at all. While the conference was largely a story of retreats, the final charter still bore some Canadian 'fingerprints. Aiming to link responsibility with capability, the delegation ensured that, when electing the non-permanent members to the Security Council, "due regard" would be "specially paid" to what a member could actually contribute. Mindful of Mackenzie King's prime foreign policy nightmare, the delegation also ensured that non-sitting members would have a say in Security Council decisions involving the members' military forces. In other words, the Security Council could not conscript Canadian forces without Parliament having the final say.[55]

Although less than what Canada wanted to achieve at the beginning of the conference, these efforts made for a worthy contribution. After all, a nation dwarfed by the Big Four still influenced a document that more than four dozen self-interested nations quarrelled over. "Canada sent a good Delegation which generally gave a good account of itself," a senior US State Department official opined. "I would not say that Canada's role at the Conference was spectacular or brilliant. It was simply good and solid." After the battle subsided, the other members rewarded the impassioned Australians, not the sensible Canadians, with election to the Security Council and later the presidency of the UN General Assembly. As John English put it, "Respectability had its price."[56]

On June 26, 1945, the now fifty members of the nascent United Nations submerged their unresolved arguments in a public show of unity to sign the compromised but tangible charter. Despite all their misgivings, the delegates had reason to celebrate, for they had, however imperfectly, resurrected a noble ideal. Ever the pragmatist, Pearson would always urge support for the union while openly acknowledging its flaws. A January 1948 speech captured his initial dismay with the fledgling organization, unable to defend its own members:

> Instead of the United Nations acting as a forum for the expression of the conscience of mankind, it is becoming a platform for the aggressive propagation of ideological passions and reactionary and revolutionary plans. Discussion is debased to the level of vilification.... In this political climate, the United Nations, even with a perfect charter, could not guarantee peace and security. In this political climate and with an imperfect charter, the structural weaknesses of the organization are becoming depressingly apparent.[57]

As he would for the rest of his diplomatic career, Pearson appealed to the disappointed and the critical to look beyond the immediate paralysis and not confuse the symptom with the disease: "The symptom is the veto-scarred record of the Security Council," he noted. "The disease is the division of one co-operative world into two opposing worlds." To the inevitable question, "Does all this mean we should give up the United Nations?" he would preach the same answer: "Not at all. That would be suicidal as well as cowardly."[58] The diplomat speaking for a middle power understood the critical need to cooperate on a very crowded planet of disparate ideologies. The son of empire had already grown up in a multi-racial assembly of unequal states and felt at home in the mosaic. The son of Methodism was blessed with the open-minded universalism needed to embrace and sustain the vision of a more communal world order. When he said, "Loyalty today should include far more than devotion to a city, a state, or even a country," he believed it. "They are inclusive and overlapping."[59]

But if in his most idealist vein he seemed to aspire to be a citizen of the world, he never forgot that national ambitions and violence remained inescapable features of the international landscape.

Pearson's insistence that Canada must remain within the UN did not blind him to the need to secure Canada's defence by moving beyond it. His willingness to create an international assembly truly capable of defending his country was evident a mere nine months after the squabbling, suspicious architects signed the charter. In March 1946, the world heard a transcendent wordsmith and warrior, Winston Churchill, Britain's leader of the Opposition, proclaim a landmark warning about the viral Soviet menace: "An iron curtain has descended across the continent," Churchill declared. "Behind that line lie all the ancient states of Central and Eastern Europe." Knowing he addressed a nation still demobilizing its armed forces and longing to lose itself in civilian pleasures, Churchill was careful not to advocate a formal military alliance. Instead he invoked the "fraternal association of the English speaking peoples" and urged the Western allies to continue their military cooperation to constrain what he called the Soviet "temptation to ambition or adventure." Churchill argued that such an arrangement, intended not to wage war but secure peace, would be compatible with the UN's charter. "If the Western democracies stand together," he urged, "the high roads of the future will be clear."[60]

From Washington, Pearson reported to Ottawa on the speech, advocating an even more sweeping response to the Soviet threat and UN paralysis:

> The United States and the United Kingdom should convert the United Nations into a really effective agent to preserve the peace and prevent aggression. This means revising it radically. If the Russians veto such a revision, agreed on by others, a new organization must be created which, as the guardian of the peace for all nations, and not merely the English speaking ones, can function without the Russians and, as a last resort, against them. All this is far removed from the more limited, but, I think, far less effective proposals of Mr. Churchill for an English-speaking association.[61]

Pearson dispatched his sweeping appeal to Ottawa, which noted and filed it away. Churchill's appeal was both praised and condemned across the global political spectrum, but it did not inspire any grand coalition. Their intensely idealistic yet practical visions, by no means unique to them, would require more time to become commonplace, and more time only confirmed for Pearson that real collective security remained virtually impossible within a United Nations that could not bridge a deep ideological schism. In 1947, a frustrated Canada began to send out public signals to allies suggesting they consider revising or looking outside the UN to protect themselves from the Soviet threat.

In a September address to the General Assembly, Louis St. Laurent, the External Affairs minister, became the first member of a Western government to call explicitly and publicly for a regional security organ-ization. His country was respected, his argument sound, but when the applause faded, the Canadian initiative was left dangling. In a bleak assessment of human motivation, Pearson would later say: "Fear is usually, in international affairs, the greatest incentive to action."[62] Through the winter of 1947 and into the spring of 1948, gnawing fear of the Soviet Union continued to edge the Western democracies closer and closer to the Canadian objective until the doubtful finally rallied to create what became NATO. His ultimate goal remained a peaceful world, but he held few illusions about the violence that was sometimes required to create peace.

In August 1945, the war in Japan ended with an obscene piece of science fiction produced by some of the greatest scientists of the day—an innovative bomb that could obliterate an entire living city. Pearson learned the news while attending a UN conference in Paris. When asked twenty-five years after the fact if he felt any kind of moral revulsion about the atomic incinerations of Hiroshima and Nagasaki, his response, though conventional for the period, remains strikingly honest for a public figure:

No, I didn't at that time. I didn't. And it's impossible to understand how you would feel about that. Some people may have had that feeling of moral revulsion. I didn't. It's impossible to understand that unless you put yourself back in the atmosphere of that moment.

We had become, of course, I was going to say captured by our own propaganda. We were certainly in the toils of wartime propaganda and it didn't need much propaganda to convince people at that time that if this war was not won by our side, the world was going to be under the control of the Nazis, the Fascists, and the Japanese military. This was enough to make me want to win this war pretty badly.

And if you add to that the propaganda which made the Japanese kind of sub-human apes in the stories that were given out at the time, and what they were doing to their prisoners, and things like that, removed any feeling I might have had—you don't usually have very much of it during wartime anyway—that our enemies were humane people that should be treated chivalrously. So I had no pity for them.

And I never interpreted this action in terms of women and children and old men being blown to pieces. I interpreted it as something that was going to bring the war to an end victoriously. And we weren't aware of that other reaction. At least I wasn't. So I had no moral feeling. I thought that this would end the war, and if it ended the war, as it did—it may have killed a hundred thousand people, but it may have saved a million people. So there you are.

War is total war now, and there is not much distinction to be made between a man, a woman, a child and a warrior in terms of destruction. Total war means that. When we were in London during the bombing, the soldiers were safe and the civilians were being killed. This was something new. And so I projected that feeling of total involvement to the Japanese and it didn't worry me very much whether, at that time, who was killed. They were Japanese. And they were on the other side and we wanted to win the war and save a lot of our people being killed. It was at that moment, it was as simple as that.[63]

FIVE

Here I Am in the Middle

It is with confidence that I look a hundred years ahead to a
class room of earnest eager young faces, their pens moving
with lightning rapidity, to catch the fleeting words that flow
from the lips of an ambitious young lecturer who is giving a
course on "The Successful Settlement of Britain's Imperial
Problems in the 20th Century."
>   —Assistant Professor Lester Pearson, 1927 course
>   "Institutions of the Modern British Empire"[1]

One evening during the 1945 San Francisco conference, Lester Pearson
joined the embattled British delegation for drinks. At the watering hole,
far away from the angry voices demanding decolonization, or as they saw
it, imperial dismemberment, the delegates may have hoped for words of
support from the British subject representing Canada. Instead Pearson
lectured them about postwar realities, unhelpfully pointing out that
Britain "obviously could not bear the imperial burden much longer, so
they would do well to recognize this and withdraw gracefully and gradually under the auspices of the UN." In a rare instance of misjudging
his audience, he hit a raw nerve. As Pearson recalled, one of the senior
British delegates, a friend, in fact, "exploded with rage and he could
hardly find words to tell me what he thought of such heretical views."[2]
The British delegates may have felt equally appalled if they grasped that
Canada too, in its own way, was undergoing a kind of decolonization.

In March 1944, Prime Minister King awoke from a dream in which
he reimagined national symbols. Quite out of character, he considered

clarifying lingering dualities by making "God Save the King" the British Commonwealth's anthem, while "O Canada" would become the national anthem. King's serpentine mind then turned to Canada's official flag on home ground, the Union Jack, waved throughout the war to celebrate victories, flown from the Peace Tower on Parliament Hill, and from schools, post offices, and homes. This was not the only flag Canadians called their own. In 1892, the country's merchant marine received permission to fly the Red Ensign, which featured a Union Jack in the canton (the upper left quarter) and the Shield of the Canadian Coat of Arms in the fly (the right-hand area furthest away from the flag pole).

In 1924, during his first incarnation as prime minister, King ordered it flown from government buildings overseas to signal a Canadian presence. Ignoring the lack of official sanction, some Canadians began to fly the Red Ensign at home. An angry debate erupted in the country between those nationalists who demanded that only the Union Jack be flown and other nationalists who insisted that no truly Canadian flag would contain any hint of Great Britain. Clinging to power in a minority government, King declined to make a decision either way. Both flags continued to fly in Canada and command overlapping loyalties.

Seeking to stand out from the Commonwealth crowd, the Royal Canadian Air Force in November 1943 and the Canadian Army in January 1944 issued orders that their forces fight under the Red Ensign. Waking from his dream that March, King wondered whether the Union Jack should become solely Britain's flag, while the dominions designed their own variation of the Red Ensign. This would, he mused, "show historical evolution and present association with the U.K."[3] However, again he held off making such a bold gesture.

In May 1945, when victory in Europe was declared, the cautious nationalist ordered the Red Ensign flown temporarily from the Peace Tower in order to, as he explained, pay tribute to the troops. Building on that precedent, the government introduced a motion in September authorizing the flying of the Red Ensign on all federal buildings inside Canada, until Parliament adopted a national flag. Hoping the Red Ensign would be chosen but keenly aware of the intense loyalty for the older Canadian flag, King addressed the House of Commons, saying: "There is no thought or suggestion that we shall cease to honour the Union Jack

(L-R) UN Secretary-General Trygve Lie, Col. W. Hodgson (Australia),
and Lester Pearson, chairman of the First Committee of the
UN's First Special Session, convened to consider the
Palestine Question, 7 May 1947 (UN Photo 325251)

as the symbol of the British Commonwealth and Empire as a whole. Our
affections are not so shrivelled or our enthusiasm so narrow that we need
denounce the one because we adopt the other. Both can have their place;
both do have their place; both will have their place."[4]

Despite his care and courtesy, the flag debate infuriated patriots in
Parliament, the press and the public, all arguing over the appropriate
symbol of unity. Having already endured one searing flag debate, the
twice-burned King retreated to a muddled status quo where the Red
Ensign would fly by default from federal buildings until further notice.
While this attempt to agree on one national symbol failed, another survived the divided body politic.

Coming into effect on January 1, 1947, the government introduced
a citizenship act that transformed people born in Canada from simply

British subjects into Canadian citizens who remained British subjects, making the dominion first in the Commonwealth to create its own, at least partially, separate class of citizenship.

This reimagining of the relationship with the Mother Country could be conducted with characteristic moderation in Canada, but across the oceans, angry demands for complete independence darkened an imperial landscape increasingly stained by British blood trying to hold back the insistent tide. The Great Britain confronted with the labyrinthine dilemma was no longer the dominant power that Lester Pearson and millions of fellow British subjects had known throughout their lifetimes. The island kingdom's sacrifice during the war left it victorious in battle but financially prostrate. Proud envoys begged under the guise of negotiation for bailouts from a rather cold-blooded Washington and a more understanding Ottawa. Even with these infusions, His Majesty's Government still struggled to make ends meet and, at times, literally keep the lights on during coal and fuel shortages. Austerities from war continued well into peace—even that essential tool of victory, the cup of tea, was rationed, along with sugar, chocolate, meat, butter, and cheese.[5] Deemed indispensable in war, Winston Churchill was not trusted in peace by enough of his fellow citizens to refashion their land into the new and socialist Jerusalem they desired. In July 1945, a laconic former barrister, social worker, and member of the wartime coalition government, Clement Attlee, led the Labour Party to a stunning majority in the general election by promising to share more of the national wealth with more of the people in an all-embracing welfare state.

Devoid of Churchill's unapologetic sense of empire, the sober-minded Attlee assumed power keenly aware that the idea of holding on was barely tolerated if not loathed in Washington and increasingly unacceptable to many at home. He had no desire to keep his exhausted nation bogged down resisting endless wars of liberation. Financially, he knew the government simply could not afford it. And so as Attlee moved to remake a more humane Britain at home, he began to deconstruct the Greater Britain overseas. He lowered the Union Jack over Ceylon, Burma, and, most devastating for true believers, India, the most treasured portion of the British map, which partitioned, with blood and slaughter, much of its Muslim population into what became Pakistan. Less emotionally fraught but no less telling was Attlee's handing over of the defence of Greece and Turkey to the US.

Pearson worried about strategic implications and political aftershocks but did not display any sentimental angst as he watched the slow disintegration of the imperial constellation that once anchored Canada's place in the world, guaranteed its defence, supplied its largest market, and shaped its cultural matrix. He became directly involved only when the United Nations suddenly had to deal with ten thousand square miles of British territory lying on the edge of the Mediterranean, seized during another world war in order to shield Egypt, the Suez Canal, and the flow of oil. In the grand relinquishment, this one piece of ground proved the most intractable and painful to leave behind.

> I shall hope to do nothing in my work here which would, to use your own words, prevent me from living with myself after I have retired from public life. It certainly is the most complicated problem that I have ever come up against.
> —Lester Pearson to a former student, May 14, 1947[6]

Thwarted ambition and other people's choices combined to land Lester Pearson in the diplomatic spotlight when the issue of Palestine reached the General Assembly in early 1947. The year before, the Soviets had blocked his bid to become the United Nation's first secretary-general, which kept him in the Canadian arena—perhaps the greatest disappointment of his career until a few years later when they vetoed him again. Then, in September 1946, Prime Minister King made him undersecretary of the department he had joined eighteen years before, becoming the government's senior civil servant on foreign affairs.

Pearson's unexpected move back home also laid the foundation for the partnership so critical to his success at Suez a decade later. He now served under the newly appointed External Affairs minister, Louis St. Laurent, a corporate lawyer from Quebec City who had left his practice during the war to join King's Cabinet as minister of justice, saying he would stay only for the duration. He ended up playing a pivotal role in the most serious domestic crisis of the war, staunchly supporting the prime minister in 1944, when, contrary to earlier promises, King introduced conscription for overseas service, outraging Quebec, splitting Cabinet, and nearly bringing down the government.

Born to a francophone father and anglophone mother, St. Laurent embodied the dominant Canadian duality. Growing up, he assumed "everybody spoke to his father in French and his mother in English."[7] Not afraid of firm decisions, devoid of King's blinding suspicions about British intrigues, he inspired profound admiration in his advisers and colleagues. Echoing the admittedly Liberal chorus, Pearson considered his association with St. Laurent one of the great privileges of his professional life. The deputy and his new minister looked at the Cold War landscape through the same lens. They perceived the same sense of threat emanating from the Soviet Union, found the alliance with Britain and America the answer to their search for security, and remained committed to the United Nations despite their qualms. They worked in tandem to keep the prime minster, now in decline, from giving into familiar but misguided impulses to retreat from the world. Within months of joining forces, they were caught up in a bitter conflict in the Middle East that strained relations between London and Washington, tested the United Nations' credibility, and threatened to inflame the entire region — all foreshadowing the crisis to come in 1956.

And Pearson would experience something unique while he grappled with Palestine. Decades later, the typically dispassionate diplomat revealed in a rare if not singular admission, "I got too personally — emotionally — involved in a very special way because we were dealing with the Holy Land and a lot of my old Sunday school stories came out of there. At one stage of my life, I knew far more about the geography of Palestine than I did about the geography of Canada. I could tell you all the towns from Dan to Beersheba but not all from Victoria to Halifax."[8]

By 1947, the Methodist minister's son had seen the mystical Biblical landscape of his youth become an unholy quagmire pitting immigrant European Jews, fleeing centuries of persecution culminating in the Holocaust, against long-conquered Arabs dreaming of independence, pitting moderates within each community against their own extremists, and pitting all of them against Great Britain, the overstretched occupying power trying to placate incompatible visions and still retain a hold on one of its last remaining spheres of influence. Each side of the schism could point to ambiguous and contradictory British promises made decades before, which appeared to offer each a homeland. Each side felt betrayed by the failure to deliver

For nearly three decades, Britain administered Palestine on behalf of the League of Nations or, more accurately, on behalf of its own imperial interests. The official mandate obliged London to guide the inhabitants towards self-government. To fulfill that obligation, the British offered to partition the territory into separate states, and when that failed, suggested a bi-national state with autonomous Arab and Jewish provinces. Every attempt to negotiate a lasting peace ended in failure.

By the end of the Second World War, London had to impose something close to a police state in Palestine, deploying an estimated hundred thousand troops, ten percent of Britain's total imperial force count—an unsustainable military and financial commitment. At times, it inflicted martial brutality to contain terrorist attacks from both sides.[9] Trying and failing to placate Arabs throughout the region and simultaneously enraging Jews around the world, London restricted Jewish immigration into Palestine, which meant, post-war, keeping thousands of Holocaust survivors languishing behind British barbed wire in nearby Cyprus or turning their crowded ships back to ravaged and anti-Semitic Europe.

Britain's attempts to maintain a fraying order were condemned by the American press, politicians, and government officials, themselves facing determined lobbying from American Jews exercising their democratic privileges to demand that Jewish survivors be allowed into Palestine. Even within American officialdom, Palestine pitted the State Department, anxious that supporting the Jewish cause would erode American influence in the oil-rich Middle East, against President Harry Truman, who was deeply moved by the suffering endured by European Jewry and mindful of retaining domestic votes and financial support for his 1948 re-election bid. "It was not just American Jews who were stirred by the prospect of a new nation for the Jewish people," historian David McCullough has pointed out, "it was most of America." Despite being infuriated at times by Jewish and Gentile lobbying (raging out loud, "Jesus Christ couldn't please them when he was on earth, so how could anyone expect that I would have any luck?"), the most powerful leader in the Western world became personally committed to establishing a Jewish homeland in Palestine—but only from a safe distance.[10]

Shortly after assuming office in 1945, Truman stated his administration's essential approach, from which he never wavered: "We want to let as many of the Jews into Palestine as it is possible." Without ever addressing the fundamental abdication of responsibility, he added, "I have no desire to send 500,000 American soldiers there to make peace in Palestine."[11] Truman compounded British agonies by publicly demanding that Britain let in 100,000 Jewish refugees. It did not escape London's notice that the superpower urging such massive immigration into a festering sectarian conflict remained itself pervasively anti-Semitic and that during the worst of the 1930s and ensuing world war, had allowed only a trickle of Jews to immigrate. With a far smaller population and geography, Britain had taken far more refugees.

After yet another round of negotiations through 1946 leading to yet another angry stalemate in early 1947, the British foreign secretary Ernest Bevin and the colonial secretary Arthur Creech Jones informed their Cabinet colleagues: "We have reached the conclusion that it is impossible to arrive at a peaceful settlement in Palestine, on any basis whatsoever, except with the backing of the United Nations." They proposed to have the international community debate whether Palestine should be partitioned into Jewish and Arab states or remade as a single unitary and therefore primarily Arab state.[12] The UN announced it would convene a special assembly to establish a committee of enquiry to study the issue and deliver a report for the regular UN session in September. All fifty-five member states were invited to attend the special session.

Just a few months before, Lester Pearson met with the president of the Zionist Organization of Canada. Unable to offer official support, he made a point of expressing, as he put it, "my own personal sympathy" for the Jewish cause. Even this modest expression set him apart from the majority of Canadians. Deep currents of racism stained the country, which made it acceptable, even desirable, for the government to close the doors to refugees in their most desperate hour. Between 1933 and 1939, an estimated eight hundred thousand Jews sought to escape Nazi Germany. Canada allowed four thousand to enter the country—the most shameful record for any of the democracies. Canadian Jews were barred or restricted from neighbourhoods, holiday resorts, universities, and professions. Certain hotels and private clubs displayed signs reading "Christians Only." An October 1946 poll ranking the most undesirable immigrants put Jews in second place after the Japanese. Of those polled, 49 percent preferred that Ottawa keep Jewish immigrants out of Canada.[13]

Against this backdrop, biographer John English calls Pearson's sympathetic attitude to Jews "exceptional" and recalled that he did not find a single anti-Semitic comment in Pearson's diaries, not even in the 1930s—which, English observed, cannot be said of some colleagues at External Affairs. Pearson's sympathies in that period also surfaced during one of his regular appearances on a BBC radio programme in London, when he argued against the stereotype that Jews refused to assimilate and viewed everything through the prism of their religion. "But even if this were true," Pearson countered on air, "who's responsible for this tendency?" He pointed to a time "when Jews were forbidden to be anything else but Jews, no matter how long they'd lived in a country. They were herded together into separate communities; they were kept there as a separate people. And it seems to me it ill becomes us now, who've been responsible for that attitude in the past, to say that they don't easily adjust themselves to the nation in which they live."[14]

His sympathies emerged in more personal fashion when he encountered the procession of Jews literally knocking on his door at the High Commission. In a 1939 letter to his mother and brother, he wrote, "I have some pretty pathetic interviews these days with refugees who want to go to Canada. I wish we were a little more generous to them. It's distressing having to tell so many of them you can do nothing for them." On one jarring occasion, he came face to face with someone he had recently worked with on refugee issues, a former member of the Czech legation desperate to flee the Nazi reach. Pearson appealed to Ottawa on behalf of this former diplomat, though to no avail, and did so again for other Jewish refugees, apparently with success in a few instances. When Pearson once again confronted the "Jewish question" less than a decade later, perhaps a lingering sense of guilt at having not done more compelled him to do something tangible. In one speech after the war, he stated that he supported a Jewish homeland "because of an underlying feeling that it had been made necessary by the slaughter of Jews in Europe during the Second World War."[15]

In April 1947, when the United Nations invited its members to set up a commission of enquiry on the future of Palestine—that is, invited members to discuss how to further discuss the situation—the immediate stakes for Ottawa were minimal. Without any debate in Cabinet or, more importantly, without Mackenzie King agonizing in his diary about nightmare entanglements, St. Laurent announced in the House of Commons that the Canadian delegation would be made up of officials from External Affairs headed by Pearson.[16] Once again, the undersecretary stepped from the obscurity of the civil service into the international spotlight.

Pearson prepared for the gathering in New York, focused on achieving the immediate goal of establishing the enquiry committee's membership and terms of reference. This would mean avoiding, he told his officials, "a debate on the substance of the Palestine question itself," already mired in violent deadlock. "If, however, a debate on substance cannot be avoided," he went on to say, "we should try to keep out of it." Rejecting an American suggestion that only smaller "neutrals" be selected for membership, and reflecting the Canadian preference to link responsibility with capability, Pearson wanted the Security Council's powerful permanent members to serve on the committee because the resulting report would bear their imprint and perhaps even oblige them to implement any proposals. Mindful of Mackenzie King's fixations and anxieties, Pearson advised that Canada not volunteer to join the enquiry committee.[17]

Ottawa's intention to remain on the sidelines proved difficult from the start. Shortly before the special session opened, various delegates informally advised the Canadian mission in New York that Canada would probably be asked to serve on one of the UN's standing committees and even on the committee of enquiry.[18] In London, one Foreign Office mandarin was already musing about Pearson as a potential president for the session: "It wd. be admirable if we cd. get him."[19] Even as External Affairs pondered how to participate without getting pulled in too deeply, the Security Council's permanent members decided amongst themselves that Pearson and Canada would play some kind of central role during the debate. When their machinations came to light, there was, surprisingly, no protest from Mackenzie King or St. Laurent. Not at all surprisingly, there was no protest from Pearson. It's impossible to know how much of Ottawa's reluctance to get involved was felt personally by him and how much of it was a shrewd bureaucratic survivor playing to his master's wishes.

So, as planned in advance by other powers, on April 28, the first day of the special session in New York, the Canadian diplomat trying to keep his country free of any responsibility found himself elected chairman of the first committee, designated to tackle the key task of defining the enquiry committee's membership and terms of reference. Pearson had few illusions about the hurdles facing the delegates. "I've heard some pretty wild speeches at the United Nations," he recalled later, "but nothing to equal the venom and the fury of the Arabs. And I don't mean that this was some kind of synthetic fury as very often [Soviet] speeches were. This was genuine. This was sincere. This was from the depths of their being. And one of the things that made this rather different from other disputes at the UN was it was the same on both sides. The Jewish feeling was equally deep and equally sincere and it wasn't diplomatic. It wasn't a diplomatic conflict. It was a conflict of life and death between two peoples."[20]

In seeking a solution to this conflict, Pearson supported independence for the Arabs in Palestine but not on their terms. He believed that some form of a Jewish state in Palestine was essential—"sine qua non" as he later put it.[21] Frail hopes for a resolution probably grew fainter in the opening rounds of the special assembly when the Arab nations called for the immediate establishment of a single unitary Palestinian state. Pearson wanted this discussed after the enquiry commission delivered its report in the fall. Canada joined with the majority at the UN to defeat the Arab resolution, in effect voting against the wishes of the majority of people living in the Middle East.

In shepherding his fellow members towards agreement on the enquiry committee's terms of reference and membership, Pearson faced multiple challenges. He wanted to avoid getting bogged down in a debate on an intractable issue, to accommodate American insistence on nominating smaller powers, and to somehow placate other member states advocating Great Power involvement while deciding whether to allow presentations from Jewish and Arab representatives, each speaking on behalf of a country that did not exist. He also needed to perform his duties with an observable air of impartiality, and he could not lose sight of Canada's private but primary domestic objective to avoid being nominated itself to the enquiry committee.

His third stint chairing a major UN issue, Pearson launched his committee work on May 6, reminding his colleagues of the pressing need for collective focus. "We must keep our remarks short and to the point," he said. "By 'to the point' I mean pertinent to the immediate problem before us." Over the next nine days, his name and statements appearing almost daily in the *New York Times*, Pearson presided over meetings and presentations with a brisk touch, stepping in when necessary to lower diplomatic temperatures, and in one instance, drawing the attention of a speaker to "the danger of making controversial statements which provoke even more controversial replies."[22] He tried to cajole the Security Council's permanent members into joining what would be officially named the United Nations Special Committee on Palestine (UNSCOP), but he had to retreat and settle for an eleven-member body of smaller so-called neutrals. The committee also agreed on terms of reference. All that remained was to find the member states willing to participate.

In this context, the middle power was deemed an ideal potential member. Pearson informed Ottawa he would continue to resist the tidal wave of pressure, "if it were possible decently and honourably to do so," but when Canada was formally nominated, he ultimately did not refuse. "There was no opportunity for me to deal with our nomination," he reported. "The discussion was at times confused."[23] His minister accepted the outcome without protest. Perhaps the two had privately agreed to do so in advance, conceding there was no way to decline membership in an honourable fashion. Prime Minister King appointed Supreme Court judge Ivan C. Rand as the Canadian member of UNSCOP.

By May 15, Pearson completed his chairmanship showered in public and private praise from the press and his peers. "The fact that we have today happily reached the end of the first stage of a difficult work," the French representative declared, "we owe also to Mr. Pearson." The delegate from the Philippines stated, "He steered our discussions...with such ability that I doubt if, without him, we could have evolved a formula as excellent as the one we approved." Most impressively, even the Iraqi delegate praised Pearson's leadership. Across the Atlantic, an official at the Foreign Office noted: "Mike Pearson came out on top, in my humble estimation." The *New York Times* reported that "a movement is developing to draft" him as the next president of the General Assembly.[24] Having worked on an attempt to shape a local peace, Pearson returned to Ottawa, by now having largely given up expecting the UN to fulfill its overarching mission to maintain a more universal peace.

Over the summer of 1947, the eleven members of UNSCOP toured the land sacred to three religions. True to the very nature of the conflict, even the commissioners sent to shape a compromise could not agree amongst themselves, and so they delivered a divided report. A seven-member majority, which included Canada, called for the partition of Palestine into Jewish and Arab states, which would share a customs and monetary union but leave Jerusalem under an international trusteeship. The minority report called for a unified federal state with Arab and Jewish provinces. The General Assembly would debate the conclusions at the UN's fall session in September.

During and after the special session in the spring, Prime Minister King appeared remarkably unperturbed by the spectacle of a Canadian diplomat generating so much acclaim while working on an explosive issue. By the fall, however, perhaps after another season of bloodshed in Palestine, he was in no mood for any more adventures in diplomacy. Pearson, of course, felt otherwise.

When the two met on the nineteenth of September, the undersecretary seemed unaware of the depth of his master's anxieties, unwisely mentioning the pressure from New York to bring him back. True to himself, King was unmoved by the needs and desires of other member states and even less by Pearson's ambitions, and advised him to refrain from taking another round in the spotlight. If he felt disappointment at being reined in, Pearson was surely gratified when King, once again, encouraged him to consider leaving the civil service for political office. This was not mere flattery on King's part, who was "wholly convinced," he later confided to his diary, "he would be the best man to succeed myself though this I do not wish to breathe to others."[25]

Consigned to the sidelines, Pearson was designated the alternate head of the delegation and would attend the first few days of the new session.

The Canadian Cabinet, which admitted it hadn't had time to read the UNSCOP report, instructed him and his fellow delegates to support any resolution that looked feasible.[26]

At the very start of the Palestine debate in the General Assembly, London undermined widespread assumptions and hopes when, without warning, it announced that it would abdicate its role as the mandatory power at a time of its own choosing, regardless of what the UN decided, and would not force any settlement upon the Arab and Jewish populations. Britain's military presence and civil administration were the only instruments staving off a bloodbath. The United States, the one other member state capable of filling the looming vacuum, stepped forward to offer sermons and advice and nothing more. The permanent members' abdication of responsibility appalled Pearson, who grumbled in an off-the-record speech that he wished he could have "dismissed the British and Americans with 'a plague on both your houses; on [Jewish] votes in New York; and oil in Arabia.' But then 'irresponsible' civil servants," he added, "can always afford the luxury of these courageous fancies." And no matter how incensed, this civil servant was not one to indulge in the impractical.[27]

Pearson soon returned to Ottawa to preside over an intense debate between his advisers to prepare Canada's position on Palestine. The senior expert on the Middle East, Elizabeth MacCallum, argued that dividing the territory into Jewish and Arab states not only lacked legal and moral validity but also would incite civil war. She posed a question Pearson never raised in public: how could Canada support a proposal that violated the hopes and dreams of the majority of people living in Palestine? Acknowledging that partition was imperfect and risky, and would lead to some "measure of disorder," the head of External Affairs' UN division, Gerry Riddell, countered that it nonetheless offered the only chance of a settlement. Riddell also put forward a strategic factor that resonated with Pearson: partition, in establishing a Jewish state, would create an ally in the Middle East with similar cultural values to the Western democracies.[28]

During this departmental contest, the deputy minister's method could seem impenetrable. George Ignatieff recalled: "Pearson tended to make decisions on the basis of intuitive judgement rather than some sort of consensus among [his] advisers or colleagues.... This instinctive approach to problem solving did not make life easy for subordinates.... On the rare occasions when he did ask for my opinion, he never let on whether or not he agreed with me. He would simply listen and ask questions and then leave me wondering what he thought of my answers."[29]

Given UNSCOP's majority recommendation for partition, which both the US and the USSR supported, and his own emotional attachment to the Jewish cause, it was hardly surprising that Pearson decided to support a separate Jewish and Arab state, albeit not without "a great deal of heart-searching," as he later wrote. "Partition was certainly no ideal solution but it seemed, certainly to me, the best that could be achieved, the only solution that might bring peace and order to Palestine, with some recognition of the just claims of both sides."[30]

At the General Assembly, following the American and Russian lead, the head of the Canadian delegation, James Ilsley, formally announced his country's position—with a marked note of ambivalence. Canada had arrived "somewhat reluctantly" at the proposal to partition Palestine, he stated, and viewed this proposal only as "a basis for discussion." Deep anxiety remained over crucial questions. Who would take over from the British when they left? How would UN decisions be put into effect if Jews and Arabs did not agree to them?[31] Following the proceedings from Ottawa, Pearson felt so compelled to help shape the answers, he seized an opening to return to the front lines, unwittingly provided by the head of the delegation.

Ilsley, a veteran and effective politician in Ottawa, proved an amateur in New York. "If ever I saw a man out of his depth it is our minister of Justice," Bruce Hutchison noted in a private memo. "He has simply lost himself in the bushes." Ilsley agonized over policy to the point of indecision. He was "the most utterly conscientious man I have ever met," Pearson later recalled. "He couldn't sleep at night because of what to do about Palestine."[32] An anecdote that Ilsley shared with Hutchison may have proved his undoing at the UN. Ilsley had fallen asleep during one meeting, his dozing head slipping off his hand just in time for the chairman to think Ilsley wanted to address the members. Duly recognized, the flustered Canadian stood up and improvised a speech while desperately fishing for notes stashed in his pockets. Unimpressed by the self-deprecating humour, Hutchison agreed not to print the story but repeated it nonetheless to his colleagues. Word of the incident probably reached Pearson through his carefully cultivated press contacts, or perhaps he heard about it from his own advisers. He clearly felt it was time for a professional to take over.

Undoubtedly with clearance from his minister, he left for New York to persuade the apparently overwrought Ilsley to take a holiday from the stressful proceedings. "Don't stay around here if it's going to worry you like this because it's just not fair," he reportedly said. Ilsley took the advice, and Pearson found himself, as he so often put it, "thrown into this rather special position."[33] Pearson now took charge of the Canadian delegation.

On October 21, the ad hoc committee dealing with Palestine established three subcommittees: one to draft a precise scheme to implement partition, a second to consider creating a unitary state, and the last to seek a peace agreement between Arabs and Jews. Canada joined the subcommittee on implementation. Pearson perhaps became in this phase, as he later put it, too personally and emotionally involved because, unlike at the spring session, he and his colleagues were confronting how to carve, legally and physically, one piece of land into two independent countries—against the wishes of the majority population.

Hoping to weave together divergent proposals and keep any resulting compromise anchored in reality, Pearson privately addressed the partition subcommittee on November 4. Tempering his language but not his point, he cautioned his American colleagues that their push to have the General Assembly preside over the transition from mandate rule in Palestine to independence ignored formidable obstacles. Pearson, siding with the Soviets on this key issue, recommended that the Security Council take the prime role in supervising what could only be a violent handover period.[34]

Given his prominence, even this informal attempt to shape a consensus hit front pages in Canada, the United States, and Britain. When the world press last reported another Canadian proposal emanating from a league of nations tackling a crisis in November, a horrified Mackenzie

King publicly repudiated the Canadian representative. Fortunately for Pearson, the prime minister was sailing to London to attend the wedding of Princess Elizabeth and probably had no idea his potential successor was making headlines on both sides of the Atlantic. In his diary for November, Mackenzie King made no mention of Palestine or Pearson's very public diplomacy at the United Nations. That would come later.

After he delivered his informal recommendations, Pearson accepted an invitation to join Russia, the United States, and Guatemala in a working group to hammer out a credible process for establishing two new states in the Middle East. For nearly three weeks, Pearson worked behind the scenes, confiding in a personal letter: "Here I am, in the middle, between an obstinate Russian and a not too skilful American, and it has been about the most exhausting experience of my life."[35] In the Pearson lexicon, "exhausting" was, of course, another word for exhilarating.

In its discussions, the working group raised the delicate issue of enforcement. The Guatemalan delegate, Jorge Garcia-Granados, suggested the Security Council's non-permanent members provide military forces to assist with the administration of a partitioned Palestine once the British evacuated. Pearson disagreed. The citizens themselves, he argued, should govern the new Arab and Jewish states, and the United Nations should intervene only if an act of aggression occurred.[36]

Part of his reluctance to see a UN agency or commission remain after partition, with or without military forces, was probably due in large part to Cold War politics. Neither he nor his allies were willing to hand the Soviet Union any opening to station troops in Palestine, even under a UN flag. The sensible civil servant also undoubtedly considered Mackenzie King's likely reaction to the prospect of Canadian soldiers landing in the middle of a distant sectarian war. But if Pearson did not, at that time on that issue, support the notion of a United Nations military force, neither, as later events show, did he dismiss it.

Watching Pearson perform, Bruce Hutchison dubbed him "the hockey player." With a measure of admiration and consternation, he noted in a private memo that Pearson was "running everything on his own. He may clear with St. Laurent. No one knows. But in any case he goes out and lays down policy and commits Canada to anything he pleases without telling [other Canadian delegates]. They never heard of the Canadian plan for Palestine till they read it in the papers." Familiar with Pearson's evasive manoeuvres, Hutchison added: "The hockey player is so very able and so nice that no one would think of checking up on him or asking him anything."[37]

Pearson may have ignored certain members of his delegation, who essentially were tourists in this arena, but the documents show him in close touch with St. Laurent, and the hockey player was no maverick about the policy directive that Canada avoid a commitment to supervise partition. In one respect though, Hutchison was absolutely right: when it came to tactics, Pearson preferred to skate solo, improvising his way through the day-to-day conflicts in informal gatherings, where delegates saw Pearson at his persuasive best.

As he endeavoured to stake out the elusive middle ground, Pearson understood that any partition plan ultimately depended on the mandatory power, Great Britain, whose public air of proper impartiality translated in private into an exasperating unwillingness to engage or contribute in any way. Worried about the corrosive effects of this on Britain's prestige, Pearson conveyed his dismay and, occasionally, even the details of his working group negotiations to British representatives, but to no avail. Pearson could not entice or shame Britain into action and his efforts, as he was well aware, rankled some members of the UK delegation. A few even accused Canadian delegates of disloyally opposing Britain's interests "in a most deliberate and offensive way," Pearson complained in a letter to colleague Norman Robertson. "I think it particularly inopportune that we should be abused for abandoning the United Kingdom line on Palestine when it was quite impossible for anyone, in public or private, to discern what that line was."[38] This refrain of misunderstanding and betrayal would return during Suez.

With Palestine on the verge of war, and delegates, journalists, and lobbyists prowling outside the working group's closed door, Pearson blended elements from the American and Soviet proposals to extract an agreement from his three colleagues over the withdrawal timeline, supervisory commission, legal issues, and Security Council involvement — no small feat in a Cold War standoff. On November 10, he presented his alchemy to the larger subcommittee and received another round of applause on the front pages of the *New York Times*, which pronounced: "The latest draft was a series of compromises that were largely a result of the tireless efforts of Lester B. Pearson."[39]

Perhaps Walter Riddell's public humiliation in 1935 after he generated headlines at the League of Nations prompted Pearson to assure Louis St. Laurent that the press coverage "may be exaggerated and misleading." He had, he said, met with journalists to emphasize that his "suggestions were put forward in a personal capacity" and not in the name of the Canadian government. And he underlined for St. Laurent his faithful adherence to Prime Minister King's insistence that Canada not volunteer to help implement partition.[40]

London rejected certain details of Pearson's compromise, forcing the working group to revise its partition scheme. "We sat in a cell-like room," Pearson recalled, "hour after hour after hour, and the press were out there in the corridor keeping a death watch. We went on all day and all night and finally worked out an agreement that the Russians and the Americans would both accept."[41] Again the man in the middle somehow encouraged a compromise between Cold War antagonists, and on November 19 he presented it to the ad hoc committee.

In this draft, the working group proposed that the mandate end no later than August 1, 1948, with the new Arab and Jewish states to be established within two months. A UN commission guided by the Security Council would administer the transition and maintain public order. Pearson and his working group colleagues acknowledged the difficulties of their proposal and recognized that the United Nations was being asked to take a calculated risk.[42] Pearson's efforts proved persuasive. The draft compromise received approval from the subcommittee and ad hoc committee and was then submitted to the General Assembly for a vote by the fifty-seven member states. The peoples of Palestine would not have a direct say in their future; foreigners would decide their destiny.

Having toiled in New York for a month to shape this partition scheme, Pearson returned to Ottawa, a chorus of praise in his wake. Norman Robertson reported that the *Manchester Guardian* was celebrating him as "the creator of these successive compromises, and this capacity to watch a plan knocked down and then set up another should give him some special sort of status with the United Nations."[43] In a gesture of admiration and gratitude, someone, perhaps a delegate or journalist, dubbed him "Rabbi Pearson," an informal honour he gladly accepted.[44] John Holmes, an important adviser during the Suez Crisis, identified Pearson's performance as "the beginning of Canada's role as a middle power." In what is still the key account of this episode, historian David Bercuson judges that Pearson "played a unique and crucial role at the UN; partition might not have been adopted without his efforts." To Israeli scholar Eliezer Tauber, Pearson's efforts on Palestine transcended his diplomacy at Suez, arguing that this "most significantly contributed to the evolvement of Middle Eastern history."[45]

Whatever private satisfaction Pearson allowed himself, he did not let the applause distract him from the probability of failure or lose sight of the larger battle facing the West. Shortly before the looming vote in the General Assembly, Pearson voiced off-the-record doubts to Bruce Hutchison, warning him of the fragility of the proposed compromise. "It is quite wrong to assume because the Russians agreed with U.S. policy in Palestine that there is any meeting of minds, or any lessening of the general tension," he cautioned. Pearson worried that the USSR might view Palestine as a potential Communist state or an opportunity to send in troops to quell the chaos they expected would erupt after partition. "Don't go out on any limbs, or sing any [paeans]," Pearson advised, "until you see what is going to happen."[46] Pearson's doubts proved all too prescient.

As the General Assembly prepared to vote on the partition scheme, Jewish lobby groups amplified their already impassioned appeals to allies in the White House, the US Senate, the House of Representatives, and the Supreme Court, which in turn moved to inspire, cajole, bribe, and, when necessary, threaten various UN delegations with economic blackmail and suspended aid.[47] Pearson was himself subjected to intense Jewish entreaties, but the rabbi was already on side.

When Britain referred the issue to the United Nations in the spring, many considered the chance of a two-thirds majority in the General Assembly voting to partition Palestine highly improbable. On November 29, 1947, that unlikely majority emerged. Thirty-three members, including Canada and other overseas dominions, the United States, thirteen Central and Latin American states, the USSR and four of its satellites, the Scandinavian countries, Iceland, France, and the Benelux contingent, supported the creation of Jewish and Arab states with an economic union. Thirteen countries opposed the plan, including all the Arab nations, recently independent India, Muslim Afghanistan, Pakistan, and Turkey. One nation, Thailand, was absent, and ten, primarily from Central and South America, abstained. The most significant abstention was Great Britain, still trying to appear completely neutral.

To those Jews who had survived the Holocaust and were stranded in refugee camps, to those attacked and even killed as they made their way back to their former homes in Eastern Europe, and to those already living in Palestine, the vote from the world assembly legitimized a collective yearning sustained through two millennia of dispersal and persecution. To the diverse Arab world, the UN vote was a blatant act of imperialism manipulated by colonial powers indifferent to the will of the majority. The attempt to make peace served to ignite the next round of violence.

The tragic momentum accelerated when Arthur Creech Jones announced that Britain would withdraw from Palestine earlier than expected; instead of August, Britain would depart "with relief, and yet with regret," as Creech Jones put it, on May 15, 1948. He reminded the international community that his government had never been "prepared to impose, by force of arms, a settlement which was not acceptable to both Arabs and Jews" and that British troops would not be used "as the instrument of the United Nations for enforcing a decision against either community."[48] That raised the question that had always complicated the debate: who would carry out in Palestine what the UN had recommended?

During the intense autumn session at the UN when Pearson's diplomacy inspired so much acclaim, Mackenzie King was an ocean away at the wedding of Princess Elizabeth. By the time he was sailing back in early December, the prime minister was growing alarmed by the grim news from Palestine. He returned to his desk bitterly regretting having ever appointed a Canadian to UNSCOP and instructed Pearson not to chair any other Palestine committee. At this point, King remained in a forgiving mood with his undersecretary, confiding to his diary: "Apparently they all use him in N.Y. to be prominent in the Palestine affair, and he being young and no doubt feeling his ability in these matters, I think lent himself perhaps too wholly to the desires of others." Intent on keeping

Canada safe from the Middle East and anywhere else, he told Pearson to, in effect, forget about any more glory in New York and to focus instead on his department in Ottawa.[49] If Pearson's finely tuned survival instincts misjudged the intensity of King's anxiety, the message was reinforced in explosive fashion two weeks later.

On December 18, making what he thought would be a routine announcement in Cabinet, Louis St. Laurent informed his colleagues that a Canadian delegate would be appointed to a UN commission dealing with the partitioned Koreas. In approving the appointment, the foreign minister had not consulted the prime minister. When he heard about this international commitment for the first time, King remounted the battlements he had guarded his entire career and lectured his Cabinet that Canada had no business getting involved in distant situations, especially where the great powers were confronting each other. "Canada's role," he declared, "was not that of Sir Galahad [to] save the whole world unless we were in a position to do it."[50]

Not one to be intimidated, St. Laurent replied that, as a member state, the dominion should assume a proper share of obligations. King came back with the argument (which to a large degree Pearson would have agreed with in principle) that "the U.N. counted for nothing so far as any help in the world was concerned." A few other ministers dared to intrude on their leader's fury, but they only irritated him even more, and by the end of his fiery sermon, King had, according to the defence minister, Brooke Claxton, given St. Laurent "a going over as if he were a naughty little school-boy who had committed a sin against the Holy Ghost."[51] Fuming in his diary, King laid some of the blame on the deputy minister: "The truth is that Pearson with his youth and inexperience and influenced by the persuasion of others around him, had been anxious to have Canada's [External Affairs] figure prominently in world affairs and has really directed affairs in N.Y. when he should have been in Ottawa," King judged. "All well meant but very much the inexperience of youth."[52] The prime minister eventually relented but his anxiety had been stoked and he would not let down his guard.

That this overwrought drama to avoid a minor UN commitment was resolved in January 1948, the very month Canada assumed its first term as a non-permanent member on the Security Council, was not lost on

Pearson. "The Prime Minister is going to watch with suspicious attention every detail of our activity on that council," he noted in a personal memo, "with the result that we may find ourselves filling too often the role of inglorious abstainers." At the same time, King recorded in his diary: "I confess the whole business has considerably shaken my faith in Pearson's judgement. It has made me feel that he is much too immature."[53] It is tempting to think these two men, so different in their personal styles, and who could clearly exasperate each other so intensely, were separated by an ideological chasm. However, Pearson's handling of the Suez Crisis essentially mirrored King's response to Chanak in 1922 and to his own Suez Crisis in 1924.

In January 1948, preparing for the upcoming Security Council debate on Palestine, Pearson wanted a clearer sense of American intentions, which would inevitably frame Canadian intentions. As he mused about how best to proceed, he appeared open to an idea he had rejected the previous autumn: sending a UN force to help implement partition. Pearson cabled Ambassador Hume Wrong in Washington, asking him to remind the State Department that Canada had predicated its support for partition, in part, on the understanding that the Security Council's permanent members would actively help to make it happen. And he had another matter to clarify.

Wary of Washington's appetite for volunteering Canada for difficult assignments, keen to make sure the greater powers made the greater contribution, Pearson wanted American officials to understand that Ottawa would not support the idea of using contingents from smaller countries in any UN force. That very evening he made a similar point in a speech to a business crowd in Toronto. "Smaller powers," he said, "should not be asked to undertake United Nations duties which their more powerful associates find to be irksome, dangerous or embarrassing. They should not be asked to play roles in the international drama which should be performed by the stars. There are times when, if it is impossible for the stars to act together, a particular play should not be staged at all."[54]

On February 4, Wrong met with the American undersecretary of state, Robert Lovett. As instructed, he ventured to point out that during the autumn, the US delegation in New York seemed to hold out the prospect of American boots on Palestinian ground. Lovett disavowed any such impression and added that the US Army's chief of staff, General Dwight Eisenhower, had already stated that sending American forces to take over from the British would require partial mobilization, a politically unfeasible proposal.[55] Yet after he learned of Washington's reluctance, the idea of some kind of UN force remained an option for Pearson, if only for private discussion.

Two weeks later, External Affairs produced a memo for Cabinet suggesting four courses of action and inaction to be pursued by the Canadian delegation at the Security Council debate on Palestine: admit failure and essentially do nothing, refer the matter back to the General Assembly, attempt another round of conciliation between the warring parties, or help establish a UN-trained and -equipped volunteer force to implement partition. It's hard to know how seriously Pearson supported the force option, because the memo undermined it by emphasizing the obstacles, at least regarding a Canadian contribution. The military would need between six months to a year to assemble and deploy any troops, far too late for the unfolding emergency in Palestine. Another complicating factor was the recurring conundrum of how to handle the enemy. Excluding the Soviets meant potentially excluding all permanent members, making it far less likely that the smaller powers would shoulder the entire burden on their own.[56]

Prime Minister King opted for the course of least involvement and led Cabinet to support a round of talks to reconcile Jews and Arabs. Whatever Pearson truly felt about the possibility of the UN creating an intervention force, his room to explore the point was almost non-existent. During a discussion on March 1 about Palestine, King stated that while voting for partition had been the right choice four months before, it was clear to him that this could not be done without force. "The Canadian people are [not] willing to participate in any force set up for the above purpose," he pointed out, "[and] therefore we have no right to support a resolution which would advise others, the Big Five, to provide the force."[57]

Declining to preach to allies what he rightly sensed his country would refuse to carry out itself, King's stance was sensible domestic and foreign policy, especially in light of the discussion in Washington that underlined the limits of even a superpower's reach. The US Defense Department estimated that fifty thousand American troops would need to be deployed in Palestine, a number which represented the country's current ground reserve. "In other words," the department noted, "there will be no troops available for deployment to any other area." An assessment prepared by the CIA pointed out that, given the strategic need to keep the Soviets out of Palestine, "it is highly improbable that an international police force will ever be formed."[58] When Washington decided it would not join or establish a UN force in Palestine, wider discussions on the topic became largely superfluous.

As the concept of an international force to keep the peace hit a dead end in this context, the drive to ensure some measure of collective security was suddenly brought to life in another by the same actors refusing to risk it in Palestine. The difference between reluctance and engagement came down to self-interest.

In January 1948, almost two years after Winston Churchill sounded his alarm about the "iron curtain" sealing off Eastern Europe, and four months after Louis St. Laurent called for a regional security organization, London dispatched a clarion call for Ottawa and Washington to join with the "ethical and spiritual forces of Western Europe" and together defend "Western civilization" against the spreading Soviet menace.[59] Canada and the United States heeded the call, and joined by much of Western Europe, began to create the most powerful military alliance in history, the North Atlantic Treaty Organization.

While these UN members worked together through 1948 to secure their own defence needs, they remained unwilling to work together through the United Nations to enforce peace in a disintegrating Palestine. Britain remained absolutely fixated on withdrawing by May 15, which would leave Palestine's estimated 780,000 Jews and 1.4 million Arabs to sort out their future for themselves, in whatever vacuum existed. Even someone so normally sympathetic to British burdens as Pearson despaired about the damage being inflicted by Britain's overriding desire for escape. "This readiness to abandon the people of Palestine to their fate after permitting a situation to develop over the years which cannot do otherwise than end in bloodshed may be perfectly justifiable in the light of the realities of power politics," he wrote to Norman Robertson.

"It is difficult, however, to reconcile this policy with professions of concern for the welfare of the United Nations [and] seems to me a pretty cynical method of behaviour."[60] But regardless of the blood being spilt in Palestine or the outrage expressed so eloquently from the sidelines, Britain was set for flight and the US, for avoidance.

From the UN's vote supporting partition in November 1947 until the spring of 1948, the violent contest between Jews and Arabs had been, as Benny Morris has written, "formless — there were no front lines... no armies moving back and forth, no pitched battles, and no conquest of territory."[61] Seeing the British military buffer melting away, fearing invasion by neighbouring Arab countries, watching with dread as Washington seemed to waver in its support for partition, Jewish militias, determined to carve out their own state for themselves, went on the offensive in April. By May, hundreds of thousands of Arabs had fled their homes, sometimes at gunpoint.

In another world, delegations at the United Nations continued debating the crisis until the very end of the mandate. On May 14, Great Britain lowered the Union Jack on three decades of thankless rule, abandoning an estimated two million people to a killing zone. Prepared for this moment, a Jewish government-in-waiting immediately declared an independent State of Israel. Minutes later in Washington, shortly after 6 p.m. local time, President Harry Truman overrode his State Department, stunned the US delegation in New York, and announced de facto recognition of the fledgling state that lacked defined borders, was represented by a provisional government, and that might not even survive. For Jews around the world, Truman had conducted a compassionate and splendid act of statesmanship. For Arabs, his unilateral move was just more betrayal. The Soviet Union and other countries quickly followed Washington's lead. Other member states, including Canada, held back.

Within hours of the Jewish proclamation of independence, Egypt, Syria, Iraq, and Transjordan, claiming to act for Palestine but in fact hoping to carve it up for themselves, launched their units against the highly disciplined and deeply motivated Jewish forces, whose cause inspired financial support, underground shipments, and volunteers from Canada, America, Britain, and beyond. In their own significant contribution, the Soviets allowed state-of-the-art weaponry to be brought in from Czechoslovakia. A local war now threatened to become a far more deadly regional conflict.

Pearson's initial reaction at seeing the Jewish kingdom of his Methodist youth come closer into being was not, as might be expected, exultation. Instead he displayed more irritation at what he saw as the erratic, self-serving diplomacy conducted by his allies. Four days after Israel's declaration of statehood and Truman's abrupt recognition, Pearson wrote to Hume Wrong: "My own impatience with the attitude and policy of both the United Kingdom and the United States toward Palestine has not been diminished by the developments of the last week." Echoing earlier criticisms, he was fed up with British support for the Arabs tied solely to "strategy and oil. On the other hand, the United States revolving door policy, each push determined to a large extent by domestic political considerations and culminating in the sorry recognition episode of last Saturday, inspires no confidence and warrants little support." Nearly three decades later, this was still the passage he used in his memoirs.[62]

For guidance on how to respond to the new state in the Middle East, Prime Minister King, judging that Washington had displayed "impetuousness and lack of real wisdom," did not look to his superpower neighbour, and instead turned back to the Mother Country. On May 17, London suggested to the dominions that recognizing Israel would constitute "a declaration of hostility to the Arab world" and that it would be "unfair and legally wrong" to support the embryonic country's admission into the United Nations.[63] South Africa disagreed and days later became the first member of the Commonwealth to recognize the Jewish state, offering to do the same for any Arab nation established in the former mandate. When New Zealand and Australia considered following suit, London mounted a counteroffensive, managing to secure a temporary delay. King was content to oblige British purposes. And Pearson, it appears, did not argue otherwise.

On May 18, a dismayed Trygve Lie, the UN secretary-general, sent Pearson a "secret and personal" letter, "from one friend to another," worrying that failure to act in Palestine mirrored the League of Nations' failure to protect China during the 1931 Japanese invasion. Lie argued that inglorious episode helped destroy the league and worried that the same pattern of inaction might do the same to the United Nations.

Lie pleaded with Pearson, the man who had been so instrumental on Palestine the year before and whose country sat on the Security Council, to do whatever he could to have the other members stop the fighting between Jews and Arabs. He even offered to meet personally or send one of his officials to Ottawa for an informal discussion.[64]

Pearson's reply is dated a cool nine days later. He concurred that the UN's unwillingness to intervene could seriously damage the organization's future. He again laid blame with familiar arguments, citing the British determination "not to prejudice their relations with the Arab states if that can be avoided while not formally opposing a Jewish state" and the American determination "not to prejudice their relations with Jewish voters, but [who] are also interested in oil and strategy in Arab countries." Pearson repeated an earlier curse, calling for "a plague on all your houses!" It was "time that someone started thinking of the [UN] edifice," he warned. "If they do not, there will be nothing left of it but ruin."[65]

But beyond that he did not go. Pearson essentially rebuffed the United Nations secretary-general's personal request to discuss the most critical item on its agenda. The essential diplomat in 1947 was now choosing to remain completely on the sidelines in 1948—hardly surprising given that he toiled in Mackenzie King's Ottawa.

That May, Lie turned to the president of the Swedish Red Cross, Folke Bernadotte, to negotiate the first of several temporary truces. Following the recent precedent set in Greece and Indonesia, the United Nations sent unarmed observers to monitor compliance with the ceasefire. They eventually became formalized as the United Nations Truce Supervision Organization, UNTSO. Their neutrality, however, meant little to Jewish extremists who, during one truce, murdered Bernadotte and a French observer, Colonel André-Pierre Serot, as they sat in their car in Jerusalem.

Through the summer and fall of 1948, the resolute, unified Jewish forces overwhelmed and pushed back the mutually suspicious, ambivalent Arab armies until they conquered far more territory than was ever allotted to them in the partition scheme. Justice for one exiled people seeking a home consigned another people to their own exile. About four hundred thousand Arabs fled to Transjordan (soon to be renamed

Jordan), two hundred thousand ended up in Egypt's Gaza Strip, one hundred thousand went to Lebanon, and sixty thousand went to Syria. Mirroring this dispersal, about half a million Jews evacuated their homes in Arab nations.[66] What the victors called a War of Liberation, the vanquished grieved as "the Catastrophe" (*al-Nakba*), which now physically divided the Arab world. And what Jews had won on the battlefield, they sought to secure in the diplomatic arena. A new government in Canada moved to join the growing chorus of acceptance.

In August 1948, Louis St. Laurent won the Liberal Party leadership. In September, Pearson was appointed secretary of state for External Affairs, and in November, Mackenzie King stepped down from office. The new prime minister and foreign minister felt no need to follow British footsteps and began the process of recognizing Israel. This involved trying to ease fractious relations between Canada's two essential allies. Washington saw Israel serving Western interests in the Cold War. Britain feared that Israel would become a Communist pawn and serve as a Soviet bridgehead in the Middle East—not that London supported an independent Palestine, which might potentially be overrun by anti-British extremists. Although the Israelis controlled land allocated to the Arabs under the UN partition plan, the US refused to make them surrender any of it. Britain wanted the Israelis to give back this territory in order to graft something of Palestine onto Jordan and possibly Egypt. Inevitably, the British were compelled to retreat from their schemes, grudgingly accepting the military facts on the ground and the immoveable force in Washington, rooted in public opinion that felt, as one scholar put it, "the valiant Jewish people in the face of great adversity were creating a state in a way perhaps comparable to the winning of the American west. They were entitled to the fruits of their victory."[67]

In November 1948, at UN meetings in Paris, Pearson worked behind the scenes to repair strained relations, urging the British to accept what they could not change. Privately he told a member of the Canadian delegation that he thought the British were making the wrong move in supporting the Arabs so vigorously. "They should aim at developing the Jewish state," he argued, "and let it get strong." He shared the prevailing sentiment in the United States that the Arabs had "walked in to fight and got a licking and Jews could not be expected to give up their gains."[68] On November 22, Pearson addressed the UN, defending the controversial partition resolution from the year before:

> Our motives in supporting it have been challenged, and our judgement violently attacked.... We were honestly of the opinion that there was no practicable alternative to partition.... Some form of unitary or federal state would, of course, have been preferable, but there was no possibility of forcing political unity on the Arab and Jewish peoples of Palestine in a form which would not have been bitterly resisted by one side or the other. In these circumstances, the only thing we could do was reconcile ourselves to the necessity of separation as the solution which seemed best in the circumstances.... Let those who charge that this decision was the cause of all the bloodshed and destruction that have degraded the Holy Land in the last twelve months ask themselves whether there would have been peace and order in the area if a unitary state had been forced on the Jewish population of Palestine, or if the Assembly had made no recommendation at all.

With typical grace, he acknowledged the losing side's grief without affirming their desiderata. "I do not deny for a moment that this is a difficult circumstance for the Arab states to accept," he said, "but it is nevertheless the case and it does not seem to me that the United Nations would be doing those states any service if it encouraged them, or even permitted them, to continue their efforts to destroy by force of arms the Jewish state." Pearson went on to urge international recognition of Israel and proposed that the UN admit the new state as a full member.[69] In December, Canada extended de facto recognition, and a month later Great Britain, New Zealand, and Australia followed. The military clashes ended in January 1949, enabling the UN to negotiate a series of armistices between the combatants now obliged to live as neighbours in a redrawn Middle East.

Established by European settlers who brought with them Western concepts of individual freedoms and representative government, the State of Israel developed into the region's only democracy, while the long-subject Arab people were consigned to endure the monarchies and military dictatorships that emerged from the vassal states of the Ottoman and British empires, all surviving by suffocating their populations' rights and freedoms, and all keeping the mass of Palestinian refugees penned up in squalid camps, to be used as pawns in the ongoing political contest.

The new minority in Israel, an estimated 160,000 Arabs, were granted citizenship and the right to vote and stand for office, but the violent nature of Israel's birth engendered its own measure of repression, as Zachary Lockman has observed: "[Arabs] were certainly not full and equal citizens. Most of them remained under military administration, their lives subject to the often arbitrary authority of (Jewish) army officers from whom permits were required for many of the activities of daily life."[70]

Supervising the uneasy state of loathing along the borderlands, the unarmed members of the United Nations Truce Supervision Organization, UNTSO, worked in small numbers, suffering injuries and death in the line of duty. No Canadians were attached until 1954, when the UN approached member states to nominate a new commander. Pearson recommended a former general and current deputy minister of veteran affairs, E.L.M. Burns. In their discussions about the potential appointment, Pearson quipped, Burns later said, "If you make a go of this, we'll recommend you for the Nobel Prize." Burns took over what he would describe as "not a peacemaking but at best a peace-keeping organization. Sometimes its members were referred to as international policemen, but they were policemen without truncheons. They were actually more like watchmen."[71]

During his tour, Burns learned that some Arabs did not see his country or his foreign minister as neutral. "There was always a tendency to [say] we were really, like the Americans, on the side of the Israelis," he noted. "It was a thing that was brought up against Mr. Pearson too." An Arab acquaintance told him that she had seen Pearson at the UN embracing Israeli Prime Minister David Ben-Gurion: "They put their arms around each other in an effusive kind of way which was not Pearson's usual style, but I suppose he couldn't refuse it if Ben-Gurion clasped him to his bosom. But anyway this was noted." A Saudi Arabian delegate to the UN told a Canadian diplomat that "he and his Arab colleagues considered Mr. Pearson the most able and fervent advocate of Zionism."

And indeed Pearson would always lavish praise on the pioneering efforts and "heroic manner in which the Jews of Palestine proclaimed and defended their State." In his written memoirs, he maintained, "I still think that [partition] was the best of all the solutions offered," but for the TV version, he allowed a note of regret and doubt, saying: "I've often looked back and wondered whether we did the right thing then. It hasn't worked out as we hoped." Speaking in the House of Commons a few months before Suez, he made the following observation on the mutually exclusive triumph and tragedy of Israel's birth and the Palestinian exodus. "Deep fear leads to desperate acts which, though they cannot be condoned, may at least be understood," he said. "It remains a difficult, complicated and controversial question. It is not wise to be dogmatic in regard to it."[72]

SIX

Same Old, Same Old

As Pearson came into the office, I was struck by his fine face
and appearance. There was a light from within which shone
through his countenance... I was immensely taken with his
whole manner which is very natural—a self-effacing one. I told
him I felt he had a great career before him.

    —William Lyon Mackenzie King, September 4, 1946,
    diary entry

"Do you know anybody in Algoma East? Have you any connection with
Algoma East?" asked the prime minister.

"Where is Algoma East?" replied the deputy minister at External
Affairs.[1]

Fortunately for Lester Pearson, previous electoral experience or any
kind of personal connection to future constituents was not considered a
requirement for public office by the outgoing or incoming prime ministers who engineered his transition from the civil service to the political
front lines. Pearson, despite the impression of jaunty indifference woven
through his memoirs, appeared to initiate this transition himself, which
was marked by striking measures of desire and hesitation.[2]

Working under Mackenzie King may have been a privilege, occasionally a pleasure, but it was too often exasperating. Pearson's qualms
about the prime minister dated back to the 1930s and his posting to
London. Journalist Grant Dexter found him in 1937 so "thoroughly dis-
heartened and disillusioned" by Canada's "do nothing" foreign policy
that Pearson thought seriously about leaving External Affairs to work in

public relations at the newly created CBC.[3] A decade later, when Pearson was appointed undersecretary, he remained uneasy about working so closely with King. "I will be on a very tough spot," he confided to his departing predecessor, Norman Robertson. "After all, you & Hume [Wrong, Robertson's right hand] have taken a beating, but there have at least been two of you. I would have no one like either of you to help...and would have the P.M. in his declining difficult months."[4] And indeed, in his twilight, King was all too easily engulfed by old demons. His reasoning and concerns were not without merit but overwrought apprehensions of phantom threats blinded him to true dangers. The year 1948 proved an especially draining ordeal for Pearson.

In January, Canada took its seat for the first time as a non-permanent member of the Security Council, but just when the dominion assumed a place of prominence on the world stage, the champion of Canadian sovereignty moved on multiple fronts to restrain his eager diplomats from joining any United Nations efforts to make peace anywhere. The year began for Pearson with an excruciating trek to Washington to persuade the State Department and a perplexed President Truman that Canada must withdraw from a UN commission on Korea. In the same month, the prime minister refused to let his country serve on proposed UN commissions dealing with Palestine and the border dispute between India and Pakistan over Kashmir. Pearson worried in a memo to King: "We may give the impression that we are unwilling to help a friendly state which has specifically asked for our good offices."[5] King could not have cared less about giving that impression.

Pearson also had to manage King's outrage at the wording in Britain's appeal for a Western defence alliance against the Soviets, which flooded the prime minister's senses with dark visions of a resurgent imperial stranglehold. The deputy minister patiently suggested that the real danger to Canada in 1948 emanated from a totalitarian Communist empire and not an impoverished and retrenching Mother Country.

Then came King's reaction to one of the most critical confrontations of the Cold War. In June 1948, Moscow attempted to force the United States, the United Kingdom, and France to surrender their occupation zones in Berlin, closing off railway lines and roads into the Allied-controlled sectors of the city and cutting off the electricity. President

(L-R) Prime Minister William Lyon Mackenzie King (left) with
Ambassador Lester Pearson at the Canadian Embassy in
Washington in 1945 (Canadian Press 08510247)

Truman and Prime Minister Attlee decided to airlift food, coal, and
other supplies to the roughly 2.5 million people now trapped behind
Communist lines. Pearson viewed this standoff as a crucial test and felt
the West could not afford to back down. Pragmatic in his appraisal, he
also accepted a fundamental factor in the country's foreign policy; while
Canada was "not responsible for the unhappy developments that have
occurred in Berlin," he noted, "there is no escaping the fact that we would
be implicated in any conflict which might result from this situation."[6]

In preparation for the massive feat of logistics, airpower and, more
importantly, willpower, UK Foreign Secretary Ernest Bevin gathered
the dominion High Commissioners in London and informally asked for
assistance. Confronted by a familiar nightmare, Mackenzie King learned
about the meeting from press reports. A headline in the *Evening Standard*
was enough to confirm all his darkest suspicions and self-justifications:

"Empire Asked to Break Berlin Siege."[7] King had spent his career making sure that Canada would be able to accept or refuse whatever the empire cared to ask. Although he knew the meeting was preliminary, informal, and leaked without sanction from the Foreign Office, learning of it after the fact drew clear battle lines in Mackenzie King's mind, and they lay not between the democracies and Communist tyranny but between his sovereign dominion and the unscrupulous, controlling Mother Country.[8] Pearson wrote King several passionate memos arguing that Canada could not and should not stand on the sidelines of this critical confrontation.[9] The prime minister could not be swayed in the slightest.

At one Cabinet meeting in late June, King outlined the pivotal connection in his own mind for those ministers who might not see it so clearly. He took them a quarter century back to his triumph at Chanak in 1922, when he defied another imperial summons and thereby saved Canada from racial discord. King gauged the mood in Cabinet with his usual accuracy, for only St. Laurent appeared to support joining the airlift. Under the prime minister's guiding hand, Cabinet agreed that while Canada could possibly offer foodstuffs to Berlin, there would be "difficulties involved" in sending any aircrew or aircraft to join the allied mission.[10] These Canadians preferred to leave it to the British, Americans, Australians, New Zealanders, and French to save the people of Berlin.

Little wonder that during the summer of 1948, even with the office of foreign minister dangling before him, Pearson held back. "I wasn't going to commit myself even to think seriously about it until I saw what happened at the [leadership] convention," he said later. "I wasn't quite sure Mr. King wouldn't be persuaded to stay on, and I didn't want to go into politics under Mr. King."[11] In August, Liberal delegates settled the matter, electing Louis St. Laurent to lead the party and the country. King would stay on for three more months to bid a long farewell and oversee one last grand backroom manoeuvre.

On September 10, Pearson, now fifty-one years old, was sworn in as secretary of state for External Affairs. His oldest friends in the department and beyond had encouraged him to make the leap, but according to one officer, Pearson's choice "to become a mere politician" dismayed some: "The young arrivals especially considered it to be something between desertion and a display of bad taste." No longer sheltered in the bureaucracy, Pearson experienced a small taste of the new hazards involved at his first press conference as a minister, which was, as he wrote in his memoirs, "slightly marred by my quip in reply to the question 'How long, Mr. Pearson, have you been a member of the Liberal Party?' 'Since I was sworn in as a Minister a couple of hours ago.'"[12]

Having anointed Pearson into Cabinet, Mackenzie King then opened the door to the House of Commons. Working closely with St. Laurent, he approved the northern Ontario riding of Algoma East, ascertained local party officials would not object, transplanted the sitting MP into the Senate, handed Pearson the nomination, and set the by-election for October

The neophyte politician required some instruction in the art of electioneering, such as waving to anyone in hailing distance, even from his moving car. He did as he was told, only too well. According to one anecdote he liked to tell, Pearson at the end of one long day dutifully waved at a lone farmer walking home. "You can stop waving now," the outgoing MP accompanying him said. "We're out of the constituency."[13]

He may have mocked himself, but the new minister was campaigning to win. The *Toronto Daily Star* noted that Pearson in the opening rounds appeared "somewhat diffident and hesitant." The "audiences were unlike anything he had experienced at the United Nations, the League of Nations or elsewhere. By the end of his campaign he was able to give both light jesting touches and grim earnest messages," the paper wrote. And when a lumberjack at a stop in Blind River "started to snore loudly, he wasn't more than mildly disconcerted."[14] Pearson, of course, had experienced these kind of rural audiences before, long ago in his youth when he watched his easygoing father in small meetings, connecting with humour and without affectation, showing the son how to spread his own gospel in a convincing and indeed winning fashion.

On October 25, a solid majority in Algoma East elected Pearson. Three weeks later, William Lyon Mackenzie King tendered his resignation as His Majesty's longest-serving first minister in Canada and stepped down from his mission to keep the country united, sovereign, and Liberal. He retired, unmarried and childless, to his country estate, respected rather than admired, leaving behind a country and a government seemingly reinventing itself on the world stage.

Pearson's true constituency and most pressing concerns lay far beyond his new riding, and within days of the by-election, he was en route
for a UN meeting in Paris, where he overturned King's previous policy
and urged international recognition of the fledgling state of Israel. In
December, the United Nations appealed for military observers to supervise a cease-fire between Pakistan and India, and Pearson again moved
away from the path of least involvement. He believed in supporting the
UN, for all its faults and limitations, whenever feasible. The UN's request
was decidedly modest, and he thought his country— "English speaking,
no immediate interest in the India-Pakistan dispute, no colonial possessions in the Far East," as Pearson noted—made the ideal observer.
He could not discuss in public the other reason for participating in this
mission, which was to provide protective cover for intelligence gathering.[15]

In January 1949, Minister for National Defence Brooke Claxton
brought the matter to a Cabinet meeting not attended by either the
foreign minister or the prime minister. Reflecting the instincts and customs of their recently retired leader, those gathered declined to make
a decision. Afterwards, Claxton told External Affairs that Cabinet was
"allergic" to the UN request, noting that minsters posed two questions
hinting of trepidation if not indignation, namely, "Why was Canada one
of the countries invited to appoint observers?" and "What other countries
had accepted the invitation?"[16]

Ignoring his colleagues' distinct lack of enthusiasm, Pearson announced that Canada would send four officers to join the United Nations
Military Observer Group in India and Pakistan. The announcement
barely made a ripple in the Canadian press or state of mind, or indeed
in later memoirs, but this unheralded decision marked the first time
that Canada joined a UN observer mission.[17] A much more dramatic
and celebrated move into the wider world was symbolized in April when
Pearson travelled to Washington to sign the North Atlantic Treaty, joining for the first time eleven other allies in a peacetime defence alliance.

For some, then and in the decades to come, the new secretary of state
for External Affairs embodied a radical break from what Pearson himself
criticized as a foreign policy "of timidity and isolation and withdrawal."
To the end of his life, he reinforced this sense of schism, writing in
retirement: "I have often wondered why [King] wanted me for the post."

The prime minister, he observed, "thought many of my ideas on foreign affairs rash and adventurous, which would lead Canada into trouble."

Looking past the mesmerizing shine of what came to be called the Golden Age of Canadian diplomacy, historians eventually perceived underlying continuities from the rule of King to the ways of Mike. They came to see that even in the most glittering period, representing a country far more open to international engagement, Pearson and his colleagues did not become "rash and adventurous," once unshackled from King's clutches, but in fact implicitly agreed that Canada's role was not that of Sir Galahad bound to save the whole world; far from it. In this rebalancing of perceptions, historian Greg Donaghy has written: "As the records of the 1940s and 1950s are progressively uncovered, King's ghostly hand seems ever more apparent. Like King, his successors possessed a shrewd appreciation of the nature of global power and Canada's modest place on this scale. Conscious of limited means, they were inclined to shun burdensome international responsibilities, followers not leaders. Their diplomacy was cautious, modest, and pragmatic."[18]

Pearson's decision to commit to the military observer group and join NATO obscured the continuities. The Americans and British continued for months to make private, informal requests for a contribution to their efforts in Berlin, but the new prime minister continued to hold back, allowing Cabinet to dither. St. Laurent even expressed concern that dispatching Canadians to fly British planes might "be interpreted in some quarters in Canada to mean that Canada was behaving very much like a colony."[19] Surprisingly given the intensity of his memos written just a few months before as undersecretary, no evidence exists of Pearson pushing either St. Laurent or Cabinet very hard to commit Canada to the airlift.

The continuity of caution and restraint resurfaced in June 1950 when Communist North Korea invaded South Korea. In the opening days of the attack, Pearson perceived and certainly felt no need for Canada to defend this distant country from aggression. He was astonished to see Washington, which had repeatedly stated South Korea was not part of its defence perimeter, abruptly overturn its own policy and rally the United Nations to assemble a credible fighting force. For weeks, as other countries, including Britain, Australia, and New Zealand, offered troops, Pearson and St. Laurent resisted making any kind of commitment to the

UN's first police action. Criticism from the Opposition and the press and, more decisively, pressure from Washington finally compelled Pearson to urge Cabinet to approve sending Canadian volunteers to uphold the principles of the United Nations—at least as interpreted by the West in this instance of selective security enforcement.

In an earlier period of conscious, tactical evasion, when the League of Nations pulled back from the brink to sacrifice Ethiopia, Mackenzie King asked a question to which arguably only one credible if unheroic answer could exist for a country of Canada's size and influence: "There is such a thing as a sense of proportion in international affairs as in all else. Do hon. members think that it is Canada's role at Geneva to attempt to regulate a European war?"[20] When King's brilliant, internationally educated cadre eventually took charge of Canada's foreign policy, they implicitly agreed with him that their country could and should not regulate vast wars and remained ever sensitive to their sense of Canada's proper proportion in foreign affairs.

In a January 1948 speech, Pearson shared his own sense of these proportions and possibilities. "Of course, we are independent now, constitutionally," he observed. "But that independence is only relative." A decision taken in Washington or London, he stated, could have the same effect on Canadian foreign policy as an act of Parliament, and he asked his audience to acknowledge the limits of Canada's reach, saying, "We needn't exaggerate our power, or deceive ourselves about it, by talk of sovereign rights and unrestricted independence." Writing in retirement, he had not altered his nuanced, pragmatic appreciation of what Canada could sensibly aim for, even in a so-called Golden Age: "I was not so naive as to think that we could decisively, or even importantly, influence the policies of the Great Powers, but I hoped we could influence the environment in which they were pursued."[21]

And when he found his country caught up in great power policies he considered unwise, he maintained continuities that Wilfrid Laurier upheld when he defied the imperial pull to South Africa, and established before that by John A. Macdonald, who refused to get involved in 1885 when London appealed for help in putting down an Islamic insurgency in the Sudan that threatened Egypt and the Suez Canal. Even though proudly born a British subject and happy to die as one, Macdonald held back. "The Suez Canal is nothing to us," he stated. "Why should we waste money and men in this wretched business?"[22] When Pearson, as foreign minister, faced appeals for help in Britain's secondary wars, he remained faithful to these sentiments and calculations.

> The quality which the Middle Eastern peoples recognise above all others is strength. If we retained our position there during the early part of the present war, it is because the Middle East never lost confidence in our resolution and in our ultimate ability to win through.
> —UK Foreign Secretary Anthony Eden to Cabinet, April 13, 1945[23]

> In peace and war the Middle East is an area of cardinal importance to the United Kingdom...a focal point of communications, a source of oil, a shield to Africa and the Indian Ocean, and an irreplaceable offensive base...our influence is greater than that of any other foreign Power. It is essential that we should maintain our special position.
> —UK Foreign Secretary Ernest Bevin to Cabinet, August 25, 1949[24]

In the spring of 1951, having glimpsed enough retreat and frailty, the government of Iran defied Britain and nationalized the Anglo-Iranian Oil Company, a sprawling masterwork of imperialism and industry, majority owned by the British government, employing some 4,500 British staff and seventy thousand Iranians, and operating vast oil fields and the world's largest refinery.

Already accused of scuttling the empire, Prime Minister Clement Attlee found his government insulted without an honourable exit route. Speaking for many an anguished patriot, Minister of Defence Emanuel Shinwell railed in Cabinet. "If Persia was allowed to get away with it, Egypt and other Middle East countries would be encouraged to think that they could try things on: the next thing might be an attempt to nationalise the Suez canal," he argued. "We must be prepared to show that our tail could not be twisted interminably."[25] Dedicated to nationalizing entire swaths of the British economy and espousing a postcolonial foreign policy built on partnership rather than coercion, Attlee maintained his preferred path of non-violence because, despite clamours in his party, in the press and across the Opposition benches, the country as a whole did not possess the stomach, let alone the budget, to risk getting bogged down in another Palestine or Malaya. Attlee was also guided by the knowledge that Britain's most important ally and financial backer consistently urged negotiation rather than invasion.

An ocean away in Ottawa, the Opposition asked Lester Pearson to respond to the crisis. Speaking to the House on May 14, the secretary of state for External Affairs declined to cheer or condemn either side, saying, "It would be inappropriate and inadvisable for one in my position to talk about this particular subject at this particular moment." Pearson saying nothing was, in itself, saying something. Instead of flying the "Old Flag," the middle-power diplomat staked out a middle ground, acknowledging and thereby seeming to confer equal legitimacy upon "the national aspirations of the Iranian people" as well as "the legitimate interests of other people who have ministered to the well-being of Iran in administering the oil industry." He was no doubt keenly aware his calculated balance would anger some sections of the electorate which heartily agreed with an editorial headline in the *Globe and Mail* condemning Iran's move as "grand larceny."[26] Fortunately for Pearson, the events were too distant to require anything more from him, and most helpfully, the British eventually stood down.

At a late September Cabinet meeting, Attlee ruled out the use of force to keep the AIOC in British hands, largely because he foresaw that the United Nations and, more importantly, the United States would condemn any such attempt. Foreign Secretary Herbert Morrison worried that if the government's response appeared "feeble and ineffective," Egypt might nationalize the Suez Canal Company. Yet however disturbing Iran's insult, he was unwilling to incur the price of exacting satisfaction and concurred with his prime minister: "We could not afford to break with the United States on an issue of this kind." The last of the AIOC's British staff departed like servants dismissed. For his prudence, Attlee saw his country endure what many perceived as another shaming surrender. By now he and his party were fighting a general election.[27]

On the campaign trail, Anthony Eden, the former foreign secretary, did not praise Attlee's conscious aversion of war but instead declared the whole affair "a resounding and humiliating defeat." That sentiment echoed through the Middle East. At least one officer in the Egyptian army, then plotting treason — or in his eyes, liberation — took a measure of inspiration from the expulsion. Speaking with a British official, Gamal Abdel Nasser remarked, "You British from that moment no longer retained any respect. If [Iran] could do that to you, why couldn't the rest of us?'"[28] And indeed on the eighth of October 1951, the Egyptian government declared that it would abrogate the all-pervasive 1936 Anglo-Egyptian treaty, which allowed British troops to stand guard on Egyptian soil, the Royal Navy to protect Egyptian waters, and the Royal Air Force to patrol Egyptian skies, all in defence of the Suez Canal.

Ever since landing troops in the late-nineteenth century to crush a nationalist threat, and despite numerous promises to withdraw, the British military presence in Egypt had sprawled symbiotically alongside the waterway into the largest base in the world that stretched nearly one hundred kilometres from its eastern to western edge and roughly 145 kilometres north end to south, and housed approximately thirty-five thousand troops and their families. "Every village in Britain," wrote journalist Elizabeth Monroe, "contained men familiar with the Canal Zone, and with keeping guard below the dun-coloured hills round Suez, 'the white cliffs of Dover browned off,' as the troops called them."[29] Now Cairo wanted them all to go home.

In the midst of an election, the Attlee government informed Cairo that it considered the abrogation invalid and would continue to maintain British troops on Egyptian soil. On October 13, His Majesty's Government in Britain dispatched a justification and appeal to His Majesty's Governments in Canada, South Africa, New Zealand, and Australia. In outlining its determination to negotiate a new treaty with Cairo, London largely ignored any notion of Egyptian choice in the matter: "We shall regard ourselves as agents acting on behalf of the free world when we say that we intend to stay in Egypt at whatever cost."[30] Unlike Abadan or Palestine or India, Attlee was not prepared to walk away from the Suez Canal. The day after the abrogation, demonstrators in the Suez Canal zone city of Ismailia, aided by helpful police officers, torched British cars, looted British stores, and tried to force their way into an apartment block for British families. Only British machine guns and bayonets persuaded the mob to disperse.

In the cumbersome machinery of diplomacy, the telegram sent from London on the thirteenth was handed to Arnold Heeney, the undersecretary at External Affairs in Ottawa, on the fifteenth, and his memo in response was presented to Pearson the following day, by which time the canal zone had become a battleground. As a middle-power diplomat sensible of limits, Heeney noted: "It would be useful to know what the United States view is [but] we should not wait on them." In the meantime, he urged, Canada must give full support to Britain's struggle to remain in the canal zone "for the security of the free world."[31]

It is uncertain whether Pearson had read Heeney's memo by the time he stood up in the House of Commons; even if he had, an exceedingly cautious minister declined to accept the advice. Pearson did not even utter supportive platitudes for a NATO and Commonwealth ally under fire, merely observing that the "difficult" situation appeared "highly inflammable." Pearson doubted the usefulness of any statement he could make at that time but noted: "If anything can usefully be said, I shall say it at the first opportunity."[32] Mackenzie King himself could not have been more evasive.

The next day, October 17, in preparation for Cabinet, Heeney sent Pearson another memo urging staunch support for Britain, rather pointedly lecturing his minister, "Moral support is of little value unless it is made public." Perhaps because they had been fellow civil servants and still friends, Heeney felt entitled to hold Pearson accountable to his own words. "Yesterday," he pointed out, "you said that 'if anything can usefully be said, I shall say it at the first opportunity.' There is therefore an opening for you to make a statement today when the House assembles."[33] Heeney's draft for this statement linked "the security of the free world" with Britain's continuing "to fulfil its responsibilities" defending the Suez Canal. Implicit in the statement was the assumption that Canada should give British and therefore Western strategic defence interests clear precedence over Egyptian sovereignty—hardly a radical notion in the midst of the Cold War.

Yet in the fractious breakup and reordering of the British Empire, Pearson felt some sympathy for subjects restless for self-rule. In a foreign policy debate later that October, he acknowledged that both Iran and Egypt arbitrarily violated agreements and undermined the rule of international law, but he pointed out that the inspiration for both disputes lay in "the natural and justifiable wish of states which have experienced periods of foreign intervention to assert their right to be masters of their domestic affairs.... It would be folly indeed to underestimate the strength of this movement, as it would be folly to underestimate the basis of its inspiration." But Pearson attached a strong caveat. "We have two blocs," he observed. "We have the bloc of freedom and we have the bloc of slavery." He supported liberation for all as long as it did not lead to a new kind of subjugation. "The tragedy for these countries," he argued, "lies in their blind refusal to recognize that, in their anxiety to gain full control of their affairs by the elimination of foreign influence, they are exposing themselves to the menace of communist penetration and absorption."[34]

On October 17, Pearson took Heeney's draft statement urging strong backing for Britain into Cabinet where, according to the minutes, "considerable discussion" ensued. Evidently, unnamed ministers wanted the draft statement revised, which meant Pearson ignored Heeney's advice to make a quick declaration of solidarity that day. He returned to his office to edit the draft himself. For the most part, Pearson simply polished the wording, but he made one significant revision that diluted Heeney's bold appeal: no attempt should be made to use force to change the situation. He did not specify which country he was addressing. Implicit in his dilution lay the assumption that Cairo was entitled to have its interests met in any new defence arrangement and that Cairo's interests deserved as much consideration as Britain's.[35]

When Heeney and others in External Affairs saw Pearson's revised statement, they were not pleased, replying to the minister: "it almost puts Egypt and the United Kingdom on the same footing. It would not be regarded as an expression of 'moral support' for the British decision to 'stand firm.'" Pearson's officials suggested tougher language, which he incorporated in the next draft.[36]

Cabinet met on the following day, by which time, as Pearson pointed out, both the French and American governments had rallied to express public support for the United Kingdom. Following in their wake with all due caution, Pearson suggested that Canada might now consider declaring its position. Reassured by the US lead, his colleagues agreed.[37] Pearson and his officials revised the statement yet again. In the meantime, in the House of Commons, Tory MP Howard Green attacked the government's silence. Pointing out that New Zealand, Australia, and the US had taken a stand, he asked: "Why is Canada waiting?"[38]

On October 19, Pearson at last offered Canada's moral support to the British cause in Egypt, stating that Ottawa regretted Egypt's action to abrogate the defence treaty. Finding shelter in the shadow of the neighbouring superpower, Pearson noted that Washington considered Egypt's act "as without validity. We agree with that view." He concluded with some of the tougher language suggested by his undersecretary, invoking "the security of the free world." And he clearly addressed Cairo when he expressed the hope that force would not be used to alter "the present regime of responsibility of the United Kingdom for the defence of the Suez canal zone."[39]

Even with this stronger language, Mackenzie King's former apprentice offered Britain only a modest measure of moral force and nothing more. A glimpse of his reasoning came to light indirectly, from a conversation in which an official from the British High Commission asked a counterpart in External Affairs, A.J. Pick, why Pearson felt the need to refer to the shared US position. Pick replied candidly "We had in Ottawa in all important matters to take into consideration the United States position." In 1951, as in any other year of Canada's existence, this sensible appreciation of continental constraints was hardly remarkable. Pick noted another, less obvious consideration: if Pearson had not stated that Canada was moving in harmony with the US, Pick observed, "there might well have been criticism from Quebec Members."[40]

Pick later raised this point with the minister himself. His assumption proved right on the mark. Pearson acknowledged that the reference to the US position had been added "to forestall any possible criticism from Quebec quarters." Pearson then went on to remind Pick of the "celebrated" Chanak crisis in 1922.[41] Nearly thirty years after that controversial British appeal for moral support inflamed Canada's racial divisions, Pearson still felt the need to factor into dealings with Great Britain potential resistance from Quebec about Canada looking like an imperial puppet. Moving in concert with Washington helped to dispel that image. Had he been alive, Mackenzie King would have applauded Pearson's invocation of Chanak and his proper attendance to the former prime minister's recurring nightmare of racial discord ignited by anglo-phones rallying to Britain's side. Pearson never mentioned his reasoning in public.

As if the foreign minister could ever forget the other equation in Canadian diplomacy, on October 8, at the outset of the abrogation crisis in Egypt, Canada's future Queen, Princess Elizabeth, and her husband, Philip, touched down in Montreal for a royal tour. For weeks, bold head-lines about London sending reinforcements to the canal zone played against front-page photographs of the princess meeting her Canadian subjects. The coverage in English Canada was predictably devotional. While this sentiment did not translate into automatic support for British foreign policy, no Canadian politician could ignore such a powerful emo-tional attachment, however indirectly and unevenly it was felt across the country.

By election day in Britain, October 25, 1951, Clement Attlee and his Labour Party had spent six years remaking a home front that "compared to the UK of 1931 or *any* previous decade, was a kinder, gentler and a far, far better place in which to be born, to grow up, to live, love, work and even to die."[42] But in retreating from so much imperial territory, they were seen to have presided over the appalling erosion of the country's inter-national prestige. The electorate was evenly divided in their judgment. Labour actually won a slight majority of votes, but the Conservatives took a thin majority of seventeen seats, bringing Winston Churchill back into power and Anthony Eden back to the Foreign Office. They inherited the crisis in Iran and Egypt, the "emergency" in Malaya, the brewing trouble in Cyprus and Kenya, and the ongoing UN police action in Korea. Like its predecessors, the new regime had no intention of settling for a lesser role on the global stage but it also understood that, in theory at least, something somewhere had to give.

In a June 1952 Cabinet memo, Eden warned that the country could barely afford its current overseas obligations and policies. If Britain was not able to reduce, share, or transfer these international burdens, he declared, "a choice of the utmost difficulty lies before the British people." They could see their standard of living fall, "or by relaxing their grip in the outside world, see their country sink to the level of a second-class Power."[43]

Eden could frame the stark choice facing his country with brave clarity but, emblematic of his peers and their moment in history, he could in the very same memo only flinch back from making the hard choice between domestic affluence and international esteem: "Once the prestige of a country has started to slide there is no knowing where it will stop."[44] Thus Eden returned to the Foreign Office, at once clear-eyed and blinded, grappling with irreconcilable objectives, and operating with only claustrophobic room for manoeuvre. His last-ditch attempt to confront that dilemma in its Egyptian incarnation would set the stage for his greatest failure and Pearson's greatest triumph.

SEVEN

One Strong Young Figure

> In the second half of the 20th century we cannot hope to
> maintain our position in the Middle East by the methods
> of the last century. However little we like it, we must face
> this fact…the tide of nationalism is rising fast. If we are
> to maintain our influence in this area, future policy must be
> designed to harness these movements rather than to struggle
> against them.
> —Anthony Eden, February 16, 1953[1]

In the fall of 1935 in Geneva, the man who did everything he could to
defuse the Suez Crisis met the man who did all he could to inflame it.
On "one grand Sunday," they took a break from the League of Nations'
contortions over Ethiopia to play tennis against each other. They were the
same age but occupied very different positions in the diplomatic hierarchy.
Lester Pearson was a High Commission official for a marginal nation.
Anthony Eden was a cabinet minister for an imperial power. The Canadian
was invisible on the world stage, whereas the Englishman glittered in the
spotlight. They did not become close friends, but their meeting marked
the beginning of a long, largely harmonious working relationship, marked
by some reservations on both sides. Writing in his diary later, Pearson
acknowledged Eden's charm, intelligence, and diplomatic skill, but he
also raised many of the doubts entertained by contemporaries and later
historians about the bright young star of British foreign policy. Eden had
so much handed to him without having to earn it—"breeding, money,
looks"—and he had been very lucky. Eden's "triumphs up to the present

are due as least as much to the misfortunes of his superiors," Pearson noted, "as to his own ability." He did not think Eden singular in any way, judging many others in British politics equally able, and concluded his diary entry with a prescient observation: "Wait till the 'breaks' start to go against him. That will be his testing time."[2] When the ultimate testing time erupted in 1956, the two sons of empire staked out diametrically opposed positions, arriving from similar trajectories. Both were born British subjects in 1897, as Queen Victoria celebrated a glorious imperial high point, her Diamond Jubilee. Both enjoyed privileged upbringings, Eden lavishly as the son of a baronet and Pearson more modestly as the son of a Methodist minister. They served in the Great War, with Eden decorated for manifest courage in the trenches and Pearson ending his inglorious military career by being hit by a bus. The war's futility did not embitter them, radicalize their politics, or turn either of them into pacifists.

They both attended Oxford, their terms slightly overlapping, although they did not meet one another. From 1919 to 1922, the more disciplined Eden read oriental languages (Persian and Arabic) at Christ Church College and achieved a first while the more distracted, sports-obsessed Pearson scored a humbler second in modern history. They both decided on diplomacy. After graduation, Eden avoided joining the Foreign Office, later writing in his memoirs: "It seemed to me, in my impatience, that responsibility in one of our embassies would be long in coming. I should be forever handing round teacups in Teheran."[3] Instead, Eden sought political office, becoming, at age twenty-six and on his second attempt, a Member of Parliament in 1923. After drifting for nearly a decade, Pearson entered the diplomatic realm through the civil service and then, after twenty years, crossed over to the political side.

While eloquent and persuasive in informal settings, they were incapable of rousing larger audiences and were reluctant to do so. However, each impressed their colleagues and superiors to such an extent that both were purposefully advanced with the thought that they might one day hold the highest office in their land, and each impressed so many on the world stage that they were both seen as strong candidates to run the UN and NATO. They were pragmatists, intuitive in their tactics and moved by a streak of idealism but never naive about the limitations of international goodwill.

British prime minister Anthony Eden (left) with External
Affairs minister Lester Pearson, February 1956, Ottawa
(Duncan Cameron fonds/ Library Archives Canada E002505455)

When they met in Geneva, Eden occupied an anomalous, frustrating
position as Minister for League of Nations Affairs; in effect, a junior
foreign minister often undermined by his superior. Samuel Hoare's resignation, after outrage greeted his proposal to carve up Ethiopia and
feed parts of it to Mussolini, made way for Eden to be appointed foreign
secretary. At thirty-eight years old, he was the youngest person to hold
the position since the middle of the previous century.

In an age when newsreels and photographs made powerful impressions on the collective attention span, Eden enjoyed movie-star good
looks, a casual elegance, and, in contrast to the greying diplomats around
him, a youthful sheen. His impeccable technique at the conference table
and a professional grasp of the issues mirrored his personal graces. "I
don't think any Secretary of State I served excelled him in finesse, or as
a negotiator, or in knowledge of foreign affairs," one permanent undersecretary later judged. "No one worked harder." In the 1930s, Eden was
a recurring and, for some, reassuring image on front pages as he faced
the two dictators slowly taking Europe by the throat. Pearson appreciated

that Eden was, at times, "forced to play a very thankless game; to keep his head and maintain his courteous composure midst the shrieks and threats of the demagogues on the Continent. A mediator can never be popular and a moderate can never be stimulating. Eden is both."[4] Almost twenty years later, Pearson would witness the moderate mediator once again enduring more thankless games. In one, Eden would keep his cool. In another, he would lose everything.

> I have just returned from a visit to Egypt where I found a terrible situation. The British are detested. The hatred against them is general and intense. It is shared by everyone in the country.... Egypt is rapidly going down the drain...and it will soon be lost unless the trend is soon reversed.
> —Burton Y. Berry, US State Department, December 12, 1951[5]

Anthony Eden began dealing with Egypt in the 1930s, when he could, through intricate backstage manipulations, largely secure Britain's imperial desiderata. He returned to the Foreign Office in October 1951, when his country was more supplicant than regent, to grapple with Cairo's sudden abrogation of a defence treaty he himself had negotiated. Given all the British hardware and manpower guarding the Suez Canal and the oil that flowed through it, Eden could not afford a permanent break with this necessary ally and needed to negotiate a new treaty in order to legitimize any future military presence. However, Egypt and indeed the entire Middle East had seen Tehran nationalize the Anglo-Iranian Oil Company and expel thousands of British expatriates without suffering any consequences. When Eden dispatched a strongly worded diplomatic note, the Egyptian government felt comfortable responding with disorder and bloodshed.

London increased the number of troops in the canal zone; by early 1952, some eighty thousand British soldiers faced a hostile population impatient for them to leave. A Conservative MP painted a grim portrait of the untenable standoff. "To sit in a sand-bagged post, illuminated at night by arc lamps, with a village 100 yards away from which shots are fired every night & quite often during the day, without the slightest prospect of being able effectively to return the fire is quite an ordeal," he noted. "The troops are neither guarding the Base nor the Canal. They are merely guarding each other."[6]

While British forces poured into the canal zone, Egyptian workers in their thousands, threatened or bribed by government agents and the extremist Muslim Brotherhood, quit their jobs. A US State Department officer reported having lunch with a senior British official, the meal consisting of "canned food which we ate at his desk. His servant had gone out to obtain fresh food and had been beaten up and warned that unless he ceased to serve the official he would be tied hand and foot and thrown into the Canal."[7] On top of fighting an insurgency, besieged troops were obliged to take over basic maintenance duties to keep the electricity flowing and water running.

The breaking point came in January 1952. British forces converged on police barracks in Ismailia to disarm Egyptian auxiliaries suspected of participating in the guerrilla warfare. From behind their walls, the police ignored appeals to surrender and started firing their weapons. The battle claimed an estimated fifty Egyptian and four British lives. The next day in Cairo, government agents incited demonstrators to loot and torch (with assistance from government fuel trucks) British and other foreign banks, consulates, bars, restaurants, and cinemas. Destroying property did not quench the lust for revenge. When expatriates tried to flee a private club that had caught fire, a mob attacked and killed them and then threw their corpses into the inferno.[8] One of the victims was the Canadian trade commissioner.

In the aftermath, Eden urged Prime Minister Churchill to pull all British troops out of the canal zone. "The plain fact is that we are no longer in a position to impose our will upon Egypt," he argued. "If I cannot impose my will, I must negotiate."[9] Eden's reasoning was entirely practical, but for diehard Conservative imperialists like Churchill, the issue was profoundly emotional. After the galling expulsion from Abadan a few months before, any hint of withdrawal was condemned as more ignominious scuttle and appeasement—the latter being perhaps the dirtiest word in the political lexicon of the 1950s. Eden, the prime minister's heir apparent, could not afford to alienate his colleagues, but neither did he want to surrender to their prejudices. For his restraint he endured a public and private torment, attacked by sections of his own party and flayed by the press. Then, the political landscape in Egypt was suddenly remade.

Close to midnight on July 22, a rolling thunder of tanks, trucks, and half-tracks moved to seal off streets and bridges throughout Cairo. Led by commanders calling themselves the Free Officers, roughly three thousand Egyptian soldiers occupied government ministries, police stations, telegraph and telephone offices, the national radio station, and army barracks, where they rounded up incredulous generals and senior officers and took them into custody. Mobilized to redeem centuries of shame, the rebels brought down an entire regime with almost no shots fired and only two fatalities, those occurring when sentries at army headquarters resisted.

On the morning of July 23, with most Egyptians unaware of what had happened, an unknown voice beamed through radios across the country. "Egypt has just passed through the darkest period of her history, degraded by corruption," the voice intoned. "That is why it has been purged." Listeners were told a popular war hero, General Mohammed Neguib, was now their leader, though in reality he was a figurehead installed to reassure a wary populace, the expatriate community, and the watching world. In another effort to soothe anxieties, the radio announcer pledged to "our foreign friends" living in the country that no harm would come to them or their property.[10]

The unknown speaker was future president Anwar Sadat, who left the radio station and drove through Cairo in awe. "I saw the streets of the metropolis crowded with people as I had never seen them before," he later recalled. "Men, old and young, women and children, were kissing each other, shaking hands, coming together." Two French reporters concurred that the coup "was welcomed with immense relief, as though some decaying whitlow had been removed." The sight of troops and tanks throughout Cairo inspired delight as crowds gathered in public squares. "The fruit-juice vendors," observed the reporters, "shrewdly patriotic but with an eye to business, offered a few free drinks 'In the name of the Revolution.'"[11]

The mastermind of this brazen revolt was a thirty-four-year-old colonel, Gamal Abdel Nasser. By circumstances of birth, he was a man of the people: the son of a postal worker. By force of character, he was exceptional: a former student radical, war veteran, and nationalist officer who had inspired and organized others like himself. Foreign journalists and officials would come to know the "tall, saturnine figure usually to be noticed at the back of the group," some even judging him a potential leader, but at first this conspirator preferred to manoeuvre behind the scenes within the rebel command structure, biding his time.[12] During the coup, one of the most telling items on his agenda was dispatching a senior comrade to the US embassy. For at least the preceding two years, embassy officials and CIA operatives nurtured clandestine contacts with Nasser and the Free Officers, some of whom had participated in military training programmes in the United States.[13]

Working to head off any potential escalation and keen to further entrench themselves, US officials obliged the rebels and delivered a message to the British Embassy. In it, the Free Officers warned they would resist any military intervention. They also emphasized their action had nothing to do with "foreign issues" and everything to do with domestic concerns. The message to stay out was reinforced in Washington when State Department officials met with British counterparts.[14] Restraining the formidable British force stationed on Egyptian soil proved unnecessary because London shared the instinct to hold back.

No doubt mindful of American opposition to the use of force, for the first time since the late eighteenth century Her Majesty's Government did not intervene in a major Egyptian crisis. The once and essential ruler of Egypt witnessed a new and unknown group of local actors take power, while the familiar and rotating cast of confidants and agents were consigned to oblivion. On the first bewildering day of the new order, the lack of violence impressed Churchill. The abbreviated notes from a Cabinet meeting showed him urging restraint: "Gt. disadv. in appearg. to seek to take advantage of domestic [difficulties] to increase our hold over E....We shd. wait until real threat to B. lives occurs."[15]

On July 26, having decided against regicide, the rebels banished their King Farouk into luxurious exile and, as promised, did not interfere with day-to-day life. In this honeymoon period, Churchill noted: "The more I read the news from Egypt the more I like the Neguib programme. We ought to help Neguib and Co. all we can unless they turn spiteful."[16]

But the mutinous officers serving on what would become known as the Revolutionary Command Council were nationalist to the core, driven by personal memories of imperial sins as well as a collective sense of grievance stretching back centuries. They had no interest in collaborating with a former master, and the initial burst of goodwill disintegrated once the new regime took up the old demand that Britain leave Egypt to the Egyptians. In early 1953, a Foreign Office official painted a gloomy picture of the prevailing mindset in Cairo, writing: "We are up against a determined anti-British movement. The young officers think we are on the decline as a Great Power; they have a real hatred politically for us in their hearts. No amount of concession or evacuation on our part will evoke the slightest gratitude in return. Whoever Egypt may want in the future as an ally, it will not be us."[17]

Anthony Eden once again entered the thankless middle ground to try to shape a compromise that might mollify the nationalists in Egypt and the imperialists in Britain. In his determination to evacuate all British forces from the Suez Canal base and establish a tolerable working relationship with the new regime in Cairo, his most formidable opponent was arguably his own prime minister. Churchill had once condemned the Attlee government because it had "had scuttled and run" from Iran "when a splutter of musketry would have ended the matter." The prime minister invoked Neville Chamberlain's appalling agreement with Hitler, saying that he "never knew before that Munich was situated on the Nile." His loyal aides expressed the view that "we should sit on the gippies and have a 'whiff of grapeshot.'" Displaying political courage and personal conviction, Eden repeatedly ignored Churchill's belligerent advice. Michael T. Thornhill argues convincingly that, in this tactical and, to some extent, generational clash, Eden was the "strong-willed realist, rather than a faint-hearted appeaser," while Churchill was "the romantic reactionary [who] wanted to turn back the clock."[18]

In February 1953, Eden delivered a masterful argument to Cabinet. "We could undoubtedly deal effectively with any immediate attempt by the Egyptians to eject us by force from the Canal Zone. But the situation which this would create would almost certainly compel us to re-occupy Egypt," he stated. "We should be likely to have world opinion against us and would find it difficult to make a case if Egypt took us to the United Nations. It is hard to see what future there is for such a policy." While some colleagues could disagree with his politics, more difficult to refute was Eden's parallel economic argument: "We cannot afford to keep 80,000 men indefinitely in the Canal Zone."[19] Eden's prudence was grudgingly accepted. Talks with Cairo began in April and lurched through fits and starts into 1954.

While Eden slogged through his party's bitter internal debates, the backstage architect of the Egyptian coup, Gamal Abdel Nasser, manoeuvred through a power struggle to unseat the regime's figurehead and emerge from the shadows to become prime minister in April 1954. To a certain extent, Nasser's "relatively restrained" rule, as Laura M. James has judged it, reflected his personality, which appeared free of megalomania and toxic greed and displayed a genuine desire to raise living standards for his people. James observes that, unlike some of his corrupt colleagues, "he enjoyed a quiet family life, [and] he had few expensive pleasures."[20] He did not tolerate a free press, free speech, free elections, or any rivals, but "it would not be accurate to describe Egypt under his rule," according to Robert Stephens, an early and sympathetic biographer, "as simply a 'police state.' There was a large element of consent, discussion and persuasion involved. Most of the aims of the regime were in line with a broad national consensus....Egypt remained a much more 'open society' than any Communist country."[21] Those Egyptians rounded up by state security forces, some of whom suffered torture, might have reached a different conclusion.

First from behind the scenes and then as prime minister, Nasser participated in the canal zone talks with Britain to achieve his lifelong dream to rid Egypt of foreign troops. Balancing national honour and practicalities, Nasser took his share of risks in persuading comrades to cede British forces the right, for seven years, to return to the base in the event of an attack on Egypt or other Arab countries or Turkey. He also agreed that British civilian technicians could remain on-site to maintain the base. However, he did not enter into any kind of formal defence arrangement with London.

In October 1954, Nasser signed the historic agreement with his country's former rulers that, at long last, would remove all British troops from Egyptian soil by June 1956. The minister of state at the Foreign Office, Anthony Nutting, remembered: "Nasser was deeply affected by the significance of this achievement and, when we met for the signing ceremonies, he gripped my hand and held it for several moments as he struggled to control his emotions."[22] But while Nasser had successfully negotiated the end of Britain's military occupation of the canal zone, he was not a hero to all his people.

Fixed on creating a puritanical religious state, the Muslim Brotherhood condemned the agreement for maintaining even a lingering entanglement with Western infidels. Days after the signing ceremony, one of their own fired a gun at Nasser while he addressed a rally in Alexandria. Despite the close range, every bullet missed their target. When the initial commotion subsided and the would-be assassin and suspected accomplices captured on the spot, Nasser regained his composure, returned to the microphone, and proclaimed, "If Abdel Nasser dies, then everyone of you is Abdel Nasser.... Each of you is Gamal Abdel Nasser. Gamal Abdel Nasser is of you and from you and he is willing to sacrifice his life for the nation." This poetic response to near death was cheered and rebroadcast to the nation. Seizing this opening to strike back at his domestic enemies, Nasser then unleashed what biographer Said K. Aburish has called "the biggest political crackdown in the history of Egypt" and "a period of official terror."[23] The Muslim Brotherhood headquarters were torched and some of their members were hanged.

In the wake of the canal zone agreement, Anthony Eden justly earned praise in some quarters for ending seventy-two years of military occupation in Egypt, but he was also put on notice when some two dozen Tory MPs voted against their own foreign secretary's diplomacy. He urged the House of Commons to believe that the agreement would help shape a new kind of partnership in the region. "It is the only way we can hope to work with those countries," Eden argued. "We cannot hope to work with them by putting 20,000, 30,000, 80,000 [British soldiers] there and telling them what to do. They simply will not do what they are told and that leads to endless trouble for us all."[24]

Despite Eden's gesture, something in the dialogue between a fading imperial power and a former vassal state got lost in translation. An anecdote from Eden's memoirs, meant as a humorous aside, serves as an apt metaphor. During negotiations for the 1936 treaty in London, Eden arranged a "special luncheon party" for the Egyptian representatives, some of whom had brought their wives. "Thinking I might add to their entertainment by giving them unusual fare, I arranged for grouse to be sent down from Yorkshire for the meal," Eden recalled. His efforts were not appreciated. "Afterwards I asked how the luncheon had gone off and received the reply, 'I am sorry, but it was not a success; the ladies complained of being given old crows to eat.'"[25]

> If we cannot hold the Suez Canal, the jugular vein of World and Empire shipping communications, what can we hold?
>   —Lord Hankey to Winston Churchill, February 7, 1953[26]

Anthony Eden met with Gamal Abdel Nasser face to face for the first and only time on February 20, 1955. They arrived at this moment from wildly incompatible narratives. As a young boy, watching an airplane soaring high above him, the Egyptian son of a postal clerk would shout out a plea at the symbol of foreign intrusion, which translated inadequately as "O, Almighty God, may disaster take the English." Within roughly the same time frame, Eden was an aristocratic MP sailing through the Suez Canal and jotting in his diary: "Did not like Port Said. The Egyptians cheeky." Eden described the 1936 Anglo-Egyptian Treaty he negotiated as "the only event which had given me any satisfaction during these dismal months." Far from the negotiating table, an eighteen-year-old Nasser raged against this shackling of his country's sovereignty. "I led demonstrations," he later wrote. "I shouted from my heart for complete independence, and many others behind me shouted, too. But our shouts only raised dust which was blown by the wind." In 1942, when the British ambassador in Cairo used soldiers and tanks to persuade King Farouk to appoint a pro-British government, Eden cheered his pluck, writing, "I congratulate you warmly. The result justifies your firmness and our confidence." An outraged Nasser vowed: "Egypt would never again suffer such a humiliation."[27]

When Eden and Nasser met in Cairo at the palatial British Embassy, they were professional, even friendly, with each other. Still, small wrinkles occurred. Nasser appeared somewhat disconcerted when Eden greeted him in Arabic and then quoted Arab proverbs. His aides had not briefed him that Eden studied "oriental" languages at Oxford. The British dressed formally in dinner jackets, while Nasser and his colleagues wore military uniforms or business suits. "What elegance," Nasser later joked. "It was made to look as if we were beggars and they were princes!" During the evening, the foreign secretary asked the prime minister whether this was the first time he had been inside the Embassy. Nasser replied that it was. "It was interesting," he said, "to see the place from which Egypt used to be governed." Eden replied, "Not governed, perhaps. Advised rather." They briefly touched on but did not get bogged down rehashing the events of 1936 and 1942 before moving on to pressing concerns.[28]

One key question hung over their meeting: where would Egypt and indeed the entire Middle East stand in the Cold War schism? Eden wanted Nasser to join an alliance with Britain's allies, Turkey and Iraq, and by implication, Britain as well. What he could not admit but which Nasser fully understood and resented was that London intended to use this pact to maintain a measure of influence in oil-rich former protectorates and mandates. Nasser stated that joining such an alliance would symbolize enduring subservience to Britain.

Locked in rjvalry with a pro-British Iraq, Nasser had already turned to Saudi Arabia and Syria to discuss a separate defence alliance. He then laid out a neutrality appalling to British ears, saying, "If the Soviet Union attacks us, we will ask you to help us. And if you attack us, we will ask the Soviet Union to help us." Looking for some kind of opening, Eden asked Nasser if he would at least muzzle his propaganda machine and "not treat this pact as if it were a crime." Laughing, Nasser replied, "But it is one."[29] Their encounter ended with little more than a cordial agreement to disagree, but a sense remained, however tenuous, that more might be possible. Eden, however, would not deviate from his goal to establish a military alliance, and this refusal alarmed and incensed the leader he hoped to befriend.

Four days after the meeting, Iraq and Turkey signed a defence agreement dubbed the Baghdad Pact. Great Britain acceded in April, Pakistan in September, and Iran in December. This agreement fuelled Nasser's apprehensions and resentments and inexorably wore away any hopes for a better working relationship between London and Cairo. In response, Egypt, Saudi Arabia, and Syria announced their own military alliance, which fundamentally undermined Eden's grand design.

In March 1955, Lester Pearson received word that the United States intended to announce strong support for the fledgling Baghdad Pact at an upcoming North Atlantic council meeting. Washington urged

Ottawa and other NATO members to offer their own encouraging words. However, Pearson appeared largely unimpressed by British tactics and judged that "it would be a mistake to read too much into the Pact as it stands or to ignore its potentially disruptive effects." He doubted that such a selective alliance would generate more stability throughout the region and noted, rightly, the pact had in fact worsened relations between Egypt and the West.[30]

Pearson dispatched a memo to Canada's NATO representative outlining Ottawa's overall position that could have been drafted by Mackenzie King and seconded by Wilfrid Laurier and John A. Macdonald. Canada's defence interests, Pearson argued, did not include the Middle East, and he did not want Canada's allies to confuse support for the Baghdad Pact with any desire to get involved in the region. Pearson made it clear he wanted "our words of welcome to be reserved in tone and to leave no doubt…that none of these treaties or pacts in any way involves an automatic extension of our obligations under the North Atlantic Treaty." At the meeting in May, however, despite his private misgivings, the good ally dutifully uttered the encouragement that Washington and London desired, though he also voiced concern about Israel, noting that the treaty had "increased Israel's sense of isolation, and had encouraged the Extremists in that country."[31] Here Pearson touched upon a volatile new dynamic inflaming the Middle East.

The partition of Palestine and creation of the State of Israel seven years earlier displaced an estimated seven hundred thousand Arabs, who languished in camps in Lebanon, Syria, Egypt, and Jordan. Some of these refugees risked their lives to cross borders that were defended but not yet sealed off. Considered infiltrators by the new state, they came, writes Israeli historian Benny "to retrieve possessions and crops, and thereafter, to steal…to resettle in their former villages and towns or to visit relatives or just to look at their former homes and lands."[32] A handful returned to strike at their enemies with deadly but futile blows. With the Nazi and even Tsarist slaughter of family and community seared into living memories, the Israelis fought terror with terror.

In February, Nasser toured a military camp in Gaza and assured his troops that the border would not turn into a battle zone.[33] Soon after, during the evening of February 28, Israeli forces attacked the camp, killing some three dozen troops and two civilians, one of them a seven-year-old boy, and wounding twenty-nine soldiers. Ever since the armistice agreements of 1949, the border had seen civilians and soldiers killed on both sides by both sides but not on this scale. Nasser knew he had to be seen to respond—in all likelihood, the last thing he wanted to do.

In the early years of his regime, Britain, not Israel, remained the great foreign enemy. What truly mattered most to Nasser was glimpsed during the 1948 war. Even in this desperate arena fighting Jewish forces, wounded several times in action, Nasser's deepest passion lay elsewhere: "We were fighting in Palestine but our dreams were centred in Egypt. Our bullets were aimed at the enemy in his trenches before us, but our hearts hovered over our distant country, which we had left to the care of wolves." When he negotiated a surrender with Jewish officers, one of them recalled him as eager to learn from their successful campaign against British rule. And despite anti-Israeli rhetoric in public and while refusing Israeli ships passage through the Suez Canal, Nasser inherited and maintained informal and top-secret contacts with his northern neighbour.[34]

At their February 1955 meeting, Eden raised the possibility of Nasser leading the Arab world towards making peace with Israel. Nasser did not, reported Eden afterwards, reject the idea; he "implied Egypt has [an] open mind." A British journalist, Tom Little, who met him several times, noted: "In private talks with non-Arabs [Nasser] seemed tacitly to accept the fact that one day there must be a peace settlement." Little cautioned, however, that "it was wrong to conclude, as some diplomats did, that he was prepared to promote a peace settlement; at best it meant that he might in certain circumstances explore the possibility."[35] Although skeptical about his intentions, London and Washington spent months encouraging Nasser to begin a peace process. Then the Gaza raid took place.

Ever since the Free Officers seized power, they had sought arms from the West, only to be offered what they considered miserly amounts. In part, this was Britain and America trying to staunch an arms race and, in part, not trusting Nasser. After Gaza, Nasser again approached Washington and London, telling the American ambassador in Cairo, "Up till now we have been asking for arms so that our army could be properly equipped. Now we are asking for them to save our lives. The situation has changed completely. Now I can't wait."[36] In the raid's aftermath, Palestinian refugees in Gaza burnt cars, vandalized buildings, and raged against Egyptian impotence. Having struggled to limit Palestinian civilians from crossing the border, Nasser's government started training Palestinians in guerrilla units called the *fedayeen* (self-sacrificers or "those willing to sacrifice themselves"), who crossed into Israel to inflict mayhem and murder. But this terror tactic was only one move in Nasser's game plan.

In September 1955, Nasser unveiled a bold act of independence, in his mind, and of alarming defiance in Western eyes, by revealing the purchase of tanks, bombers, fighter jets, and artillery from Czechoslovakia—in the Cold War, another word for Communist Russia. US Secretary of State John Foster Dulles fumed about the perceived betrayal with his UK counterpart Harold Macmillan but admitted that if Nasser caved in to Western pressure and rejected the arms deal, "he may well be overthrown and we could get someone worse." Macmillan observed: "The world will not allow the USSR to become the guardian of the Suez Canal. We could make life impossible for Nasser and ultimately bring about his fall by various pressures."[37] The two left that question open for the time being.

Throughout 1955, Pearson met with emissaries from the remote conflict and added his voice to the calls for peace and to the argument that a Jewish state remained essential. In June, the Egyptian foreign minister, Mahmoud Fawzi, visited Ottawa, making the predictable public case that Arab governments would not recognize Israel. In private, however, he implicitly conceded that Israel would remain a fact on the ground. In line with secret British-American proposals, he suggested that any settlement depended on financial compensation for the displaced Palestinians and that Israel should cede land in the south to link Egypt and Jordan. He called this a small price to pay for peace. Pearson agreed these were moderate demands but worried that Israel would find these concessions difficult to accept, and they could lead to "extremists taking over if they were attempted." When Pearson asked how Arabs would react to a proposal that didn't meet their full demands, Fawzi replied they could be persuaded to accept a compromise. Pearson noted that this moderate Arab voice was strictly unofficial and not for quotation. His report of their meeting concluded with regret: "If [Fawzi's] views prevailed in Arab policies, we would have far more ground for optimism over developments in that part of the world than is at present warranted."[38]

In November, Pearson stopped in Cairo for a meeting with Nasser and Fawzi. Given the geographic distance and insignificant trade between the two countries, the stakes in this encounter were negligible. As he did so often with Western officials, the Egyptian prime minister made a favourable first impression upon Pearson, who noted: "I found Colonel Nasser quite as impressive and attractive a personality as I had been told he was. He is certainly plain and blunt in words, but friendly and modest in manner. He gives an impression of sincerity and strength, without any trace of arrogance or self-assertion." Pearson asked Nasser whether Arab governments would ever recognize the State of Israel. Nasser replied they would but stated there would have to be "important changes" on the borders and that Palestinian refugees would insist on returning to their former homes. When Nasser cited what he saw as Israeli aggressiveness, Pearson countered, "While there were extremists in Israel, as in all countries, there were also moderate men there doing their best to avoid extreme courses."[39]

The next morning, Pearson met with E.L.M. Burns, the chief of staff of the United Nations Truce Supervision Organization. The previous week, on November 4, travelling through London, Burns had met with Anthony Nutting, Britain's minister of state for foreign affairs, and they discussed increasing the UN presence in the region to provide a more effective buffer. This was an unremarkable, almost obvious suggestion, given that UN observers were already patrolling the Israeli-Arab borders, but it would be incredibly difficult to implement. Having witnessed over the preceding year the intense hatred dividing Jews and Arabs, Burns said that it would require major players intervening first to set the stage for any UN forces to move in and the Arabs and Israelis to step back. Burns and Nutting concluded that, for the time being, UNTSO's unarmed observers were as much as the warring parties would tolerate; they left unstated that it was also as much as the most powerful members of the UN would support. The next day, Burns received a last-minute invitation to lunch with Anthony Eden, who had replaced Churchill as prime minister the previous April. Regarding the interjection of UN troops between Arabs and Israelis, he and Eden reached, Burns recounted, "the same conclusion — or lack of conclusion," that little was possible at the present time.[40] When Burns met Pearson in Cairo just seven days after these talks, their friendship made it likely that Burns shared with Pearson his discussions with Eden and Nutting. Pearson made no written record of his meeting with Burns, but he probably left Cairo with the suggestion, or some variant, to station a larger UN force along the Israeli-Egyptian border.

In London, Pearson met with his old tennis partner from the League of Nations. After a tortuous wait stretching back to the war's end, Eden had finally become prime minister, a position he craved as intensely as Churchill had been reluctant to relinquish it. The unpretentious minister's son got on well with the aristocrat, though, as John English notes, Pearson "never liked Eden's propensity to greet him with 'Oh hello, my dear.' He much preferred Ernie Bevin's working-class twang: 'Gddy, me boy.'"[41] However, Pearson appreciated the mastery in Eden's method.

On November 14, Pearson spoke with the British prime minister at No. 10 Downing Street. Having both so recently met with General Burns, they inevitably discussed the Middle East. At some point, Pearson judged it potentially useful to mention informally the idea of a UN force already raised by Burns. According to British records of the discussion, Pearson offered to suggest or to support someone else suggesting "that some form of international force should be interposed between Israel and Egypt with a view to eliminating border troubles."[42] This was the essence of the deceptively straightforward peacekeeping proposal he would present in a year's time, almost to the day, at the UN General Assembly. The prime minister asked his officials to give the matter some thought. Interposing a larger force in a hostile setting was hardly a new idea, really more a variation on existing practices; diplomacy typically and properly works by building on established precedents and working within continua.

The British officials designated to examine Pearson's suggestion politely and firmly tore it to shreds. They cited the reluctance of UN members to dispatch military forces to Palestine in 1948 and worried that a larger force might further antagonize the antagonists. The Foreign Office advisers were especially reluctant to involve British troops that already bore the stigma of occupation from Britain's mandate in Palestine, because this opened the door to those British troops fighting Arabs — and, the advisers noted bluntly, "might jeopardise our oil interests."[43]

Given that Pearson's idea hardly served British interests, Eden's officials advocated no British participation and suggested to simply wait and let the Canadians raise the matter again, if they so wished. Eden accepted the advice to leave the Canadian suggestion unmolested, and minuted in agreement, "We would not be part of it nor any of [the] great powers."[44] The idea raised by two senior Canadians went dormant but would resurface soon enough. And the Arab Israeli dilemma continued to show up on Pearson's agenda.

In early December, just three weeks after hearing "the usual intractable Egyptian case" in Cairo, Pearson heard from the other side of the divide, and in equally uncompromising tones, when the Israeli foreign minister, Moshe Sharett, visited Ottawa. Sharett expressed skepticism about Nasser's claim to want peace, given that the Egyptian prime minister made speeches that attacked Israel. "Nasser would like to see Israel cease to exist," Sharett stated bluntly. "I agreed that was probably his ultimate desideratum," Pearson replied, "but I thought this was simply the highest bargaining point, and that he would be prepared to negotiate."[45]

Sharett also stated that Israel could never allow Palestinian refugees to return to their former homes, but he indicated his government would offer them financial compensation and assistance with settling somewhere else. Handing over a corridor in the south to link Jordan and Egypt was out of the question, he said, but his colleagues might contemplate "territorial adjustments" at certain points along the border. Finally, Sharett said that if he had known Pearson was going to be meeting with Nasser, he would have asked him to warn the Egyptian leader to stop the *fedayeen* raids into Israel or "there might be serious trouble." Pearson replied, "Nasser had told me almost exactly the same thing. He had said: 'Tell your Israeli friends that if they don't stop making provocative raids on Egyptian territory, we will have to take strong measures.'"[46]

Pearson could offer no acceptable answers for enemies determined to survive each other's defensive and offensive manoeuvres. But in eleven months he would find himself at the centre of the storm at the United Nations as the world tried to stop an Israeli invasion of Egypt from spreading across the region. And then his simple idea would become the rallying point for the skeptical and the desperate reaching for any kind of solution.

EIGHT

All Good Reasons

It is important to reduce the status of a megalomaniacal
dictator at an early stage. A check to Hitler when he moved
to reoccupy the Rhineland would not have destroyed him, but
it would have made him pause...some say that Nasser is no
Hitler or Mussolini. Allowing for a difference in scale, I'm not
so sure.
　　　—Anthony Eden[1]

Despite the fraying relationship between Britain and Egypt, now a happily
supplied consumer of Soviet weapons, Anthony Eden saw no choice but to
remain in the bidding game for influence and favour. His last-gasp efforts
centred on Gamal Abdel Nasser's dream project, the Aswan High Dam,
which would, if ever built, become the world's largest civil engineering
venture and bestow tangible benefits to the Egyptian people: more electricity, more irrigation, more arable land, and more protection from the
Nile's floods. The Soviet Union had begun to dangle promises of financial
aid, and Eden was adamant the West must fend off any further infiltration.
"If the Russians get the contract," Eden declared, "we have lost Africa."[2]

In December 1955, Washington and London presented a joint loan
proposal to Cairo and launched a serious courtship. But at the same
time, Eden worked against these efforts and pursued his goal to bring
Jordan into the Baghdad Pact. Nasser condemned the British-led regional
defence alliance as British imperialism in another form. Despite repeated entreaties, Jordan's young King Hussein declined Eden's advances,
in large part so as not to antagonize Nasser and his supporters in the

(L-R) Lester Pearson with Egyptian prime minister Gamal Abdel Nasser
and foreign minister Mahmoud Fawzi in Cairo,
November 1955 (Corbis 42-71277268)

Jordanian government. At the same time, he struggled to resist Nasser's
pressure to align his country with Egypt. The year ended with virulent
propaganda from Cairo, which caused riots in Amman that brought
down cabinets and even threatened to topple the king himself. London
deemed Nasser the principal arsonist in this conflagration, which was
subdued only with difficulty (but not quenched) by the Arab Legion,
a twenty-thousand-strong force of Jordanians commanded by British
officers and paid for by London.

The year 1956 opened much as the old year had ended: with Britain
anxious and uncertain how to maintain its tenuous presence in the Arab
labyrinth. Jordan still hovered on the brink of chaos, obliging Eden and
his officials to debate sending in reinforcements. Writing in his diary
on January 12, Harold Macmillan, now chancellor of the exchequer,
mused about what Jordan's rejection of the pact meant for the larger and
undeclared contest. "We have lost the first round. However, the game is
not over yet and we have *got* to win," he observed. "For the stakes are very

high—no less than the economic survival of Britain. For [if] we lose out in the M. East, we lose the oil. If we lose the oil, we cannot live."[3]

Almost inevitably for this generation of politicians and officials, their experiences in the Second World War framed their struggle during the 1950s in the Middle East. Both Eden's foreign secretaries viewed Nasser through that prism. Macmillan described him as "an Asiatic Mussolini," while Selwyn Lloyd "thought that the comparison with Hitler was more apt." The leader of the Opposition, Hugh Gaitskell, perpetuated the historical equation. "It is all very familiar," he observed during one parliamentary debate "It is exactly the same that we encountered from Mussolini and Hitler in those years before the war."[4] Eden's reflex response to link a dictator in the 1950s with the ones he faced during the 1930s was perhaps more intense, more personal, because he was also confronting his own legend, anchored in his resignation from Neville Chamberlain's Cabinet over the policy to appease Italy, which Winston Churchill later described in a passage that elevated the moment and the man into the stuff of myth:

> I must confess that my heart sank, and for a while the dark waters of despair overwhelmed me. . . . From midnight till dawn I lay in my bed consumed by emotions of sorrow and fear. There seemed one strong young figure standing up against long, dismal, drawling tides of drift and surrender, of wrong measurements and feeble impulses. My conduct of affairs would have been different from his in various ways; but he seemed to me at this moment to embody the life-hope of the British nation, the grand old British race that had done so much for men, and had yet some more to give. Now he was gone.[5]

Churchill's prose obscured the convoluted circumstances surrounding Eden's resignation, which at the time baffled some Cabinet colleagues who did not perceive any serious divergence in overall approach between the prime minister and his foreign secretary. In the collective memory, however, Eden became bathed in a righteous light for rejecting the government's "drift and surrender," and afterwards escaped the period untarnished, even though he as foreign minister had played a central part in formulating the well-intentioned policies that enabled Nazis and Fascists to get away with murder.

Lester Pearson also initially supported appeasement, and he shared the generational sense of failure for supporting such misguided efforts, but he did not invoke the lessons and language of the 1930s to frame the threats emanating from the Middle East in the 1950s. With no economic or direct military interests to defend in Egypt or national prestige on the line, he could view the struggle with emotional detachment. He could also understand that anti-colonial nationalism was not necessarily a Communist plot. Yet even this distant region could still generate political headaches at home.

On January 11, 1956, Pearson was asked in the House of Commons whether Ottawa had allowed the export of training airplanes to Egypt. At first, Pearson replied that he didn't know of any shipments and would seek confirmation from the relevant departments. Six days later, he informed the House that Canada had sent fifteen used and unarmed Harvard training planes to Egypt. These Second World War–vintage planes were not, he insisted, combat worthy, and they could not be armed. The very next day, newspapers made a mockery of his response by printing Department of National Defence photos showing the supposedly inoffensive Harvard mounted with rockets, bombs, and machine guns. The Opposition accused Pearson of evasion, of arming a country that was also receiving weapons from the Soviet Union, and of pursuing policies that would inflame an already turbulent region.[6]

On January 24, Pearson responded at length, outlining government policy on arms shipments in particular and on the Middle East in general. During the previous two years, he said, Canada sold just over $2 million worth of arms to Israel and just under $800,000 to Egypt. He did not see these modest sales as incitement to war but as necessary for keeping the peace. Indeed, he argued, a general embargo on all shipments might prove counterproductive: countries would not be able to defend themselves, as they had a right to under the UN Charter, and an ongoing imbalance between neighbours might generate the fear and insecurity that leads to aggressive acts. Acknowledging that Egypt had purchased Communist weaponry, Pearson urged continued engagement. "If our response to recent Soviet moves in the Middle East were to abandon friendly relations with the Arab states and support Israel completely and exclusively, with our diplomacy and our arms," he pointed out, "then we should indeed be playing the communist game."[7]

Turning to the political impasse, he expressed, in equal measure, sympathy for Israel's sense of fear and sympathy for those Arabs who had "been made homeless." He offered conventional proposals to facilitate a peace between these neighbours who loathed each other. Arab governments, he said, should accept and recognize Israel's existence, and Israel should allow some refugees to return to their families and former homes. The rest could receive financial compensation for their losses.[8] Coming from a respected but inconsequential player in the Middle East standoff, these words merely evaporated into the official record. However, an idea he raised privately two months before in London was already being worked into the public discourse.

On January 24, the same day that Pearson defended Ottawa's arms shipments to the Middle East, the new foreign secretary in London, Selwyn Lloyd, was floating the force idea to pacify the same patch of ground. Some observers and colleagues viewed Lloyd's recent promotion as an unsettling turn of events, and their reaction ranged from puzzlement to contempt. In their view, the prime minister had reached into the second division to fill the most glittering position in Her Majesty's still-imperial government. However outwardly unassuming, Lloyd was no novice. Churchill appointed him to the Foreign Office in 1951 as a minister of state, where he tackled files on Iran, the Sudan, disarmament, and the Suez Canal base, and he demonstrated a steady, solid competence. Eden had never fully trusted the independent-minded Macmillan, who, in turn, resented what he viewed as constant interference from the prime minister. "He really should have been both PM and Foreign Secretary," Macmillan later observed. This, in effect, is what Eden achieved when he replaced the assertive Macmillan with the compliant Lloyd. "Macmillan conceived the Foreign Secretary as being a sun among the planets; Selwyn knew that the Foreign Secretary was but one of the planets that revolved around the sun, but was not the sun itself," wrote D.R. Thorpe, biographer to all three men. "This suited Eden."[9]

In the British House of Commons in January 1956, the newly installed Lloyd praised and pointed out the limitations of current UN observer missions in the Middle East. Their mandate, he pointed out, was simply to report after the fact; they were not designed to prevent an act of aggression. Lloyd suggested the UN go further, proposing the establishment of "some bodies of United Nations derivation" to keep the peace in demilitarized zones. Lloyd stated that he had put this same suggestion to Dag Hammarskjöld, the UN secretary-general, as recently as some ten days before, but they judged that too many obstacles stood in the way.[10] He did not acknowledge, perhaps because he did not know, that Lester Pearson and General E.L.M. Burns had separately raised this idea with Prime Minister Eden just weeks before.

Shortly after his speech in Parliament, Lloyd flew with Eden to Washington, where they met with President Dwight Eisenhower and Secretary of State John Foster Dulles. They mulled over what to do about the problematic Egyptian prime minister, still considered a potentially useful player in their schemes for peace, influence, and communist containment. As Eden observed, "It was difficult to know whether Nasser could be dealt with. If so, our course of action in the Middle East could go one way; if not, it should go another." Eden described him as "a man of limitless ambition."[11] They did not reach any conclusion on the nagging question.

In keeping with such private gatherings, part of the talks were leaked to the press, which reported that the British had raised the idea of stationing some kind of armed UN force on the Israeli-Arab border, but the American response had been unenthusiastic. This was an election year in the US, and committing American troops abroad might be a tough political sell to the electorate. However, in the final joint communiqué released on February 1, the UK and US leaders declared their full support for General Burns and his UNTSO team, and even went so far as to state that the two governments would be open to strengthening the observer mission.[12]

That evening in Ottawa, Opposition MP John Diefenbaker asked Pearson about a news report that Canada and the Netherlands might join a UN force to police demilitarized zones along the Arab-Israeli borders. In his response, Pearson dealt first with the formidable practicalities. The boundaries in question were established by armistice agreements following the 1947–1948 war and remained unratified. A UN attempt to guarantee these tenuous borders would face angry opposition from the Arab peoples and their governments, and Pearson could not support pitting UN troops against any one party. The more palatable and practical solution, he stated, would be to use the UN force to buy time "as a provisional measure to keep the armies apart while peace can be secured." Echoing Laurier and Mackenzie King's resistance to involvement in imperial engagements,

Pearson the sovereignist refused to make any troop commitments in advance. The internationalist in him, however, declared that if war did break out, the United Nations should be involved and Canada would support the UN. Canada would not lead the way, he emphasized, telling the House, "It is a matter principally for the big powers who have the most important interests in that area."[13] The key phrase in Pearson's sentence was "provisional measure." For him, any UN force, whether unarmed observers in Indonesia, Greece, Kashmir, and the Middle East or the fully armed divisions sent to Korea, should never be considered the end point; he inevitably looked beyond the distractions of any immediate emergency towards reaching a political settlement.

On February 3, Pearson discussed the matter with Michael Comay, the Israeli ambassador to Canada. Comay preferred quick intervention from the US, the UK, and France over waiting for a United Nations response, which, he pointed out, would be blocked by the Soviet veto in the Security Council. Pearson admitted, "The situation was so complex that it would be difficult for anyone to say what was the right thing to do," and concluded that the Arab recognition of Israel was fundamental to an eventual settlement.[14]

Later that day, Eden and Lloyd arrived in Ottawa. The press reported that they would discuss the vague idea of a UN force, very much a British-driven idea at this point. On February 6, Diefenbaker asked Prime Minister St. Laurent if the government had received and considered a request to contribute Canadian troops. St. Laurent replied that no such request has been made. On the same day, addressing a packed House of Commons, Eden publicly suggested strengthening UNTSO's presence and stated that his government would "wish to be guided by General Burns, a brave Canadian soldier who is resolutely carrying out this thankless task."[15] Eden did not mention that Burns and Pearson had proposed this idea back in November; perhaps he was requested not to do so by Pearson, who would have been briefed in advance on the contents of the speech.

On February 7, Pearson and St. Laurent met with Eden and Lloyd for their formal talks. In a wide-ranging discussion, they spent most of their time on the Middle East and much of that clarifying the UN police force notion. Sounding a touch defensive, Eden said that London had merely been considering increasing the number of observers and not the scope of their mission or their powers. Lloyd acknowledged that "it was impossible to have...a police force which would prevent aggression," but nonetheless repeated the suggestion to significantly increase UNTSO's numbers from the current roughly fifty observers up to one thousand. The Canadian and British records of this discussion do not show Pearson making any response to the idea, either to praise it or dismiss it, even though he had raised a similar proposal with Eden just three months before.[16] And although he would have been aware of all the difficulties in creating a more powerful UN force in the Middle East when he first mentioned it, and suggested it nonetheless, for reasons unknown in February 1956, Pearson had decided to pull back.

At a press conference in which he inevitably fielded questions about strengthening UNTSO, Eden, the consummate diplomat, let the Canadian government off the hook. "I have never heard of any specific proposal—certainly we did not have one in mind—to allot some special task to Canada," he said. The additional observers would come from a number of different member states. Lloyd backed up that implicit assurance to Ottawa, telling reporters, "There was no idea of sending an actual national contingent." Speaking directly to Israelis and Arabs, he added, "There is going to be no attempt to impose on an unwilling people something which they do not want."[17] And that seemed to apply in equal measure to the unwilling Canadians who, without making unnecessary noise about it, had informed the British that they had no interest in being allotted any special tasks.

For now, the UN force idea was consigned to the sidelines. Writing a few weeks later to T.W.L. MacDermot, the Canadian ambassador in Greece, Pearson despaired: "there doesn't seem to be much hope, as I see it, for the parties getting together. The best we can do is to hope that they don't get together in the wrong way by shooting at each other."[18] By the time he wrote this, his worst fears were already taking shape.

On March 1, the British government was insulted before the entire Arab world when a country it had invented after the Great War and supported financially and militarily abruptly dismissed the British commander of the Arab Legion, General John Bagot Glubb. Reviled by some Jordanians as a puppet master, celebrated in Britain as another Lawrence of Arabia, Glubb Pasha, as he was known, had commanded the legion since 1939, but in a matter of hours the iconic figure was history. Threatened by nationalist discontents and relentless Egyptian propaganda condemning him for being too subservient to his foreign lifeguard, King Hussein was in no position to resist. For supporting his government's decision to dismiss Glubb, he was cheered in the streets, probably saving his throne. In London, the dismissal was taken as both betrayal and portent. "For A.E. it is a serious blow," a foreign office official noted of the prime minister. "He wants to strike some blow somewhere."[19]

Hounded by the press and the Opposition, Eden considered cancelling economic subsidies to Jordan and even reoccupying the Suez Canal zone, but his officials and Cabinet colleagues urged him, as he himself had done so often with Churchill, to restrain his hand. Even Glubb, the object of the insult, counselled a stiff upper lip. "It would not be right to come down on Jordan like a ton of bricks," he said, urging Eden to "let the dust settle down."[20] Eden accepted the advice, conceding, "It was an occasion for doing nothing."[21]

When Eden responded to the crisis in the House of Commons, he did not denounce King Hussein or punish Jordan financially, but neither did he offer a firm lead out of the morass. Instead he urged an impatient Opposition to hold its breath. If he were to lay down "immediate definite lines of policy," he said, the rush to action "would be not only premature but probably dangerous to our own interests." Struggling against a loud, contemptuous reception, he used this moment to sound a warning to Nasser. "If the Egyptians generally want friendly relations with the Western Powers, they can be obtained," he declared, "but not at any price." Taunted and shouted down, Eden, uncharacteristically, lost his temper in public and delivered what even he considered one of the worst speeches in his long parliamentary career. One British newspaper described the "silent devastated ranks on the Conservative benches" and warned: "If the year goes on as it has begun, it will not be Sir Anthony but Mr. Harold Macmillan who reigns in Downing Street." One of Eden's most senior advisers, Evelyn Shuckburgh considered the speech "absolutely right and courageous" but nonetheless judged the prime minister had "made an ass of himself." Eden, Shuckburgh lamented, "seems to be completely disintegrated—petulant, irrelevant, provocative at the same time as being weak. Poor England, we are in total disarray."[22]

The day after Eden's speech, one week after Glubb's dismissal, Pearson spoke in the Canadian House of Commons about the "tense and difficult" situation in the Middle East, and perhaps to send an informal plea for restraint to a beleaguered ally. "War would be disastrous to all concerned," he said. "It would result in the mobilization of world opinion, in the United Nations and elsewhere, in condemnation of the aggressor and in support of the victim of aggression. I cannot believe that this is a situation which any country in the Middle East wishes to bring about."[23] But even as he was speaking, Britain had begun to incite all those appalling consequences.

Anything in our power to hurt Egyptians without hurting ourselves?
  —Anthony Eden, June 1955[24]

At some point in March 1956, the minister of state at the Foreign Office, Anthony Nutting, prepared what he thought an "unexceptionable" memorandum on how to salvage Britain's disintegrating position in the Middle East: basically offer more economic and military aid to true allies in order to isolate the Egyptian prime minister. While dining out, Nutting was called to a public phone and heard the prime minister's voice on the other end of the open line.

"What's all this poppycock you've sent me?" he demanded. "I don't agree with a single word of it."

Nutting tried to defuse his master's irritation, but Eden would not relent.

"What's all this nonsense about isolating Nasser?" Eden raged. "I want him destroyed, can't you understand? I want him removed."

Nutting argued that removing Nasser would only cause anarchy, to which Eden apparently shouted, "But I don't want an alternative and I don't give a damn if there's anarchy and chaos in Egypt!"[25] Eden had reached an emotional and political turning point.

The draft minutes of a March 21 Cabinet meeting show Eden and Lloyd making the case for removing someone they once considered their "best bet" in the Middle East. Nasser was moving into the Russian orbit and was refusing to make peace with Israel. Although he had promised to relent, he maintained his radio and press attacks on Britain and its allies in the region. "We must therefore assume his [continued] hostility," Lloyd declared. "We must therefore go for him, recognising he will be a formidable opponent."[26]

Lloyd then outlined an intricate pan-Arabian stratagem: provide more aid to members of the Baghdad Pact, bring Iraq and Jordan closer together, and establish a more friendly government in Syria. Britain would exacerbate Saudi fears of Nasser's ambitions to overthrow and replace the region's monarchies with a union of Arab states under Egyptian leadership, thereby prying Saudi Arabia away from Egypt. The Anglo-American financial package still on offer to help build the Aswan High Dam would be withdrawn, and this highlighted an essential factor in the far-ranging scheme: London must enlist Washington's support and cooperation. And while this grand plan unfolded, there should be no open break with Nasser. He must be kept guessing.

Giving his blessing, one minister piped up, "Write him off and see him off, using all practical means. Pity we didn't decide earlier to take this line." After hearing Eden and Lloyd's case, Cabinet expressed its full support for these tactics to destroy a foreign leader, and then moved on to discuss the export of tractors to China and other items such as quality control in husbandry and estate management.[27]

This operation would clearly take some time to arrange and conduct. In the interim, an impatient prime minister quietly turned to other devices to get rid of his Mussolini on the Nile. Here the story inevitably sinks into murky terrain where little was committed to paper, where colleagues were kept in the dark by counterparts and associates, where not even superiors were entirely sure what their juniors were up to. Over the months to come, British secret agents and at least one MP approached resentful Egyptians who lived in self-imposed exile or had been cast aside at home — ex-ministers, military officers, politicians, members of the Muslim Brotherhood — to try to assemble a rebel force to topple Nasser and establish a government to fill the ensuing vacuum.[28]

Assassination was also explored. Operatives conducted trials to put poison into a popular brand of Egyptian chocolates. Another idea involved hiding canisters of nerve gas in the ventilation system of an office where Nasser worked. Both schemes were rejected because of the potential to kill members of his staff. A package of cigarettes was fitted to fire poison-tipped darts, which in one experiment successfully hit and killed a sheep. A botched attempt was made to bribe Nasser's doctor to administer poison. Presumably Eden was not speaking entirely in metaphor when he told Shuckburgh that Nasser "must be got rid of," warning: "It is either him or us, don't forget that."[29]

As the British turned, so did the Americans. At some point in this period of disenchantment, Eisenhower told his officials he wanted a combined US-UK "high class Machiavellian plan to achieve a situation in the Middle East favourable to our interests."[30] In a detailed response to this presidential request, the State Department outlined its own economic and political manoeuvres to isolate, weaken, and erase Nasser's regime from the map.

On March 28, Pearson dined privately in Washington with John Foster Dulles, flanked by their respective ambassadors. The day before they had discussed the British prime minister, Pearson saying he was "very much concerned and particularly worried" that Eden was "not reacting very well to the strains and pressures of the present situation." Dulles found him "rather jittery" and "doing a number of things rather hurriedly and without any prior consultation." Pearson observed that Eden's father had been "quite eccentric" — possibly an allusion to stories told in a memoir by Eden's brother, Timothy, about their high-strung father and his "terrible tornado of oaths, screams, gesticulations and flying sticks" at the most minor of provocations. Pearson may have even seen firsthand that the father's taut emotional wiring ran through the famous son; it certainly seemed common knowledge within the Foreign Office. In 1955, Eden's incoming press secretary, William Clark, was warned about Eden's "quite extraordinary fits of temper. He will denounce you in a way that will make you want to slap his face." Eden would eventually apologize, Clark was told—although, as someone added acidly, "That is the nastier part of it." Another official compared Eden to one of his predecessors, noting: "Bevin wouldn't throw a book at your head."[31] Whatever Pearson knew of the outbursts, he still admired Eden's many impressive qualities.

The official record of Pearson's dinner with Dulles notes only one topic of discussion. For over a year, Israel had made several informal enquiries to Ottawa about purchasing Canadian-built F-86 Sabre fighter jets. Pearson noted the Canadian manufacturer obviously wanted the business but equally obvious were the tangled politics surrounding the business. The American secretary of state seized upon the Canadian dilemma as a potential opening to ease a thorny and parallel issue for the US administration. Moving indirectly but with clear purpose, Dulles mentioned a talk that afternoon with Abba Eban, the Israeli ambassador to the US, who had pleaded for more and heavier weapons. Dulles replied that American arms supplies to Israel had been "relatively trivial" because to give more would seriously weaken whatever influence the US retained with Arab governments. However, Dulles went on to tell Eban, Washington "would see no objection to the Israelis shopping around various other countries." In sharing the content of this talk, Dulles gave Pearson a green light. Pearson did not indicate what Ottawa's final decision might be and noted without going into detail that arms shipments to Israel had political implications in Canada as well as the US.[32]

Pearson had little time to contemplate those implications. Six days later, on April 3, the Israeli ambassador to Canada, Michael Comay, presented a formal request to Ottawa to purchase a squadron of twenty-four F-86 Sabre jets, a significant escalation from earlier Israeli orders for ammunition, electronics, and spare parts for tanks, vehicles, and aircraft. His childhood imagination shaped by stories from the Old Testament, Pearson admired Israel as the fulfillment of the Jewish dream to return to the ancient holy land. As a foreign minister in the Western alliance, he appreciated the country as the only pro-Western liberal democracy in the Middle East. But he was anxious not to inflame the region's climate of fear and loathing.

Bringing the matter to Cabinet two days after receiving the request, Pearson opened with a strong pitch to approve the sale. Egypt would soon take delivery, he said, of Soviet Ilyushin bombers and MIG fighters, which could reach Israeli cities within minutes. He spoke from intelligence reports that indicated the Soviets were also supplying "sabotage material" to Arab states and training Egyptians as commandos. Selling the F-86 jets to Israel would not only help correct this imbalance but, Pearson suggested, might also calm the extremists in Israel who were pushing to launch a pre-emptive strike. He had already expressed a variation on this concern at an earlier Cabinet meeting in March, when he said that "the greatest immediate danger in the Middle East could be a feeling of despair and frustration in Israel." Yet for all the arguments he made in favour, Pearson deemed it "undesirable" to agree to export the jets while the UN secretary-general was touring the region on a peace mission. "A definite stand," he concluded, "would have to be taken."[33]

Inevitably, sensibly, Pearson stayed in close touch with the emerging dominant power in the Middle East to gauge its reaction to a potential Canadian arms sale. Ambassador Arnold Heeney reported from Washington that the American secretary of state, also playing safe, had expressed hope that Canada would permit the sale because it could do so with less political fallout, domestically and regionally. Dulles indicated that the US government would support the decision but would not want to be publicly associated with it.[34] Such self-protective encouragement did not inspire Pearson to move out front, and he waited until a NATO meeting in May in Paris to resume the matter face to face.

The US, said Dulles, was shipping only modest military material to Israel because of the "anxiety not to be identified conclusively with the Israeli side." He was also concerned that an escalating arms race between Israel and Egypt would, in truth, be more of a race between Moscow and Washington. Yet still wanting Canada to help maintain the balance of arms and lower Israeli anxieties, he again encouraged Pearson to release the F-86 Sabres. With far less at stake in the conflict, Canada had more room to manoeuvre. In this instance, Pearson judged it right to use that room to support his key ally. He replied that while Canada "was not any more anxious than the United States to become identified with one side or the other in this quarrel," he agreed it would make for good policy to enable Israel to rectify the perceived imbalance of power, albeit as a temporary measure until a more lasting political settlement could be reached.[35] Their meeting ended with the decision waiting to be made.

On his way home, Pearson stopped off in London and saw Prime Minister Eden and found him, "not surprisingly, nervously and physically exhausted and therefore, somewhat overwrought, though as friendly and charming as ever." Eden had his own reservations about the Canadian foreign minister. Within days of their meeting, *The Times* reported Pearson was considered the probable next secretary general of NATO. "I had not heard this story about Mike Pearson," Eden wrote to Selwyn Lloyd in a "strictly personal" dispatch. "I confess that my enthusiasm would be very limited. We know the family's views on Colonial questions."[36] Eden did not elaborate on his oblique criticism, but Pearson clearly was not behaving as a family member should.

While the British prime minister grappled with frayed nerves, assassination schemes, safe-guarding imperial prestige, and his own personal legacy, the Canadian prime minister was running on automatic pilot. The seemingly invincible Liberal Party had held power without interruption since 1935, and St. Laurent since 1948. Now seventy-four years old and physically spent after a draining world tour, he made the cardinal mistake of ignoring his own instincts to step down. Disengaged, he allowed manageable business to collapse into disaster.

In May, the government introduced a bill to build a natural gas pipeline from Alberta to central Canada. Anxious to meet the construction timeline, the government immediately invoked closure. Typically, the heavy-handed device had been wielded sparingly to shut down long-winded debates, but here, an out-of-touch leader and colleagues employed it in the very opening rounds. The issue was no longer the pipeline but the government's contempt for free speech. The Opposition unleashed a ferocious uproar, arguably unparalleled in Parliament's history. Pearson dutifully did his turn defending the government's dubious position, but he had no stomach for the sordid theatre. He even seemed to seriously consider leaving Canada to become NATO secretary general.

Later, in retirement, while being interviewed about this episode for his television memoirs, he thought the camera was turned off and answered candidly, "I would have been glad to have taken it on then, in a way because we were having such a.... I was so fed up that summer but I couldn't walk out on the Party and the government on the eve of an election, where we were going to have a rough time. So I...." Here the interviewer interrupted him to pick up the thread of their earlier conversation, and Pearson realized the camera was running. He abruptly switched into cheery public mode. "I wasn't available to be secretary general," he said "I was too happy being secretary of state for External Affairs."[37] And for the most part, he was.

As the government forced the pipeline bill through Parliament, Pearson continued to deal with the Israeli request for fighter jets. A departmental memo dated May 14 weighed the tangled options for him. On one hand, selling the jets would be "a simple act of justice to enable Israel to defend itself" and would give Washington some breathing room. Another argument in favour, and which probably resonated heavily with

Pearson, since it was exactly the kind of advice he used to give Mackenzie King, was that Canada had nowhere to hide. "It is not right to think in terms of 'pulling American chestnuts out of the fire,'" the memo argued. "The chestnuts in this dangerous area are as much Canadian as they are American or British, because we would be inevitably involved in the consequences of war." Significant risks lurked on the other side of the diplomatic ledger, however. Without question, Canada's selling arms to Israel would offend Arab governments. The sale might also damage the perceived neutrality of UNTSO's General Burns and his five Canadian officers. The memo warned that the damage could extend to the country's future diplomatic effectiveness, continuing, "One should not dismiss lightly the possibility that we could play a very useful role of mediation in the right circumstances."[38] Caught between perfectly defensible options, Pearson continued to hold back from making a decision either way. Israel could not afford that luxury and continued to press Ottawa.

In a May 21 meeting with Ambassador Comay, caution pervaded Pearson's explanation for the ongoing delay. Releasing the jets, he argued, would generate headlines, and might aggravate an already controversial issue. He was also concerned about not aggravating historic tensions at home, saying, "Canadians would resent any implication that their government was acting on behalf of the U.S. in the same way as Czechoslovakia had acted for the U.S.S.R."[39] He was clearly reluctant to disappoint the Israeli government, but Pearson continued to hesitate. It was no surprise that someone who had proved critical a decade before in persuading the UN to advocate a Jewish state should feel compelled to emphasize that the delay did not reflect the lessening of Canada's support for Israel's existence.

Dulles and Pearson returned to the seemingly inescapable topic at a June 11 meeting in Washington. Now it was time to disappoint the Americans. Despite months of polite pressure, Pearson said Ottawa remained unwilling to "take such a 'dramatic' step" and would do nothing for the time being. The US secretary of state acknowledged the intense political heat bearing down on the administration to sell more arms to Israel and confided that President Eisenhower "was probably the only person who could hold the line against such pressure." The willingness to continue resisting, Dulles added, may not survive what was an election year. Definitive rejections are difficult to express, let alone hear, in diplomatic exchanges, and as the meeting drew to a close, Pearson allowed that changing circumstances might create a future opening to sell Israel the jets. Dulles asked whether Canada could train Israeli pilots and technicians on the F-86s as an interim measure, and Pearson agreed to consider the request.[40]

Over the next few weeks, seeking to balance American needs, Israeli fears, and his own concerns, Pearson decided, in a very Canadian tactic, to seek camouflage in numbers. Ottawa might now, he thought, offer to release a smaller number of fighter jets as part of a larger cache from allies already shipping arms to Israel. In a memo to Cabinet, he suggested initiating discussions to sound out this proposal, arguing that "collective action should follow a collective decision." Pearson's tactical shift failed to persuade Dulles, who cabled the US embassy in Ottawa on July 18 to relay his doubts. He understood the "Canadian desire for joint respons- ibility" but still advocated "piecemeal" sales. The US, UK, France, and Italy were already supplying arms to Israel, and the Netherlands was considering making a sale as well. A more formalized "collective action," Dulles warned, would reinforce the unhelpful impression of an organized arms race.[41]

On July 19, the US ambassador, Livingston Merchant, met with Pearson to convey Washington's well-known view and provide the hope- fully welcome information that the US would be releasing helicopters, machine guns, and scout cars to Israel, although this would be done as quietly as possible and not all at once. This was far from ideal for Canada, but Pearson, by temperament and experience, generally consigned him- self to working within the possible. Bowing to the American preference for piecemeal shipments, he acknowledged that it would indeed be un- wise to create the impression of a concerted Western arms effort, but he still hoped for, at the very least, a coordinated announcement, "so that Canada," as he put it, "would not be left out alone too long."[42]

Mere hours after this meeting to ease Middle East tensions took place in Ottawa, another occurred in Washington that lit the fuse to the Suez Crisis. Just after 4 p.m., Dulles received the Egyptian ambassador, Ahmed Hussein, who had recently returned from Cairo, where he had persuaded a skeptical Nasser to reject Russian advances and finally accept the US-

UK loan for the Aswan High Dam. Taking pains to deliver bad news as courteously as possible, Dulles informed the ambassador that the US was withdrawing its offer. The secretary of state cited the crushing burden that building the dam would impose on the Egyptian people and, more to the point, underlined the intense hostility coming from Congress. A dismayed Hussein was powerless to reverse the decision.

After four years of trying and failing to use each other for their own ends, each side perceived little but betrayal. Nasser resented the West for not giving him the arms he wanted, for always supporting Israel, and for trying to divide the Arabs with the treacherous Baghdad Pact. In Western eyes, Nasser's sins were legion: he bought arms from the Soviets, professed the heresy of non-alignment, kept up his relentless propaganda assault on London, continued working to undermine Jordan, steadfastly supported Algerian rebels in their anti-colonial struggle against France, and declined to lead the Arab world to make peace with Israel. In one of his final acts of treachery, Nasser had, just two months before, recognized the Communist government in China and announced he would even travel there. Presented with such behaviour, Dulles could cancel the loan offer with absolutely no domestic political cost.

The Foreign Office knew the move was coming but not exactly when. Eden had already decided to withdraw the British portion of the loan, but he was hoping to play the delay out a bit longer. After being informed about the American decision, he apparently said, "Oh good, oh good for Foster. I didn't really think he had it in him." After a brief pause, he added, "I wish he hadn't done it quite so abruptly."[43]

The day after meeting with the Egyptian ambassador, Dulles gloated that his reversal amounted to "as big a chess move as US diplomacy has made in a long time." Even if the Soviets picked up the tab, he could tell the Egyptian people, "You don't get bread because you are being squeezed to build a dam."[44] At least one diplomat was unimpressed by the American play. When he met with State Department officials, the French ambassador, Maurice Couve de Murville, expressed some concern about the potential Egyptian response, only to be dismissed with, "What can they do?"

"They will do something about Suez," the ambassador replied. "That's the only way they can touch the Western countries."[45]

NINE

Egypt for Egyptians

October 1915
Alexandria, Egypt

They sailed from Canada under the British flag, which they considered their own, to volunteer in a global war for a British King and a British Empire that they also called very much their own. Marching beneath the Egyptian sun through ancient streets, an eighteen-year-old Lester Pearson and his brothers in arms sang an unofficial Canadian anthem that celebrated a dauntless British general who shaped the fate of their continent when he "planted firm Old England's flag on Canada's fair domain/ Here may it wave, our boast, our pride." The locals who watched these foreign soldiers striding past without invitation or second thoughts also lived under the political and military shadow of that same flag, as did nearly a quarter of the world's population. However, they did not celebrate that fluttering reminder of imperial intimacy. Within living memory, British cannon balls had smashed through stone and flesh in this city to command a submission that continued to this day. As the Egyptians endured what they could not change, and while the loyal Canadian troops sang "The Maple Leaf Forever," who could doubt that the Union Jack would continue to fly in Egypt for as long as the British desired?

***

July 26, 1956
Menshiyeh Square, 7:30 p.m.
Alexandria, Egypt

Beneath a cooling twilight sky, vast crowds flowed across the enormous square to mark the fourth anniversary of a seismic event—the day a group of patriotic army officers banished the king into exile and restored the national sense of honour. One Egyptian newspaper claimed that a quarter of a million people gathered in the square, but an American diplomat estimated the count to be between sixty thousand and ninety thousand.[1] Earlier in the day, cars and vans mounted with loudspeakers drove slowly through the streets announcing that a warning would be delivered to the foreign powers hovering over Egypt's destiny.

The man expected to deliver that warning stood on the balcony of the old stock exchange building, illuminated by towering arc lights, flanked by foreign dignitaries, protected by bodyguards scanning the sea of faces in case another religious extremist tried to assassinate him. Tall, dark, and charismatic, the thirty-eight-year-old-year-old leader of Egypt looked more like a matinee idol than a military dictator. His very presence embodied a political miracle. The simple fact that Gamal Abdel Nasser, recently elected to the office of president, had been born in Egypt and governed an independent country shattered a legacy of imperial rule by foreign-born conquerors stretching back 2,500 years to the Persian invasion in the sixth century BC, which in turn gave way to a procession of formal and informal rulers from Greece, Rome, Byzantium, Arabia, Turkey, France, and Britain.

Dressed in a dark suit, Nasser started talking at about 7:40 p.m., improvising from scribbled notes, though he knew exactly where he would end, as did his Cabinet ministers, who were nervous about the unintended consequences his words could unleash. Naturally, he honoured the recent revolution, saying, "We succeeded in raising the Egyptian flag above Egypt's sky." He boasted that the country had dared to embrace "an independent policy which emanates from Egypt and not from London, Washington, Moscow, or any other country." On the evening of July 26, 1956, Nasser seemed to Nicholas Lakas, the American consul watching with binoculars from a hotel window, like a man reborn. Compared to

Nasser on the train to Cairo, July 1956, after nationalizing
the Suez Canal Company (Canadian Press/ AP 08516085)

a speech from the previous year, where Nasser "exhibited considerable
nervousness and apprehension," Lakas felt that he now "exuded confidence" and noted that "his hands, as he drank a glass of water, did not
tremble." At times, Nasser broke away from the classical formal Arabic
typical in official pronouncements and addressed the crowd using a
colloquial style that Egyptians call *baladi*. He even turned jester and
mimicked foreign diplomats ordering him about. Two French journalists standing on the balcony near him were pleasantly astonished by the

waves of laughter washing in from the vast square. "The crowd hangs
on his every word, every nuance," they wrote. "We came here expecting
a monologue with tragic overtones; instead we are getting comic relief.
This timid, self-conscious man has finally discovered how to speak to the
people—with humour."[2]

The crowd would soon learn, this was mere preamble leading towards
a spectacular finale. As he finished the second hour of the speech, Nasser
checked his watch repeatedly. Just before 10 p.m., he turned his focus
to the negotiations with the World Bank, Washington, and London regarding the Aswan High Dam. The protracted discussions had ended
abruptly, just days before—though not to Nasser's surprise. As relations
with the West deteriorated during the negotiations, he came to expect
his request for funding would be rejected. Faced with this public insult,
Nasser decided to hurl back a stunning reply.

Drawing the audience towards his denouement, Nasser railed against
a lingering symbol of foreign intrusion, the Suez Canal, still operated by
La Compagnie Universelle du Canal Maritime de Suez, owned primarily
by the British government and French shareholders, headquartered in
Paris and run by mostly French executives. Nasser invoked a powerful
sense of collective grievance. "[We Egyptians] dug the canal with our
lives, our skeletons, our bones and our blood," he declared, "[yet] Egypt
became the property of the Canal."[3] He then conjured up the spectre of
Ferdinand de Lesseps, the retired French diplomat who either inspired
or conned the Ottoman viceroy into giving him the concession to build
the canal, and who then sold the scheme to investors all over Europe—a
scheme that still enriched the West while allowing only a fraction of the
profits to trickle back into Egypt. Even now, Lesseps's statue loomed like
an unwelcome ghost at the northern entrance to the canal. Nasser repeated the hated name over a dozen times in his speech. He was not being
obsessive; this was the code word to launch his incredible gamble—as
monumental as dethroning a king.

Far from the crowded square in Alexandria, armed military teams
stationed from the north to the south end of the Suez Canal had been
listening to Nasser's speech on radio, waiting to hear him say "Lesseps."
As soon the name was uttered, they entered canal company offices and
installations at Port Said, Port Tewfik, Ismailia, and Cairo, informing

shocked technicians, administrators, and even the chief executive officer that they now worked for the Egyptian government.

At roughly 10:10 p.m., Nasser announced to the crowds in front of him, as well as to his opponents and allies abroad, that their government was nationalizing the company that managed and operated the Suez Canal and would henceforth use the canal dues to build the Aswan High Dam. For a few seconds, a silence stilled the human sea. Then they took in what Nasser had just done and lost themselves in a vast communal convulsion, weeping, dancing, and grabbing each other. Nasser beamed with delight and relief, even laughed uncontrollably, now that he had shared his secret with his country and the world. Watching from a balcony, the two French reporters observed that even "journalists whom we knew to be sceptical of the government were standing on their chairs, shouting enthusiastically."[4]

Stung by the West, Nasser had hit back. Still, paying heed to business conventions, he waited until stock exchanges in Europe and New York closed before announcing the nationalization, informing shareholders they would be reimbursed at the day's closing price. By 10:30 p.m., Egyptians now held the canal company that had been owned and managed by Europeans since the 1870s; held initially, it must be noted, at gunpoint. Threatened with imprisonment if they walked off the job, canal employees were ordered to keep working as if nothing had happened. Critical to Nasser's gamble was proving that Egypt could run the great waterway like a business, not a political weapon. He suspected some kind of diplomatic and perhaps even military storm was going to break over him. He judged his best countermove was to play a waiting game as long as possible and keep the canal traffic flowing smoothly between the Mediterranean and the Red Sea. In the meantime, as he tried to leave the square, crowds danced and proclaimed, "Long Live Nasser, Lord and Savior of Egypt and the Arabs." Some even tried to touch and kiss him and climb into his car.[5]

While scenes of jubilation erupted across Egypt, the sound of Nasser's voice had already carried out into the summer night to far-off hand-held transistor radios in Lebanon, living room sets in Jordan, glowing car radios in Syria, crowded cafes in Iraq, and across North Africa into Morocco, Tunisia, and Algeria. Although divided by geography, dialects, tribal loyalties, and ancient variations in how they worshipped from the same holy book, countless millions throughout the scattered Arab world rejoiced to hear spoken out loud a subversive defiance in which one of their own dared to redeem a collective history of subservience. While British battleships patrolled Mediterranean waters, Royal Air Force jets remained at rest beneath the Arabian night sky, and thousands of British troops stood watch over their kingdom's economic and political interests, the oscillating waves of sound were tearing through the lingering mirage of Great Britain's hold on the Middle East.

Frankly I am not content, and none of us should be content to leave the protection of a vital artery, the jugular vein of the British Empire, to the good will of the people of Egypt. I hope we claim that good will and get it, but we certainly should not be justified for one moment in leaving the defence of the Canal to the occasion of that good will.

—Anthony Eden, House of Commons, December 23, 1929[6]

July 26, 1956
No. 10 Downing Street, just after 10 p.m.
London, England

While President Nasser consciously made history in Alexandria, Prime Minister Eden was tending his country's network in the Middle East. His guest of honour was King Faisal II of Iraq, a primary ally in the region and thus a rival to Egypt. The young king was accompanied by his uncle, who had served as prince regent during his childhood, and by a veteran survivor of numerous government intrigues and shuffles, Prime Minister Nuri al-Said, who had first met Eden in the 1920s. Eden was fond of the Iraqi king, of whom he later wrote: "He seemed to me the best type of young ruler, caring for his people, modest in his living and direct in his approach."[7] In two years, all three Iraqis would be murdered in a military coup. At about a quarter past ten, an aide walked through the after-dinner conversations and quietly informed Eden that Egypt had, so to speak, taken the canal.

In 1956, over half of Britain's oil imports were shipped through the

Suez Canal. Other supplies surged via pipelines snaking across Syria and Saudi Arabia, both of them allies of Egypt. Roughly a third of the ships using the waterway were British, and they carried nearly a quarter of all goods destined for the island kingdom—which as its leaders could never forget, could not feed its population, power its industry, or fuel transportation with what was produced on home ground. If Nasser blocked the Suez Canal, oil reserves would run out after six weeks; Western Europe would go dry even sooner. With a menace suddenly looming over all these convoys, Eden declared at some point during the evening that Nasser could not be allowed "to have his hand on our windpipe."[8] From that premise, everything else was to follow.

On the surface, Eden responded to the shocking news like the veteran diplomat he was, gracefully underreacting. The leader of the Opposition, Hugh Gaitskell, a guest that night, spoke briefly with him and Selwyn Lloyd. Their conversation foreshadowed all the complications lying in wait. Eden wondered out loud whether he should refer the matter to the United Nations. Gaitskell asked what would happen if Nasser ignored the UN. Lloyd interjected, "Well, I suppose in that case the old-fashioned ultimatum will be necessary." Rather than rebuke the foreign secretary for making a threat, Gaitskell urged that, whatever they chose to do, they move quickly, and encouraging Eden even further, declared that the country would stand behind them. Almost an axiom in British postwar foreign policy, he also suggested that they "must get America into line."[9]

Eden received other advice that night. Before leaving No. 10, the Iraqi prime minister apparently told his host and military supporter how best to deal with Nasser: "Hit him hard, hit him soon, and hit him by yourself."[10] This was exactly what Eden wanted to hear. He had already instructed his country's secret services to try to destabilize the Egyptian regime and bring down the president. For Eden, the nationalization was not so much the insufferable last straw as it was the much-needed opening to launch a public campaign to destroy the enemy.

Wasting no time, Eden summoned his senior military officials, Chief of the Imperial General Staff Gerald Templer and First Sea Lord Louis Mountbatten—titles perhaps better suited to a true imperial power—who joined Chief of the Air Staff Dermot Boyle already present from the dinner. Rallying allies, Eden called in the French ambassador and the American chargé d'affaires and, with his foreign secretary and other ministers around him, presided over a meeting that lasted into the early hours of the morning.

They immediately dismissed the notion of referring the crisis to the Security Council, with its predictable Soviet veto, which would risk this critical confrontation becoming "hopelessly bogged down." Instead, Eden explored another option: invading Egypt and physically retaking control of the canal. The military men were cautious in their advice. They were all too aware of their country's limitations, made even more limited thanks to the agreement Eden had negotiated to withdraw some eighty thousand British troops from the Suez Canal base. The last British troops had left Egypt just weeks before. The Royal Navy could reach the canal in a matter of days with 1,200 marines picked up in Cyprus, but they could not, the advisers argued, secure the entire canal. To achieve that objective, the senior command would need an estimated seven weeks to prepare, assemble, and transport the appropriate invasion force. And regarding the central question in Eden's mind—taking Nasser down for good—he was apparently told, "Prime Minister, we can take Cairo, we cannot hold it." Thus, at the very moment Eden wanted an intimidating display of power, he learned he could do very little. Attending the late night discussion, Eden's press secretary, William Clark, captured the dilemma in his diary. Britain "could not deal militarily with a little local episode in the eastern Mediterranean. I felt ashamed that our nakedness should be thus revealed to the French and American representatives present."[11] Eden, however, did not flinch. Nothing he heard from the military chiefs that evening tempered in any way his decision to settle things with Nasser once and for all.

I asked Pearson what were the present limits of Canadian interests. He said "Western Europe"—not the Mediterranean or the Middle East. They'd proposed $25 million a year (he thought from memory) to the Colombo Plan, but apart from this their interest in South-East Asia was nil. They'd be interested in the Northern Pacific if that area became active.

—Australian foreign minister R.G. Casey, November 15, 1951[12]

House of Commons
Ottawa
July 26, 1956

Lester Pearson sat at his desk in the front row of the government benches, engaged in the mundane miracle of representative democracy. The
Speaker of the House acknowledged in the visitors' galleries the presence
of the Australian prime minister, Robert Menzies, who received a round
of applause from his fellow members of the British Commonwealth
of Nations. Then Her Majesty's Loyal Opposition began to probe Her
Majesty's Government for failures of action and lapses of judgment. At
about 11:20 a.m., Pearson rose from his seat to answer a question about
two Canadian UN observers seriously injured by a landmine while on
patrol near the Israel-Jordan border. He told the House that the host
government had provided these UN officers, one francophone and the
other anglophone, with the protection available but conceded that, given
the nature of their duties, these observers could never enjoy complete
protection. Prime Minister St. Laurent then fielded a question about
Canada possibly exporting F-86 Sabre jets to Israel, explaining that no
final decision had been made. Next, an MP asked whether the government was considering a reduction in the number of troops stationed
in Europe as part of Canada's NATO commitments. St. Laurent again
relied on the parliamentary art form to reveal as little as possible in as
few words as tolerable.[13]

The Opposition's hunt for errors and omissions digressed from one
topic to another, but although the questions were routine, the concerns
raised in this microcosm reflected the macrocosm in which the North
American dominion operated: a transatlantic defence alliance, an assembly of former British colonies, and a somewhat global league of nations.
The country exported military arms and, at the same time, sent unarmed
UN observers to monitor hostile borderlines. The old racial divisions that
haunted Laurier and Mackenzie King so deeply had largely dissipated
because, in this Cold War, francophones and anglophones shared the
same desire to eradicate the Communist virus.

After routine business in the House, Pearson joined his colleagues at
a 1 p.m. luncheon for Menzies in the Parliament building. Four hours

later, in Alexandria, Nasser announced the nationalization of the Suez Canal. Word probably reached Canada by early evening, by which time Pearson was attending a reception for Menzies at the Ottawa country club. But however and wherever he learned that Great Britain had just lost control of one of its economic lifelines, the news did not make an impact powerful enough for him to leave any written or oral record of his first reaction — not in his memoirs nor in any interviews afterwards. Neither did any of his colleagues in External Affairs or the Prime Minister's Office. Their emotional distance from Egypt reflected their geographic and political distance.

The nature and importance of the clash between Egypt and Britain shifted in the eye of each beholder, viewed as another manifestation of the Cold War schism, an expression of anti-colonial nationalism, and a test of democratic resolve in the face of tyranny. In Canada, all these views came into play. The country's history also provided another lens to view the conflict.

I had to speak in the House this afternoon on the Royal Style and Titles. . . . It is interesting to think that 15 years ago a vote on a bill of this kind which established The Queen as Queen of Canada, and which firmly and irrevocably divided up the monarchy, would have caused not only general interest, but excitement and controversy. It didn't cause a ripple of either this afternoon. Does this mean we are growing up?
    — Lester Pearson, February 3, 1953[14]

In 1956, Canada remained a nation still being consciously constructed. Even its borders had been redrawn when a new province, Newfoundland, entered Confederation just seven years before. This unfolding evolution in the northern half of North America, to a large degree, entailed remapping and reimagining the enduring relationship with Great Britain.

Presiding over what most Canadians perceived and celebrated as the rightful odyssey "from colony to nation" was a francophone prime minister whose family roots in Quebec dated back to the seventeenth century. Anchored in such deep personal history, Louis St. Laurent "felt no nostalgia for the old lands of Europe," observed journalist Bruce

Hutchison, and remained untouched by "the emotional claims of other countries that always tugged at his predecessors, even King."[15] St. Laurent sought greater and greater sovereignty to serve his one country. In 1949, Ottawa abolished the right of Canadians to appeal civil cases to the UK's Judicial Committee of the Privy Council, making Canada's Supreme Court truly supreme, and patriated from the British government the power to amend the constitution in areas of federal jurisdiction.

Moving onto contentious ground, St. Laurent modified the country's title, dominion, chosen in the 1860s by the Fathers of Confederation as they sought a name for their political experiment that was neither a colony nor completely independent. Made in Canada by Canadians for Canadians and then adopted by the other self-governing members of the Britannic family, this unique designation had come to sound, at least to Liberal ears in the 1950s, somewhat retrograde. According to Cabinet minister Jack Pickersgill, the prime minister certainly felt the title suffered from "a colonial or quasi-colonial connotation." Yet, wishing to avoid a backlash from the many Canadians who felt no such colonial cringe, Ottawa began, without fuss or debate, to remove the offending word from government documents, statutes, buildings, and simple usage (dominion-provincial conferences became federal-provincial conferences) — although it still remained the country's title. The Conservative Opposition deplored the move, but the approving majority dismissed their voices.[16] While sensitive to the racial division that lay beneath the debate on symbols, St. Laurent was nonetheless undeterred and maintained the momentum to reimagine the national state of being.

In 1952, he made a landmark recommendation to George VI, who appointed the first Canadian-born governor general, Vincent Massey. The decision itself and the choice of individual were widely praised, but the change was not universally welcome. A Gallup poll from the previous August showed that a quarter of respondents wanted to retain the tradition of a British-born governor general.[17]

At the press conference announcing Massey's appointment, St. Laurent felt compelled to defend himself on several fronts. Regarding appointing a Canadian to Rideau Hall, he offered an irrefutable case: "I would not like to admit that Canadians, alone among His Majesty's subjects, should be considered unworthy to represent the King in their own country." Regarding the slow erasure of "Dominion" from government discourse, he tried to persuade reporters that the matter was all about semantics and not politics: "Canada is a Dominion but its name is not 'the Dominion of Canada' any more than the name of Ottawa is 'the City of Ottawa' or the name of Ontario is 'the Province of Ontario.'" In the course of the press conference, however, he tipped his hand, by saying, "The word dominion does suggest to many good and loyal Canadians that our country occupied a somewhat inferior status." Even London, he pointed out, had changed the name of the Dominions Office to the Commonwealth Relations Office. "We have got to some day grow up," St. Laurent declared, unintentionally adding a measure of insult to the injury felt by the many other good and loyal Canadians who did not find their attachment to their heritage infantilizing. "There will be a time when it won't be necessary for us to have apron strings tied to us."[18] The prime minister did not elaborate which apron strings he meant, but some could not be so easily cut away.

Canada's flag in the 1950s, the Red Ensign, displayed the Union Jack in the upper left-hand corner and the Shield of the Canadian Coat of Arms, made up of British and French iconography. For some Canadians, the Canadian flag was not British enough. A May 1953 Gallup Poll showed thirty-eight percent of Canadians preferred to fly the Union Jack as the country's flag. And one overarching connection remained: the monarchy, which no prime minister would dare to cut, especially as it had been revitalized by the recent accession of a young new queen. Indeed, Pearson noted in his diary that St. Laurent was "a devoted admirer of the Royal Family in general and the Queen in particular, and thinks that the monarchy is more solidly established than ever. There is something about the atmosphere of a Throne!"[19]

The enduring constitutional and emotional web between Britain and Canada was reinforced by the sheer power of immigration. For the first half of the decade, roughly a quarter (and in 1956 alone thirty percent) of all immigrants came from the British Isles, by far the largest source of all newcomers.[20] They arrived in a country that shared the same head of state, whose familiar face featured on the currency; the same form of parliamentary government; the same language and social customs; and membership in NATO, the United Nations, and the Commonwealth.

Small wonder then that the diplomatic relationship with Britain remained "so cordial and intimate...taken for granted," as John Hilliker and Greg Donaghy write, that "External Affairs did not create a separate British desk for another decade.[21]

Pearson might be entranced by the sheen of majesty but not by the lure of closer imperial attachment, nor was he dismayed by the empire's slow fade. His lack of sentimentality was evident just three months before the Suez Crisis when he wrote to Arthur Irwin, Canadian High Commissioner in Australia. Irwin had reported on an informal but heartfelt talk with Australia's foreign minister, R.G. Casey, someone considered fairly liberal in his outlook regarding the new state of Commonwealth affairs, relative to his Cabinet colleagues. Casey had ruminated about postwar humiliations suffered by the British, which prompted Pearson to observe:

The nostalgia of the British Conservative for the empire of the past is quite understandable and perhaps not unhealthy, but it does seem to me that an essential basis of any wise approach to relations with India, Pakistan and Ceylon is to believe, or at least to make oneself believe, that the 'empire' has progressed into a higher rather than a lower existence.... There are certainly people in Canada who think the empire has gone to pieces, but I think the great majority of Canadians who have opinions on the subject and those in authority honestly believe that, to cope with the problems of to-day, the new type of Commonwealth is an infinitely better institution than the old.

In observing the nostalgia, Pearson did not indulge in assumptions of Canada's moral superiority and instead underlined the link between geography and emotional detachment.

It is of course true that we in Canada can take a somewhat more relaxed view of developments in Asia than can the Australians. All of us profess to believe that the Far East is of direct importance to us, but I suppose we never feel in our bones the fears and anxieties which Australians must have when they look towards their Near North. This makes it easier for us to appear "sympathetic and understanding," and makes us, consequently, pretty popular in that part of the world;

especially as we can give material assistance too. The absence of immediate pressures and specific problems is always a great asset in becoming popular; or at least in avoiding dislike and suspicion.[22]

Lacking the fears and anxieties felt in Australia, New Zealand, and Britain would allow Pearson to confront Egypt's act of defiance with far greater understanding of what was sensible and practical—though this same understanding would make him extremely unpopular with many at home and some of the very people he was trying to rescue.

July 27, 1956
London, England

A packed House of Commons met at 11 a.m. looking to, as one MP put it, "repair this injury to our honour and interests." The model of restraint, Eden made a brief, bland statement criticizing Egypt's unilateral action and said he would consult with the other canal users about "the wider questions" now raised. Opposition and government MPs immediately raised those wider questions. Leading the choir of indignation, Labour leader Hugh Gaitskell denounced the seizure and then, as he had the night before at No. 10, asked Eden if he was referring the matter to the United Nations. The prime minister declined to commit himself. A Labour MP compared Nasser's methods to Hitler's and wondered if Eden grasped "the consequences of not answering force with force until it is too late."[23] The prime minister again played it cool in his response. Watching from the galleries as a junior parliamentary clerk, future biographer Robert Rhodes James saw that Conservative MPs appeared let down by their leader's tepid statement. Having said very little, Eden left for his first full Cabinet meeting of the crisis, and as MPs dispersed, Rhodes James recalled walking past "anguished discussions in the Lobbies and corridors; if there were any voices raised in defence of the Egyptian action, I did not hear them. The mood was one of outrage at an act of international piracy."[24]

Eden sat down at the Cabinet table committed to seizing triumph from insult. "Colonel Nasser's action [has] presented us with an opportunity," he declared, "and we should not hesitate to take advantage of it." This posed a bit of a dilemma because some in Cabinet acknowledged their "weak ground" if they simply framed the nationalization as illegal. They were dealing, after all, with a registered Egyptian company. Nasser had said he would reimburse the shares. "From a narrow legal point of view," one minister conceded, "his action amounted to no more than a decision to buy out the shareholders." Eden dismissed the legal view and, looking ahead to the necessary task of rallying allies in the Commonwealth and NATO, especially the essential government in Washington, elevated his case to a more exalted plane, as a critical challenge confronting the international community.

With little debate, his colleagues decided they would ignore geography and national sovereignty and argue that the Suez Canal belonged to the world and therefore should be operated by an international agency, which would grant Egypt a seat at the table. To achieve this, however, Eden preferred to avoid working through the world assembly with its Soviet veto. In discussing how to impose a political solution with no solid legal foundation, "the fundamental question," Eden said, was "whether they were prepared in the last resort to pursue their objective by the threat or even the use of force, and whether they were ready, in default of assistance from the United States and France, to take military action alone."[25]

Debating the use of force against Egypt was hardly a novel question for a British Cabinet. In order to command the strategic passage between three continents, Britain had meddled with, protected, fought over, and controlled Egypt in varying degrees since the Royal Navy attacked the French fleet in 1798 at the Battle of the Nile. All through the nineteenth century, London ensured that this precious gateway to India remained nestled within the feeble and therefore malleable Ottoman Empire. During the opening decades of the century, Britain loosened the political leash, but only just. The military presence imposed in 1882 had ended only weeks before Nasser's nationalization. Therefore, the collective decision in the face of the most recent threat was hardly surprising. "Our essential interests in this area must, if necessary, be safeguarded by military action," the Cabinet concluded. "Even if we had to act alone, we could not stop short of using force to protect our position."[26]

With Cabinet on side, Eden turned to another critical factor in his war against Nasser: harnessing the most powerful member of the Western alliance. He promptly dispatched a passionate appeal to his old wartime comrade US president Dwight D. Eisenhower, addressing him as "Dear Friend." In confronting the threat to Britain's economic lifeline, the prime minister declared, "We should not allow ourselves to become involved in legal quibbles." This challenge before them was manifold: protecting oil supplies, preserving what was left of British prestige, and not replaying the sins of past appeasement. Without a firm response, Eden warned, British and American influence in the Middle East would be finished. Then he laid down a marker with unmistakeable clarity. "We are unlikely to obtain our objective by economic pressures alone," he wrote. "My colleagues and I are convinced that we must be ready, in the last resort, to use force to bring Nasser to his senses."[27] The president's reply expressed concern but not alarm and so lacked Eden's intensity, and it urged a peaceful resolution. This clear divergence in tone, perception, and approach grew only more dramatic over the coming months, and from this moment forward, the former general did everything he could to restrain the former diplomat from using brute force to bring Nasser to heel.

> It is almost platitudinous now to state that Canada's position becomes impossible if Great Britain and the United States drift apart on any major issue. Like many other platitudes, however, this one involves a fundamental truth. Canada is a British Dominion. She is also an American state. She cannot permit herself to be put in a position where she has to choose between these two destinies. Either choice would be fatal to her unity, indeed, to her very existence as a state.
> —Lester Pearson, *Foreign Affairs,* April 1935[28]

July 27, 1956
Ottawa

The moment that enthralled Egypt and enraged Great Britain was overshadowed on the front pages in Canada by a disaster at sea off the northeastern US coast. A luxury liner, the *Andrea Doria*, collided with another ship, killing close to fifty passengers and crew, and injuring hundreds more. Possibly to the delight of newspaper editors across the country, Canadians were discovered on board, including a heroic nun who, in her life jacket, apparently calmed terrified passengers by praying for them as the ship listed.[29] In Ottawa, MPs did not discuss the Suez Canal but instead debated various items, such as a tax on advertising revenues, quotas for grain farmers and the preservation of the old Supreme Court building.

In this deceptive lull, Lester Pearson formulated the first public, official Canadian response to what had happened in Egypt and, equally important, to what was unfolding in the United Kingdom. On arriving at his office, he almost certainly read ticker tape reports or was briefed about Eden's statement branding a legal if brazen act of nationalization as expropriation, and warning that the government would deal with "the wider questions" raised by this theft. Pearson likely would have asked his officials dealing with the Middle East to begin drafting a statement. At 10 a.m. he attended a Cabinet meeting where the ministers covered a wide range of topics, beginning with amendments to market regulations for Ontario peach growers. According to the minutes, they did not discuss the events in Egypt at all. The key Middle East issue facing Canada remained the sale of fighter jets to Israel.

In making his presentation, Pearson noted existing and future US and French arms shipments to Israel, as well as Communist shipments to Arab states, and recommended the immediate export of twelve F-86 jets, with the balance of the request to be considered at a future date. Some ministers expressed doubts about Washington following through with its own shipments, which would leave Canada exposed, and pointed out that the Americans also wanted as little publicity as possible. Pearson was instructed to consult yet again with the US and emphasize the fact that Canada would wait to announce any sale only after US arms shipments become public knowledge.[30]

At some point around midday, Pearson received a cable from the High Commissioner in London, Norman Robertson, reporting on a morning meeting of his counterparts at the Commonwealth Relations Office, presided over by Alec Douglas-Home, the commonwealth secretary. The High Commissioners read an advance copy of Eden's statement to the House of Commons before engaging in what Robertson described as a "brief and desultory" discussion. Friends and colleagues for nearly thirty years, Robertson and Pearson had been shaped by the same generational anxieties and imperatives. Thus the High Commissioner felt confident in expressing, without first consulting Pearson, historic Canadian caution in the face of British ambitions. To his Commonwealth Relations colleagues, Robertson said he assumed London would discuss whether to take the canal crisis to the Security Council, clearly implying he thought this was the right thing to do. Robertson added, "I hoped the United Kingdom would not be too quick to gather too many spears to its own bosom."[31] Robertson's cable did not record any reply from Douglas-Home. The Canadians had no idea that Eden and his ministers had that same morning already decided to use force to protect British honour and interests.

To craft Ottawa's formal response to Nasser's move, Pearson no doubt factored in Eden's statement in Parliament, Robertson's report from London, and the all-important American reaction. At noon, the State Department issued a brief press release labelling the nationalization a seizure, but it did not call for any strong measures. The restrained US voice would have reaffirmed Pearson's instinctive reaction to the distant crisis. Rather than speak in Parliament, the foreign minister issued his own brief understatement. "While Canada has no share in the ownership of the Suez Canal Co., as a trading nation," he stated, "we have a very real interest in the efficient and non-discriminatory operation of this waterway of great and historic importance in peace and war. We would regret and be concerned about any action which interfered with such operation."[32] Only a handful of newspapers picked up the statement, which was buried away from the front page.

With these deceptively bland words, the first official Canadian response, Pearson staked out in the very opening rounds of the crisis a highly contentious position. He did not condemn Nasser. He did not describe the nationalization as theft or threat. He wouldn't even, as he told Ottawa's *Journal*, be making any formal "representations" to Egypt on the matter.[33] And the final line contained a striking ambiguity. When Pearson expressed concern about potential actions that could interfere with the canal's operation, it was not at all certain whether he was concerned about potential Egyptian action or potential British action. What was clear in his first statement on Suez, however, is that he declined to wave the old flag and cheer the march to war.

TEN

Seen but Not Heard

Each part of the Empire...has its own sphere. But at certain
points the arcs cut, the interests become common. There
are issues which are of fundamental concern to all parts
of the Empire; and with these all parts of the Empire must
deal.... It is true that there is no clear cut and enduring line
of demarcation between these fields...no foreign question
affecting one part of the Empire is without its influence on
other parts, however small and indirect that influence may
be...it is a question of degree.
     —William Lyon Mackenzie King, Imperial Conference,
     October 8, 1923[1]

It took two days, once the Egyptian government nationalized La
Compagnie Universelle du Canal Maritime de Suez, for the political
repercussions to reach Canada. On July 28, at a brief morning meeting,
Livingston Merchant informed Lester Pearson that Washington had now
decided to delay arms shipments to Israel so as not to encourage "the
extremists" there or in Egypt. Having pressed Ottawa for months to sell
F-86 Sabre jets to Israel, the ambassador hoped that Ottawa would also
hold off approving the sale. Pearson readily agreed, assuring Merchant
that he would remain in close step with the US before proceeding. Having
dealt with the unavoidable gravitational pull from one imperial sphere,
Pearson moved to confront another.[2]

The House of Commons met at eleven o'clock. Her Majesty's Loyal
Opposition, the Progressive Conservatives, which had ignored Suez the

day before, now made the crisis its lead point of attack. Pearson took the first question, posed by his future nemesis, perhaps the only man he would ever at times truly hate, John Diefenbaker—devoted believer in the British connection, a master of rhetoric and invective, and one of the most effective and even electrifying campaigners the country would ever see. In the realm of political theatrics, he utterly outclassed Pearson. Suez marked the beginning of a personal and increasingly bitter duel that would spill into the next decade as they each vied for and attained the office of prime minister. At this point, however, relations were cordial.

The jousting opened with Diefenbaker asking Pearson whether Canada would condemn Cairo's "perversion of international contracts." Pearson agreed that the violation of the concession established in the late nineteenth century was to be condemned and acknowledged that, having blocked Israeli shipping, the Egyptian government had violated its pledge to guarantee free passage through the canal. However, Pearson avoided Diefenbaker's bait and refrained from criticizing Nasser personally or labelling the nationalization a military threat. Instead, he suggested it was premature to go beyond his statement from the day before in which, purposefully bland, he merely noted that Canada had "a very real interest in the efficient and non-discriminatory operation of this waterway."[3]

Conservative MP Howard Green followed to stress the critical importance of the canal to the United Kingdom and Commonwealth, and urged Pearson to have Canada "stand beside them and let the whole world know that she does." The foreign minister again offered a tepid reply.[4] The Opposition saw all too clearly that he did not intend to make any kind of call for Commonwealth unity nor wage a war of words against Egypt for perceived crimes against Britain. The first skirmish in Parliament over Suez was framed from the very start by the implicit question of loyalty.

The UK High Commission reported the disappointing proceedings to London, observing that Pearson showed no interest in taking "a more positive attitude." When he read about the unmistakable lack of enthusiasm, Eden wrote one word on the telegram: "Miserable." Another report from the High Commission, summarizing press coverage, brought Eden another measure of grief. Although eastern Canadian newspapers criticized Egypt and stood by Britain, discordant voices could be heard. One professor argued on CBC radio that Britain had provoked Nasser, and

Anthony Eden (left) with Louis St. Laurent, February 1956, Ottawa
(City of Ottawa Archives/ MG393/ CA024855/ Newton)

the very liberal *Toronto Daily Star* posed the appalling question: "If the
Canadian section of the St. Lawrence waterway were today owned and
controlled by foreign interests, as a result of a British deal 100 years ago,
would Canada feel content with the deal?" Seeming to think Ottawa held
editorial sway over the public broadcaster and the country's most widely
read newspaper, Eden minuted to the commonwealth relations secretary:
"Please speak. This is Canadian government again. We must react."[5]

And indeed what Pearson could never divulge to the Conservative
Opposition and its sizeable constituency was that, at this early point in the
standoff, he was far more concerned about overreactions from London
than from Cairo. Before speaking to the House, Pearson had walked
into the prime minister's office and found him reading a short message
from Eden, also dispatched to the other members of the Commonwealth.
In this first missive from London, laying out clear intentions and using

much tougher language in private than anything so far expressed in public, Eden seemed alarmingly disinclined to employ diplomacy to settle the matter. He preferred, instead, to dangle a noose over Nasser's head. "We cannot allow him to get away with this act of expropriation and we must take a firm stand," he wrote. "If we do not, the oil supplies of the free world will be at his mercy." Without indicating any role for Egypt to play in the process, Eden declared his intention to put the Suez Canal permanently under "proper international control," and wrote that while he hoped political arm-twisting would do the trick, "it may be that this will fail and that in the last resort force may have to be used to secure Egyptian agreement."[6]

What he read deeply alarmed Pearson. He was perhaps more disturbed by what he foresaw. Before replying to this thinly disguised threat, he composed a long cable to Norman Robertson in London—the first in a series of what J.L. Granatstein has rightly called "extraordinarily prophetic" arguments and observations[7]—and expressed his skepticism and anxiety about Eden's intentions:

> Surely with the Russians dissenting and supporting Egypt, the UK do not think that this can be done, as they profess to hope, "by political pressure" alone. There remains force—which they visualize as a last resort. But is it not clear that to be effective enough force would have to be used to destroy the Nasser Government and take over Egypt? Any effort to use force, in fact, would in all likelihood result in an appeal by Egypt to the UN. That would be bringing the UN into the matter with a vengeance, and by the wrong party.[8]

Pearson was absolutely right in his calculation that taking back control of the canal would require using enough force to destroy Nasser. Eden shared that assessment and had already appointed an inner circle of ministers to a so-called Egypt committee, assigned an explicitly stated goal: "Our immediate purpose was to bring about the downfall of the present Egyptian Government." If the internationalist in Pearson was appalled by the risks Eden and his Cabinet appeared willing to take and the violence they were prepared to inflict, the realist in him was, at the same time, concerned about a glaring flaw in Eden's approach. "I doubt very much whether he will receive strong support from Washington in the firm line which he proposes to follow," Pearson wrote to Norman Robertson. "Surely the UK Government will not do anything which would commit them to strong action against Egypt until they know that the US will back them. Pearson reiterated the same concern in a phone call that same day to Australian prime minister Robert Menzies. "Talk of using force would be a bluff," he said, "unless the United States also were willing to adopt the same policy."9

Pearson's strongly felt and repeatedly expressed concern about how, not if, Britain might use force without American support reveals a fundamental factor in his thinking, an almost amoral ambivalence, that he could conceivably support "strong action" against Egypt if Washington were to back London. One of his closest and most perceptive advisers during the Suez Crisis, John Holmes, later wrote in admiration: "His approach was ruthlessly pragmatic." Pearson, explains political scientist Denis Stairs, was "a realist in the conduct of foreign policy. He understood that power is a fairly fundamental currency of international politics. He was constantly aware of limits. His test, I think it's fair to say, in the conduct of foreign policy, was not whether it was right in principle but whether it was effective."10

Pearson's dispassionate calculations were evident throughout the Suez Crisis and were strikingly apparent in a personal letter written after the worst was over. Even with civilian casualties in Egypt, he did not express any emotional or moral condemnation about the unjust and deadly use of imperial force. "My only quarrel with the British and the French is that they have not themselves shown any awareness of their own limitations of power in the protection of their interests—political and economic—in the area. Without American support—and they must, or at least should, have known it was not forthcoming—they never really had any chance of success," Pearson wrote. "It is not a question of right or wrong, but of the wisdom or unwisdom of policies and tactics." He prudently added: "It is something that I cannot say publicly, of course."11

Although London had not requested a reply to Eden's blunt declaration of intent, Pearson decided to answer the alarming memo with a short message of concern about entirely predictable consequences: "The use of force in present circumstances—even as a last resort—will be surrounded by risks and difficulties, one of which might be the submission of the matter to the United Nations by the wrong party." He dispatched this on the same day St. Laurent received Eden's telegram, July 28, to Norman Robertson to forward to the Commonwealth Relations Office, though Pearson specified that Robertson should deliver the reply only if he thought it would be helpful. Prime Minister St. Laurent did not want "to be intervening with advice which would be too negative in character to do anything but irritate."[12]

The Canadians dealing with London surely knew this appeal for caution and negotiation would not go down well at No. 10 Downing Street. Indeed, St. Laurent decided Robertson should deliver a more muted message. To make sure that Ottawa's real feelings did not go unheard, however, and in a sign of the intimacy between Canadian and British officials, Robertson discreetly showed the original draft along with his own earlier and more critical cables to Norman Brook, the British Cabinet secretary, who presumably shared them with others in Whitehall.[13]

The senior dominion was, of course, but one voice from within the family that London had to take into account, even if only to ignore. With roughly two-thirds of Australia's imports and exports passing through the Suez Canal, the country's external affairs minister, Richard Casey, sharply criticized Cairo's "abrupt and high-handed action" and the ensuing sight of Egyptian forces patrolling the canal. He called for international control of the waterway, declaring that Australia's trade could not become subject to "capricious or arbitrary action." However, firm language was as far as Canberra wanted to go for the moment. In private, Casey admitted: "The main policy question we have to decide is whether we're going to be tough or soft with Egypt. Little as one may like it, I can see no future in being tough." His mandarins supported his assessment. As one historian has written: "In the department, the 'doves' were in the ascendant." Most importantly, Robert Menzies, the prime minister, shared their view. Echoing Canadian calls for restraint, Menzies told the British ambassador to Washington, Roger Makins, "It was quite true that in days gone by military force would have been the appropriate reply to Egypt, but in present circumstances resort to it would split the Western world." Menzies suggested calling an international conference to deal with the crisis, but he also left the door open to a stiffer response down the road. If Egypt ignored the conference's recommendations, "a new situation would be created."[14]

Speaking for the most geographically remote but arguably the most emotionally attached of the "white settler" dominions, New Zealand's prime minister, Sidney Holland, pledged his country's unwavering support: "Where Britain stands, we stand; where she goes, we go, in good times and bad." From the other end of the emotional spectrum, South Africa's prime minister, Johannes Strijdom, summed up his government's attitude with a pithy disavowal: "It is best to keep our heads out of the beehive." South Africa held no shares in the Suez Canal Company and so was not affected by the nationalization. That was a purely domestic issue "in which South Africa would not presume to intervene," the foreign minister Eric Louw stated. Privately, however, he and the prime minister told the British that they were worried the crisis might escalate into "a wider conflagration."[15]

Predictably, a difference in tone and assumptions coincided to some degree with the colour divide in the Commonwealth. The first prime minister of an independent India, Jawaharlal Nehru, the Cambridge-educated voice of anti-colonialism, immediately sided with Egypt, like India a former British pawn struggling to escape the last vestiges of the imperial game. He knew Nasser relatively well from their alignment in the non-aligned movement and strongly supported the nationalization. Like Pearson, Nehru judged that the danger to international peace came not from Cairo but from London.

Ceylon's prime minister, Solomon W.R.D. Bandaranaike, a graduate of Oxford, worried to the British High Commissioner about the Middle East going up in flames and how this might affect his country's trade, eighty percent of which, he estimated, passed through the Suez Canal. But he did not question the legitimacy of Nasser's action. Pakistan's foreign minister, Hamidul Haq Chowdhry, expressed privately to British officials his "acute anxiety" that Egypt would mismanage the canal and, worse, wield it as a political weapon. But his government, he said, found itself "in a difficult position," unsure how to voice its disapproval over what Cairo had done without being criticized by the press and public for not showing "sympathy with another Muslim people."[16] Thus, in the opening days of the crisis, most of the Commonwealth had little to offer Britain beyond deep concern and unwanted words of caution. On the other hand, Britain's historic rival in the Middle East shared the same hunger to destroy Nasser.

In the summer of 1956, the spectre of ever-diminishing grandeur haunted France. The country had limped from the humiliation of wartime surrender, occupation, and collaboration to the loss of empire in Indochina and the release of its formal grip on two long-held protectorates, Tunisia and Morocco. Now France was fighting for what was left in North Africa, which was perhaps most precious of all. Conquered in the 1830s, Algeria was not seen as merely an overseas possession but considered and indeed administered as home ground. Some 1.5 million French and European settlers lived there, some for generations, and along with nine million Muslims, boasted French citizenship. A quarter of a million French troops were fighting Algerian rebels seeking independence. Egypt supported the rebellion with weapons, training, and propaganda. That was reason enough to despise Nasser even before he nationalized the Suez Canal Company.

If not quite the emotional "lifeline of Empire," the French-conceived canal symbolized a grand triumph from a more glorious past. The canal company was registered in Egypt, with offices in Cairo, but it was headquartered in Paris, run by French managers, and supervised by a predominantly French and British board. For generations, the canal remained financially meaningful to roughly a quarter of a million individual shareholders. French parents gave canal company shares to their children as christening and wedding gifts.[17] From the very start the French body politic saw the Suez Crisis as one with the battle for Algeria, and it rose without hesitation to join the British crusade to uphold honour, international treaties, and oil supplies.

Within forty-eight hours of the nationalization, France and Britain worked in tandem to launch an economic campaign against Nasser, freezing the canal company's funds and assets in their respective countries and blocking all pending weapons and materiel exports to Egypt. British banks imposed controls on Egyptian sterling accounts held in London.

France would have attacked Egypt immediately, but Britain felt constrained to consult and co-opt the dominant power in the Western alliance. And so began an unhappy, mutually frustrating minuet in which Washington expressed concern and outrage, acknowledged the potential threat to Western strategic interests, even voiced hopes for Nasser's downfall but, nonetheless, argued consistently against the use of force—except as a last resort. For Washington, the Suez Crisis was one battle in an ongoing war. For the British and French, this was their last stand. Each side hoped or assumed the other would eventually retreat from their clearly stated positions. It is still difficult to say precisely what was genuinely misunderstood, what was said simply to placate and buy time, what was taken out of context for self-serving purposes, and what was wilfully ignored. The unspoken but perpetual canker in the so-called special relationship was that the British needed the Americans far more than the Americans needed the British.

On August 1, John Foster Dulles arrived in London, bringing his outrage but also an unwelcome plea for calm negotiation. He agreed on the end goal but differed on the means, saying, "A way must be found to make Nasser disgorge. We believe, however, that force is the last method to be tried....We believe that Nasser can be forced to disgorge by means other than military."[18] Over several meetings, he urged Britain and France to mobilize world opinion and make genuine efforts to reach a diplomatic solution. He reminded his allies that no popular or Congressional support existed in the US for what would seem like an old-fashioned colonial assault.

Governing a nation dependent on the oil flowing through the canal, Eden was unswayed. Revealing just how far he was willing to take this fight, he hoped out loud to Dulles that, if things got out of hand, Washington "would take care of the Bear."[19] At every point, Dulles found himself facing a phalanx of unflinching warriors, their attitudes forged and hardened by their self-perceived failures to confront an earlier generation of tyrants. "We just could not afford to lose this game. It was a question not of honour only but of survival," Harold Macmillan told Dulles. "We must either get Nasser out by diplomacy or by force."[20]

Despite the hunger to strike at Nasser as soon as possible, London and Paris gave into American insistence for a show of diplomacy and reluctantly called a conference of canal users for mid-August. These shipping nations were invited to establish an international agency to operate what Egypt now considered Egyptian. The US hoped this meeting would help bog down impatient allies in protracted negotiations that would dull the march to war. The British and French saw the conference as annoying but unavoidable theatre. According to the script they were enacting, Nasser would reject international, or rather, foreign control of the Egyptian canal, and his rejection would allow them to launch an assault on behalf of the international community.

While the British government prepared to kill time, the British military prepared to invade. But the abrupt call to action had caught one of the world's largest armed forces off guard, and planners scrambled to deal with a maze of complications, including shortages of sufficiently trained paratroopers, air transport and landing-crafts, and Valiant bombers with up-to-date targeting systems, and a lack of airfields within range of the Suez Canal. The readily available British island of Cyprus did not have a harbour deep enough to accommodate an invasion fleet, so instead Malta, just over nine hundred miles away, was chosen as the launching base. Codenamed Musketeer, the assault was set for September 15 on Port Said, at the northern entrance to the Suez Canal.[21]

As the two permanent members of the UN Security Council worked to keep passions inflamed, Nasser ensured the Suez Canal, under its new management, continued to operate like a business, and as he had promised, cargo ships and oil tankers plied the hundred-mile waterway as if nothing had happened. Playing with a weak military hand, Nasser decided to gamble on a waiting game, hoping that every day of smooth sailing made reprisals less and less likely. He knew his opponents depended on the shipments. Their need played into his plan. After the initial burst of indignation, coupled with threats to recall the non-Egyptian staff and pilots, the old management calmed itself and requested all crews to remain on duty in order to keep the traffic moving. In the meantime, "long files of delighted Egyptian motorists drove down from Cairo and the cities of the delta and valley to park alongside 'their' Canal and wave handkerchiefs at passing ships," according to a *New York Times* report. "Overnight the Canal became a tourist attraction for Egyptians and a place of patriotic pilgrimage."[22] With every passing peaceful day, Eden's sense of emergency seemed less and less convincing. The would-be champion of international order and stability desperately needed a persuasive reason to disrupt the orderly flow.

On August 1, Pearson made a long, unemotional statement on foreign policy in the House in which he mentioned Suez only briefly. While acknowledging that Cairo's "sudden arbitrary move" had caused deep concern about the future use of the canal, he declined to offer anything beyond general support for the principle of international control, possibly under the aegis of the United Nations. In his response, John Diefenbaker employed the vivid metaphors and imagery that Pearson avoided. Nasser's nationalization speech, Diefenbaker charged, displayed "all the exuberance, all the flamboyance and all the threats that were common to Mussolini." The Egyptian president "has taken to himself the garb of a dictator, as did Mussolini and Hitler." In language that would have delighted the British government, he proclaimed: "If the canal is closed the danger to Britain's lifeline and to freedom's defence is fearful to contemplate." Other Conservative MPs rose to criticize Pearson for letting Great Britain down and for "adopting...a lofty attitude of distant spectators." Making an argument that could only fail to impress opponents who wanted bold, clear denunciations, Pearson pointed out that no other government had offered blanket support, either. In any crisis, he preferred to hold back from taking definitive stands too early in the game to allow maximum room to manoeuvre down the line. But this diplomatic tactic was impossible to translate with any credibility in the parliamentary arena. The diplomat merely sounded vague when he remarked, "I do not think at this time we would be helping anyone by expressing more detailed views."[23]

That evening, Pearson met with the UK High Commissioner to Canada, Archibald Nye, and expressed his support for the international conference still not officially announced. Even though Canada barely used the Suez Canal, Ottawa would be willing, Pearson said, to consider attending. Beyond this, the rest of the meeting must have disappointed the High Commissioner. Pearson would not pressure Canadian banks to freeze Egyptian holdings in the country, and he told Nye in no uncertain terms that this political problem could not be solved with military measures. "The use of force could only be effective if the whole of Egypt and not merely the Canal were occupied," Pearson argued. Nye dispatched a report of the meeting to the Commonwealth Relations Office. "While there is a general feeling among the public that Canada should back up our efforts and while the Government is not indifferent to these views," he concluded, "I think they will act with typical Canadian caution."[24] The High Commissioner knew his host country all too well.

The next day in the British House of Commons, Prime Minister Eden announced that the government was recalling reservists and ordering Royal Navy, Royal Air Force, and army units to unspecified positions in the Mediterranean, in order to strengthen, he said, "our ability to deal with any situation that may arise."[25] Having brandished one military threat, Eden offered up another, though he disguised it as diplomacy. Later that day, the UK, US, and France announced a conference to establish international control over the Suez Canal. In Cairo, the British embassy advised British expatriates to consider leaving the country.

On August 3, Queen Elizabeth issued a royal proclamation declaring, "The present state of public affairs [does] in our opinion constitute a great emergency" which would require "the protection of the interests of the Commonwealth and Empire." This assumed conjunction of interests set off alarm bells in External Affairs. Pearson complained to Norman Robertson that the proclamation's language put Canada "in an unsatisfactory and somewhat ambiguous situation." He worried that the linkage of Commonwealth and imperial interests could make matters even more difficult for the government. He instructed Robertson to make clear to the British government that the proclamation reference to a military response "does not apply in any way to Canadian forces." Whitehall duly noted Canada's alarm; one official minuted with a touch of condescension, "a soothing reply will be prepared."[26]

Yet little in the first days of August soothed Pearson's sense of foreboding. Based on leaks from contacts in the British defence establishment, Canada's chairman of the chiefs of staff, General Charles Foulkes, advised External Affairs: "It is not a case of whether military action will be taken but rather a matter of how and when." Plans for an aerial and ground assault on Egypt had been drawn up and approved, a commander appointed. The invasion force could be ready in roughly six weeks. And the general raised a spectre probably already flitting through Pearson's mind. If London took military action against Egypt, Foulkes warned, "this would provide a great temptation to the Israelites to strike at the same time and might really start a flare-up in the Middle East."[27]

The chances for that flare-up probably seemed all the more likely when Pearson read the next telegram from Eden, which stated that, in calling the international conference, London would concede no further. Shutting down any other options, the prime minister openly hoped the gathering would compel Nasser "to disgorge his loot." But his greater hope was more obvious. When presented with the conference's presumed recommendation to place the Suez Canal under international control, Eden confidently asserted, the Egyptian president "will seek in some cunning way to evade it. Our preparations are against this danger."[28]

"I could see trouble developing," Pearson later recalled. "I wasn't thinking of trouble in terms of a war in Palestine. I was thinking of trouble in terms of a grave difference of opinion between London and Washington. That always gives a Canadian nightmares." In a joint TV and radio address on August 3, President Eisenhower said he was "vastly disturbed" by Nasser's actions, and Secretary of State Dulles struck the same notes played by the British and French, declaring it "inadmissible" that one country be permitted to selfishly exploit a waterway ("the world's greatest highway," he said) internationalized by treaty. Nationalization of the canal, he charged, was not simply an economic decision but, as Nasser himself described it, "a blow" against Western imperialism, "an angry act of retaliation." Letting this seizure go unanswered would undermine the international interest. But then, without naming names, Dulles publicly and explicitly repudiated the British and French push for military retaliation, which would, he warned, contravene the spirit of the UN Charter and possibly escalate to a wider war. Instead, Dulles placed his faith in the impending international conference and the "moral forces which are bound to prevail." In the event that the conference failed, he promised his audience, especially in Congress, that the administration had made absolutely no commitments in advance.[29] Even with all the verbal camouflage, the split between Washington and London was clear.

The next morning, the Canadian ambassador in Washington, Arnold Heeney, met with the deputy undersecretary of state, Robert Murphy, who had been dispatched to London to gauge British and French resolve. After intensive discussions, Murphy returned convinced that the two governments were "deadly serious" in their willingness to use military force. Eden had said to him, "If Nasser got away with this current action, the UK would 'be just another Netherlands'" — a seemingly unforgiveable fate for that generation of Britons.[30]

Heeney heard much the same assessment and alarm when he spoke with Dulles three days later. During his short stay in London, Dulles understood that Eden and his colleagues would never accept a dictator reducing their country to the status of "a second-rate power," even if this risked nuclear war. Needing an ally in his mission to constrain other allies, Dulles regretted that Canada had not been invited to the upcoming conference in London. He asked Heeney if Ottawa could direct its "considerable Canadian influence" towards a peaceful resolution. Heeney noted later in his report to Pearson: "Your anxieties seem to coincide exactly with those of the Secretary of State." As Washington appealed to Pearson to lend a restraining hand upon London, Eden was instructing the British High Commission in Ottawa to rouse the tepid Canadians: "Do anything you can to keep them up to the mark and to get them to take a more positive attitude."[31]

Regretting Nasser's actions without condemning them, and supporting the principle of international control but not the use of military force to impose it, Pearson occupied a tenuous middle ground. Never one to miss an opportunity to embarrass the government, Diefenbaker asked him in the House whether "Canada's official stand follows that of the United Kingdom and France or that of the United States." It was not a question Pearson could answer truthfully, or rather, fully without incensing large sections of the anglophone electorate and so he replied, with calculated evasion, that there wasn't "necessarily any difference of policy" between the country's key allies. He hoped the London conference would find a way to safeguard free passage through the Suez Canal and restated in public what had already been conveyed in private to the Eden government: military force should not be used to solve the crisis. Diefenbaker, determined to make him squirm, asked yet again how Canada was supporting Britain, given the divergence with the United States. Pearson replied with more platitudes, which he himself could scarcely have believed.[32] The next day, August 7, Pearson was far more candid in Cabinet, predicting the conference would end in failure because Cairo would never yield operation of the Suez Canal to an international agency. And if the conference failed, he had no doubt that Britain would forcibly seize the canal zone. "The whole Arab world would rally in support of Egypt," Pearson predicted, "and the Commonwealth would be split as would the United Nations." Pearson's pessimism and anxiety were evident in the telegram to Norman Robertson drafted that same day: "I hope I am wrong but if not, where do we go then?" He was too experienced a diplomat to censure friends in public to no effect, noting, "We have no desire to be critical unless and until we can come up with some constructive ideas of our own."[33]

In the midst of drafting this telegram, Pearson suddenly grasped at a diplomatic straw, the only thing left to grasp, and proposed to Robertson that London consider recognizing the nationalization. This might induce Cairo to accept a "continuing committee," perhaps composed of ambassadors who would ensure that, even with Egyptian ownership and operation, the principle of complete freedom of traffic would be upheld. Robertson presented the Canadian proposal, and British officials agreed to consider it, but in private they sounded rather affronted and immediately dismissed Pearson's suggestion, as he most probably assumed they would.[34]

On the evening of August 8, Eden addressed the nation and the world via the BBC (broadcast in full across Canada on the CBC), intending to project an image of determined statesmanship. However, revealing his real objective to topple Nasser, his language was provocative, insulting, and more of a threat than an invitation to negotiate. With the conference just eight days away, with Nasser still debating whether he himself should attend, Eden framed the crisis as a confrontation between a dictator and democracy. He referred to Nasser as "colonel" rather than "president" and indicted him as a thief who, "for his own ends," would "snatch and grab and try to pocket what really belongs to the world." Urging his country to view the challenge of 1956 through the prism of the 1930s, Eden intoned, "We all know that this is how fascist governments operate and we all remember only too well what the consequences can be in giving into fascism." Invoking his legacy as the heroic anti-appeaser, the prime minister made it clear he would not give in to the current threat emanating from the military regime in Cairo, declaring in stark, undiplomatic language: "This is a matter of life and death for us all." In jarring contrast to the dominant tone of his address, Eden concluded: "We do not seek a solution by force but by the broadest possible international agreement."[35]

Pearson seemed to take some comfort, or perhaps just said he did, from Eden's speech. Not wanting to antagonize an ally under great stress, he cabled Robertson, "It would probably be best not to say anything more formally to the Foreign Office at this time about our apprehensions." In this tactical retreat, he simply asked the High Commissioner to convey "our relief at the improved atmosphere" and with Eden's stated goal to seek a peaceful solution. Robertson quickly followed up on these instructions and, perhaps, exceeded them informally. When Douglas-Home asked him if Canada would support Britain's using force, Robertson replied that Ottawa had not dispatched formal instructions but "felt the answer would be 'no.'"[36]

When Eden learned what Robertson had said, he wanted this taken up with Pearson. "It is far worse than anything the United States Government has ever said," he fumed. After drafting a telegram to the High Commission in Ottawa, Douglas-Home, no doubt foreseeing the probable unpleasant response from Canada, argued it should not be sent at all. Eden conceded the point, saying, "Very well we will not follow up. But I see no advantage in asking Robertson his opinion any more." Eden's sense of betrayal and dismay had seeped beyond the prime minister's office. In his diary, Harold Macmillan complained, "The Canadians are very wet."[37] Unfortunately for Eden, it wasn't just the Canadians who were letting the side down.

By early August, the Labour Party began backing away from its initial support. Letters to *The Times* indicated a shift in public opinion. "The first fine careless rapture in the press has almost entirely died away," William Clark, the prime minister's press secretary noted, privately, "and the weasels are at work asking why we should be so bold." The public was getting on with its summer holidays and, as Conservative Party chairman Oliver Poole shrewdly understood, clinging to irreconcilable hopes: "The majority of people in this country want the best of both worlds. They want negotiations with Nasser to end in a diplomatic victory for this country with as much loss of face to Nasser as possible . . . and at the same time they are unwilling to take the final step of military intervention, particularly if this is to be done by Great Britain on her own." Eden had to grapple with ever-shifting delays to the invasion date, changes in the landing site from Port Said to Alexandria and then eventually back to Port Said, military planners trying to work out how to bomb Egypt by air and sea with minimal civilian casualties but with enough force to win the match, and Cabinet members, so staunch at the outset, visibly beginning to lose their nerve. Walter Monckton, the minister of defence, declared his doubts and moral qualms in a "painful and rather disturbing" outburst in Cabinet and was gracefully shuffled to a lesser post. First Sea Lord Louis Mountbatten had to be talked out of resigning. At times, the stress on Eden was all too evident. One private secretary working at the prime minister's country retreat endured, according to Clark, "terrible tantrums over the weekend with [the PS] slamming the door and [the] PM bouncing out of bed to shout at him."[38]

And there was still all the diplomacy to deal with.

On August 16, exactly three weeks after the nationalization, representatives from twenty-two nations gathered in London. In Egypt's absence, two approaches were put forward. Not unlike what Pearson had suggested to Britain in private, the USSR, Indonesia, Ceylon, and India proposed that Egypt continue to own and operate the canal company in consultation with an association of user nations. John Foster Dulles proposed that an international authority should operate the waterway, reserving a seat on the board for Egypt. Eighteen nations endorsed this plan and chose Australian prime minister Robert Menzies to lead a delegation to convey the statement of views to Nasser in Cairo.

Pearson informed his Cabinet colleagues that he and Prime Minister St. Laurent had decided to endorse the eighteen-power proposal, even though, he conceded, Nasser was unlikely to accept it. Despite his faint hopes, and revealing just how cut off he was from British thinking, Pearson's earlier pessimism had dissipated, and he told the Cabinet that he "doubted if really serious trouble would occur."[39]

Speaking at a press conference the next day, he praised the proposal and urged Nasser to accept the invitation to talk. The Suez Canal, he said, should be run without any political interference, for the benefit of all trading nations. Then in language that would not please London, he also took care to acknowledge the legitimate "desire of Egypt to safeguard its sovereignty and its national dignity." And in another direct rebuff

to British and French assumptions, Pearson stated that, in the upcoming negotiations, "there is no take it or leave it attitude, no question of
imposing something." Foreshadowing what was to come over the next
two months, the *Globe and Mail* speculated that Pearson might be called
in as a mediator, given that Canada barely used the canal and had not
participated in the London conference.[40]

Pearson left for Paris to attend a series of NATO meetings. En route he
stopped off in London and on September 3 met with his British counterpart, Selwyn Lloyd. It was the first time Pearson had sat down with a
member of the UK Cabinet since the crisis began, and the talk reinforced
his deepest misgivings. He found Lloyd feeling more sinned against than
sinning and seemingly baffled that London's approach had "aroused
anxieties in the minds of [its] friends." Lloyd rejected the charge of
sabre-rattling and insisted that force had only ever been contemplated as
a last resort. The economic sanctions, the naval and troop movements to
the Middle East, and the calling up of reserves were simply precautions.
And yet the foreign secretary also declared that his government still felt
"as strongly as ever that Nasser's efforts to establish control of the Suez
Canal must be defeated, and [that] they were resolved to do everything
possible to bring this about."[41]

Pearson raised with Lloyd the dismaying prospect that London and
Paris might act without taking the matter to the United Nations or without
American backing. Lloyd replied that the Americans shared the British
determination to stop Egypt, or more precisely Nasser, from running the
canal. After the meeting, Pearson dispatched a gloomy report to Ottawa.
London's handling of the crisis suffered from "a lack of imagination
and skill. . . . a lack of direction and no sureness of touch." Like Norman
Robertson's inability to influence thinking in the Commonwealth
Relations Office, Pearson failed to give Lloyd pause in the escalating
confrontation.[42] Nonetheless, the middle-power diplomat continued to
voice his preference for a diplomatic solution.

At a NATO meeting in Paris two days later, he restated the Canadian
position, adopted from the very beginning of the crisis: "We must rule
out force except as a last resort and use it only in accordance with the
principles we have accepted in the NATO Pact and the UN Charter."
His was one more voice in a prevailing chorus of alarm ignored by the

British government. But one allied voice was not so easily ignored. On the same day Pearson addressed his NATO colleagues in Paris, President Eisenhower informed a press conference in Washington that the United States remained committed to a peaceful solution to the Suez Crisis.[43] That peaceful solution seemed even more doubtful when, on September 10, Robert Menzies and his delegation left Cairo in failure. The Egyptian president declined to accept a proposal from eighteen foreign powers to yield control of the waterway that ran through Egyptian territory.

Dulles had seen this coming and, looking for any kind of roadblock, suggested setting up an association of users to run and operate the canal themselves, hiring the pilots and collecting the tolls, from ships stationed at either end of the canal, literally floating beyond the reach of the Egyptian government. Dubious, impatient, but not ready to break off completely on their own, Paris and London sensed a chance to entrap Washington in a device that could ultimately serve more forceful methods, and so agreed to sign on. Dulles saw his plan in a rather different light.

On September 12, the secretary of state met with Ambassador Arnold Heeney and did not hold back about his frustrations and disappointments. Britain and France, Dulles complained, had made little effort to find a course of action between capitulation to Nasser and the invasion of Egypt. He candidly admitted that he had devised his users association proposal as a "makeshift arrangement" intended to bog down London and Paris in more negotiation and assured Heeney that, if necessary, the US would send its tankers around the Cape of Good Hope rather than "fight our way through the Canal." Dulles's conversation with Heeney took place at about the same time that Anthony Eden was to announce the users association proposal in London. Dulles was still unsure how Eden would present the new plan. "If it was interpreted as a punitive action against Egypt, the scheme would in all likelihood fail," Dulles told Heeney. But if Eden presented the plan as a step towards negotiation, it could succeed.[44]

That afternoon, Eden stood up in the House of Commons to announce "a provisional organisation" that was, he said, "designed to meet an emergency." It became clear all too quickly that the prime minister was not making a suggestion. If Egyptian cooperation was not forthcoming, Eden warned, "Her Majesty's Government and others concerned will be free to take such further steps as seem to be required either through the United Nations, or by other means, for the assertion of their rights." For this scarcely veiled threat, Eden was cheered by the so-called Suez rebels in his party, diehard imperialists, and attacked by Opposition MPs shouting out "Deliberate provocation!" "What a peace maker!" and "You are talking about war!"[45] The effect of their sound and fury was nothing compared with the calm, measured words uttered the following day in Washington.

As worked out in advance with his allies, Dulles delivered a prepared statement to the press outlining the user association plan and then fielded the inevitable questions about having to use force if Egypt interfered with canal traffic. His answers faithfully reflected what he had told Heeney the day before. The proposal was in no way meant to be an enforcement mechanism, and if the Egyptians offered any kind of resistance, Dulles said, American ships would avoid the Suez Canal and instead sail around the Cape of Good Hope. He ended the press conference by saying, "The United States did not intend itself to try to shoot its way through the canal."[46] Dulles had done what he felt he must. In London and Paris, his statements were felt like a stab in the back.

Even before this all came to pass, Pearson, still in Paris at a NATO meeting, had privately dismissed the plan as ill conceived and unworkable. It would fail even as a makeshift device, as he noted in one memo, because the proposal required Egypt's technical assistance, and far more importantly, Egypt's consent to succeed, which he judged extremely unlikely. Pearson outlined, with striking accuracy, the overarching factor complicating the proposal's already slim chance for success:

> There is, I think, a real danger of a split developing between the USA and the British and French on the presentation and the application of the new proposal. Mr. Dulles, for instance, may think that Eden has put it forward in too forceful a way in London. The USA Government may be able to divert American shipping around the Cape if there is trouble — as Dulles proposes — but that may well be interpreted over here as a weakening of a scheme of which he was the main author, with the British and French left to deal with Egyptian obstruction by other and more positive means.[47]

When he looked beyond this makeshift scheme, he saw little but disaster ahead. "What is the next move?" he asked, fearing the answer. "Force, without USA support or approval?" There remained one move that Pearson wanted to see, going to the UN—the same move that London had put off for as long as possible.[48]

That move had hung over the British government from the very beginning of the crisis, most acutely for Anthony Eden, who was palpably reluctant to debate the canal company nationalization at the world assembly he helped to create and where Britain sat as a permanent member on a Security Council pledged to help maintain international peace and order. "Moderate opinion at home and abroad would be outraged if we were to attack Egypt without having made some gesture towards the UN," Selwyn Lloyd cautioned in a memo weighing the move. "Our choice," he stated, "is a choice of evils. To go to the Security Council is full of risks; not to do so would be certain to have consequences of the greatest gravity."[49]

Anxious to accommodate the shifting military timetable, London and Paris agreed they could no longer avoid the diplomatic detour and, on September 23, requested the Security Council to inscribe the Suez question on the agenda for debate in October. Even framing the question was fraught with contradictory objectives. London and Paris wanted to put Nasser on trial. Washington, not to mention Ottawa, wanted conciliation. Cairo wanted exoneration and to see the former colonial powers compelled to retreat. Moscow wanted to see maximum discord in the Western alliance.

Approaching the debate, Pearson received troubling reports from Robert MacKay, head of Canada's permanent mission at the UN, describing the diplomatic landscape awaiting the contenders. The African and Asian members saw Nasser as a heroic underdog daring to stand up to powerful "white imperialists." On the other side of the divide, MacKay warned Pearson, Anglo-French assumptions were hopelessly out of touch, too provocative, obsessed with "the idea that Egypt is to be 'hauled into court.'" One member of the Australian mission, MacKay reported, had even bragged that the upcoming debate was going to be a "bashing session," with Egypt as "the intended victim," and that the British UN mission had been urging allies on the Security Council to "go in with flags flying." MacKay's telegrams prepared Pearson for the worst, and he was likely entirely in sync with his minister's mindset when he wrote: "France and the UK, but particularly the latter, seem bent on humiliating Nasser and perhaps showing the helplessness of the Security Council in this matter."[50] A helpless UN would, of course, provide the excuse needed to bash Nasser into submission.

In parallel fashion, Canada continued to dismay Britain. One High Commission official in Ottawa conjured up a potentially distressing spectacle: "I think that Canadian officials... have an idea that the time may come when Canada could play a mediator's role, and that there is some danger that, in order to do so, they take up an attitude of neutrality as between ourselves and the Egyptians. This will not, of course, matter so far as the Security Council debate is concerned, but there is of course the [General] Assembly to follow."[51]

And that is exactly what came to pass.

ELEVEN

In Sorrow and Anger

> How do we act if Nasser refuses and on what "pretext" or on what "principle" can we base a *casus belli*. How do we get from the Conference leg to the use of force? British opinion is uncertain.... Yet, if Nasser 'gets away with it,' we are done for. The whole Arab world will despise us.... It may well be the end of British influence and strength forever. So, in the last resort, we must use force and defy opinion, here and overseas.
>
> —Chancellor of the Exchequer Harold Macmillan,
> August 18, 1956 diary entry[1]

On October 5, ten weeks after the military dictatorship in Egypt nationalized the Suez Canal Company, envoys from the three countries most concerned finally gathered face to face at the Security Council—not to negotiate a settlement but to see if they could even agree on a framework to begin negotiations. After all, they desired incompatible outcomes. Egyptian foreign minister Mahmoud Fawzi insisted that the Suez Canal be shielded from foreign interference. British foreign secretary Selwyn Lloyd and French foreign minister Christian Pineau demanded that it be protected from the unilateral control of any one country. Their show of diplomacy was qualified by their thinly veiled desire to overthrow Gamal Abdel Nasser and complicated by the Egyptian president's shrewd tactical response in ensuring that all canal traffic continued to flow peacefully between the Mediterranean and the Red Sea. One British official summed up his country's dilemma to a reporter: "We would like to be beastly to Nasser, but we haven't figured out a sensible way to do it."[2]

Watching from Ottawa, Lester Pearson knew full well the British and French had come to the Security Council with the greatest reluctance, and very late in the game. Just days before the session was due to open, Canada's High Commissioner to the UK, Norman Robertson, reported from London a "short and troubled" talk with Lloyd, who "said that he himself was as ready to bash the Egyptians as anybody but he had to ask himself where this country and the Commonwealth would stand after the job of bashing had been done." Small wonder that at the outset Pearson feared little more would emerge beyond a Security Council resolution that pleased no one followed by "a period of fruitless negotiation" leading to a debate in the General Assembly.[3]

After the predictable posturing in the Security Council, the three antagonists met for private talks presided over by the Secretary-General Dag Hammarskjöld. In this more intimate setting, perhaps admitting to himself that the moment for a military strike may have passed, Lloyd appeared to make a credible effort to shape a compromise. Despite stubborn interference from his French ally, he secured agreement with Fawzi on a tentative set of principles centring on free and open transit insulated from politics, fairly negotiated tolls, and the creation of a mechanism for resolving disputes between users and the operator. The hard question of who would ultimately operate the Suez Canal was left hanging, but the three foreign ministers agreeing on this much was no small feat. On October 13, the Security Council unanimously endorsed this glimmer of peace. In the final weeks of his re-election campaign, Dwight Eisenhower expressed delight at the apparent return of sense to his unruly allies. Even Anthony Eden seemed to think that a basis for future discussions had been established.[4] On October 14, he cabled Lloyd suggesting they approach Egypt to resume talks in Geneva.

In the wake of the talks, Canada's UN ambassador, Robert MacKay, reported from New York that a senior member of the British mission had advised him not to draw any optimistic conclusions, as "the parties were far apart on questions of method." Still, Pearson chose to echo the sense of relief rather than reinforce the doubts, and told his Cabinet colleagues that the Suez Crisis seemed to be calming down. His optimism proved premature.[5]

(Clockwise from bottom left) Anthony Eden, UK foreign secretary
Selwyn Lloyd, Lester Pearson, Louis St. Laurent, February 1956, Ottawa
(City of Ottawa Archives/ MG393/ CA036737/ Newton)

On October 26, Pearson learned that Hammarskjöld had been trying
to resume the peace process, but London was holding back because
Egyptian counter-offers were deemed "somewhat obscure." Worse,
an official at the High Commission in Ottawa told Pearson that the
secretary-general's efforts would come to nothing.[6] Escalating tension
between Jordan and Israel inevitably amplified tension surrounding the
Suez Canal. Through September and October, both sides inflicted savage
cross-border raids against each other, killing civilians, including children,

and leading an anxious Jordan to ask Iraq for reinforcements, which in turn raised the alarming prospect that Britain might get pulled in to protect them from Israel.

While allies and opponents worried over France and Britain's defence of honour, influence, and oil in the Middle East, another, far more brutal sphere of imperial interest drew international attention. On October 23, thousands of students assembled in the streets of Budapest and dared to call for the basic political freedoms denied them in a Communist state. Faced with the prospect of its own extinction, having noted that shooting their people in broad daylight did not crush the hunger for freedom, the Hungarian government appealed to Moscow, which unleashed troops and tanks to restore submission. On October 28, Security Council members convened to praise and condemn the revolt, which would have dominated the proceedings if other events had not come into play.

On the morning of October 29, the US ambassador to Canada, Livingston Merchant, met with Pearson, looking for answers. Washington, he said, felt cut off from British thinking over Suez and could not understand why London showed no interest in resuming talks with Cairo. Feeling equally cut off, Pearson offered to have Norman Robertson informally root around Whitehall for anything that might shed some light and ease anxieties.[7] The much-vaunted role of North Atlantic go-between was suddenly more fact than fiction.

At roughly the same time as Pearson was being asked about British thinking in the Middle East, the aftermath of that thinking was about to convulse the region. After a ninety-minute flight at low altitude to avoid radar detection, sixteen Dakota transport planes reached a mountain range in the southwestern Sinai Peninsula, deep inside Egyptian territory. At 4:59 p.m. local time, 395 Israeli paratroopers began dropping down to the eastern approach of the Mitla Pass, some thirty miles to the east of the Suez Canal. Transports returned to drop jeeps, mortars, guns, and ammunition. That same day, at three other points, Israeli ground forces backed by armoured units rumbled across the border into the Sinai. The first reports of this assault baffled the Egyptian military command. "Something very strange is happening," Nasser reportedly told a confidant. "The Israelis are in Sinai and they seem to be fighting the sands, because they are occupying one empty position after another."[8]

Some thought the enemy was making a feint to divert attention from a coming attack on Jordan or the Gaza Strip. Whatever the obscure Israeli objective, Egyptian forces engaged the enemy.

It took some eight hours for the news to reach North America. Pearson later said that, at first, he had been relieved the Israelis had not attacked Jordan, which could very well have pushed Britain to rally to its ally's defence. External Affairs was compelled to respond quickly to the one issue directly affecting Canada. In late September, Cabinet had approved the sale of twenty-four F-86 Sabre jets to Israel, to be shipped in small batches, starting in a few weeks. On the day of the Israeli attack, the department released a brief statement saying that shipment was now under review.[9] Beyond this, no one had reason to think Canada would become further involved in the distant battle.

> If the only alternative is to allow Nasser's plans quietly to develop until this country and all Western Europe are held to ransom by Egypt acting at Russia's behest, it seems to us that our duty is plain. We have many times led Europe in the fight for freedom. It would be an ignoble end to our long history if we accepted to perish by degrees.
> —Anthony Eden, September 6, 1956[10]

For a few moments on the morning of Tuesday, October 30, the diplomatic world still made sense. The Security Council convened at 11 a.m. and the US ambassador, Henry Cabot Lodge, called on Israel to cease all military action in Egypt and withdraw its forces. In a rare instance of agreement, Soviet ambassador Arkady Sobolev supported the American call for peace. In more customary fashion, he then attacked Western intentions, asserting that Israel would not make such a risky move without the encouragement of certain nations looking for an excuse to move their own troops into Egypt. Switching to English, Sobolev read a news wire report of a statement Anthony Eden had just made at Westminster. The contents stunned the room.

According to the report, the governments of Great Britain and France had issued an ultimatum to Egypt and Israel, demanding that their troops lay down their weapons and withdraw ten miles from the Suez

Canal. If this was not done within the next twelve hours, Eden warned, an Anglo-French force would force compliance. It was clear that Eden was not asking for permission from the UN to make peace in Egypt. The British mission, appalled by the position it had been thrust into without warning, requested and received an adjournment of the Security Council until later in the afternoon so instructions could be received from London.

Within the same time frame, Pearson received word in Ottawa of the British-French ultimatum from Norman Robertson, who had quite possibly watched Eden deliver it in the House of Commons in London.[11] Thus, like every other member of the UN, NATO, and the Commonwealth, the Canadian foreign minister learned about a major decision taken by two key allies before any official communication had been delivered in advance through the proper diplomatic channels. That decision became all the more troubling once the implications of Eden's ultimatum began to register.

The compliance demanded was breathtaking in its bias: London and Paris had ordered the Egyptians to stop defending themselves from a large-scale assault. If Israel complied and withdrew its forces ten miles from the Suez Canal, they would remain deep inside Egyptian territory. If Egypt complied but Israel did not, the Anglo-French force would still land to impose a ceasefire. There was no mention of London and Paris coordinating the ultimatum with the United States or of working through the United Nations.

In a diplomatic career marked by the dismaying decisions and actions inflicted by close allies without warning, this moment had few equals. Pearson did not wait to shape a formal reply. He immediately asked Robertson to convey Ottawa's "grave anxieties" to London, although he undoubtedly expected his words would, once again, have no effect; all summer and fall, his advice on the crisis had been politely noted and pointedly ignored. In his phone call with the High Commissioner, Pearson perceptively highlighted Sobolev's accusation that the British and French were using the Israeli attack for ulterior motives and acknowledged that he too suspected they had been "cooking this up in their recent conversations." That same day, he dispatched a telegram to the Canadian embassy in Paris asking for any information about French attitudes regarding the Israeli attack, writing: "I have an uneasy feeling that there is something going on between the French and the Israeli governments which the French have not bothered to tell us."[12] Pearson was not alone in his suspicions that the Israeli invasion seemed far too convenient. In this instance, the conspiracy theorists were absolutely right.

Two weeks before, on October 14, Anthony Eden spent the weekend at Chequers, the prime ministerial country retreat. He had just sent a cable to Selwyn Lloyd at the UN suggesting that talks with Cairo resume in Geneva. Here was the recognizable, veteran diplomat pragmatically inclined to accept a compromise. Then, within hours of sending this message to New York, Eden embarked upon the most controversial decision of his career, one that effectively renounced the possibility of a peaceful resolution to the Suez Crisis. On that Sunday in the country, Guy Millard, a private secretary, and Anthony Nutting, the minister of state for foreign affairs, joined the prime minister. At 3 p.m. Eden welcomed two last-minute guests from France, the minister for social affairs, Albert Gazier, and General Maurice Challe. Only a handful of people in either capital knew this meeting was taking place.

Once the pleasantries were over, Eden turned to Millard and said, "There's no need to take notes, Guy."[13] The French emissaries then outlined the plan to provide Eden with the pretext that would allow him to place the Suez Canal under international control and overthrow his nemesis: Israel would invade Egypt and incite a small war, and British and French troops would intervene as peacemakers to separate the combatants. Back on Egyptian soil, they could secure the waterway physically and, regardless of what the Egyptian government might have to say on the subject, secure it politically.

Eden was visibly intrigued. Nutting was horrified. The counter-arguments were many. Britain's historic allies in the Middle East were Arab states. Collusion—a word that has since lost its stench but then was politically toxic—and collusion with Israel no less, could wreak havoc on the fragile web of alliances. Iraq's prime minister, Nuri al-Said, had stressed on several occasions not to get involved with Israel in order to deal with Egypt. Collusion would entail deceiving the US, Britain's essential ally, on a policy it strongly opposed, and it would blatantly violate the terms of the 1950 Tripartite Declaration, in which Britain, the US, and

France pledged to control the arms race in the region and defend Israel or Arab states from invasion. Yet, according to Nutting, Eden promptly "made up his mind to go along with the French plan." In his account of the crisis, he asked with evident anguish: "How and why was this mortal decision arrived at? And how and why did the man, whose whole political career had been founded on his genius for negotiation, act so wildly out of character?"[14]

Eden had his reasons. Seeing a dictator he did not trust seize control of the world's most important waterway genuinely appalled him. He was determined not to repeat the sins of the 1930s, and he was deeply concerned that the Soviet Union, already supplying Egypt with weapons, might achieve dominance over Britain's last sphere of influence and source of oil. Eden knew the Americans wanted Nasser gone, even if they refused to lend a military hand. He was feeling intense pressure from France to move before all was lost, and he had already made a public show of mobilizing British troops and ships into the region. Finally, he had framed the confrontation in very personal terms and thus had staked his reputation and possibly his political survival on standing firm. And then there was his drug intake.

Perhaps all of this unfolded as it did because three years before, a nervous surgeon dropped a scalpel during surgery. In April 1953, Eden underwent a gallbladder operation. Harassed over several weeks by a meddling but genuinely concerned Prime Minister Churchill, the surgeon became so flustered by the prospect of operating on such an illustrious patient that he needed an hour "to compose his nerves" before starting to operate. Then he punctured Eden's bile duct, nearly killing him. The assistant surgeon had to complete the procedure. Two weeks later, the follow-up operation, as biographer D.R. Thorpe writes, "proved even more tense than the first, and Eden was within a whisker of death at several stages." To patch up this mess, Eden went through a third operation in which the surgeon gave him a fifty-fifty chance of dying on the operating table. Lucky to have survived all three ordeals, Eden's health was permanently compromised. His principal private secretary from 1951 to 1954, Evelyn Shuckburgh, wrote that Eden "was constantly having troubles with his insides. We used to carry around with us a black tin box containing various forms of analgesic supplied by his doctor, ranging from simple aspirins to morphia injections, and we dealt them out to him according to the degree of his suffering."[15]

Six decades later, analyzing how Eden's health affected his decision-making abilities during the Suez Crisis, David Owen, a medical doctor and a former foreign secretary, discovered a letter from one of Eden's physicians revealing that throughout 1956 the prime minister often took an amphetamine tablet in the morning. This drug can produce a sense of "overconfidence and euphoria," as well as side effects such as sleeplessness, restlessness, and nervousness. Eden also took painkillers and sleeping pills. The drugs, Owen concedes, probably did not affect the essence of Eden's Suez policy, which was founded on entirely predictable and defensible factors, but they did impair his "judgement and decisions"—that is, his conduct of policy—and made him "more changeable and unpredictable from one day to another, depending on whether he was under greater influence of their stimulant or their sedative actions." Afterwards, some colleagues remarked on this already high-strung man seeming even more so, conducting Cabinet meetings in a "fairly restless fashion," according to Alec Douglas-Home; appearing "very jumpy, very nervy, very wrought" to the senior official in the Ministry of Defence; and acting "during the final days like a prophet inspired," in the opinion of Air Chief Marshall William Dickson, "carrying all by his exaltation."[16]

Pearson was already familiar with Eden's finely tuned temperament. In early November, he was apprised of a confidential talk between an official at the Canadian High Commission and a contact at the Foreign Office who described Eden as "highly emotional," "highly worried and uncertain," and even "neurotic." The report also cited senior officials in other departments who described the prime minister as "wrought up" and "difficult." In his memoirs, Pearson would only venture to write, "No doubt many a battle has been lost because the General had a bad night and a worse breakfast. The Suez operation demanded strong, vigorous health and this Mr. Eden did not have."[17]

During the crisis, sheer exhaustion likely also affected Eden's judgments and decisions. Just before he took the fateful decision to work (or conspire) with the French and Israelis, he collapsed from a debilitating fever and spent a weekend in hospital, returning to work still drained. The following weekend he met with the French at Chequers, "more susceptible to the simple attractions of the French plan," David Dutton argues, "and less conscious of its equally obvious drawbacks than he would otherwise have been."[18] And while some historians have portrayed the plan as unthinkable, it would have sounded familiar to Eden, regardless of his health, because it had been tossed around informally for years.

In December 1951, then Foreign Secretary Eden was discussing his travails over Egypt when Winston Churchill suddenly growled, "Tell them that if we have any more of their cheek we will set the Jews on them." In January 1954, still incensed, Churchill mused about joining with Israel to invade Egypt and seize the canal. In November of 1955, one of Eden's key advisers on the Middle East, Evelyn Shuckburgh, pondered two options that might resolve various matters: "the death of Nasser [or] a free hand to the Israelis." At the end of July 1956, during planning sessions for the assault on Egypt, military officials suggested they might need to use the Israelis in some capacity, and in early August, Harold Macmillan presented a memorandum to the Egypt Committee, the inner Cabinet dealing with Suez, arguing that Britain "*must* make use of Israel against Egypt." Eden rejected the idea when he heard it, but when the French foreign minister, Christian Pineau, raised the possibility, Eden "reputedly responded in a flaccid tone that he was not opposed to this provided Israel did not attack Jordan."[19] So by mid-October, when Eden met with the French, it was hardly a novel proposition. And however much exhaustion, illness, and pills may have blurred Eden's judgment, he still managed to convince healthy Cabinet ministers, Lloyd (initially skeptical if not hostile to the idea) and Macmillan among them, to accept this pretext in the defence of the realm.

Over October 22-24, the scheme was discussed in detail and in utmost secrecy at a villa in the French town of Sèvres, just outside Paris. The French premier, Guy Mollet, and his foreign minister, Pineau, were in attendance, as was the Israeli prime minister, Ben-Gurion, but not the person most in need of an excuse to invade Egypt. The discovery that he was working with Israel to attack an Arab country would have finished Eden, so he sent the ever-loyal Lloyd, "a sacrificial lamb," as D. R. Thorpe has observed, "expendable no doubt if things turned nasty." Straightforward and decent, Lloyd accepted the premise but could only bring himself to attend one session and looked to the Israelis as though he was engaging in something so sordid that he wanted to wash it off as soon as possible.[20] To Eden's later horror, the agreement was put down in writing and signed by representatives of all three governments, the British signature coming from a senior official in the Foreign Office.

To the end of their days, Eden and Lloyd denied that they had conspired to do anything in advance. The most they would ever admit was that they had discussed potential reactions to possible events. Their denials were not persuasive. Eden's last appearance in the House of Commons, in December 1956, saw him trying to refute the charge that his government had "engaged in some dishonourable conspiracy." This, he said, was "completely untrue, and I most emphatically deny it." He was pummelled that day, and tragically for someone who had served his country honourably for decades, in war and in peace, his very last words spoken in Parliament were far from the truth. "I want to say this on the question of foreknowledge, and to say it quite bluntly to the House, that there was not foreknowledge that Israel would attack Egypt—there was not," Eden stated. "But there was something else. There was—we knew it perfectly well—a risk of it, and in the event of the risk of it certain discussions and conversations took place, as, I think, was absolutely right, and as, I think, anybody would do."[21] Only the diehards would have agreed or believed.

Fifteen days after Eden's conversation at Chequers, less than a week after the meeting at Sèvres, the Israeli government kept its end of the bargain and sent forces into the Sinai. This large-scale assault provided Israel with the chance to destroy Soviet equipment in Egyptian hands, to eradicate *fedayeen* bases in Gaza used to launch deadly cross-border raids, and to break the Egyptian blockade at the southeastern edge of the Sinai Peninsula and allow Israeli shipping back through the Straits of Tiran, into the Gulf of Aqaba, and up to the Israeli port of Eilat. Israel had another reason for taking on the unpalatable role of aggressor. When informed of this high-stakes plan, Ben-Gurion replied: "This is the birth of the first serious alliance between us and a western power. We can't not accept it."[22] He did not trust Britain, bound by treaty and self-interest to defend Israel's hostile neighbours Jordan and Iraq, but he was determined to strengthen the critical relationship with France, which was already supplying the country with Mystere fighter jets, AMX and Sherman tanks, and artillery, and would eventually share nuclear secrets. Even before the fall of 1956, Israel and France concluded they shared the same enemies—pan-Arabism, Nasser, Algerian rebels—and were willing to endure international condemnation for using force to defend themselves.

October 30, the day after the Israeli invasion, the day Eden announced the ultimatum, Lester Pearson still worked only from the sidelines of the bewildering crisis. At 3 p.m. he spoke on the phone with a "greatly concerned" John Foster Dulles, who described the ultimatum "as brutal as anything he had seen." Pearson dismissed it as stupid. Both men noted their suspicions of collusion. And the timing, Dulles observed, was terrible. Just when the West was condemning the Soviet Union for trying to crush democratic forces in Hungary, he said, "We come along with action as bad or worse." Pearson could only concur with his counterpart, and after their talk he remarked that Dulles had spoken "in a state of emotion and depression greater than anything I have seen before in him." In a cable to Norman Robertson, Pearson reiterated the need to convey to the British government Ottawa's "feeling of bewilderment and dismay." The great nightmare of Canadian foreign policy—a serious break between London and Washington—was now erupting in full view of enemies and allies. He ended his dispatch stating: "There is nothing but pessimism around here."[23]

The mood in External Affairs must have darkened even more when at 5 p.m. Louis St. Laurent received a cable from Anthony Eden laying out the official justification for the ultimatum, which he had learned of only from a wire report. "Needless to say," Pearson noted dryly in his memoirs, "he was not very pleased about the state of Commonwealth consultations."[24] Now, at the end of an appalling day, St. Laurent was confronted with a palpable lie.

Endeavouring to appear surprised by the turn of events, Eden claimed his government was anxious and committed to ending the fighting and protecting the Suez Canal and would eventually raise the matter at the United Nations. Each word carefully weighed, the telegram stated that Britain presumed it could at least "look for," rather than "expect," Canada's support and understanding. "Clearly there are risks in intervention," Eden's telegram concluded "But the risks of hesitation and delay are in our judgment greater." When he finished reading Eden's telegram, a "still simmering" St. Laurent threw it on his desk, writes Terence Robertson, and "then exploded he was so mad." The prime minister summoned Pearson. "I'd never seen him in such a state of controlled anger," Pearson later recalled. "He was shocked, as he had every right to be shocked, and so was I."[25]

That initial shock did not obscure tactical imperatives. Pearson knew his country's focal point in the escalating crisis. "Our immediate problem was to let Mr. Eden know that he couldn't count on our support automatically," he noted. "This wasn't a situation of 'ready-aye-ready.' And this telegram had to be answered at once, clear up that point."[26] But while he would not blindly follow the old flag, neither did he wish to condemn publicly two NATO allies, no matter how disturbing their actions. Underlying his impulses and actions to safeguard Canadian sovereignty lay parallel, fundamental objectives to shield the Western alliance. In this instance, that meant encouraging and even facilitating the British and French to stand down with as little humiliation as possible and, of course, to repair the breach between London and Washington.

Seeing that St. Laurent was "prepared to send a pretty vigorous answer," Pearson asked for time to work on his own draft, and the prime minister took the sensible advice. Crafting an official response that balanced disagreement and disappointment without offending wide sections of the country would be no easy task. Later that evening, a visibly distressed Pearson confided to Ambassador Merchant the difficulty he faced in discouraging St. Laurent from "criticizing [the] Franco-British move against Suez in immoderate terms."[27]

That afternoon in New York, the Security Council reconvened to debate the Israeli attack and the disturbing British-French threat to intervene. Although Eden had promised Ottawa that he would raise the whole issue at the UN "in the most appropriate way," what unfolded stunned the international community. Henry Cabot Lodge introduced a resolution calling on Israel to cease fighting and go home. When called to vote, the Security Council's representatives, seated around the horseshoe-shaped table, raised their hands in the air to be counted. In another display of agreement, the USSR voted to support the American resolution. China and the council's non-permanent members, Cuba, Iran, Peru, and Yugoslavia, also voted in favour, while Australia and Belgium abstained.

Even though their governments had publicly ordered the Egyptians and Israelis to cease hostilities, in effect mirroring the American resolution, Britain and France vetoed this call for peace. A junior member of the British mission and a future foreign secretary, Douglas Hurd, could hear "a gasp in the public gallery as the British and French raised their hands against the American resolution."[28] This was the first time Great Britain had wielded the loathed veto.

Making the most of an open wound, the Soviet ambassador amended the defeated resolution and resubmitted it. Late in the evening, Britain and France again vetoed a Security Council resolution calling for a cessation of hostilities—an abysmal spectacle for Britain's friends and a severe ordeal for members of the British mission. First Secretary Peter Ramsbotham could feel the dramatic fall from grace. "Up to then, the only country which ever used the veto was the Russians," he later said. "We never had to nor the Americans because we had these big majorities. There we were, confronted with a situation which we never had before." In retrospect, he concluded, "it was probably good for our souls because up to then we had been rather smug. We were the people who ran the place. We half invented the United Nations."[29]

In Ottawa, Pearson very consciously tried to avoid taking a firm stance on either side of the growing divide. At about 6 p.m. he walked into a hastily convened, packed meeting with the parliamentary press gallery. Many of the members were his admirers and even partisans, some of whom he had known since he was an obscure junior diplomat in London in the 1930s. Over the decades he shared insights and leaked information, off and on the record, to promote his career as well as the government's agenda, and also, genuinely important for him, to sustain an informed populace. This would be one of the most difficult sessions of his career, and he could not pretend otherwise. He had to convey displeasure with his allies without condemning them. He had to indicate disagreement with London without angering those Canadians who supported it. He needed to let those Canadians who were incensed by Britain that he shared their dismay. The *Vancouver Sun* reported that he looked "obviously ill at ease." The *Calgary Herald* confirmed the impression. "Pearson was nervous, jumpy, more harassed than veteran reporters had ever seen him," the paper reported, noting that he was "quite evidently anguished at the major split between Canada's major Allies."[30]

When asked whether he had comfort or anxiety to report, Pearson replied with disarming frankness, "Mostly anxiety." With every carefully chosen word, he tried to blunt edges while acknowledging grave reservations. "I'll go this far," he began. "I regret—as do all others—that Britain and France found it necessary to take this action while the UN Security Council was discussing this matter." He did not venture beyond this fairly mild reproach but revealed that Ottawa had told Paris and London it preferred and hoped the matter would be solved without the use of force. He admitted with "ill-concealed annoyance" that Ottawa had not been consulted, and he tried to make allowances, saying the speed of events made consultation difficult. Reporters asked him about the delayed sale of Canadian-made Sabre jets to Israel and wondered whether the Israeli attack was the kind of action the jets might be used for in the future. Pearson "gulped twice, smiled broadly and replied he 'wouldn't attempt to answer' that question."[31]

At the end of the press conference, several journalists gathered around him to confirm their interpretation of certain remarks as a criticism of Britain. He strongly denied it and asked them not to frame his comments in that light. But he was fighting a losing battle on that point and in the end only reinforced existing positions, reflected in the next day's press coverage, which ranged from approval to accusations of betrayal and acting like a lap dog to Washington. The *Calgary Herald* proclaimed, "Canada stands with the United Nations, not Britain." The *Vancouver Sun* railed, "Canada Not Backing U.K."

Later that evening, at 10:30 p.m., Pearson appeared on the CBC TV public affairs show *Press Conference*. He explained to his divided country that while Canada strongly disagreed with Britain and France, it did not condemn their actions, not even their unprecedented use of the veto. He refused to comment on whether Israel's assault constituted an act of aggression, saying, "I am satisfied in my own mind Israel has suffered a great deal of provocation over the years from her neighbours." He also avoided speculating whether or not Britain and France had colluded with the attack. Despite intense pressure from the interview panel, he refused to take a definitive stance and suggested more time was needed to understand what was going on.[32]

At 11:30 p.m., by which time Pearson had likely left the TV studio and was heading home, the twelve-hour British-French ultimatum ran out. In Cairo earlier that evening, President Nasser informed the British ambassador that Egypt rejected the foreign demand to stop defending itself. This was exactly what Britain and France needed to hear.

On the afternoon of October 31, Eden rose before a skeptical, angry Opposition to defend his unilateral threat to intervene in the Sinai, where, he claimed, Israeli forces were converging on the Suez Canal. He presented himself as a leader unwilling to rely on a dithering world organization to defend the peace. "Can anyone say that we and the French Government should have waited for a satisfactory resolution by the Security Council authorising definite action to stop the fighting?" he asked defiantly. Eden laid the blame squarely on the victim of aggression. "There is no Middle Eastern problem at present which could not have been settled or bettered but for the hostile and irresponsible policies of Egypt," he insisted.[33]

Unconvinced by these arguments, mindful that the government's ultimatum had already expired, the Opposition wanted to know if British troops had landed and were engaged in combat with Egyptian forces. Eden declined to give a direct answer of any kind. Labour leader Hugh Gaitskell abandoned his early support for tough words and tougher action and now criticized Eden for wrecking the basis of the country's postwar foreign policy. Citing one example that a defensive Ottawa would not have appreciated, he noted that the Canadian government, through Lester Pearson, had "expressed in the coldest possible language their regret at the situation which has arisen. They have also made it plain," he pointed out, "they were not consulted in advance before this ultimatum was sent." Gaitskell then went after the most vulnerable point in the government's position and referred to a *Washington Post* article that claimed Britain, France, and Israel had conspired to arrange the assault. Taking up the reply, Selwyn Lloyd dutifully kept a straight face and dodged the truth. "It is quite wrong to state that Israel was incited to this action by Her

Majesty's Government," he declared. "There was no prior agreement between us about it."[34]

From Washington, Ambassador Arnold Heeney reported in a gloomy cable to Pearson on the prevailing mood in the American capital, which he summed up as "a combination of anger, disappointment and depression." Heeney cited the same *Washington Post* article, which boasted the damning headline "British, French, Israeli collusion on moves in Mid-East now seen." After talking with senior officials, Heeney wrote: "Of French collusion they seem quite convinced. The circumstantial evidence against the British has to many seemed strong but I think most would be willing to give London a day in court."[35]

In New York, the Security Council remained suspended in confusion and stalemate. Allies were no longer working together or explaining their actions to each other. Washington felt compelled to move in concert with Moscow to restrain the drive to war. To circumvent the British and French veto, Yugoslavia, with American encouragement, introduced the so-called Uniting for Peace resolution, designed to move a debate from the Security Council to the General Assembly. The British and French delegations tried to block the manoeuvre, but this was deemed a procedural motion and their veto did not apply. A General Assembly emergency session was called for the following day, November 1.

To tackle the situations in Hungary and Egypt, St. Laurent called a special Cabinet meeting for 11 a.m. Journalists and photographers thronged the corridor outside the Privy Council Chamber. "Smiling at first," St. Laurent offered up an evasive "No comment, gentlemen." When someone asked for his thoughts on Australia and New Zealand announcing support for Britain and France, his mask fell. "That is their affair," he snapped. "We have no criticism or comment to make of what other governments choose to do." He smacked down a question about Canada's supposedly undefined position with "No decision has been made yet and I'm not going to comment until a decision is made." Even an innocuous query about whether Suez would be discussed in Cabinet brought a sharp retort: "That is our business, sir. We'll deal with it in its proper order." The exasperated prime minister walked through the swinging doors that lead to the council chamber, then reappeared right away, fuming. "It's too bad you can't come inside and tell us what to do," he told the press. "But we members of the Cabinet happen to be the ones who are responsible to the Canadian Parliament and the Canadian people." With that he re-entered the Cabinet room. The press reported his bad temper in full.[36]

In Cabinet, Pearson dealt first with Canadians wanting to fight in Hungary and then turned to the Middle East. He informed his colleagues that Norman Robertson had already, albeit informally, conveyed Ottawa's dismay to London and that the American secretary of state had asked him to help repair the breach between the US and UK. St. Laurent then raised the question of the formal reply to Eden's appeal for support and understanding. The minutes do not record that any discussion took place, but some ministers were clearly anxious about Ottawa's moving in any way to criticize the Mother Country.[37]

According to one of St. Laurent's principal assistants, Minister of Finance Walter Harris cautioned that criticizing Britain "would cost the Liberals forty seats in Ontario at the next election." Public Works Minister Robert Winters voiced concern about the cost in the Atlantic provinces. St. Laurent apparently replied to his anglophone colleagues, "You're just talking with your blood."[38] But the prime minister was also talking with his own newly found heat. Just four months before, with his government mired in the interminable pipeline debate, he seemed adrift and indifferent, at some points even sitting in the House of Commons, a vacant expression on his face, reading a book. The confrontation between faded colonial powers and former vassals brought the tired leader back to life.

While Her Majesty's Government in Canada agonized over how to express its disagreement without implying criticism, its task suddenly became infinitely more difficult. Roughly fifteen minutes after Cabinet met, Canberra and Valiant bombers from the Royal Air Force began dropping bombs on military airfields around Cairo. By mistake, they hit Cairo International Airport. The Egyptian air force did not engage them but instead withdrew its Soviet jets to safe havens well beyond the capital and into Syria and Saudi Arabia. When word reached Cabinet that London was attacking a country already defending itself from an Israeli assault, there was a shocked hush in the Privy Council Chamber. Paul Martin, the health and welfare minister, was the first to speak, and then only to say that he could not believe what he was hearing.[39] Over the course of some two to three hours, the Cabinet agreed to temporarily suspend the export of F-86 Sabre jets to Israel and hold off on other arm shipments to the Middle East. Drafting the formal reply to London would be left in the hands of the St. Laurent and Pearson.

Pearson met with the UK's acting High Commissioner, Neil Pritchard, at 5:30 p.m. He planned to give Pritchard an unofficial and general preview of the pending reply to London. First, however, Pritchard relayed a message from the Commonwealth Relations Office, offering up another hollow justification for military intervention. Claiming itself trapped by Cairo's refusal to stop fighting, London declared it had "no choice in these circumstances but to proceed, though with the greatest regret, to the action to secure compliance." The British record of the meeting does not indicate a reply from Pearson on this dubious point. Instead he prepared London for more disappointment, telling Pritchard that Ottawa would not offer the support and understanding that Eden had sought.[40]

Pearson then indicated the key concerns that would be addressed in the reply: the deplorable impact on the UN and the Commonwealth, and the "extremely depressing" effect on the Anglo-American relationship. Trying to sound a wake-up call, he told Pritchard that the reaction in Washington was "extremely strong and indeed violent. Dulles had telephoned...and spoken very emotionally." Perhaps he was simply being polite in the presence of a British official, perhaps this was a true blind spot for him, perhaps he was speaking with an irony lost in the recording, but Pearson went on to say that while Ottawa was cross with the French government—assumed to be "secretly arranging things with Israel"—he suggested that Britain had not expected the Israeli attack. Pritchard does not appear to have responded to this line of discussion.[41]

As the meeting drew to a close, Pearson admitted that the Canadian government was "depressed." Properly loyal to his government, Pritchard offered that the "cataclysm created [the] possibility of a thorough and stable settlement in the Middle East." Glimpsing an opening, Pearson replied, "That might be a gleam at the end of the corridor." And indeed, it seems he tucked this idea away for later. He then went on to say that his immediate concern centred on the debate moving to the General Assembly, where Russia would try to brand Britain and France as aggressors. Pritchard ended his report to London noting that Pearson "did not know how it might best be handled."[42]

But Pearson had not shown his full hand. He was in fact already considering a way to defuse the looming confrontation. He did not appear to mention it in Cabinet, nor are there documents at External Affairs indicating that he discussed it with his officials. He believed that a real crisis provided the ideal setting to get creative, and so he did.

After his meeting at the British High Commission, Pearson telephoned Norman Robertson at about 7 p.m. Ottawa time, midnight in London. He asked him to sound out informal reaction to an idea he and UNTSO's General Burns had spoken of with Anthony Eden the previous November and that Selwyn Lloyd had mentioned briefly in January: the creation of a UN police force.

The idea itself was hardly original or overly complex. The UN began weaving the embryonic strands of modern-day peacekeeping unintentionally and haphazardly back in 1947, when a UN commission reported to the Security Council on the tense border situation between Greece and her neighbours, Albania, Bulgaria, and Yugoslavia, all charged—correctly—with supporting Communist forces in the Greek civil war. The report proposed the creation of a committee to monitor the area and included a modest suggestion to attach a corps of military observers to keep watch over the border and record any incursions. That same summer the Security Council also managed to secure a ceasefire between former Dutch colonial masters and newly independent Indonesians, and in August 1947 the UN established a consular mission made up of diplomats to monitor the fragile peace. Within weeks, four Australian military officers arrived in Batavia (now Djakarta) at the diplomats' request to function as observers.

The General Assembly established the United Nations Special Committee on the Balkans (UNSCOB) in October. By the following January, observers "equipped only with notebooks and pens" and using "jeeps, mules, and rigorous footwork" to patrol the treacherous Greek borderlands, shone an international spotlight on guerrilla infiltrations. To the Greek government's immense frustration, illumination was all these observers could provide.[43] They had no mandate to intervene or make peace, and no authority to force their way into the three hostile

Communist neighbours refusing them entry. Despite the limitations of this innovation, UNSCOB's observers in Greece and their counterparts in Indonesia embodied and helped to legitimize a physical UN presence in the midst of crisis.

To some historians and even the UN, these "early experiments with a non-fighting military presence" are not the first peacekeepers. The reasons for the exclusion seem to be, partly, appearances (no signature blue helmets or white jeeps) and, to a certain extent, semantics. One history has pointed out that unlike peacekeeping missions, the UN Secretariat did not assemble and administer these operations, while another has noted, "The observers functioned under the aegis of their consular missions."[44] Regardless of how they were outfitted, classified, organized, or administered, in 1947, impartial, unarmed observers were monitoring conflicts in Greece and Indonesia on behalf of the United Nations, their lack of hard power reflecting what a divided world assembly could tolerate.

Attempting to build on those precedents would, however, require something of a diplomatic miracle, one that would involve serious polit-ical muscle, the kind Canada did not possess, not even at the height of its international reputation. So Pearson made another phone call that evening, this one to Arnold Heeney, asking him to float the suggestion in Washington — the indispensable factor in any major diplomatic or military solution.[45] On the night of October 31, 1956, Pearson was quietly trying to set something in motion: vague, informal, sure to undergo multiple revisions as it unfolded, if it ever did. He had no clear-cut, linear, logical path to reach his objective. He would simply, as he quipped on other occasions, jump off that bridge when he got to it.

TWELVE

Eye of the Storm

The alliance of England and France has derived its strength not merely from the military and naval power of the two states, but from the force of the moral principle upon which that union has been founded. Our union has for its foundation resistance to unjust aggression, the defence of the weak against the strong.... How could England and France, who have guaranteed the integrity of the Turkish Empire, turn around and wrest Egypt from the Sultan? A coalition for such a purpose would revolt the moral feelings of mankind, and would certainly be fatal to any English Government that was a party to it.

   —Prime Minister Lord Palmerston, March 1, 1857[1]

May I recommend to the very special kindness of those with whom he will be dealing, Pearson of the Department of External Affairs, whose assistance to us during the past year has...been invaluable. A student at Oxford and one who has come away imbued with a great affection for Great Britain, he has taken considerable risks on several occasions in order to impart to us information which otherwise would never have reached us....He is a man...in whom our departments can place implicit confidence.

   —British High Commission, January 1930[2]

On November 1, the Canadian High Commissioner in London, Norman Robertson, enclosed a confidential report for Lester Pearson, which had been prepared by one of his officers after full and frank talks with senior contacts in Whitehall. One at the Foreign Office painted a bleak picture of the feeling inside the Cabinet and No. 10 Downing Street towards the senior dominion. "The bitterness about the Canadian attitude on Suez was as great as that against the Americans," the Foreign Office official said. Canada had recently decided to sell wheat to Egypt, which was "regarded as a stab in the back in a moment of Britain's crisis and need. In all this," he judged, "Canada had been even softer than the Americans."[3] These observations could not have surprised Pearson. He knew he had disappointed his ally, but that didn't stop him from wondering how to rescue the country he admired so much from suffering any more self-inflicted wounds. The country's government was beginning to ponder this same question.

On November 1, 10 a.m. GMT, Selwyn Lloyd joined his permanent undersecretary, Ivone Kirkpatrick, and other senior officials to plot out another day in diplomatic hell. Twelve hours away loomed the UN General Assembly emergency session, convened to debate the Israeli attack on Egypt and Britain and France's disturbing ultimatum. Conducting a similar kind of operation in Hungary, and facing a similar global chorus of outrage, a totalitarian dictatorship like the USSR could safely defy world opinion, and indeed the opinion of all those trapped within its borders, for as long it wished. This kind of defiance was far more difficult for a democracy like Britain to pull off for very long.

During a pause in the morning discussion, Lloyd mentioned the expected confrontation at the UN, where Asian, Arab, and African delegates would likely declare Britain and France to be aggressors—a serious charge in diplomatic language as it carried, at least in theory, the potential for sanctions. His senior mandarin, Kirkpatrick, shared the deep concern about the "almost ferocious way [Washington] was leading the opposition to us." No shrinking violet, even he conceded to Lloyd that unless some alternative was found, Britain confronted highly unpalatable choices: withdraw from the United Nations, or remain to be kicked out by angry members. Trying to find some breathing room, Lloyd reframed an idea he had raised in the House of Commons months before and

Lester Pearson in UN General Assembly at Canada desk,
November 1956 (UN photo 121723)

wondered whether handing over what he called Britain's "peacekeeping function" would improve the nation's position.[4]

The prime minister's press secretary, William Clark, offered a shrewd spin to make the proposition more attractive. "We might say—on the Korean analogy—that we had acted for the UN and would be glad to accept a UN commander eventually," he suggested. This expectation of an eventual and preferably drawn-out handover seemed to generate support for this idea; with any luck, the UN might not be able to actually take on the role. Not everyone at the table wanted to risk bringing in a meddling organization. Clark observed that defence minister Antony Head "kept on reminding us that the first objective of this whole operation was to get rid of Nasser, and that would never be done by the UN." With the General Assembly scheduled to convene in less than twelve hours, however, and with the government facing a motion of censure in the House of Commons that same afternoon, Lloyd went to talk with Prime Minister Eden.[5]

When presented with the idea, "Eden willingly agreed," Lloyd later recalled. "It was very much in accord with his own thoughts." William Clark, however, remembered things differently. According to him, the foreign secretary left the meeting with Eden in defeat, the prime minister responding with words to the effect that letting the UN move in was "simply to thrown our hand in and wasn't it to keep the United Nations out of this, that we have done this?" Informed of Eden's rebuff, Clark assumed the idea was now "a dead duck" and "went away very sorrowful."[6] But very soon afterwards, Eden completely changed course. Something or someone persuaded him to announce that Britain would hand over the police action in Egypt to the United Nations.

In his memoirs, Eden did not adequately explain his abrupt reversal. He claimed that "to have proposed a United Nations force in advance of the outbreak of hostilities would have evoked no response" — true, but still evasive.[7] To cover himself, he also claimed that he had long championed the idea of an international force going back to the League of Nations and had, more recently, suggested ramping up the UN's military observer mission in the Middle East — again all true, and again, an incomplete response.

Not present during the discussions and asked decades after the event, former private secretary Guy Millard said that Eden was probably relieved, given the terrible circumstances, to turn to the idea of a UN force as "a way out with minimal loss of face. From Eden's point of view, it was an attractive proposition, a graceful exit." Selwyn Lloyd's assistant private secretary, Donald Logan, doubted very much that Eden "readily agreed" to hand over military operations, especially as he had resisted going to the UN from the beginning. "But by then," Logan said, "he was desperate because his alibi had been rumbled." Logan thought that Eden would have needed to be pushed into accepting the idea, for his own good: "Lloyd and Kirkpatrick were anxious to get Eden out of the woods — it was their duty."[8]

Perhaps the tipping point on that November 1 came, as Keith Kyle has written, from the home front. The Cabinet minutes from the following day, November 2, show the leader of the House of Commons, R.A. Butler, noting an improvement in the government's position in the

House, suggesting that "this was undoubtedly the result of the Prime Minister's offer to transfer the responsibility for policing the Suez area to a United Nations force." Kyle argues this shows that Eden made the offer because of pressure from Butler, anxious to mollify the Opposition, not to mention anxious Conservative backbenchers.[9] The beleaguered prime minister needed to deflect tempers, regain some sense of moral stature, and above all, buy time so his armada sailing the nearly one thousand miles from Malta would actually reach Egypt and retake the Suez Canal. Whatever the precise reasons that led Eden to invite the United Nations into his contrived theatre of war, he unwittingly unleashed a set of circumstances that Lester Pearson would seize and transform into a plausible exit route, whether Eden liked it or not.

All my life I'd been working on forms of words to make things possible.
— Lester Pearson, May 6, 1970[10]

The secretary of state for External Affairs was said to make a habit of devouring the morning newspapers. On November 1, he likely read the editorial pages of the *Globe and Mail*, a staunchly large "C" conservative paper. Three days after the Israeli incursion into Egypt, and the day after the British and French started bombing the country, columnist George Bain dissected with surgical precision all the contradictions in Pearson's painstaking attempt to walk fine lines: the government had declined to condemn the Israelis formally yet delayed shipping them the F-86 fighter jets, which implied some kind of displeasure; the government declined to condemn Britain's use of force but still did not support it; Ottawa said it was dismayed by the lack of allied consultation and the flagrant snubbing of the UN but had not uttered any blatant criticism of those tactics. Bain deplored the government's dithering foreign policy, which, he wrote, "rests so largely on speaking last on any subject, speaking meekly, and frequently not speaking at all." Another faithful voice in the choir of Conservative indignation, the *Calgary Herald*, charged that just when Britain and France were trying to bring peace and stability to the Middle East, Canada "ran out." It continued: "What sickening tale is this that Canada is 'hacking out a stand of her own'? Is it not more accurate to say that Washington has nibbled out, not hacked out, a place for us to stand among its puppets?"[11]

Not all press opinion or the popular feeling it reflected was so hostile or ill informed. Pearson had his champions, especially the *Winnipeg Free Press*, the *Toronto Daily Star*, and the *Halifax Chronicle Herald*. The divergence across the nation on a matter as fundamental as loyalty to the Mother Country was so vast, however, there was little he could do in the short term to bridge the chasm.[12] And on the morning of November 1, he was already staking out a path that would harden the division, because by then he was already trying to work out—without knowing the British were doing likewise—whether he should propose the creation of a UN police force to separate the Egyptian and Israeli armies. He didn't want to discuss this in public just yet; continuing to say as little as possible remained one defensible option. His ultimate response would depend on how events played out in Cairo and London and New York and Washington. In the meantime, he would circle the storm, judging the parameters of the possible.

Constantly weaving around obstacles as he looked for working compromises or simply a palatable stalemate, Pearson was inclined to let go of positions leading nowhere and improvise his way towards fluctuating transition points, which is what so much diplomacy amounts to. His weaving approaches were evident on the ice when he played for Oxford against Swiss teams in the 1920s. One fellow Oxonian (and future governor general), Roland Michener, remembered Pearson as "a good stick-handler" who "would swerve back and forth across the rink—he often started from defence position. So the Swiss in their sports columns called him Herr Zigzag, which was typical of his play." Diplomat Charles Ritchie observed with admiration that Pearson "approached his objectives indirectly, not by method of head-on confrontations. He was incredibly persistent. He would back away from something and then come back to it, come around to it again. It was fascinating to watch. It was a form of gamesmanship of a most accomplished kind and his footwork—not a bad analogy for him with his interest in football—was expert."[13]

Pearson's weaving could irritate his more linear, logical colleagues. The Canadian ambassador in Washington during the early 1950s, Hume

Wrong, once got off the phone after discussing some point with him and apparently erupted, "The trouble with Mike is that you never know what principle he is acting on." Wrong likened Pearson to the legendary escape artist Houdini: "Tie him up in knots, drop him in the middle of an international mess, and he'll not only get himself out of it but transform frustration into triumph." And here was the most annoying quality in this process for Wrong: "Ask him how or why he did it—and he can't tell you."[14] Or wouldn't tell; Pearson was far too experienced not to know how he skated to his compromises.

Pearson's assistant undersecretary during Suez, John Holmes, pointed out another fundamental aspect in how he played the game. Pearson was not really "an original thinker," judged Holmes. "I think essentially he was a brilliant tactician." he said. "After all, that's the essence of diplomacy." He also recalled two other elements in Pearson's method. "The great thing about working for him," Holmes said, "is if you had a bright idea, he gobbled them up. He'd read pages of memoranda and you always felt that, no matter how far out your idea was, he'd love to taste it and test it. He wasn't going to mark you down as an idiot." Then, when Pearson heard an idea with actual potential, he would raise doubts and questions, which Holmes understood was not "negativism." It was, he observed, "clearing away the obstacles." The clearing away typically took place each morning in what those at External Affairs dubbed "prayer meetings."[15]

At the November 1 gathering, Pearson may have discussed his UN force idea with others in the department. He may have kept it to himself. When asked about it later, John Holmes could not identify who first put the idea forward. "None of us who were involved could say at one moment somebody proposed it," Holmes concluded. "It was there in the air. I say this because somebody's written something saying I was the author of it and I was certainly not. I was part of the spontaneous combustion."[16]

During the morning, Pearson read yet another cable from Norman Robertson reporting on yet another meeting at the Commonwealth Relations Office in which the High Commissioner again expressed Ottawa's "misgiving and dismay" to no effect. Robertson departed on a note of palpable regret. "The UK and France had somehow got themselves into a truly tragic position," he told those present. "Neither of them had any closer friend and ally than Canada, but at this pass I could not see what we could do to help." In his report to Pearson, Robertson did not indicate that he raised the possibility with Whitehall of creating a UN force. According to one account, the night before, Pearson had suggested he do this.

That morning Pearson telephoned Robertson. Without question, Pearson asked Robertson to float the force idea, if he hadn't already done so. Hoping to take advantage of the immediate crisis to reach a greater goal, he also wanted Robertson to get reaction to the possibility of setting up a major diplomatic conference to establish a true peace in the Middle East. Theirs had to be a brief phone call because Pearson was late for a Cabinet meeting that had already started.[17]

The fighting in Egypt was the fourth item on the lengthy agenda. Louis St. Laurent began by reading a draft of the official reply to Eden's disingenuous telegram from the day before. Seen by some as a grey, aloof "chairman of the board," by others as the genial national uncle, St. Laurent apparently composed the reply, as his biographer wrote, "in a highly agitated state of mind," telephoning the minister of finance and a key party broker in Ontario, Walter Harris, multiple times during the evening to make sure no offence would be given, no doubt either to London or to Liberal voters across the country. He also spoke with Pearson, who felt compelled to urge (in his own words) "some changes to make the tone somewhat softer expressing more regret than indignation." The draft was finalized sometime around midnight.[18]

This official reply from Ottawa to London was first and foremost a message from within the family that took pains to underline the two countries' "very special relationship of close friendship and intimate association." In the face of obvious deceit and bewildering diplomatic tactics, the tone was impeccably restrained and even generous. Ottawa was still willing to give London the benefit of some doubt regarding motives, allowing that "your own information is much more complete than ours." But St. Laurent's and, by extension, Pearson's profound disagreement was made unmistakeably clear.[19]

The telegram laid out three areas of "particular anxiety" caused by the crisis: the "most regrettable" effect on the United Nations, blatantly ignored, with the "equally regrettable" and unprecedented use of British vetoes in the Security Council; the corrosive and potentially lethal effect on the Commonwealth; and finally and most critically, the "deplorable divergence" between Canada's two closest allies. "Anglo-American co-operation and friendship is the very foundation of our hopes for progress toward a peaceful and secure world," the telegram stated. "It would be a tragedy beyond repair if it were now to disappear, or even to be weakened. It is hard for a Canadian to think of any consideration—other than national survival or safety—as more important."[20] Canada's message was delivered to the UK High Commission at 11:30 that morning.

That hurdle cleared, Pearson turned Cabinet's attention to the UN emergency session scheduled to convene in approximately six hours. He outlined his intentions to try and shield two NATO allies from the anger in the General Assembly, which he feared might pass a resolution condemning Britain, France, and Israel. The last was not a NATO member but, in Pearson's mind, still deserving shelter from the storm. "It would be embarrassing," he said, "to be faced with a motion drafted in extreme terms by the Arab-Asian bloc and endorsed by the communists." He would try to dilute and deflect any condemnation by including "a reference to the provocation which had led Israel and the U.K. and France to act in the manner they had."[21] If that failed, he would attempt to delay the vote itself.

And then Pearson made an astonishing move. At some point during the Cabinet meeting , he received information that almost certainly came from Norman Robertson, either in a telegram composed shortly after their earlier trans-Atlantic talk or possibly in a follow-up phone call. It was probably the single most important communication in his decision to go ahead with the UN police force plan, because it offered the first glimmer of a way out.

Robertson had managed very quickly to get through to Ivone Kirkpatrick by phone and inform the permanent undersecretary that Pearson was thinking about proposing a diplomatic conference to tackle sweeping regional issues beyond Suez. Part of this approach would entail setting up a UN military force to separate the Egyptians from the Israelis, while a peace settlement was negotiated. This was the first notice London received that Pearson was considering a strikingly similar approach to defuse the conflict in Egypt and, unstated but equally important, the conflict at the United Nations.

Kirkpatrick told Robertson that Eden would announce in Parliament that afternoon that London was offering to hand over the British-French police action in Egypt to the UN. He stressed to Robertson that any such force "would have to be to a substantial and properly supported international force…and not just a notional force thought up as a diplomatic gimmick to meet this evening's diplomatic requirements." Perhaps Kirkpatrick was aware of the irony in his dismissive tone, since Eden was using the UN force idea precisely as a gimmick to meet immediate diplomatic emergencies. In his telegram to Pearson, Robertson allowed only faint hope regarding the reaction from the Foreign Office's senior mandarin. "This is not much," he wrote, "but it is something."[22] For Pearson, however, it was almost everything he had to work with. He now knew that the country his proposal was truly meant to serve would not instantly reject it. He was, moreover, already looking beyond the emergency to use the improbable idea to try to bring a lasting peace to the Middle East.

Armed with this information, Pearson told his Cabinet colleagues, "It might be that the U.K. government would soon welcome a proposal calling for the cessation of hostilities, the convening of a widely-based conference on Middle Eastern matters and, in the interim, the provision of substantial police forces stationed on the Israel-Arab borders to keep peace."[23] Pearson then offered to make that proposal himself, and his colleagues gave their blessing, or at least, did not resist. No doubt the prime minister's unflinching support allowed the foreign minister to take this critical step.

Pearson left the Cabinet meeting and caught a flight to New York with John Holmes. "On the way down in the aeroplane, I kept wondering what I would do," he remembered later. "[The UN force idea] was in my mind from the very beginning, but I wasn't going to tell anybody about it until I sensed the atmosphere in New York." Holmes worked on a draft speech during the flight, which Pearson "as was his wont…adapted and improved considerably." He continued to revise until just before he delivered the speech from the General Assembly rostrum.[24]

In London that day, opposition parties put the government on trial in the House of Commons for "bombing Egypt not in self-defence, not in collective defence," Labour leader Hugh Gaitskell charged, "but in clear defiance of the United Nations Charter." The debate was "quite the most shattering experience I've ever sat through," a senior editor from *The Times* remembered. The Conservatives sat in silence "but at each word the whole of the Labour benches rose like a wall. No longer shouting, they were howling with anger and real anguish," he said. "It really was a most terrible, terrible spectacle."[25] The rage became so intense, the Speaker suspended the sitting for half an hour.

After the debate resumed, Eden rose just after 5 p.m. GMT — 12 p.m. EST — to explain that while Britain was "in an armed conflict," the country was not in a state of war. Pressing on through interruptions and accusations, he threw out the tactical distraction urged upon him earlier that day by his foreign secretary. "Israel and Egypt are locked in conflict," he said. "The first and urgent task is to separate these combatants and to stabilise the position. That is our purpose. If the United Nations were then willing to take over the physical task of maintaining peace in that area, no one would be better pleased than we. But police action there must be to separate the belligerents and to prevent a resumption of hostilities."[26] As these words were transmitted around the world, Pearson was en route to the UN.

Delayed by fog, Pearson's plane finally touched down at 4 p.m. By the time he reached the UN building in downtown Manhattan, at about 5:25 p.m., the General Assembly had been meeting for almost half an hour. A senior adviser with the Canadian mission, Geoff Murray, recalled: "It was near hysteria in the building. The Assembly was in a high state of nerves." Murray and Robert MacKay met Pearson and Holmes at the bottom of the escalators leading up to the second-floor entrance to the General Assembly, and Pearson unveiled his idea for a UN police force. To establish it in time, he said, would require using the closest troops at hand, which might mean the British armada currently sailing from Malta for Egypt or French forces in North Africa or their allies in the region. Pearson's willingness to harness the two countries bombing Egypt in obvious collusion with Israel alarmed his audience.[27]

MacKay, the senior person in the Canadian mission, "sort of shuffled his feet and then looked down and cleared his throat a couple of times," Murray recalled, and then "turned to me and said, 'Well, Geoff, what do you think? You've been in the lounge all day.'" The floor of the General

Assembly provided the platform for official, public declarations. The delegates' lounge allowed for casual, honest talks over drinks. Murray was thirty-eight years old. Pearson was fifty-nine. The young adviser had never held a conversation with his minister, but he must have known that Pearson was not someone who wanted to be coddled, so Murray did not hold back. "I just said point blank that it wouldn't work at all," Murray noted, "It would simply not work. It ran in the face of this near hysteria that existed in the General Assembly." He also stressed that the African and Asian members saw the British and French assault as an appalling return to "old time colonialism and gun boat diplomacy," something Pearson already appreciated and indeed, personally agreed with.[28]

Pearson had not even entered the General Assembly and already he was told, in no uncertain terms, that a key element in his plan would be shot down, possibly taking the entire idea with it. Murray did not remember Pearson saying anything in reply to this. The minister simply took it in, nodded his head in acknowledgement, and then turned to Holmes to say he had better speak with Norman Robertson. Pearson faced a critical, possibly insuperable dilemma. Britain and France, ironically, had the closest troops at hand. If they were not allowed to serve in the police force, the British and French would never cooperate with the UN and bring it into being. But to persuade other members to accept these would-be aggressors as peacemakers would require him to blur the facts. Fortunately, his gift for letting go of impractical or what he termed "unwise" positions would serve him well through the next forty-eight hours.

When he finally assumed his seat at Canada's desk near the front of the vast hall, Pearson caused a visible stir. Anxious delegates from member states and officials from the UN Secretariat had already circled John Holmes asking, "What's he got? We hear Mike's got a proposal. It's high time. Can he do it?" Murray shared the same memory of Pearson's effect on the assembly. "There were people coming up from the other delegations, mostly from the missions, but also ministers," Murray later said. "They came there for advice. They came for information. They came to try to find out what he was going to do." They converged on Pearson because he helped shape the UN's first major agencies during the Second World War; because he was instrumental in guiding the UN to support the partition plan for Palestine; because he served as president of the General Assembly during the Korean war. "By the time Suez occurred," quipped Murray, "he had become a household god in the United Nations."[29] They also knew that the well-connected Canadian foreign minister could reach anyone in the State Department, the Foreign Office, the Commonwealth, and NATO, if only to be heard. And while he wasn't considered neutral, he spoke for a country with no colonial history in the Middle East and with no economic or military stake in the Suez Canal.

When the UN emergency session opened, Egypt was the first to speak. Ambassador Omar Loutfi denounced Israel, Britain, and France's assault on his country and poured scorn upon the ultimatum demanding that Egypt stop defending itself so that the aggressors could impose their own peace. "I was amazed," he declared, "that [London] could have thought for a single moment that Egypt would agree to Franco-British forces landing on its territory against its will." The representative from Ceylon, Senerat Gunewardene, spoke next. "It is to me a matter of profound grief that I should have to perform this duty," Gunewardene lamented, but perform it he did, condemning Britain for wanton disregard of the UN charter and Egyptian sovereignty. "No nation, however powerful, can turn back the clock in Africa and Asia and resist the inexorable march of events," he warned his fellow member of the Commonwealth. "The spirit of Asia and Africa can never be crushed."[30]

Britain's permanent representative, Pierson Dixon, had not been warned in advance of the indefensible position he was given to defend. Impeccable, soft-spoken, scholarly, he showed himself a consummate professional able to submerge personal angst to serve a policy he privately loathed. "The effort of concealing these feelings and putting a plausible and confident face on the case was the severest moral and physical strain I have ever experienced," he wrote in his memoirs. The same could probably be said for every member of the mission. First Secretary Peter Ramsbotham saw Britain's standing eviscerated, as he remembered in retirement. "There we were, entering a dog house where we became the pariah delegation. It was a very uncomfortable feeling. I've never felt anything like it, I think, since. The American delegation who had been our very close friends for all those years wouldn't be seen drinking with us. We made ourselves untouchables"—but not to Canada. John Holmes later wrote: "When we got to New York, we discovered that our friends in the UK mission were even more upset than we were with what the government had done and only too anxious to reach for a path of retreat."[31] Pearson was determined to carve out that path for the British, and he would employ the person who had caused the mess in the first place.

During the early afternoon of November 1, the news wires had brought word of Eden's offer in the House of Commons to step aside in Egypt to make way for the United Nations. Ramsbotham said, "When it came over to us—I remember seeing it on the ticker tape in the UN—it came as a merciful message." Like Pearson, he grasped the potential for cover and retreat even while understanding that this was "not what Eden really wanted, of course. He wanted the troops to go in and Nasser to fall. [There was] a certain amount of duplicity behind that." Acknowledging and sidestepping that duplicity, Ramsbotham decided to use Eden's offer as if the prime minister had actually meant it.[32] Pierson Dixon, his superior, evidently approved of this approach.

One of the first to speak in the emergency session, Dixon ended his implausible defence to the General Assembly by repeating Eden's invitation word for word: "If the United Nations were then willing to take over the physical task of maintaining peace in that area, no one would be better pleased than we. But police action there must be to separate the belligerents and to prevent a resumption of hostilities."[33] The members of the British mission then reinforced this cry for diplomatic help by appealing informally and personally to the delegation they thought most able and most willing to save Britain from its leaders.

Early in the evening, parallel or even simultaneous discussions unfolded. Properly seeking out someone on the Canadian side of roughly equivalent rank, someone he knew and trusted, Ramsbotham approached Holmes. "I came to him with this [Eden's statement] at once," Ramsbotham recalled. "I think I made it clear that we really wanted to use it. Whether Eden was keen about it or not, he'd said so. This is what we wanted to press for." The British in New York did not have to press too hard because Pearson was thinking along similar lines. He spoke directly with Pierson Dixon, someone he admired as the best of a political culture he greatly respected. Pearson told Dixon that he was "contemplating" proposing a UN police force. He found a receptive audience for his idea.

The British and Canadians tacitly began working together, Ramsbotham remembered, "It was like a joint operation, really."[34]

At some point that evening, Pearson witnessed the intolerable pressure bearing down on his embattled allies. Perhaps unaware of what had already transpired or perhaps uncertain of the Canadian commitment to help, one of the senior members of the British mission came to speak with Pearson. Murray was sitting behind the minister and was surprised at first by the official's open display of emotion. "He was a very sort of cynical guy most of the time and took kind of a lighthearted view of the UN and the way we went about business there," Murray said. "But when he was trying to explain to Pearson directly—he didn't talk through me or John Holmes; he spoke directly, sort of knelt at the side of the desk—I could see his face from where I was sitting immediately behind Pearson. He was in tears, I mean, quite literally in tears, streaming down his face."[35]

Pearson undoubtedly understood that the delegation was acting well beyond its instructions, something he had done himself in the past. While anxious to help Canada's NATO partner, Commonwealth ally, and Mother Country, and while he had seized on the same potential opening in Eden's speech, he had also been told by Murray that the assembly would never accept the British and French armies acting under the UN flag. Pearson may have had a maverick streak, admittedly one unleashed only behind the scenes, but this coexisted with an equally innate caution. In his memoirs, Pearson once advised, "Never to go out on a limb, above all formally and officially, from which you are likely to have to crawl back or be cut down."[36]

The dominating power in the Western coalition would, Pearson knew, inevitably determine what he could achieve. John Foster Dulles was circulating a resolution calling for an immediate ceasefire and withdrawal, and he intended to press for a vote that same evening, an unusually accelerated pace for the deliberating body. Dulles "had become a statesman in a hurry," Pearson commented in a rare snide note. "I was disturbed by this, but it was apparent that there was no way to deter him and I did not try." Dulles legitimately worried that a harsh resolution might be introduced. However well intentioned, Pearson felt the American effort was inept because "it carried with it a strong flavour of censure [and] was needlessly clumsy," as it flew in the face of Eden's stated position.[37] And at this point, Pearson was thinking about long-term solutions, which an American focus on the immediate emergency did not serve.

The last delegate to address the General Assembly before the break, Dulles began with obvious emotion. "I doubt that any delegate ever spoke from this forum with as heavy a heart as I have brought here tonight," he said. "The United States finds itself unable to agree with three nations, with whom it has ties of deep friendship, of admiration, and of respect, and two of whom constitute our oldest, most trusted and reliable allies." But, he noted, these allies had to be stopped. If the UN did not act quickly enough "what has been called a police action may develop into something which is far more grave."[38] Dulles introduced his resolution calling for an immediate ceasefire and withdrawal, to be voted on that evening. At 7:40 p.m., the sound and fury inside the hall subsided for dinner.

A resolution introduced by a superpower is no easy thing to ignore or deflect, but Pearson decided to discuss the Canadian option privately with Dulles — not someone he was personally close to. Geoff Murray had the impression their relations were, "in the words of the trade, 'cool.'" Pearson recorded his ambivalence towards Dulles, shared by other diplomats, in his diary. "Dulles is a most rigid and unsympathetic person at these social gatherings," he wrote. "He is also pretty inflexible in his Presbyterian mind, and while intelligent and informed leaves you with a feeling of uneasiness at his ability to adapt himself to changing circumstances and to accommodate himself to anybody else's views."[39] They may not have been friends but they were professionals, capable of working together despite the personal distance, and on this evening Dulles revealed he was perfectly able to adapt when he felt he needed to.

The two men talked at the US desk in the full glare of the dispersing General Assembly. Pearson would work around the American resolution and so prepared Dulles for the alternative Canadian game plan. There was no point, Pearson told him, in simply returning to the status quo. He might therefore advocate "an international police force for maintaining strict order along the demarcation lines in Palestine," he said, "during the painful process of negotiating an overall settlement." Folded within this ambitious scheme was the more immediate objective, candidly stated:

the UK and French governments needed to be able to withdraw from Egypt "without losing too much face."[40] Their methods were different but their end goal was identical. Dulles said he would press ahead with his ceasefire resolution but encouraged Pearson to attempt his rescue plan. Another major obstacle was cleared away.

Even with superpower approval, the middle-power diplomat still had to prepare the ground ahead. He understood the majority of delegates would refuse to make the French and British aggressors the standard bearers for the United Nations. He also knew the boundaries of his influence. Not everyone celebrated his work at the UN promoting the partition of Palestine. "He was not entirely trusted by the Arabs, and I emphasize 'entirely,'" noted Murray. India's de facto foreign minister, Krishna Menon, viewed Pearson not as a neutral mediator but as a loyal member of the Western alliance, indeed as "NATO personified." Pearson, he said, "had his limitations. Whatever happened he could not get away from the United States." In Menon's view, this personal limit applied to the country as well. "Canada did not play a United Nations part," he judged. "In all questions in which they were not particularly involved they simply voted with the Americans."[41]

Whatever his shortcomings in some eyes, on the floor of the General Assembly, no one was better placed than the moderate, mediatory Canadian to propose solutions that might be accepted across great divides. From the Canada desk, Pearson dispatched Holmes and MacKay to discuss his UN force idea informally and sound out reactions through the assembly hall, in the corridors, and in the lounges. Murray, more familiar with the new members admitted the year before, remained behind with Pearson.[42]

While his advisers circulated, Pearson politely deflected appeals from other delegations, especially Pakistan, the Scandinavians, and Turkey, to support the US ceasefire resolution; he kept an eye on the ever-shifting list of speakers as delegates changed their place in the lineup; and most importantly, he continued to ponder if and when he should actually put forward his proposal. Late in the evening, Pearson may have displayed some hesitation, because Ramsbotham remembered encouraging him to persist in his course more than once. "I did at one time think that John Holmes and I had made a helpful contribution at a midnight hour in the General Assembly," he later recalled. "John and I had helped to persuade Pearson that he could go ahead with his proposal without Eden's objection." The British mission's support was unquestionably a factor in Pearson's calculations but not the dominant factor.[43]

Through the night, the Canadian advisers shared informal reactions to the force proposal, and as Pearson sifted through the maze of opinions and interests, he sensed the prevailing tide was in his favour. "By midnight," he later said, "we had a pretty good idea that this might get a good deal of support." With the vote approaching on the US ceasefire resolution, he reached a turning point. "It had become quite clear to me that if Canada was going to play any part in this, she had to detach herself from both sides at the beginning," he later said. "In other words, we couldn't support this US resolution and expect to get a very sympathetic hearing in London or Australia, New Zealand." But he also recognized that "if we opposed it, our standing with the other members of the Commonwealth, the Muslim world, and the US would have disappeared, and we would have no further capacity for useful service in this emergency."[44] Pearson decided that Canada would take the highly controversial position of abstaining on the vote, which was not the same thing as claiming neutrality.

In a tactical move noticed by other delegations, he did not speak during the debate when the session resumed at 9:50 p.m. He remained at the Canada desk drafting one of the most significant speeches of his entire career and, as Murray marvelled, continuing to revise it while "frequently interrupted by urgent consultations and messages, always in the din of debate.... Few public servants I have known, even seasoned United Nations pros had the power of concentration to work so effectively in that kind of turmoil." Unlike foreign minister counterparts who were political appointees, Pearson had spent twenty years in the bureaucracy at External Affairs, drafting speeches, memos, and policy papers. He was particularly skilled at shaping diplomatic language. According to Murray, Pearson himself wrote virtually every word of the speech he would make after the vote, and when shown the text, Murray judged that nothing needed to be changed or added.[45]

At about 2:30 a.m., now November 2, the members of the United Nations voted on the US ceasefire resolution. Sixty-four nations supported the hurried call for peace. Still in the midst of attacking Egypt, Britain, France, and Israel, voted against the resolution, joined by Australia and New Zealand, faithful to the Mother Country. Luxembourg was absent. The remaining six members—Belgium, Laos, the Netherlands, Portugal, South Africa, and Canada—abstained. After the vote was announced, the Italian delegate made a brief appeal on behalf of the people of Hungary, who were being dragged at gunpoint back into the Soviet scheme of things. At about three in the morning, the Canadian foreign minister, who had attracted so much attention when he entered the assembly, finally stood up to address the international community. He was the first speaker in the resumed debate. "I asked for the floor to explain my abstention and I wandered on about, 'We didn't have enough time to consider everything. You shouldn't rush a thing like this through.' This wasn't my real reason at all," he later said. "I couldn't explain why in tactical terms I was abstaining."[46]

Striving not to alienate belligerent allies or outraged members who wished to condemn them, Pearson expressed "a feeling of sadness, indeed even distress, at not being able to support the position taken by two countries whose ties with my country remain close and intimate." He praised some aspects of the US resolution but deemed it inadequate to deal with the deeper conflict. "A ceasefire will be only of temporary value at best. Surely we should have used this opportunity to link a ceasefire to the absolute necessity of a political settlement in Palestine and for the Suez," he said. "We need action, then, not only to end the fighting but to make the peace."[47]

Pointing towards a transformative goal for the region, Pearson posed a fundamental question to the assembly. "What then, six months from now? Are we to go through all this again? Are we to return to the status quo? Such a return would not be to a position of security, or even a tolerable position, but would be a return to terror, bloodshed, strife," which, he candidly acknowledged, the current observer mission, UNTSO, "would be powerless to prevent and possibly even to investigate." As the UN Secretariat and General Assembly, especially the British and American delegations, had been primed to expect, Pearson then said he wished the secretary-general had been authorized to begin establishing a UN force. "My own Government," he pledged, "would be glad to recommend Canadian participation in such a United Nations force, a truly international peace and police force."[48]

Pearson was one of the most experienced and respected diplomats in the emergency gathering, but that was only a starting point. He could not enforce or demand or even insist. He could only inspire, suggest, and persuade. At this critical point in the crisis he ensured the General Assembly saw that he was not speaking in isolation.

Shortly after Pearson returned to his desk, Dulles walked down the long aisle to the rostrum and expressed his complete support for Pearson's desire to make a larger peace in the Middle East. Adding even more weight to his words, Dulles announced that he had spoken with President Eisenhower, who also supported this approach. "The United States delegation," Dulles declared, "would be very happy indeed if the Canadian delegation would formulate and introduce as part of these proceedings a concrete suggestion along the lines that Mr. Pearson made."[49] Now the entire assembly knew the middle power moved in step with the superpower. Seemingly in an instant, though in fact he had manoeuvred quietly the entire evening, Pearson had shaped an entirely new agenda from what was unfolding some twelve hours before. It helped that the proposal itself was not a radical proposition.

In the 1920s, the League of Nations had come close to sending an international force to help resolve the clash between Poland and Lithuania over the city of Vilnius. In 1934, the League managed to dispatch an international police force composed of 3,300 British, Dutch, Italian, and Swedish troops to supervise a plebiscite in the Saar region contested by France and Germany. As one historian noted, "the Saar Police Force had no coercionary powers and functioned mainly as an international representative, keeping order by its mere presence and prestige."[50] That force successfully kept the peace without firing a single shot.

This impetus continued in the postwar period when the League remade as the UN sent observers to Palestine, Greece, Indonesia, and Kashmir. However, there would be limits to how far member states were willing to go. In 1948, Trygve Lie, then the secretary-general, tried to establish a United Nations Guard Force composed of up to five thousand troops but could not rally the necessary support in the Security Council.[51] In 1950, with the Soviets boycotting the Security Council, the UN sent a true army to protect South Korea from a North Korean attack. The force was largely an American project launched, primarily though not exclusively, to protect American interests in the region, but it also made the UN's promise of collective security, ever so briefly, a reality.

At times exasperated and even enraged by American tactics, Pearson still took a measure of gratification from the compromised outcome, although his words damned slightly with faint praise. "A United Nations command had been set up which made it, in theory at least, a United Nations command. I consider this all to be in theory a very important episode in history because for the first time, so far as I know...an assembly of nations, democratically chosen...had formally voted against an aggressor and unlike the League of Nations, in '35 and '36, they followed through," he later said. "I felt at the time, really pretty excited about this precedent in history and I've always felt since that however it worked out in practice, it was a very valuable precedent for the future of the United Nations."[52] All these precedents, familiar in varying degrees to his generation of diplomats, laid the foundation for Pearson's force proposal on the night of November 2, which was not an end in itself. In his eyes, in this crisis, any force was a support act, a potentially useful tool to serve his greater agenda to negotiate a more permanent peace in the Middle East. With this proposal now in play, the session adjourned at 4:20 a.m.

During the morning of November 2, operating with very little sleep, Pearson worked through hastily arranged meetings at his hotel. In one, the Pakistani ambassador, Mohammed Mir Khan, conveyed his government's support for the Canadian plan and expressed its deep concern that Ceylon and India might leave the Commonwealth if the British did not pull back. "The pressure on us to do the same," Khan added, "will be irresistible."[53] At the same time, cables and phone calls from Norman Robertson in London that indicated just how difficult it would be to get London to pull back heightened Pearson's consternation at the prospect of Commonwealth dissolution.

Robertson had met that day with Selwyn Lloyd, who, on the one hand, professed that he was "very seriously interested" in the force proposal. When Robertson urged the foreign secretary to accept an immediate ceasefire, however, Lloyd demurred, citing, according to Robertson, "the virtual impossibility of suddenly putting into reverse the elaborate combined schedule of air and sea movements by two forces."[54] Lloyd would be meeting with the French foreign minister, Christian Pineau, at end of the day, and no decision could be made until then. In the meantime, the armada would continue to sail towards the Suez Canal.

Robertson encountered more obstruction when he spoke with the permanent undersecretary at the Foreign Office and, perhaps trying to apply some pressure, said that Pearson might introduce his UN police force resolution that same day. Ivone Kirkpatrick moved in like a vigilant headmaster to dampen Canadian enthusiasms and strongly advised Canada "not to plunge" but rather "to proceed in an orderly manner" while the foreign secretary formulated a proper reply. Perhaps applying his own measure of pressure, Kirkpatrick proceeded to disparage the Canadian initiative. As he recorded in a memo afterwards, Kirkpatrick told Robertson that it was "highly unlikely that we could agree to anything quite so flabby as a ceasefire accompanied by no more than an invitation to the United Nations to constitute an international force." Robertson seemed "very reluctant" to acquiesce, and worse, as Kirkpatrick noted with palpable irritation, was "anxious to rush us into a ceasefire."[55]

Kirkpatrick's and, more importantly, Lloyd's desire to stall Pearson's initiative was not universally shared through the Foreign Office, quietly reeling from the resignation just two days before of Anthony Nutting. When the news was made public, Douglas Hurd at the British mission in New York concluded in dismay, "If there were a master plan he would have known it. Nutting had left; so there was no master plan, no aces, no trumps; just deception." Eden would also lose William Clark and a junior minister but rising star, Edward Boyle, the economic secretary to the Treasury. Others in the civil service contemplated or actually drafted letters of resignation but never presented them. One of the senior mandarins at the Foreign Office, Paul Gore-Booth, wrote a private memo to Kirkpatrick describing the mood of his colleagues as "perplexity turning into despondency and resentment." Now, having rebuffed the Canadian High Commissioner, Kirkpatrick was forced to endure a passionate appeal from one of his own people contradicting the official line. "[I] wanted to express urgently the hope that we could work ourselves out of our present position through the lifeline now extended by Mr. Lester Pearson," Gore-Booth implored.[56]

At 1 p.m. in New York, the keeper of that lifeline lunched with Secretary-General Dag Hammarskjöld in his offices on the UN's thirty-eighth floor. It is unclear whether this was the first time they had talked during the emergency session. They had known each other at least since Pearson, as president of the General Assembly, presided over Hammarskjöld's swearing-in ceremony in 1953. Although they were very different personalities—the Swede being something of a mystic, poet, and ascetic—they admired and trusted each other. In fact, Hammarskjöld and his advisers in the Secretariat considered Pearson "one of us," which was "no mean accolade," according to Geoff Murray, who later served in the Secretariat and felt that the high officials maintained a distinct divide between themselves and the delegates of the member states.[57]

During their lunch meeting, a depressed Hammarskjöld appeared "quite cool to our idea," Pearson remembered, "and very pessimistic about our chances of success. He did not reject the idea but spoke almost entirely of the difficulties." Underlying his mood was the sting of personal betrayal. One of his advisers, Brian Urquhart, recalled that "Hammarskjöld regarded the European powers as the example to the world, the forerunners in everything that was sensible like the Marshall Plan and European unity, which hadn't come about then but was being sought. He was appalled that the two countries he admired most, the two permanent members of the Security Council he most felt at home with, would have done something which was not only stupid but extremely shoddy."[58] If Hammarskjöld did not encourage Pearson's idea for a UN police force, at least he did not obstruct it.

Pearson then met with an "uncertain and dispirited" Pierson Dixon at 3 p.m. Britain's permanent ambassador was "hardly more encouraging," Pearson later wrote. His entirely understandable depression suffused a cable he had sent, just hours after the emergency session, adjourned to his masters in London. "Even our closest friends here are becoming intensely worried," he warned, "that our open defiance of the United Nations may be compounded to the point where we have no option but to leave the organization." In this desperate hour, the Canadian was as good a friend as the British could ask for, which Dixon noted in a follow-up telegram: "[Pearson] made it clear that his main preoccupation was to be helpful in finding some bridge between the United States and ourselves. He certainly would not make any proposals without first ascertaining from us what was the position."[59]

Already thinking beyond the current position, Pearson told Dixon that in two days' time Louis St. Laurent would likely make a nationwide address supporting the force proposal. Dixon could not offer any formal support, as he remained suspended, waiting for instructions, struggling to carry them out faithfully, and perhaps even wondering whether he could remain at his post. "I don't have the slightest doubt at their private meeting that he would have let his hair down," Geoff Murray judged, "and probably say, 'Mike, what do you think I should do?'"[60] Dixon remained for the entire ordeal but his devotion to duty would be tested again and again.

During the afternoon, Pearson talked with Ambassador Heeney in Washington to discuss American intentions and what that would mean for his own. The US, in turn, was keenly interested in what Canada was going to do. John Foster Dulles summoned Heeney to meet just before 5 p.m. Dulles still supported Pearson's proposal but was doubtful that a force could be created soon enough. Heeney agreed and said it was vital to secure London's approval. The force might help to make a temporary peace in Egypt, but critically for Pearson, it was needed to help make peace between Britain and the US. And Heeney did not forget the other role the force could play, saying, "Pearson's objective is to help get the British and French 'off the hook.'"[61] In terms of the larger challenge for the region, a UN force remained a secondary element.

Coming into sync with Pearson's original thinking, Dulles outlined a proposal to establish separate UN commissions on the Suez Canal and Palestine. He wanted Pearson to tackle the canal issue and was considering introducing the resolutions within the next forty-eight hours. Heeney indicated that Pearson was also considering convening a conference or small committee to work on a peace settlement for the Middle East but admitted that Ottawa's thinking on this was "still somewhat vague." Faced with a tangled political landscape made only more complicated by the current crisis, Heeney made an observation which perfectly encapsulated Pearson's tactical approach: "It was important to avoid taking up a fixed position too soon until sufficiently wide support was reasonably assured."[62]

After less than thirty hours away, Pearson arrived back in Ottawa at 6:45 p.m. Despite his exhaustion, he headed straight into a press conference. "We are going to see if it is a practical idea. We are going to try to work it out," he stated. He told the reporters that he had no idea whether Egypt would even accept a UN force and that only the US had publicly supported his proposal. Working to lower expectations, he cautioned, "If you don't see much about Canada's plan in the next few days, you'll know that it is not generally acceptable." Trying to downplay the unhelpful reality that the British and French armada was still sailing for Egypt, Pearson asserted that the landing would not "invalidate" his idea. This was a necessary evasion. He had no illusions about his very small window of opportunity. As he put it, "The next two days will tell the tale."[63] Earlier in the day, he had said to Heeney that he was planning to introduce his resolution during the following week. He didn't know yet that he would have to shift diplomatic gears and bring that plan forward in the next twenty-four hours.

THIRTEEN

Off the Hook

It is difficult to see what part we can play, unless our position
as a smaller state without ties gives us a chance to say some
things that the great powers or the little powers tied to the
great ones would not dare to.
— Lester Pearson, September 29, 1931[1]

The fact is that it rarely ever happens that a foreign
government gives up its selfish interests, its
passions or its prejudices to the force of argument or
persuasion.... Persuasion seldom succeeds unless there is
compulsion of some sort, nearer or further off behind it.
— Prime Minister Lord Palmerston, September 3, 1850[2]

On November 3, just after 12 p.m., Anthony Eden rose in the House of
Commons to defy the world for another day. The British and French
"police action" sailing towards the Suez Canal to make peace, he declared, "must be carried through" until the proposed UN force was
established and accepted by Israel and Egypt. Asked about consulting
with the Commonwealth, he noted briefly and without endorsement "Mr.
Pearson's observations" from the night before. Britain "should naturally
not expect to be excluded from it. We should want to be a part of it,"
the prime minister said, complicating Pearson's mission. "I should hope
that the House would feel that I was not unreasonable."[3] His opponents
sitting in front of him and at the General Assembly and foreign ministries

around the world would judge Eden's expectations, more accurately, as completely out of touch with political realities.

In Ottawa, at 9:15 a.m. EST, Pearson met with Neil Pritchard, the acting UK High Commissioner, and was shown Eden's statement, which elicited his "intense satisfaction." Unspoken objectives and self-serving caveats notwithstanding, London had publicly implied its support for his proposed UN force. Having tactfully begun on a positive note, Pearson then turned to the "main difficulty" with Eden's approach: the assumed and desired inclusion of British and French forces. Wanting to accommodate this assumption and somehow defuse the anger in the General Assembly, Pearson was anxious for London to contrive, as the meeting notes put it, some "cover" for this sticking point. He suggested that London and Paris could place their intervention force formally under UN command, to be joined by troops from other member states as soon as possible. Without this, he cautioned, "resistance might build up in [the] United Nations." Pearson advised Pritchard that this point "demanded most urgent consideration." In other, less diplomatic, words, Eden's refusal to accept these suggestions for cover could destroy Pearson's still tenuous lifeline.[4]

Not wanting to alienate or abandon London, and needing American support, Pearson next asked Arnold Heeney to inform the State Department that the formal Canadian proposal might include British and French contingents. Suspecting this would not be received with any enthusiasm, Pearson had started working in advance to manage expectations.

At 10 a.m., Pearson attended Cabinet and briefed his colleagues about his next move: the formal presentation at the General Assembly of a proposal for a UN police force to be initially composed of troops immediately available — in other words, the British and the French — who would be joined as soon as possible by American and Canadian troops, and then by forces from other member states.

With Cabinet still in session, Heeney took this proposal to senior State Department officials to secure US agreement in principle; John Foster Dulles was unavailable, having been hospitalized with what appeared to be appendicitis but proved to be cancer. The proposed UN force, Heeney emphasized, was being put together "on a crash basis." The Americans

UK ambassador to the UN Sir Pierson Dixon (left) with Lester Pearson,
November 1956, United Nations (UN photo 121724)

shared the objective to extricate the British but not the method proposed.
The African and Asian members would see the Canadian plan "as a
device to get the British and French off the hook and nothing more than
putting a UN cloak over military aggression," argued C. Burke Elbrick,
the deputy assistant secretary. "Any support we might give to such a plan
would be taken as US collusion." Heeney did not deny these charges;
he knew this was exactly what Pearson was trying to do. Canada was,
he acknowledged, "suspect as a member of the Commonwealth," but
nonetheless "something must be devised at once to bring the situation
under a UN cloak."[5]

Regardless of how Canada ultimately proceeded, Elbrick replied,
Washington would move ahead with its plan to introduce resolutions
calling for parallel commissions on Suez and Palestine. The allies appeared to have switched emphases: the US now focused on a political
settlement, and Canada on setting up the police force stop-gap. Elbrick

ended the meeting reiterating that the US must "avoid giving the impression that we [are] working in collusion with Canada to get the British and French off the hook." Washington was not alone in its reservations. Indian prime minister Jawaharlal Nehru, the key voice in Southeast Asia and the non-aligned world, informed one of his ambassadors that India would "strongly oppose" an international police force.[6]

Even with Heeney's discouraging report, Pearson decided to ignore Washington's central concern for the time being and see if he could persuade the General Assembly to even temporarily tolerate British and French contingents in the proposed force. He drafted a resolution calling for the General Assembly to recommend "that a Committee of Five Members of the Assembly be appointed to submit to it within forty-eight hours a plan for the setting up in the Middle East of an emergency international United Nations police force recruited from national military forces immediately available and adequate in number to carry out the purposes of Resolution No. _____."[7]

The draft was sent to Heeney in Washington and Norman Robertson in London for informal circulation. Robertson had also been assigned the difficult task of suggesting to Her Majesty's Government to delay military landings until after the General Assembly debated the Canadian proposal. That evening, Eden made a major statement on television and radio, and restated his earlier overture: "If the United Nations will take over this police action, we shall welcome it," he said, but added "until the United Nations force is there, ready to take over, we and the French must go on with the job, until the job is done."[8]

At 4:30 p.m., bearing his problematic resolution, Pearson left Ottawa for the UN emergency session, scheduled to resume in a few hours. One journalist on board the flight remembered him sitting "alone in a private cabin looking out the window. No aides in discussion, though they were on the plane. No documents, no notes, no memo pad." The minister was uncharacteristically withdrawn, as even he later acknowledged. "Press men [were] with me on the plane and they wanted to talk to me and I wanted to look out and think of what I ought to do and how I ought to do it," he remembered. "It was a rough flight. I was so preoccupied by what was going to face me in New York that I forgot to be airsick as I always used to be."[9]

While Pearson mentally mapped out the night ahead, Arnold Heeney showed State Department officials Pearson's draft resolution. The Americans called it promising, and one they could support if enough members rallied to it but, consistent in their concerns, suggested Ottawa delete the line inviting "national military forces immediately available." They also suggested including a caveat that the UN would act only "with the consent of the parties concerned." Heeney said he would convey these comments to Pearson, en route to the General Assembly, poised "with pencil in the air."[10] After the meeting, the Canadian idea was outlined to President Eisenhower, caught up in the final days of his re-election campaign and operating without his hospitalized secretary of state. Henry Cabot Lodge, the US ambassador to the UN, served as the American point man in the debate to come.

At 7 p.m., just before Pearson reached the UN, the president spoke on the telephone with Lodge. Eisenhower was unhappy about the impending British and French assault, "a great tragedy" if it was to happen, and wanted someone and something "to stall this landing." That someone should be Dag Hammarskjöld, and the something was the UN force plan. He informed Lodge that Canada was bringing a resolution calling for a five-member committee to establish the force, but he preferred "to get the Secretary-General into the act, [as he] could act more freely than a committee of 5 would." Events were moving so quickly that Lodge learned only during the phone call that the State Department had drafted a resolution for this purpose. What he didn't know was that Canadian arguments and even wording had influenced American thinking. The American draft resolution expressed the Canadian idea with one significant difference: the force's composition. The president instructed the ambassador "to see the Secretary-General, sell it to him, and then sell it to Pearson when he arrives."[11] Lodge received a copy of this draft resolution, most likely by teleprinter, right after his conversation with Eisenhower.

In later interviews, Lodge would sometimes characterize himself as the hinge of fate because he had personally chosen Pearson to front the so-called American resolution. In one version, Pearson happened to walk into his office, and in a second, they bumped into each other in a hallway, at exactly the moment Lodge was looking for a sponsor. He would recount that he marvelled at how Pearson — a mere passerby — read the

US resolution in a flash, immediately grasped all its implications, and then right away strode off to propose it from the floor of the General Assembly. "It was the quickest thing I've ever seen in my life," Lodge enthused later. "Really, my hat was off to him."[12] But this only shows how out of touch Lodge was with the rapid-fire decisions being taken in Washington in response to the drafts from Ottawa and the meetings with Heeney, let alone everything else Pearson had been working on for the last three days. Lodge's memo of his talk with Eisenhower establishes that the president instructed him to sell the American draft specifically to Pearson. Lodge's version also glossed over the primary fact that Pearson had already presented the idea of a UN force forty-eight hours earlier. The piece of paper Lodge handed over was a function of that Canadian initiative, and not the other way around.

And Pearson did not, as Lodge remembered, just saunter off to the assembly hall, bearing the draft to a foregone conclusion. He had to navigate a long, uncertain night before he felt ready to approach the rostrum, and even after that landmark moment, he faced further hurdles that very few diplomats could have cleared. Lodge graciously acknowledged that Pearson deserved "the lion's share of the credit," but years after the event he could also be heard to complain that he had held the precious piece of paper that established the UN force, and he had happened to hand it to Pearson, when it could have been someone else, and that's how Pearson happened to win the Nobel Prize.[13]

Unaware of the phone call between Lodge and Eisenhower, Pearson reached the UN building at about 7:30 p.m., half an hour before the assembly was due to reconvene. Geoff Murray immediately briefed him about reactions to his draft proposal. In London, Norman Robertson discussed it with Selwyn Lloyd, who in turn spoke with Eden. Their overall impression was favourable, which was not surprising since the plan would allow British contingents to join the proposed UN force. However, Eden still declined to support the resolution formally in the General Assembly or, more importantly, to call off the imminent landing in Egypt. Furthermore, he requested changing a handful of words that would, most unhelpfully for Pearson, recast the force's mission. Eden would not have the UN force, as the Canadian draft proposed, "carry out the purposes of" the American ceasefire resolution, because ceasing to fire would not allow his troops to overthrow the Egyptian government, his true objective. Instead, he wanted the resolution to instruct the UN force "to procure a cessation of hostilities between Egypt and Israel pending a general settlement of all outstanding problems in the area." This could mean that British and French forces would remain on Egyptian soil indefinitely, and with the blessing of the United Nations.[14]

Before walking into the Assembly hall, Pearson headed for the American mission's tiny secondary office in the basement. As Geoff Murray recalled, "Almost the first thing that happened once we got in the door, [was] Cabot Lodge produced a piece of white paper with blue printing on it."[15] This was the just-received American draft resolution that the ambassador had been instructed to sell to Pearson, who in turn produced a copy of his own resolution, which he wanted to sell to Lodge. Looking at the American draft, he must have been gratified to see that Washington endorsed and echoed the core premise in the Canadian proposal, the creation of a UN force. Washington's preference to have the secretary-general oversee the report to create that force was not only easy to accommodate but also sensible. The American draft, however, did not contain the line "recruited from national forces immediately available." This omission would unequivocally shut out the British and French troops. Here the central British requirement collided with unyielding American objection. Pearson had to choose which of these allies he could afford to disappoint. He clearly did not waste much time deliberating.

Then and there, with the emergency session due to start in less than thirty minutes, the two diplomats reworked the language from their two drafts into a single resolution. Pearson barely mentioned this meeting in his television memoirs and brushed over it in his autobiography, simply noting that the American "text was simpler than ours and with some minor alterations we adopted it as our own." He did not mention that, in an instant, he dropped the Canadian resolution's provocative phrase "recruited from national military forces immediately available," obviously concluding that the Americans were simply not going to budge on this point. He knew the change would require some very heavy persuasion to sell to the British and that there was no guarantee he would prevail. Having worked with Lodge to craft the revised resolution, Pearson still made no promise to submit it to the General Assembly.[16]

As soon as he finished with the Americans, Pearson walked across the narrow hall to the British "cubbyhole" to talk with Pierson Dixon. The delegation was, Murray saw, "in quite a nervous state." With the General Assembly about to resume in mere minutes, "they didn't know what was coming next." They almost certainly did not expect their next blow to come from the amiable Canadian with whom they had been working in secret to get their government off the hook.[17]

For the last forty-eight hours, Dixon had reprised Eden's public line that "no one would be better pleased than we" to hand over the tough fighting in Egypt to the United Nations. For the last forty-eight hours, Dixon and his officials hoped and expected to seek shelter and redemption within the proposed UN force. For the last forty-eight hours, Pearson said he would provide that cover. But now, without warning or discussion, he had thrown that cover aside. After the British ambassador looked over the revised resolution, the watchful Murray remembered him saying something along the lines of, "Well, this is not quite what we had been looking at before Mike," and Pearson replying, "No, but it amounts to the same thing. It's a little simpler than ours," which was "something of a diplomatic understatement," as Murray recalled with a smile.[18]

Having delivered a devastating blow, Pearson imposed further still and asked Dixon to abstain. "Pearson didn't expect that they would vote in favour," Murray said, trying to explain Pearson's tactics. "He didn't need them to vote in favour. It mightn't have been a good thing if they voted in favour. Dixon didn't commit himself, but in effect he said, 'We'll just have to see, Mike; perhaps I won't have instructions,' which is always an out for abstaining."[19]

Pearson left the British with their quandary, took his place at the Canada desk in the General Assembly, and against the backdrop of angry speeches from the rostrum launched his campaign to persuade as many of the seventy-five delegations as possible to support his call for a UN police force. First, he touched base with the man who, if the resolution passed, would bear the greatest responsibility for bringing it to life, someone who was extremely pessimistic when they last spoke just over twenty-four hours before. Murray was the messenger. When approached, Hammarskjöld simply replied, "Tell Mike I'll be in touch shortly."[20]

Mirroring tactics from the previous emergency session, Pearson sent adviser John Holmes and Permanent Representative Robert MacKay to delegation desks, hallways, and lounges to once again sound out opinion, drum up support, and smooth away obstacles before they were made public. The third secretary to the Australian mission, Michael Wilson, recalled: "People were just not sure what it meant, and they didn't know what it would consist of, and they didn't know who would be involved in it, and they didn't know who was going to pay for it. You get all these sorts of bread-and-butter questions from diplomats when they suddenly think, 'My God, my country's going to have to pay for this and that.'"[21] At one point, a Secretariat official "carrying a small notebook," pulled Holmes aside, ready to write down the "concrete ideas we Canadians had for this force we were proposing. The truth was that we hadn't gone that far."[22] The Canadians were asking for a huge leap of faith.

During multiple informal encounters, where the assembly became a kind of trading floor, Pearson secured Norway and Colombia as co-sponsors, which would lend the resolution a more multilateral frame. Word reached him that, along with the American push for commissions on Suez and Palestine, nineteen Asian, Arab, and African states, including Egypt, were circulating their own draft resolution calling on Britain, France, and Israel to comply with the existing ceasefire request within twelve hours. India's permanent representative, Arthur Lall, a driving force behind this resolution, was scouting for votes and therefore was open to supporting the Canadian resolution in return for Canada's bringing over as many votes as possible to support his. Pearson was privately "somewhat doubtful" about the "unrealistic" request to have Britain and France stand down within twelve hours, but given the potential of picking up Asian, African, and Arab votes, his pragmatism prevailed, and he offered Canada's support. During the evening, Lall also passed on crucial unofficial information from Cairo that President Nasser had agreed in principle to accept a UN force on Egyptian soil.[23] This added more momentum to the emergency meeting's promising opening note when the Egyptian ambassador announced that Cairo would agree to a ceasefire if Britain, France, and Israel did likewise.

In a vivid break along Commonwealth colour lines, Pearson's collaboration with India could not extend to other imperial offspring that had staked out a diametrically opposed position. In Canberra, Prime

Minister Menzies unapologetically affirmed the British intervention as a legitimate police action that would protect the Suez Canal. To Eden he privately wrote, "You must never entertain any doubts about the British quality of this country." New Zealand's permanent representative to the UN, Leslie Munro, likewise defended the Mother Country in the General Assembly. "Our ties are never closer than in times of stress and danger," he stated and proclaimed without apology that his government "does not accept any charge or imputation of insincerity" in the United Kingdom's motives.[24]

Despite staunch popular and official support, some dismay coursed through the respective UN missions. Australian delegate Michael Wilson, noting his third secretary rank as "the lowest form of life [in the mission], there to make notes and do what I was told," accepted that personal reservations could not interfere with professional conduct: "You're employed by the government. It's your job to represent the government's view. If you disagree with the government's view as it's coming in by telegram, you can argue, by all means. You can telephone, if you insist on doing so. But in the end, if the government wants X, you provide X." First secretary in the New Zealand mission Malcolm Templeton also struggled with his government's position, aware that some of his colleagues "would have liked to have gone along with the Canadians one hundred percent, but public opinion was against us. Whatever we might have felt as professionals about the damage to UN principles, the predominant feeling in New Zealand was 'Wherever Britain goes, we go.'" In similar fashion to his Australian counterpart, Templeton's personal qualms were inevitably submerged to punishing professional demands: "Basically we were too bloody busy working to be having these philosophical thoughts. We were working eighteen hours a day and doing our best to make sure that our government's views were put across in a fair way."[25]

During the haggling around the Canadian proposal, a semantic fire ignited over Washington's insertion of the phrase "with the consent of the nations concerned." Did this consent, delegates asked, apply to the nations contributing troops to the proposed UN force, or to the three aggressor nations? Pearson did not have the answer, and the delegates wouldn't allow him to take refuge in ambiguity. Egypt, especially, insisted on clarification. After several discussions with the American delegation, the Canadians let it be known that the consent in their resolution applied to the nations contributing troops to the force. The aggressor nations would not be allowed to dictate terms to the General Assembly. Cast aside in this backstage manoeuvring was Pearson's desire to link his proposal with a commitment to negotiate a more lasting peace. It was important to Pearson, as John Holmes wrote later, to "exploit the crisis to get ourselves out of the mess that had been perpetuated. However, we were always up against the insistence of the Asians and the Africans, who could command majority support in the Assembly, that any settlement under those circumstances would mean a reward for Israel's aggression."[26]

On the surface, the middle-power diplomat exuded endless patience. He understood he could, as always, only suggest, persuade, divert, or encourage. At times, however, Geoff Murray glimpsed his limits. "It is not that he was never irritated, never impatient," he wrote. "He reacted angrily at what he regarded as unjustified suspicion of the Egyptians. He resented persistent Israeli pressure to drive him into a corner even on debating points. He was caustic about British condescension and American haste."[27] Long before this crisis, the professional diplomat had learned the value of masking his feelings in public.

With the outcome still uncertain, Pearson's operation received a public sign of official favour when Hammarskjöld walked over to the Canada desk and spoke with him so that all could see—a simple gesture but one meant to be noticed. "My own belief," said Murray, "is that he did that to demonstrate to the Assembly that their secretary-general was in touch with the proposer of the force. I think it was quite deliberate."[28] Perhaps it was during this brief talk that Hammarskjöld, despite his initial pessimism, told Pearson that he now felt that creating the force might actually be possible, and as proposed in the revised text, he would take on the central role to establish it.

At about 10:30 p.m., Pearson took his turn at the rostrum to address the delegates. He noted the immediate purpose of the meeting, to secure a ceasefire and withdrawal of troops, and the long-term challenge, to shape a settlement in the Middle East. He praised the Asian, Arab, and African proposal supporting the former and the American draft resolutions addressing the latter. Then he formally submitted the resolution his advisers had been circulating throughout the evening.

The General Assembly,
Bearing in mind the urgent necessity of facilitating compliance with
the resolution of 2 November 1956,

Requests, as a matter of priority, the Secretary-General to submit to
it within forty-eight hours, a plan for the setting up, with the consent
of the nations concerned, of an emergency international United
Nations force to secure and supervise the cessation of hostilities in
accordance with the terms of the aforementioned resolution.

In a repeat performance from the previous meeting, and quite possibly
orchestrated in advance, the American ambassador Henry Cabot Lodge
spoke right after Pearson to bestow the superpower imprimatur critical
to the resolution's approval and implementation. "We should like to see
it acted on quickly this evening," he stated, "because it contains a real
hope of meeting the very grave emergency." Then Israel's representative,
Abba Eban, announced his government had agreed to accept a ceasefire,
providing Cairo did the same.[29] Suddenly, Britain and France's already
dubious reason to continue their military assault seemed even more so.

But before the vote could be called, questions lingered. Indian delegate Arthur Lall addressed the assembly, requesting public confirmation
of private assurances that the resolution's reference to "the consent of the
nation concerned" meant the nations that would contribute the troops.
He also made it very clear that India would not tolerate British and
French contingents in the UN force. Finally, he cautioned that a vote in
support of the resolution was not an automatic commitment to establish
the force, only a vote to ask the secretary-general to submit a report.[30]

Returning to the rostrum, Pearson assured delegates that what was
said in private stood in public. There would be no question of needing to
ask consent from Britain, France, or Israel to implement a UN force and,
likewise, the secretary-general should not be empowered to name any
countries to the force without their consent. Pearson invoked Canadian
insistence flowing back three-quarters of a century and stated that requiring the UN to seek consent from member states "may seem an obvious
point but our own experience in the past has shown that it is just as well
to make it quite clear, because it has happened that…Governments have
been named at international meetings not only before they had agreed

but even before they were consulted on the subject, and these words are intended to make it doubly sure that will not happen on this occasion."[31]

After a final speaker, the vote on Pearson's resolution was called, the order drawn by lot. In a fitting coincidence, having guided the General Assembly to this moment, Canada was first to vote on an idea that had evolved from the League of Nations in the 1920s and 1930s through to the UN observer missions of the late 1940s; that General Burns and Pearson raised in private in November 1955; that Selwyn Lloyd suggested in January and London, Washington, and Ottawa discussed and set aside in February; and that, finally, in a play for time and cover, a cornered Anthony Eden offered up just three days before.

In a matter of minutes the voting was over and the tally read out from the rostrum. Not a single member voted against the Canadian resolution. Nineteen abstained, the most important being Egypt, Britain, France, and Israel. A negative vote from any of these governments would have derailed if not shut down any possibility of moving forward. The remaining fifty-seven members delivered the two-thirds majority needed to pass the resolution.

The result was a stunning triumph for Lester Pearson. There was arguably no other diplomat who could have orchestrated this improbable result, for there were no other diplomats who combined his tactical finesses with his depth of experience, particularly at the UN; who could claim his range of close contacts in the capitals that mattered; and who was simultaneously a member of the Commonwealth and NATO. Pearson represented a country not so large that it was threatening nor so small that it could be easily dismissed, and which was not clouded by a direct economic or military stake in the Middle East. Yet once the applause and congratulations faded, hard realities remained. The Canadian had shaped a brilliant victory in the General Assembly, throwing out a lifeline to two critical allies, perhaps even launching a new security experiment for the world organisation, but he had not made peace in Egypt.

With the British-French armada sailing through the Mediterranean towards the Suez Canal, and Israel and Egypt declaring they would accept a ceasefire, Anthony Eden had to decide whether to stand down or carry on. Pierson Dixon bluntly warned him: "If we bomb open cities with resulting loss of civilian life or engage in battle with the Egyptian forces, there is not the faintest chance of this move receiving any sympathy," he said. "The only honest course for Her Majesty's Government and the French Government would be to withdraw their representatives and leave the United Nations."[32] At the same time, Dixon alerted Eden that the government faced something far more punishing than harsh sermons from the world community. Serious talk of economic sanctions was circulating in the UN. When he heard this, Harold Macmillan, the chancellor of the exchequer, described as "wanting to tear Nasser's scalp off with his own fingernails," who had bragged that he was willing to risk war with the Soviets, and who had urged Eden to engineer an Israeli attack as a pretext for invading Egypt, now exclaimed in anguish, "Oil sanctions! That finishes it!"[33] But Eden was not for turning just yet.

The British Cabinet assembled at 6:30 p.m. on November 4 to debate the stark choice facing Her Majesty's Government. Muffled roars and shouts reverberated into the meeting room from thousands of demonstrators in nearby Trafalgar Square, demanding "Law not war!" Eden noted a letter from Hammarskjöld that placed the responsibility for ending the conflict squarely with London and Paris. "It would be difficult to deny," he frankly acknowledged, "that the purpose of our intervention in Egypt had already been achieved." One of his most senior colleagues, R. A. Butler, agreed with that judgment. If Israel and Egypt were willing to lay down arms, "we could not possibly continue our expedition," he said. "We had no justification for invasion." When Eden asked each minister to declare himself, the prime minister found a Cabinet almost evenly divided between those who wanted go to on and those who urged a temporary or indefinite halt. Eden "wrestled for hours with Cabinet," as he later wrote in his diary, to drag the doubters back into line.[34] At some point in the long meeting, he took aside Butler and Macmillan and told them that he would resign if Cabinet did not support the landings.

The impasse lasted until about midnight. Eden was saved when news arrived from the Israeli government, continuing to serve as a good ally, that it now attached numerous conditions to its acceptance of a ceasefire, that it refused to withdraw from Egypt, and that it refused to accept a UN force on its newly conquered territory. Happily for the remaining hawks, a state of conflict still existed and thus required a British and French peace to be imposed. According to Clarissa Eden, who must have heard this from her husband, when the Israeli news came through, "everyone laughed and banged the table with relief," except for two ministers "who looked glum."[35] With the pretext still conveniently in place, Cabinet decided to carry on with the landing of British forces on Egyptian soil, there to remain until the UN was able to establish its own police force. Pierson Dixon, it was agreed, would speak in favour of the Canadian resolution but with reservations, which would oblige Britain to abstain from formally supporting it.

Eden phoned the delegation in New York to speak with Dixon, who had First Secretary Peter Ramsbotham listen in on an extension. As Ramsbotham recalled the phone conversation, "There was this euphoric voice, this First World War clipped voice talking excitedly: 'the paraboys are going in!' My heart sank, you know, because this was not in keeping at all with what was happening in our part of the United Nations. No mention of Lester Pearson. No mention of the UN force. Nothing. Dixon wished him well on the telephone and said he could just hold the position for another three or four days before we'd be kicked out of the United Nations."[36]

While Eden and his Cabinet colleagues agonized through November 4 into the night about whether to land their troops, Lester Pearson began his day confronting the pressing need to create a different kind of intervention in Egypt. Words of support filtered in from around the world, even from countries that abstained on his resolution. Australia's government would "await the concrete development of Mr. Pearson's helpful proposal," Robert Menzies announced, "with most sympathetic interest." New Zealand's prime minister, Sidney Holland, issued a press statement in which he welcomed the Canadian initiative, even if he also saw it as "a vindication of the Anglo-French contention that police action in the area had been urgently necessary." His Department of External Affairs cabled the New Zealand mission in New York. "Pearson's proposal," it conceded, "may well offer the prospect of a solution."[37]

At 11:30 a.m., Pearson joined counterparts from Colombia, India, and Norway at UN headquarters to discuss a task that, as he described it to them, "seemed almost impossible." In a supremely fortunate alignment, however, the gamble of creating a UN police force virtually from scratch had been handed to Dag Hammarskjöld. The austere, enigmatic Swede had begun to reimagine and remake his role and, as Douglas Hurd saw first-hand, "to place himself on a different moral plane to the representatives of temporal governments. He alone was the custodian of the United Nations Charter." The junior member of the British mission discerned the interweaving elements of Hammarskjöld's personality—"his moods and his obscurity and his pontifical outlook," which could be exasperating, but also the skilled command, wisdom, and integrity. "When he talked," Hurd wrote, "you knew you were in the presence of an exceptional, perhaps a great human being."[38] Pearson shared this admiration.

At the 11:30 meeting, perhaps overly anxious to see a force of any kind established on the ground as soon as possible, mindful he had to present a report to the General Assembly in less than forty-eight hours, Hammarskjöld surprisingly suggested including British and French troops. India's Arthur Lall absolutely rejected such heresy. These aggressors, he declared, must be considered "untouchables." Perhaps hinting at his own personal suspicions, he said their presence would make it seem as if the UN force had been proposed merely "to cloak with respectability the impending occupation of Egypt." This was no doubt cutting too close to the bone, and Pearson did not engage Lall on this. "This Indian reaction was of course to be expected," noted an External Affairs record, "and we have no reason to doubt that Lall was saying moderately what the Egyptians and others would denounce in violent terms."[39]

The argument apparently settled, Pearson articulated his sense of the nascent force's purpose and function, and with impressive prescience, the dead ends that must be avoided. Canada "would be very reluctant to participate," he said, "if we thought it would develop into a long-term commitment which might result in little more than maintaining the unsatisfactory status quo, perhaps until another explosive situation developed in future." Returning to his original objective, he advocated linking the proposed force with a more lasting political settlement. This appeal did not generate much, if any, reaction, and the meeting remained focused on the mass of problems generated by the immediate emergency. The improbability of this mission's success was underscored by the fact that all present concurred that the "toughest problem" ahead would be securing Israel's withdrawal from Egyptian territory.[40]

One detail not mentioned in the Canadian record of this morning meeting, which perhaps Pearson handled himself privately, involved the question of the force commander. His choice was perhaps obvious: fellow Canadian and UNTSO chief E.L.M. Burns, who was already monitoring the Arab-Israeli border. Apparently, Hammarskjöld had doubts about him and wanted "to introduce someone new." Pearson persisted, however. "We had no time to hunt around," he later said. "We had a first-class field officer on the spot with United Nations experience, therefore we should use him."[41] Acknowledging the tight timeline, Hammarskjöld agreed.

Looking ahead to the next emergency session on Egypt, scheduled for later in the evening, Pearson prepared to introduce a draft resolution establishing a command structure for the UN police force. He decided to co-sponsor the resolution with Norway and Colombia and planned to include India, but Pakistan complained bitterly about the place of prominence extended to its rival. Therefore, to eventually make peace in Egypt, Pearson was obliged first to make peace within the United Nations. Moving behind the scenes, he soothed Pakistan's anger by quietly facilitating India's removal as a co-sponsor. He also had to endure "a very discouraging talk" with the Israeli ambassador, Abba Eban, who criticized "the unwarranted interference of the UN with Israel's sovereign rights."[42] Pearson could see all too clearly that, enjoying a strong military position, the Israelis would not surrender any newly captured Egyptian territory unless they were politically compelled to do so. This, he knew, could only come from Washington.

At 4 p.m., the General Assembly convened an emergency special session to debate the crisis in Hungary. Delegates from the Eastern bloc offered support for the brutality carried out in their empire's name. Those from the other side of the Iron Curtain demanded that Russia stop killing comrades who did not wish to remain locked up inside a Communist state. The limits of middle-power diplomacy were on undeniable display as Pearson appealed to Moscow to support the creation of some kind of UN machinery and allow it to enter Hungary. Like everyone else pleading for decency, he spoke in vain. The totalitarian dictatorship was too powerful to be compelled to apologize, explain, or retreat. The one UN member state able to make a difference, the United States, could not encourage any strong measures without risking a world war. Without superpower backing, all the well-intentioned sermons counted for nothing. The meeting on Hungary ended just after 8 p.m. The delegates were due to return in less than two hours for the next round of the emergency special session dealing with Suez.

From Ottawa that evening, Louis St. Laurent delivered a nationwide radio and television address, reportedly his first before live cameras. On the subject of Suez, the prime minister restated all the essential points Ottawa had made for months. He regretted the use of force but understood the provocations that led up to that use, he supported the sovereign rights of Egypt as well as the rights of nations that used the Suez Canal, and he hoped for a wider settlement for the region, preferably one negotiated under the aegis of the United Nations. He praised Pearson's work in the General Assembly and, working to maintain momentum for the proposal, declared that his "government is ready to recommend Canadian participation in such a United Nations force if it is to be established and if it is thought that Canada could play a useful role."[43]

In New York, the emergency session on Suez resumed at 9:45 p.m. Less than 24 hours after Pearson had proposed the request, Hammarskjöld delivered his report, which he called self-explanatory and not requiring "any special comments" from him; in other words, he did not want a lengthy debate. Norway's Hans Engen sponsored, with Canada and Colombia, the draft resolution embodying the principal points from the secretary-general's report. Carrying significant influence with Arab, Asian, and African delegates, Arthur Lall rose to support the resolution. Isolated, Israel's Abba Eban followed to defend the principle of national sovereignty and consent, which, he insisted, must take precedence over the power of the UN to station forces on any member's territory. The French and British ambassadors announced they were still awaiting instructions, but Pierson Dixon indicated, without knowing the ultimate decision had already been taken, that London had "been giving most careful consideration" to the UN's debate.[44]

During this late Sunday night, Hans Engen recalled he, Hammarskjöld, and Pearson felt "pretty desperate." The three men shared "a sort of despairing hope," Engen said, that the British and French "would stop rather than allow the situation to collapse into impossible chaos."[45]

After the majority vote in the General Assembly the night before, which Britain did not oppose; after encouraging words from London, and after the Israeli and Egyptian offers to cease fire, the three diplomats could hardly be faulted for hoping that two permanent members of the Security Council, supposed to uphold the principles of international order, would finally make a gesture of some kind to the world community, most especially to their anxious allies—even a momentary pause.

At about 11 p.m., preparing to address the General Assembly, Pearson was suddenly called away to take a telephone call from St. Laurent, a signal interruption from someone who had allowed Pearson full rein throughout the crisis. The news from Ottawa was devastating. The prime minister had just met with Neil Pritchard, the acting High Commissioner, who hand-delivered a message from Anthony Eden announcing that Britain and France had decided to land their forces in Egypt. Eden described the decision as difficult, even agonizing; he did not mention his Cabinet ministers cheering and pounding their table in delight when they finally made that decision. In his explanation, Eden dismissed the Israeli ceasefire offer as qualified by too many conditions, and he restated the familiar argument that if the Anglo-French force did not intervene to make peace, he foresaw "a major conflagration." While London had not heeded the UN's appeal to stand down, Eden expressed his debt to Pearson for his "skill and energy" but observed that it would take days "for the United Nations force to come into being. This makes it imperative for us to take a grip of the situation."[46]

This fateful decision, and no doubt the palpably disingenuous justification, caused St. Laurent to respond, as Pritchard recorded, "under obviously great emotion and indeed anger." The incensed Canadian prime minister seized in particular on one sentence in Eden's message that claimed that if London did not act, "Nasser's position will be strengthened." Mindful of the unstated but unrelenting British desire to overthrow the Egyptian president, St. Laurent "repeated twice emphatically" that his government could not support that premise and its implications. The prime minister "had nothing good to say about Nasser but Canada could not accept the idea of using armed force to get rid of him." The late-night meeting concluded with St. Laurent declining yet again to offer any support for a military solution to this political crisis.[47]

Pritchard conveyed St. Laurent's displeasure to the Commonwealth Relations Office, adding a private warning that, despite some calls in certain Canadian newspapers to delay judgment, "we should be misleading ourselves if we do not recognise that Mr. St. Laurent is accurately reflecting the general attitude of his Government which is deeply disturbed and, I must say frankly, mistrustful of our motives and our wisdom." Pritchard perhaps strayed beyond the bounds of his position with the personal suggestion that military operations should end swiftly and that London "make way for a U.N. police force with expedition and enthusiasm."[48]

And so in the midst of the debate to establish a UN command for the proposed force, Pearson learned that London and Paris were proceeding with their military expedition in Egypt, despite all of Ottawa's clear but measured appeals over the last four months, despite the anger generated in the Commonwealth and throughout the Middle East, despite the strain inflicted on the Western alliance, despite all of his inspired and politically costly diplomacy at the United Nations. There is no record of Pearson's conversation with St. Laurent, but he must have felt betrayed, even devastated. Journalist Terence Robertson, who later interviewed him, wrote with marked understatement: "Pearson, in particular, was deeply affected."[49] More than any other Commonwealth and NATO diplomat, the moderate mediator had toiled for months in the thankless middle ground, only to be accused at home of betraying the very ally and Mother Country he had done everything to protect.

The official response from Ottawa to Eden's distressing message must have captured something of Pearson's feelings. "We will continue to do our best to be of whatever assistance we can," St. Laurent concluded to Eden, "but I would not wish to leave you with the impression that as seen from here the situation appears other than tragic." After the telephone call, Pearson privately informed Henry Cabot Lodge of the news from London. They then spoke with Hammarskjöld and decided it was best to vote on the resolution as soon as possible. They even discussed transporting Canadian troops stationed in West Germany to Egypt.[50]

When he spoke from the rostrum, near the end of the debate, Pearson decided not to inform the General Assembly what he had learned; the appalling news might enrage the delegates and derail his entire game plan. Whatever he was feeling, he merely made a brief, unemotional statement urging them to press ahead with establishing the force and restated, virtually word for word, what St. Laurent announced a few hours before: Canada was willing to volunteer troops for the proposed UN force. In keeping with the informal agreement, Lodge spoke next, and invoking the urgency of the hour, moved that the debate be closed and the vote taken, obliging the beleaguered British and French delegates to plead for time to receive instructions. In a quick discussion with his Norwegian and Colombian co-sponsors, Pearson agreed that delaying the vote could serve no purpose. Britain and France would either support it or oppose it, and if they opposed it, "it was all the more important to proceed with the plan." British and French pleas for a delay were denied, and the draft resolution was put to a vote at 12:15 a.m., now November 5. The results revealed a clear majority in the General Assembly: fifty-seven member states, with nineteen abstentions and no opposition, endorsed the secretary-general's report to establish a United Nations command for the proposed emergency force. No one was using the terms "peacekeeping" or "peacekeeper." That would come later. Fulfilling Pearson's hopes and backstage lobbying, General Burns was appointed the chief of the command, authorized to immediately recruit officers from his existing observer team. In an unmistakeable rejection of British and French wishes, the force would not contain any troops from the Security Council's permanent members.[51]

This verdict represented the culmination of all Pearson's intensive efforts over the last frantic four days, in the course of which he had suggested a UN police force, seemingly as an afterthought, then shaped it into a formal request to the secretary-general to present a preliminary report, and finally brought it before the General Assembly for its endorsement. John Holmes said later, "The idea was not important; the execution was." Holmes credited Pearson's "extraordinary quarterbacking" for the resolution's success. "His footwork was so fast I couldn't keep up.... His genius was as a strategist." The *Globe and Mail* reported: "Although the idea of a police force seemed to many delegates to be the obvious answer from the start, it remained for Mr. Pearson to make the first concrete suggestion and for Canada to take the initiative in shaping a resolution. Coming from almost any other country, [a Danish delegate] said, such a resolution and such an idea could not have had... the same impact that it had coming from Canada."[52]

The meeting adjourned at 12:25 a.m. As they drifted out into the cold New York night, departing delegates had no idea that while they had been talking about how to make peace in Egypt, just minutes before, at the northern end of the Suez Canal, close to seven hundred British paratroopers had dropped onto a small airfield west of Port Said. Five hundred French paratroopers landed close by to the south at the Raswa bridges and, as one soldier recalled, "machine-gunned every living thing ahead of us."[53] Egyptian forces engaged the invaders in combat, and the land war had begun.

However appalled, Pearson remained determined to save the British from themselves, the Western alliance from more corrosion, and the UN from more blatant insult. He spent the late morning and early afternoon of November 5 with Hammarskjöld and Secretariat officials discussing logistics and tactics for what came to be called the United Nations Emergency Force (UNEF). "Pearson was extremely important in bringing along governments who were nervous about a new experiment and explaining to them also Hammarskjöld's extremely complicated prose," Hammarskjöld adviser Brian Urquhart later said. "Hammarskjöld's English was at a level of a sort of metaphysics which was pretty difficult for the ordinary person to understand, and Pearson was wonderful about that."[54] Submitting himself to a familiar ordeal, Pearson met in the afternoon with Krishna Menon, India's roving alternate envoy, self-styled champion to the non-aligned movement, and for many in the West, an infuriating prima donna.

Throughout this crisis, Pearson was ever mindful of Indian concerns and suggestions, for he understood that as Canada remained the vital link to London, India maintained the critical line to Egypt. Nasser and Nehru were known to be personally close and politically united in their desire to remain above what they saw as the primitive schism between the democracies and the Communist states. Having been tolerated and essentially dismissed in his earlier uninvited attempts to mediate the conflict in the later summer and early fall, arriving at the UN only after all the key debates and votes had taken place, and seemingly unaware of all the compromises employed to reach the precarious accommodation, Menon "stormed" into a meeting of Arab and Asian delegates to denounce UNEF as impossible. He was brought, if only momentarily, down to earth by his colleague, Arthur Lall, who informed him that, except for Egypt, which abstained, the Arab, African, and Asian members had endorsed the emergency force, and Nasser had accepted it, something that even Menon could not circumvent. Denied the chance to put the imperialists in the dock, Menon suggested to Pearson that he would introduce a resolution in the General Assembly condemning Britain and France as aggressors and demand an immediate withdrawal. Pearson promptly warned Hammarskjöld.[55]

That evening the Security Council convened to debate the ongoing state of undeclared war in Egypt. The Soviet Union's Arkady Sobolev alarmed delegates when he proposed that the United States join his country and other members to push back the British and French forces. During this bluffing game, Pearson was advising Hammarskjöld on the follow-up report to the General Assembly. In the midst of this they received a copy of Menon's resolution denouncing the French and British, which neither man could ever support. Pearson felt it was imperative to somehow delay the approaching General Assembly meeting, because there would be, as he delicately phrased it to Ottawa, "intemperate language." Moving to provide temporary breathing room for the British and French, Hammarskjöld, with Pearson's encouragement, "prevailed upon" the General Assembly president to postpone the meeting and thus spare the their allies another round of invective.[56]

Knowing the collective outrage had merely been suspended, Pearson worked on the other side of the lingering equation, trying to secure the elusive British acquiescence. He spoke late in the evening with Pierson Dixon about the force proposal, urging that the British government "now take this way out of their difficulties," and then remained with Hammarskjöld, finishing the report at around 2 a.m.[57] But London did not want to take Pearson's way out just yet. Toppling Nasser seemed beyond reach, but a useful bargaining position could still be seized physically and held.

On November 6, as Pearson toiled in New York, a vivid red dawn emerged over the northern entrance to the Suez Canal. British and French aircraft carriers, destroyers, cruisers, minesweepers, tank landing craft, troop vessels, tankers, and supply ships prepared to enforce peace upon a country that had already declared it would accept a ceasefire.

Just before 6 a.m. local time, the deafening roar of battle began with a rain of shells tearing up the breakwater and beach at Port Said, followed by strafing sweeps from the Royal Air Force. A black torrent of smoke unfurled skywards from a bombed oil facility. Tanks and armoured carriers thundered over the beaches. Assault helicopters hovered overhead. British commandos advanced into Port Said and the French into adjacent Port Fuad, fighting street to street, building to building, not entirely sure whether they were killing soldiers or clumsy civilians who had bravely, foolishly taken up arms. A French paratrooper recorded the scene: "Palm trees are blazing like torches. The whole city reeks of fire, grease, metal, gasoline, powder, and carrion." A British military doctor saw Egyptian corpses arriving, as he reported, in "trucks, hearses, ambulances, and even a Coca-Cola lorry. Loads and loads of bodies, of all ages, and both sexes. They were buried in roughly bulldozed mass graves." However stubborn and lethal in some clashes, the outnumbered Egyptian resistance was professionally crushed, and by the end of day, units in the 22,000-strong invasion force reached twenty-three miles south along the Suez Canal causeway to El Cap. In the midst of the carnage loomed the towering statue of Ferdinand de Lesseps, the man who made the Suez Canal a reality, who dreamed his waterway would unite East and West and remain forever neutral in war and peace.[58]

In London, at 9:45 a.m. GMT, six hours after the Royal Navy began shelling Port Said, Prime Minister Eden assembled his Cabinet in his House of Commons room to confront the enduring dilemma: to carry on or stand down? At this juncture, with both Israel and Egypt offering unconditional ceasefires, he had lost any plausible reason for maintaining his uninvited police force. The prime minister was still prepared, however, to continue military operations. Harold Macmillan was not, and he began to undermine Eden's faltering support around the table. Now as untouchable as the government it represented, the British pound had been thrown overboard in overseas money markets, draining the country's gold and currency reserves. Then he delivered truly horrifying news: he could not prop up sterling by drawing from the International Monetary Fund because Washington was blocking the request—unless London announced a full ceasefire.

Although the tidings were undeniably grim, Macmillan, it later turned out, had so seriously exaggerated one set of recent losses that some could say, as indeed they did, he deliberately misled the prime minister and his colleagues. Other actions, or lack of them, would also later raise questions that cannot even now be fully resolved. Unlike the French, he had done nothing to prepare for this entirely foreseeable emergency, such as borrowing from the IMF well in advance, before Washington was in a truly punishing mood. He returned from a September meeting with Eisenhower, whom he had known since the war, and in a complete misreading of the president, assured Eden, "I know Ike. He will lie doggo!"[59] His prime motivation was almost certainly to serve and save his embattled country, but there is more than a distinct possibility that in the crisis Macmillan had also quietly and skilfully served his own longed-for advancement up the greasy pole of British politics by facilitating Eden's fall.

On the morning of November 6, Her Majesty's Government confronted an unforgiving cacophony: a letter from Moscow that threatened nuclear war, which unnerved some ministers but not Eden; the latest warning and plea received just hours before from Dixon in New York; a secretary-general impatient for Britain's formal acceptance of the UN force; an unrelenting Opposition representing a divided country; and a clearly vindictive Washington. All these factors could be deflected for another measure but not the apparently imminent threat of a crippled currency.

For the pound to survive, London needed all the financial resources at Washington's disposal. "While Britain could forgo American approval and friendship, it could not forfeit American money," historian Diane B. Kunz argues. "For the previous decade, it had been conducting a foreign policy beyond its means, relying on the United States government to pay the bills." On the morning of November 6, Eden found that almost all his Cabinet had abandoned him; the bills, financial and political, could no longer be put off. One minister captured the dominant tone of that morning: "We have played every card in our hand, and we have none left."[60]

Eden was obliged to make a painful call to his French comrade-in-arms, Premier Guy Mollet, whose government was financially more secure and less emotionally and militarily tied to the US, and who therefore wished to carry on, if only for a few more days, in order to seize the whole canal and so as not to be seen as weak—particularly while the French army waged a parallel war in Algeria. But Eden had to insist on calling a halt, and Mollet had to acquiesce. Eden was already looking ahead to the diplomatic negotiations to be waged against opponents and, more importantly, against allies. With troops on Egyptian soil and a formidable armada floating off the northern entrance of the canal, he still felt that he held "a gage."[61]

At 12:30 p.m., Eden met Norman Robertson, whose opinion he had written off three months before, and gave him advance warning of the decision to cease fire. No public announcement could be made until Mollet secured approval from his own Cabinet. The prime minister said that he was "very grateful for Canada's steadying influence" at the United Nations and then made two requests of the country he had so studiously kept in the dark. The first almost went without saying. He hoped Canada would help to create an effective UN force. The second request was the true objective: despite all the predictable "political and psychological objections," Eden wanted Canada and the US to persuade the General Assembly, Egypt and India in particular, to have the British and French engineering crews already on the ground start removing the sunken ships and obstacles from the canal.[62] Eden shared the prevailing assumption that the UN would not be able to establish its own force for some time, and clearing the canal would lend a gloss of legitimacy to the remaining British and French troops.

That evening, just after 6 p.m., Eden announced in the House of Commons that British and French forces would cease military operations at midnight. Hard economic blackmail from an ally accomplished what all the sensible advice had not. The immediate reaction from the House was loud, grateful elation for some and utter despair for others. To his future biographer, then a junior clerk, Robert Rhodes James, the prime minister looked "aged and ill, defeated and broken."[63]

Immediately after his brief meeting with Eden, Norman Robertson telephoned Pearson in New York with news of the ceasefire. In his subsequent report to Ottawa, Pearson did not express his reaction, but at last he must have felt some glimmer of relief and perhaps even encouragement.[64] The ongoing complications of assembling a UN force did not allow for much celebration. Pearson was dealing with the need to ensure that as many of those troops as possible came from Western or neutral members. He telephoned Ottawa, warning that Soviet allies were already coming forward to volunteer. Cabinet was expected to discuss a Canadian offer the following day, and Pearson hoped that the troops would be ready for departure within two weeks. That same afternoon, Defence and External Affairs officials met to discuss preliminaries. For now, they candidly acknowledged to each other, they were working in the dark, without clear objectives or established practices.[65] On November 7, the world woke up to the awkward sight of British and French troops on the ground in Egypt—but not fighting. They were waiting in a kind of limbo for the first United Nations police and peace to arrive; still very far from certain that this would ever happen.

FOURTEEN

Triumph and Disaster

The idea of an international force behind international law
goes back to the very dawn of history. It has been an ideal
which has inspired many men all through history, from the
days of the Greek leagues to the Holy Roman Empire, through
the middle ages with the grand design of Henri Quatre, on
to the Holy Alliance of the nineteenth century, a kind of
autocratic expression of the whole idea, until we reach the
League of Nations.
—Lester Pearson, August 1, 1960, House of Commons[1]

"Mike's done it again!"

Those words were reportedly uttered all around Ottawa in November
1956, though not everyone would have said it with approval.[2] Lester
Pearson's very public role in orchestrating the General Assembly's support
for a UN police force had divided his land like no other international
event since the Second World War. More precisely, it divided English
Canada against itself, even in areas of intense British allegiance.

In the Maritimes, the *Halifax Chronicle Herald* supported the government, stating: "Canada once more has risen to her widely regarded
post-war role as a leading peacekeeper." Fredericton's *Daily Gleaner* and
the *Telegraph-Journal* of Saint John criticized it for perceived betrayal. In
Toronto, a bastion of imperial sentiment, Pearson predictably endured
condemnation from both Toronto's *Telegram* and the *Globe and Mail*, yet
was championed in the same city by the *Toronto Daily Star.* In the west, the
Winnipeg Free Press proclaimed, "Mr. Pearson Speaks for Canada," whereas

the *Calgary Herald* titled one editorial "The Shameful Day That Canada
Ran Out." As anglophones argued with each other, Quebec remained
united in supporting a native son, Prime Minister Louis St. Laurent, who
kept faith with Wilfrid Laurier's legacy of skepticism and resistance to
imperial summons. The crisis roused the country's only living former
prime minister, Arthur Meighen, who, remaining faithful to another legacy, resumed his call from 1922 and Chanak to stand "Ready Aye Ready"
for the Empire. He urged the entire Commonwealth to support Anthony
Eden "in his endeavour to maintain Britain's honour and place in world
affairs." The agitated national argument seemed to reverberate through
the entire country, as James Eayrs noted. "It is not often in Canada that
one hears foreign policy being talked about on street corners and in the
lobbies of hotels," he later wrote of this time. "Churchmen preached
sermons on the issue; university students debated and passed resolutions;
trade union councils were aroused to petitioning pitch." Canadians wrote
to newspaper editors and their MP, and deluged External Affairs itself
with the largest wave of telegrams and letters since Pearson took over
eight years before.[3]

In the meantime, the British subject charged with disloyalty was doing
what he could to provide shelter for his embattled ally. Over November
6 and 7, Pearson worked to moderate an Arab-Asian draft resolution
demanding the British immediately withdraw from Egypt. Knowing this
was logistically impossible and therefore impractical, he threatened to
abstain, but sensitive to the fact that "some still remain suspicious that the
[proposed UN] force is a smokescreen," he offered to deliver Canada's
support as long as the word "immediately" did not mean "right away."
His prestige was such that the threat of a Canadian abstention caused
enough consternation in the General Assembly to allow a more flexible
interpretation regarding the British and French departure. Thanks to
Pearson, "immediately" would be understood to mean "as quickly as possible" and would be implicitly linked to the UN force arriving in Egypt.
In winning this semantic skirmish, he had very consciously shielded his
allies from those he called extremists, but it was a victory that earned
him no honour.[4]

Instead, an embarrassing story that again called the government's
loyalties into question captivated the national attention span. On

THE RIGHT ROAD IS STRAIGHT AHEAD

Les Callan, *Toronto Daily Star*, November 28, 1956.
(Reprinted with permission—Torstar Syndication Services)

November 8, Canadians learned from the press that British Labour MP
Patrick Gordon Walker had read one of the telegrams that St. Laurent
sent to Eden and described it as "the most blistering personal message
that has ever passed between two Commonwealth leaders." The Canadian
prime minister insisted "I have never had anything but friendly, though
frank, communications with Sir Anthony Eden." His denial failed to convince his opponents, who added this perceived insult to the growing list of
Liberal sins. Ottawa discussed but then declined to publish the secret telegram; perhaps that was the wiser course of action. "London was 'aghast'

at its tone," a senior official from the British High Commission privately told an officer at External Affairs. "It had come as a great surprise to London."[5] And yet, despite all the criticism from conservative quarters, and in one of the most striking ironies of the entire crisis, Pearson and St. Laurent could see widespread support for Canadian participation in the experiment in international security. Indeed, a starring Canadian role was assumed. These assumptions triggered the next ordeal for Pearson.

Even before the General Assembly formally established a UN command, St. Laurent announced Canadian troops would be made available. On the day he was due to return to Ottawa, November 8, Pearson spoke on the phone with the minister of national defence, Ralph Campney, who informed him that the troops would come from the First Battalion of the Queen's Own Rifles of Canada. Pearson said he "shuddered" when he heard the regal name that highlighted historic and ongoing ties between Canada and a Mother Country that had just invaded Egypt. He would have preferred, he later quipped, "the First East Kootenay Anti-Imperialist Rifles." Pearson voiced his concerns, but Campney's response was "so immediate and violent" he let the matter drop.[6] The next morning, front pages trumpeted the proposed Canadian contribution, displaying photographs of the aircraft carrier HMCS *Magnificent*, designated to transport the Queen's Own Rifles to Egypt. In the happy clamour, the obvious was not noticed: these Canadian soldiers, like all Canadian soldiers, wore uniforms identical to British uniforms, sailed under a flag that included the Union Jack, and were dispatched by a country that belonged to the Commonwealth and had sworn allegiance to a sovereign residing in London. The Egyptian government would notice the obvious.

Pearson flew back to Ottawa the evening of November 8, and on landing, gave one of his tactical press conferences, warning reporters, "We're not out of the woods yet." And he wasn't simply talking about logistical obstacles. Moscow was now offering to send volunteers to Cairo to expel the British and French aggressors. An unapologetic NATO member, Pearson felt no need to avoid discussing a parallel objective, which was to wield the United Nations Emergency Force, UNEF, as a shield against Soviet insinuation in Egypt. "As soon as the UN can operate there, the less tempting it will be to anyone else to move in," he told reporters, and then added, "I hope." In his brief return to Ottawa to meet with officials and the prime minister, the keynote was guarded optimism. "I don't know what we have started here," he admitted. "It is a pretty far reaching development and I only hope it will succeed. If it does it will establish a precedent that might be useful in the future." After less than seventy-two hours, Pearson returned to the United Nations. Characteristically trying to make light of his political trials, he was heard at one point to joke, "I just came down from Ottawa, where I am known as an Israeli stooge, and when I come to New York, I find I am Nasser's cat's paw. I must be doing something right."[7] But if he seemed too pro-Arab for some, too pro-Israeli for others, too anti-British for many, Pearson would discover his country was also deemed too British by the very government that had to tolerate one set of foreign troops to dislodge another.

The same night he arrived, November 11, Pearson met with Egypt's permanent representative, Omar Loutfi, who introduced "a somewhat delicate matter." The ambassador, "acutely embarrassed," informed Pearson that although Cairo agreed to accept the UN force, was anxious to see General E.L.M. Burns assume command, and was "very appreciative" of Pearson's role in the crisis, it nonetheless felt that Canadian troops were another matter. He then laid out his concerns: Canada's political and military links with the country that had attacked Egypt, the identical uniforms, the shared sovereign. "Egyptians would want a neutral force," he concluded.[8]

What was entirely defensible from Cairo's point of view raised a potential nightmare for the Liberal government in Ottawa and for Pearson in particular. He told Loutfi these concerns put him "in a very difficult— indeed an impossible position." The Canadian government, he asserted, had taken an independent stance and was being severely criticized at home for having done so. Sympathetic to Pearson's dilemma, Loutfi suggested that Canadians might be satisfied to have one of their own, General Burns, in command of the force. Deciding to play hardball, Pearson replied that perhaps Burns might no longer be able to assume the command. Loutfi did not budge and merely agreed to convey Pearson's dismay to Cairo.[9]

Immediately after this meeting, Pearson joined representatives from Denmark, Finland, Norway, and Sweden, to receive a collective dose of bad news from Secretary-General Hammarskjöld: Cairo would not accept troops from any countries involved in military pacts with the British. "The Scandinavians reacted very violently to the exclusion," Pearson recalled, "just as I reacted equally violently to the exclusion of Canadians." Due to leave for Cairo in a few days, Hammarskjöld said he would press Nasser to accept the troops on offer, but this would be no easy task. The secretary-general had no authority to impose any conditions on any member state. Pearson understood this fundamental restriction and mapped out his own response accordingly.

He knew the Egyptian position would outrage Canadians, so the immediate priority was damage control at home, which meant keeping the story buried for as long as possible. St. Laurent agreed with this advice. Pearson then mounted an international backstage campaign, revealing just how tough he could be when it came to protecting his own position and that of his country—in this instance, intimately intertwined. To apply pressure to Cairo after a direct appeal failed, Pearson used a shrewd and essential middle-power tactic: harnessing larger powers to apply the pressure. He already had the UN secretary-general on side and built from there. He asked Arnold Heeney in Washington to persuade Canada's most powerful ally to "go to bat for us." In New Delhi, Escott Reid, Canada's High Commissioner, was dispatched to see a support-ive Prime Minister Nehru, who had already been alerted that Canada might be in trouble. Nehru appreciated that Canada had been UNEF's strongest advocate and had "taken up a very critical role against Britain and France." He sent a message to Nasser urging him to reconsider. Less influential but useful nonetheless, Canada's ambassador in Cairo, Herbert Norman, who had taken up his post almost a month after the nationalization and who had met only once with Nasser, back in early September, was also instructed to add his voice to the choir. He saw Egyptian officials and assisted Hammarskjöld, but did not attend the face-to-face talks with Nasser.[10]

Against this backdrop, Pearson's concerns as a domestic politician inevitably played into his role as an internationalist genuinely keen to strengthen the United Nations. At a meeting of the secretary-general's hand-picked advisory committee on November 14, Pearson noted that Egyptian sovereignty should not be infringed, but he was clearly exasper-ated by Egyptian insistence on exercising that sovereignty. Accepting the country's right to veto the force's composition and decide when UNEF would ultimately withdraw struck him as intolerable. He added with obvious impatience that Egypt should view the contingents serving under the UN flag as a truly international, that is, neutral, force.

In the course of the meeting, India's Arthur Lall interjected to defend his ally in the non-aligned movement, stating that Egypt "on the whole had behaved with great restraint" and that it would be "equally intolerable" if UNEF's composition and tour of duty were decided without Egyptian consent. In an unprofessional flash of irritation, Pearson snapped back that the UN was not trying to impose any terms. "We are trying to help Egypt, and Egypt has accepted certain conditions itself," he said. "It accepted the UN Assembly resolution and we are operating within that resolution. That is all." But of course that wasn't all. While he was undoubtedly sincere in his internationalism and properly concerned about establishing precedents that could undermine future missions, Pearson nonetheless expected Egypt to accept conditions that neither Canada nor any other member state would easily, if ever, tolerate. And over the years, Pearson, the staunch NATO supporter, had never viewed Soviet forces in proposed UN operations as immaculately international; he typically argued in favour of excluding Soviet troops. And while he was also concerned about a member state undermining a potentially useful experiment in collective security, he was undeniably anxious about the domestic political fallout if Cairo refused to accept Canadian troops. The meeting resolved little. Caught between the need to create a credible international police force and the need to placate the host country that must accept this force, Hammarskjöld concluded that all they could do for the moment was to proceed with a certain amount of ambiguity and good faith.[11]

Despite British expectations and hopes that the UN would flounder for some time to come, Hammarskjöld and his officials managed to assemble an emergency force on the fly. "We had to improvise everything," Brian Urquhart recalled. "We found that we couldn't get enough blue berets in time, so we got all these helmet liners off the United States forces in Europe and dipped them in blue paint, which was very quick and very easy. We rationed the force by buying the supplies off the ships stranded in the Suez Canal." One of the secretary-general's more unpleasant tasks was turning down troop offers from countries tainted by their voting record, such as New Zealand, or made redundant because neighbours had been invited and fulfilled geographic quotas. Hammarskjöld and his advisers also had to deal with members who wanted their troops to fly their national flags. "This was a terrible idea," Urquhart noted, "because this was not a national expedition. That took quite a lot of arguing with armies and with governments, but finally they adopted it."[12]

Unlike the UN's military observer missions, this force would operate in much larger numbers, be lightly armed, and be authorized to use weapons in self-defence. At the same time, it would be administered in a different fashion than the operation to defend South Korea six years before, which, as Pearson judged, "while a United Nations action in initiation and authority, was not genuinely international in control, administration, or participation." The United States controlled that operation and therefore, he said, was "not the best model" for what was coming to be called peacekeeping. Unlike Korea, UNEF would be organized by and operated under the aegis of the UN Secretariat answering to the Security Council and General Assembly.[13]

Watching this experiment unfold hour by hour and not knowing whether his own country's troops would be included, Pearson was not always able to mask the strain. In New York to advise the Secretariat, Canada's chief of the general staff of the army, Lt. General Howard Graham, saw him "sitting in an anteroom of the General Assembly" and "take a cigarette from a packet and rather clumsily light it. 'I didn't know you smoked, Mike,' I said. 'I really don't, but I'll be taking dope if we don't soon get this show on the road,' he replied, shaking his head as if in desperation."[14] With the Queen's Own Rifles standing by in Halifax, suspended in an increasingly obvious limbo, Pearson's dilemma was amplified when Cairo relented and accepted the Scandinavians. To much fanfare in the international press, the first UNEF units, from Denmark and Norway, arrived at their advance base in Abu Suweir, just west of Ismailia, on November 15, eleven days after the General Assembly first requested the secretary-general to examine the Canadian proposal, and weeks since the Israelis attacked the Sinai. Colombian troops followed the next day.

Despite the pressure brought to bear from Ottawa and Washington and New Delhi, Nasser continued to decline ground troops from a country so closely allied with the aggressor. Finally, during face-to-face talks in Cairo, Hammarskjöld succeeded in securing consent for Canadian air transport. This compromise, luckily for the dominion's honour, dovetailed with real needs and paved the way to placing Canadian boots on Egyptian soil. Working on logistics in New York, General Burns concluded he had more than enough offers of infantry. What he really needed were the "absolutely essential" technical and administrative troops: signals, ground transport, engineering, ordnance, mechanics, food, and medical — the unsung personnel who actually enabled military forces to perform their missions.[15]

To meet these legitimate requirements, Burns was also able — and this could not have been far from his mind — to rescue Pearson and their country from complete humiliation. On November 17, the Canadian general met with the Canadian foreign minister and made his request for technical and support troops. Not one to hold fixed positions if this risked losing the end goal, Pearson seized on the offer and immediately sought approval from the defence minister and Prime Minister St. Laurent, who bestowed it with little discussion. Then the story, suppressed for almost a week, broke out into the open.

On November 19, angry headlines announced Nasser's defiance and Canada's submission. Even supportive newspapers like the *Toronto Daily Star* compounded the government's misery by citing unnamed officials who conceded that choosing the Queen's Own was "one of the administrative *faux pas* of the century." Echoing the jibe heard from Vancouver to St. John's, a *Star* article headline summed up the snub: "Canada Limited to 'Typewriter' Army by Egypt."[16] At press conferences, Pearson did his best to spin the compromise, but even he couldn't persuade reporters that Egypt's reaction was anything less than demeaning or that Burns's request wasn't contrived convenience. However, national indignation eventually gave way to national pride.

Canadian troops departed for a staging base in Naples, reaching Port Said on November 24. They would eventually number close to 1,200 in a force that, by February 1957, reached some six thousand soldiers, volunteered by Brazil, Colombia, Denmark, Finland, India, Indonesia, Norway, Sweden, and Yugoslavia. Despite all the angst and grumbling, the Canadian contribution proved critical. As historian Michael K. Carroll has noted, "Canada was one of the few nations with a well-trained and professional cadre capable of supplying specialized support troops. While this contribution may not have been deemed glamorous, it was vital to the success of the mission."[17] This humiliating episode reinforced in Pearson a long-held desire to establish a more distinct set of symbols for Canada, which he would implement as prime minister when he introduced the Maple Leaf flag, the Order of Canada, and the redesign of the armed forces' uniforms.[18]

Dormant since August, the government called a special session of Parliament to approve funding for the country's contribution to UNEF. On November 26, Louis St. Laurent faced an Opposition looking to draw blood. The acting leader of the Opposition, Earl Rowe, moved an amendment charging the government with inflicting "gratuitous condemnation" upon the United Kingdom and France, alleging that it had "meekly followed" the United States and "placed Canada in the humiliating position of accepting dictation from President Nasser." After months of restraining himself, St. Laurent momentarily lost his composure during the debate, and accused Britain and France of taking "the law into their own hands." And he did not stop there. Uttering the most memorable, and to Conservative ears, notorious line of his entire time in office, he declared: "The era when the supermen of Europe could govern the whole world has and is coming pretty close to an end."[19] Placing Britain and France on the same moral plane as Communist dictators sent a collective shudder through the Liberal benches, reinforced the darkest suspicions in Conservative ranks, and guaranteed front-page headlines across the country.

The debate resumed the next day. The *New York Times* described it as "almost disorderly with members shouting and booing the Government benches." The most extreme language came from a senior Conservative MP, Howard Green, charging the government with being "unbelievably soft" on Egypt but "right up there in the front rank attacking the United Kingdom and France." He railed that "Canada has been a better friend" to a "tinpot dictator" and nothing more than a "chore boy" to the United

States. "It is high time Canada had a government," he stated, "which will not knife Canada's best friends in the back."[20] When Green sat down, having delighted his fellow Conservatives, the question of loyalty stood front and centre.

The architect of Canada's painstakingly crafted yet divisive policy followed to face his accusers. "It is bad to be a chore boy of the United States," Pearson acknowledged. "It is equally bad to be a colonial chore boy running around shouting 'Ready, aye, ready.'" Despite the inflammatory language from the other side, he declined to retaliate in kind and presented a thoughtful, nuanced case, speaking "without rhetoric, recrimination or blame...without emotion." A friend and admirer, *Winnipeg Free Press* columnist Grant Dexter, judged it "perhaps the greatest speech of his parliamentary career."[21]

Going back over the previous four months, Pearson had beheld interweaving nightmares—the United Nations humiliated, the Commonwealth on the brink of dissolution, the Washington-London axis in crisis, a cross-border attack threatening to escalate into a regional conflagration—all unleashed by a country he admired and where he felt at home. He patiently laid out his motivations, his objectives, his fears and his hopes, which shaped his efforts to undo the damage. Even now, he laid no blame or expressed no moral outrage. Much of what he shared fell on deaf ears.

When discussing the UN police force he had helped to launch, taking pains to cite the historical precedents that foreshadowed its creation, an innate modesty and honesty precluded Pearson from claiming sole authorship. "Of course, there was nothing new in either this idea or in its proposal," he stated. "I hope it was valuable but it certainly was not novel; except in the sense that it was adopted, but in no other respect."[22] He never wavered from this view. In his memoirs, despite numerous enthusiastic and exaggerated claims made on his behalf, he faithfully echoed what he had said in Parliament: "the idea was not novel and had received considerable circulation over the years as a talking point. Only in acceptance would it become unique."[23]

Pearson's masterful defence appeared to Grant Dexter, a not entirely objective observer, to have "disarmed" the Opposition and calmed the debate. In a contradiction never acknowledged out loud, Conservative condemnation of his diplomacy did not extend to the outcome of that diplomacy. On November 29, the Liberals, already commanding a comfortable majority in the House, secured the backing of the two smaller parties, the right-of-centre Social Credit and the left-of-centre Co-operative Commonwealth Federation, and defeated the Conservatives' amendment by 171 to 36. Then MPs on both sides of the House, "who had been at each other's throats at the opening of this special session," joined to approve funding for UNEF. Enduring opponents like the *Calgary Herald* lashed out at the "degrading story" presented by a "government clutching wildly and pathetically at anything that might save it from its own ill-conceived policies." A common observation running through much of the press commentary held that the debate was not over and would play into the next federal election. The *Herald* warned, "One thing is sure: the government cannot escape the reckoning forever."[24]

While one son of empire emerged from the Suez Crisis tainted for some but celebrated by most, another saw his long, remarkable career culminate in a very personal disaster. Anthony Eden had calculated that a twenty-thousand-strong assault force holding the Suez Canal provided him with a formidable bargaining position. Even though barred from UNEF, he expected that, at the very least, British salvage units would play a role in clearing the blocked canal. He expected the Americans would open the financial taps to staunch Britain's financial haemorrhage. In fact, the true punishment was about to begin.

The newly re-elected President Dwight Eisenhower, initially so grateful for the ceasefire, quickly accepted Eden's request for a face-saving meeting but then, dissuaded by horrified advisers, just as quickly began to stall and delay, ultimately refusing to be seen in public with his ally. With Eisenhower's consent, Washington inflicted an economic blockade over the course of November that finally forced London to capitulate and, alongside a resentful France, withdraw its forces from Egypt in late December. The retreating invaders handed over their self-appointed task of supervising the ceasefire to the waiting United Nations police force. An intransigent Israel held on until the glare of US diplomatic pressure made it withdraw from the Sinai in March 1957.

More than relinquishing India and surrendering Abadan—the former seeming inevitable if not sensible, the latter generating little collective angst—the ruthlessly compelled retreat in full view of the world was for many in that generation of Britons the most visceral, emotionally devastating sign that their long game had been played out. Britain retained imperial holdings east of Suez, held a permanent seat on the Security Council, and boasted one of the largest economies and military forces in the world, but being made to step down to second class felt like relegation to something far less.

As if reflecting the nation's decline, Eden's health was so ravaged by the ordeal that his doctors ordered him in late November to take a rest. He left the government in the hands of colleagues who wanted to see him gone forever. When Pearson stopped over in London in December, three key ministers—Macmillan, Selwyn Lloyd, and R.A. Butler—treated him to "almost embarrassingly frank" ruminations on their leader's state of health, state of mind, and choice of actions, which they had all supported in public and now disdained in private. Pearson was told in no uncertain terms "the failure of the policy should result in the departure from office of its author." Yet even now, the colleagues unburdening themselves did not make a full confession. Lloyd categorically assured Pearson that London "did not know in advance of the Israeli decision and had done nothing to influence that decision or assist it by promises of military support." In his report to Ottawa, Pearson claimed to believe this, but given the stream of revelations in the press that had started trickling out from the start of the crisis, perhaps he was being diplomatic. He clearly understood, as he put it, "the real, less publicized reason for the action, to destroy Nasser," and can only have been further dismayed when the senior people he met failed to answer a fundamental question: "If you had destroyed Nasser, who could have taken his place and would you be better off?"[25]

Pearson found the ministers' willingness to disparage their chief "strange—and a shade unhealthy."[26] He felt sympathy for Eden, whom he had known for decades and, on the whole, admired, but he concluded that the impending change in leadership was desirable. Eden's failing health proved the deciding factor.

In January 1957, the prime minister informed his Cabinet that he was suffering from insomnia and fevers and had "considerably" increased his dosage of sleeping pills as well as the stimulants required to offset the drowsiness. This generated, he said, "an adverse affect on my rather precarious inside."[27] Eden tendered his resignation on January 9 and, after a canvassing of Cabinet opinion, was succeeded by the irrepressible Harold Macmillan, who had not missed the opening to secure support from disgruntled backbenchers, disillusioned Cabinet colleagues and, very shrewdly, a Washington keen to see a change in leadership. Eden never apologized for his decision to use force to try to place the Suez Canal under international control. Even weeks before his death in January 1977, he was still justifying his armed intervention. Nor did he ever explicitly thank Pearson for throwing out the diplomatic lifeline that had offered a bare but merciful modicum of cover. In his memoirs, Eden noted only that he shared Pearson's reservations about the limited American resolution to call for a ceasefire and wished that the US had been "willing to play a part as balanced as Canada's." During a 1959 interview on CBC television, he again declined to express direct appreciation and echoed what he would write in his memoirs: "If the United States had taken the line that Canada took, the position in the Middle East today would be very much better than unfortunately it is. And beyond there I won't go."[28]

In his retirement, Eden and Pearson did not correspond beyond thank-you cards and acknowledgements, nor do they appear to have met and discussed the events of 1956. When asked to comment on Pearson's death in 1972, Eden described it "as a loss to the whole world." He wrote Maryon Pearson a gracious letter of condolence, recalling "Mike's invaluable help" over the years and noting, "It was typical of him to be ready to help where he had no obligation to do so, but was just being a true friend."[29] Eden singled out Pearson's support during the difficult 1954 Indochina Conference. He made no mention of Suez.

Cabinet colleagues who survived the crisis with their reputations and political careers intact could afford to do so. "It's a pity that the British have never publicly acknowledged the debt they owe to Mike," Selwyn Lloyd told George Ignatieff at a dinner party in the 1970s. "He really saved our bacon." The US, Eden's press secretary, William Clark, recalled "led the pack in their attack on Britain and France. Mike was the only person who sought to try and find a happy issue out of all our troubles." The greatest beneficiary of the Suez Crisis, Harold Macmillan, offered the greatest public tribute. "Britain owes much to Pearson," he wrote in his memoirs. "Both by his personal powers of negotiation and by the respect in which he was held, he was able to exercise throughout the crisis a moderating and humanising influence."[30] But these tributes would not be made public for some time, and in the interim, and perhaps always for some in Canada, Pearson and the Liberal government retained the stench of disloyalty.

While Britain's new prime minister and government grappled with the fallout from Suez and the prospect of a lesser role on the world stage, the first months of 1957 saw Pearson work at the United Nations to compel an Israeli troop withdrawal from Egypt. He did so while still moving, with characteristic balance, to moderate the anger in the General Assembly that threatened sanctions on the remaining aggressor. In this period, he put aside his earlier grand objective in the crisis. When he first proposed it, Pearson envisioned using UNEF as a means to support a wider peace settlement. In a cable to Norman Robertson in January, however, he conceded that "the present atmosphere is not conducive to constructive discussion of these broad political questions. The apprehension and uncertainties…which contributed to the violent outburst of last October and have been intensified by that incident, must be given time to recede."[31] But those apprehensions would never recede enough for any kind of lasting peace to be shaped, then or later.

On April 4, a different issue from the Middle East entangled Pearson on the home front. Canada's ambassador to Egypt, Herbert Norman, committed suicide in Cairo by jumping from the roof of the Swedish embassy. Norman was a specialist in Asian affairs, in itself cause for suspicion in the fog of Cold War fear. When advising the US occupation force in Tokyo on how to treat imprisoned Japanese leftists, Norman seemed too forgiving. He was eventually hounded by American witch-hunters, who, despite a fervent hunt, never uncovered any evidence that Norman had ever been disloyal. After being investigated and exonerated, an ordeal never considered rigorous enough by American and Canadian accusers, Pearson refused to expel Norman from External Affairs and instead posted him first to New Zealand and then to Cairo, where he took his own life after old smears were dredged up again.

Methodist born and raised, educated at the University of Toronto and in Britain like Pearson, his death hit hard. Years later, Pearson would still say, "I don't think I'd ever reached a lower point in my public career in my feelings." He paid tribute to his colleague, denounced the allegations, and protested to the State Department, dispatching what he later described as "the strongest note" of his career.[32] Yet he was criticized in the press and the House of Commons for not doing more to defend Norman. Then he muddied the story by revealing that Norman had, like so many in his generation, actually been a Communist sympathiser at university. Pearson was suddenly on trial for not being fully forthcoming. Doubts were left dangling, and for some never went away.

The nation's attention shifted on April 12, when Louis St. Laurent prorogued Parliament and called an election for June 10. After twenty-two years of Liberal rule, the press and public complacently assumed Canada's "natural governing party" would prevail over the Conservatives, now led by a long-term MP but novice chief, John Diefenbaker. The underdog opponent proved to be one of the most effective, even electrifying, campaigners of the twentieth century, at his best on the platform, sensing and speaking to intangible yearnings. In dull contrast, the prime minister, while still able to exude the avuncular charm that inspired the nickname "Uncle Louis," was a spent force. Many in the party knew it but decided they would harness him for one final campaign, even if, as one Liberal stated, "we have to run him stuffed."[33] And so St. Laurent performed dutifully, without passion. As with most campaigns, foreign policy played a minor though recurring theme, refracted through a predictable prism.

At the Conservative campaign's opening rally in Toronto, Diefenbaker took time from proclaiming the greater destiny awaiting a Tory Canada to remind the faithful, "In the tradition of this Party, we did and do resent the British people being castigated and derisively condemned as those 'supermen' whose days are about over." At campaign stops across the country, he attacked St. Laurent for abandoning the British people "when Britain had her back to the wall" and allying itself with Russia. Twisting words out of context, a necessary tool of the trade for some, he asked his audience, "Do you agree with the Prime Minister when he referred to those 'supermen' whose days are about numbered? We do not believe that. We believe that the Commonwealth still has a responsibility for freedom in the world." Days later in Victoria, hecklers taunted St. Laurent. "Why did you vote with Russia against England?" they demanded. In Guelph on May 13, Diefenbaker incited supportive boos from his audience by invoking the "supermen" slur and charging that Canada had, he declared, "found itself allied at the United Nations with Russia." In Richmond Hill, Ontario, he railed against the government for not supporting "our good friend the Israelis, where if we had left them alone, we would have had no trouble." Occasionally, his attacks fell flat. As James Eayrs observed, "In Minnedosa, Manitoba, not altogether surprisingly, there was less interest in Suez than in wheat."[34]

The only really glittering Liberal candidate in the campaign was dispatched across the country to insist that he and the government had not slavishly followed American orders; that they still believed in the Commonwealth; that he had done everything he could to shelter Britain from the worst of international furies; that his policy had been truly made in Canada. He was even able to quote words of gratitude from Britain, France, and Israel. The public applauded Pearson in person, but not the party he represented. Ultimately, the skirmishes over Suez were tangential in the larger contest between safe, grey continuity and the nagging desire for something more.

Going to print before voting day, the lead editorial in *Maclean's* magazine summed up the blinding conventional wisdom: "For better or for worse, we Canadians have once more elected one of the most powerful governments ever created."[35] Louis St. Laurent began the evening of June 10 fully expecting to return to work the next day in a still-Liberal Canada. Instead, he watched his party eke out a razor-thin majority of the vote, 2.7 million (40.5 percent of the electorate) versus 2.6 million (38.5 percent) for the Conservatives. The conversion of these votes into parliamentary seats, however, overturned the government: 112 for the Conservatives, 105 for the Liberals, and the remaining forty-eight scattered amongst third parties and independents. The results were made more dramatic by the defeat of Cabinet heavyweights in defence, finance, public works, justice, and trade and commerce.

A post-election poll suggested the bitter pipeline debate, a stingy increase in pensions, and a desire for change played the major role in the upset. Fortunately for the foreign minister, less than eight per cent of those surveyed cited Suez as a factor in their decision.[36] Untainted by the aura of arrogance and apathy, Pearson held his northern Ontario riding of Algoma East and found himself, after nearly thirty years of ascension through External Affairs, a backbencher in Her Majesty's Loyal Opposition. Demoralized by the loss, St. Laurent tendered his resignation to make way for the first Conservative government in a generation.

Some voters rejoiced to see that Pearson no longer spoke for the country, but admirers around the world, including the *New York Times*, felt his departure was "a loss to more than Canada." The *Manchester Guardian* ascribed "the world-wide interest" this election had generated to the lamentable fall from office of someone who was "probably the most generally respected and trusted" foreign minister anywhere. Pearson was "one of the few bridges between the divided nations at the height of the Suez crises," the *Guardian* stated. "He will be sorely missed."[37]

The assistant press officer at the Canadian consulate in New York, Margaret K. Weiers, witnessed first-hand the post-election incomprehension. "When the General Assembly opened in the fall of 1957, the foreign correspondents could not understand that Pearson would not be part of the Canadian delegation," she recalled. "They were really quite baffled. They kept asking me, 'When is Mr. Pearson coming?' I replied, 'There is a new government in Ottawa and to the best of my knowledge, Mr. Diefenbaker will heading the delegation himself.' They hadn't ever known anyone else." Neither had many working in the UN Secretariat, including Secretary-General Hammarskjöld, who wrote Pearson afterwards to lament his loss of office. Brian Urquhart, one of Hammarskjöld's key advisers, remembered Pearson as "a person without pretensions. He was a person with very little — well, I don't know whether he had no ego, but it was certainly extremely well in control. He was a person who didn't much mind who got the credit. He was interested in problems and doing something about them." In a more humorous vein, the Canadian ambassador to Denmark, H.F. Feaver, an old friend of Pearson, wrote from Copenhagen to say he had been meeting with Prime Minister Hans Hansen. Disappointed by the election results, Hansen, with "a twinkle" in his eye, asked Feaver to convey an offer to Pearson. "I'd like him to be Foreign Minister of Denmark," the prime minister said. "All he has to do is become a Danish citizen and he'll be appointed the next day."[38]

Not surprisingly, even in defeat, there was little question about Pearson's future. He was already looking ahead to the next game, the outcome almost a foregone conclusion. Serious and more likely contenders for the Liberal succession had quit the field a few years before or had just lost their seats. Surveying the wreckage, influential reporters, party officials, and surviving colleagues overwhelmingly decided that he must be crowned. Raised to view any signs of overt ambition as sinful and groomed in a profession that considered it gauche, Pearson did not declare himself formally but rather let his numerous allies lay the groundwork.

Parliament met on October 14 with the novel sight of a Conservative prime minister in power and Queen Elizabeth II delivering the Speech from the Throne. Long dreamed of, long denied, the day should have belonged entirely to Diefenbaker, but Pearson, in his uncanny way, stole some of the spotlight. At one point, the former foreign minister descended to his new basement office and took a telephone call from a reporter asking for a comment. Pearson expressed puzzlement and was then informed that he had been awarded the Nobel Prize for Peace. "You mean that I have been nominated," he corrected the reporter. "There are many nominations every year." The reporter read the wire report from Norway. Pearson's initial response was, apparently, one word: "Gosh."[39]

The press gallery immediately shifted its focus, compelling Diefenbaker in his moment of glory to share precious air time, front page headlines, and national attention with his rival presumptive. The next day, the prime minister made the appropriate noises, calling Pearson a personal friend, despite their political differences, and even stating that the Nobel Prize was "a tribute to him and an honour to Canada."[40] Perhaps it was easy to be gracious so early in their contest, though the charade proved difficult to maintain.

Just a few weeks before, Diefenbaker had emerged from a swearing-in ceremony with his new foreign minister, Sidney Smith. After months of press speculation wondering who could ever fill the Pearsonian void, and feeling the need to reach beyond his inexperienced caucus, the prime minister had turned to the former University of Toronto president, even though Smith had committed the political transgression of supporting Pearson's stand during Suez. A crowd of reporters naturally asked the new minister if he had changed his mind. The novice Smith honestly but rather carelessly replied that he still agreed with Pearson. Sensing a mess in the making, the hovering Diefenbaker moved in right away, clearly annoyed. There was no departure, he insisted, in the government's foreign policy from what it had espoused in opposition.[41]

Diefenbaker and more than a few of his fellow MPs never changed their minds about the treachery they thought Pearson had perpetrated. At a UN General Assembly meeting in 1958, a Canadian diplomat mentioned the Nobel award to a Conservative MP on the Canadian delegation. "The MP snorted with contempt," reported *Maclean's* columnist Blair Fraser. "'Nobel Prize,' he said scornfully. 'That was just Pearson's reward for voting with the Russians.'" In November 1959, at a large party gathering in Toronto, Diefenbaker denounced the Liberals for placing Britain and France "in the same bag as aggressors with the USSR" and promised that a Conservative government would never commit such a travesty. This prompted an unusually angry rejoinder from Pearson, stung as well by the parallel accusation that Canada's international standing "had sunk so low" during his time in office, and that the lowest point had come during Suez. Speaking in the House of Commons in January 1960, he quoted words of thanks from Britain and said he hoped the prime minister would not make any more "stupid and false allegations." Diefenbaker remained unrepentant. On New Year's Eve 1972, as Pearson's body lay in state on Parliament Hill, a reporter sat with the old chief, once again an Opposition MP, to capture some heartwarming anecdotes to balance the bitter public record. Ensconced in his living room near a Christmas tree, Diefenbaker, true to form, "scowled, 'That man never should have won the Nobel Prize!'"[42] On that specific point, however, and right from the start, most of the country disagreed.

A nationwide chorus of praise followed Pearson as he flew to Oslo in December 1957 to receive the glittering prize. He returned anointed, enjoying a virtual lock on the Liberal succession. In January 1958, a majority of delegates made him leader of the party and Her Majesty's Loyal Opposition. Until Suez, he had served as an MP for almost a decade largely unscathed by the domestic fray. Now he was playing a very different game, where certain personal qualities, some irrelevant, some essential in diplomacy, had become liabilities: his pronounced lisp and weak voice, his utter lack of stage presence, his instinct to avoid simplistic answers, his unwillingness to paint opponents in crude strokes, his talent for compromise. All too quickly, he seemed fumbling, ineffectual, out of his element. Journalist Robert Fulford remembered, "Along with a lot of other people, I thought 'Here's a diplomat, an External Affairs minister. He's trying to be a party leader and he's not interested in domestic Canadian politics.' Because he'd spent a lot of his life abroad and when he wasn't abroad he was worrying about abroad or he was down at the UN and I think we had the idea that he was some sort of representative to Canada from the international diplomatic community and not a 'real' Canadian."[43]

Smelling weakness, Diefenbaker called an election for March and, with spellbinding performances, inspired the most devastating majority ever seen in Canada, taking 208 out of 265 seats. The Liberals were cut down to a then-inconceivable forty-eight MPs, elected in only four provinces. The CCF was reduced to a shadow with eight members. The Social Credit Party vanished from the House of Commons.

On election night, in Algoma East, returns were slow in coming. Pearson and his wife dared to hope that he might lose his own riding, be released from his unseemly ordeals, and return to the world stage where he properly belonged. However, late in the evening, they learned he had been re-elected. For Maryon Pearson, this was the final straw. "We've lost everything. We've even won our own seat!" she lamented.[44] However tempted by offers of escape, and there would be many, the vanquished leader felt duty bound to remain and begin the grinding odyssey to rebuild.

Yet while the people had rejected Pearson the politician for the foreseeable future, his diplomatic legacy began to resonate more and more deeply in the collective Canadian consciousness, and to such an extent that it came to define how Canadians wanted to act and to be seen in the world and how they wished to see themselves — for better and for worse.

***

> This is no time nor is this an occasion on which to adopt an attitude of superior
> virtue or smug complacency over the righteousness of our own position.
> — Lester Pearson, November 27, 1956, House of Commons[45]

Lester Pearson's diplomacy during Suez divided the country. His Nobel triumph shaped a national vision. The prize, however, did not suddenly create this desire to embrace the mantle of peacekeeper; it echoed and amplified older currents flowing through the collective mindset.

In the late nineteenth century, this was a country where the well-intentioned celebrated the imperial "White Man's Burden" to spread civilization to savages and launched missionary campaigns to bring Christian salvation to heathen lands; a country where, in between the world wars, many recoiled from the self-serving militarism of the great powers; where during the Cold War many believed that staking out the middle ground as peacekeepers offered the most sensible path to survival. A decade before the Nobel Prize, those impulses were already singled out and encouraged.

In March 1946, the departing UK High Commissioner, Malcolm MacDonald, bid farewell with properly glowing and finely attuned hyperbole that highlighted his audience's aspirations. MacDonald likened the postwar dominion to "a new planet...working its distinct contribution to maintaining order and cohesion amongst the heavenly bodies" and praised Canada's foreign policy for exuding "a sanity, a wisdom, a true statesmanship." He went further and rejoiced that "a new moral force has grown in the world." There was the telling phrase. Once this moral impulse was distinctly religious, then imperialist, then quasi-isolationist—until a second world war redefined how this morality might be wielded. In that postwar period, one of the country's most eminent historians, Arthur Lower, envisaged a new mission for this nascent moral force, writing: "We have only one international interest, and that is peace. Surely our role then must be that of an international peacemaker."[46]

A decade later, Suez and the Nobel Prize seemed to fulfill that promise. In November 1956, columnist Grant Dexter reported from the United Nations: "Canada is almost a magic word here." That same month, the *Manchester Guardian* stated: "The Canadians have frankly taken over the moral leadership of the Commonwealth from us; the best hope is that others, with ourselves, will fall in behind their flag." In January 1957, *Saturday Night* magazine gushed: "There has been a kind of break-through to new levels of responsibility for Canada in the world." During a foreign policy debate in March, a British MP suggested reversing an age-old formula. "If we want to make our weight felt," he urged, "we must get a common policy with Canada." In September 1957, the *Globe and Mail* reprinted an editorial from the *New York Times*, continuing to restate what Canadians delighted in reading. "Until recent years, the appointment of a new Canadian Secretary of State for External Affairs would have been of minor interest," it noted. "Now it is front-page news. This is simply a recognition of the fact that Canada now plays a role in world affairs which is of great importance." For Canadians who "found or hoped to find an identity through foreign policy," these were beguiling voices.[47] From this mesmerizing period onwards, Canadian governments began to reach for their own Pearsonian moment in the sun.

John Diefenbaker may have denounced Pearson's stance during Suez, but he embraced the security mechanism it created and the glow it bequeathed. Indeed, his transport minister, George Hees, declared in the 1958 election that Pearson had stolen the force idea from Diefenbaker himself. Sharing prevailing expectations, the Conservative government volunteered Canadian troops to UN missions in Lebanon 1958, the Congo 1960, and West New Guinea 1962. During the Cuban Missile Crisis, when nuclear war loomed between the West and the Soviets, External Affairs prepared a memo for the prime minister explicitly citing Suez and musing, in almost reflex fashion, about the role Canada might play. Department officials suggested that Diefenbaker propose a UN committee to mediate and even laid out a game plan if the crisis was taken to the General Assembly. The memo, one of Diefenbaker's biographers has noted, "used language that was bound to alert Diefenbaker's interest. Here, it implied, was Diefenbaker's Suez; his chance to match the achievement of Mike Pearson; his chance, perhaps, to win a Nobel Prize."[48] He never came close.

In 1964, Prime Minister Pearson faced his own request from the UN to send peacekeepers, this time to Cyprus. He did not automatically leap to attention nor did he feel any burning need to see his country take on a by-now-familiar role. The public and press, however, hankered to resume the mantle. So did his foreign minister and onetime rival for the Liberal leadership, Paul Martin, a dedicated UN and NATO internationalist but also a domestic politician aiming for the political pinnacle. Peacekeeping historian Alan James wrote, "Thoughts of how a comparable role over Cyprus might lead to comparable results for him could not—so it is widely assumed—have been far from his mind."[49] Martin tackled the issue with vigour and skill but, alas for him, without attaining Nobel glory.

Pierre Trudeau began his reign as prime minister, to Pearson's intense distress and even anger, dismissing Canada's role as a "helpful fixer," questioning the country's membership in NATO and the Commonwealth and even disparaging External Affairs itself. Having publicly snubbed the Pearsonian legacy—nothing personal, as Trudeau inevitably brought his own baggage of priorities and methods—he eventually followed traditional Pearsonian patterns by agreeing to contribute Canadian troops to four peacekeeping missions and remaining in NATO. He even ended his tenure in a rather mediatory, missionary fashion, touring world capitals, calling for peace—exactly the kind of thing many Canadians felt their leader should be doing. The media discussion surrounding his motivations assumed, in part, the equally appropriate Canadian desire for another Nobel Prize.

The national devotion to peacekeeping continued through Brian Mulroney's time in office and reached a high point of troop commitment during his last year as prime minister, 1993, when an astonishing ten percent of all UN peacekeepers, some 4,300, came from Canada. Reflecting the widespread cultural and emotional attachment to the blue berets, images of peacekeepers, not unlike images of the royal family at the turn of the century, were engraved on currency and stamps, celebrated in citizenship guides and school books, and honoured in a striking monument unveiled in Ottawa in 1992.

Of all the international roles that captivated national imaginations, the desire to keep the peace must stand as one of the most humane and decent. However, it also proved problematic because it perpetuated an incomplete if not distorted portrait of the country and the people.

The mantle of moral power, of neutral peacekeeper, had resonated so profoundly with Canadians that it overwhelmed if not erased any real awareness of or pride in Canada's much larger contribution to facing the Soviet threat in Europe. This distortion also obscured the country's impressive military history, reflected to some degree in the way Canadians remembered Pearson, largely forgetting that the United Nations man par excellence and Nobel laureate had played a central role in calling for and building the Western defence alliance. He had no problem sustaining the seeming paradox; it took a while for the country to catch up.

Looking back at the Mulroney era and its UN highpoint, two academics wrote: "It is almost impossible to imagine an elected government openly opposing or fundamentally questioning the importance of peacekeeping in the country's foreign policy."[50] But soon enough the unimaginable became routine. Over the decades since 1956, the national faith in peacekeeping was invariably tested, occasionally faltered, but it only suffered deeper and more lingering doubt in the 1990s when the UN failed to prevent ethnic cleansing in Yugoslavia and genocide in Rwanda, and when a handful of Canadian soldiers in Somalia tortured and murdered a young local man after he infiltrated their base. At the same time, as a recession drained the federal budget, Canadians gradually learned they could no longer afford to practise what their leaders had preached so religiously.

Arguably the national wake-up call sounded in 1996, when Canadians watched their prime minister, Jean Chrétien, try to launch a peacekeeping mission to protect refugees in Zaire (now the Democratic Republic of Congo). The attempt was widely cheered. After all, it seemed so right, so noble, so Canadian, though not everyone was impressed; one military officer grumbled off the record to a reporter that "the prime minister was out to win himself a Nobel peace prize."[51] Despite the good intentions and high-level commitment, the country did not see a repeat of 1956 when Canadian forces reached the UNEF base in Egypt within days of receiving clearance. Instead, Chrétien's humanitarian gesture stumbled, stalled, and never took off, partly because of poor planning, partly because regional governments did not want any foreign troops involved—not even a supposedly benign middle power—and partly because from the outset Canada lacked the necessary hardware and manpower. The proposed mission ultimately proved unnecessary because the Africans themselves moved in to protect the refugees. Canada was not needed. And even when it was called upon to serve, the country had less and less to offer.

However much he invoked his government's commitment to peace-keeping, Chrétien slashed military spending (until the September 11 terrorist attacks), allowed equipment and infrastructure to deteriorate, and therefore eroded the military's ability to answer the UN call. By December 2003, the month he stepped down, a mere 233 Canadian civilian and military personnel were serving in UN operations. Canada ranked a distant thirty-eight behind the front-runner, Pakistan, which boasted 6,248 peacekeepers, and the second-highest contributor, Bangladesh, with 4,730.

The slow, undeniable fade-out of Canadian blue berets from UN missions paralleled a growing, anxious sense in the press and academia that the once-indispensable middle power was itself fading into irrelevance. In 2003, Canadians witnessed yet another reverse image of the triumph at Suez when two permanent members of the Security Council declared they would invade a country in the Middle East to topple a military dictator for the good of the people. The Anglo-American march to war in Iraq divided the United Nations, strained the Western alliance, and inflamed tensions in the region. Once again, Canada entered the maelstrom with a proposal to inspire peace. The effort made headlines at home, a ripple overseas, and was then brushed aside by allies hungry for war. A noble effort had culminated in more galling evidence that Canada was no longer a magical word in the Security Council or General Assembly or perhaps anywhere.

As fewer and fewer Canadian peacekeepers stood watch around the world, Canada's largest international commitment was unfolding in Afghanistan, under the auspices of a UN-mandated but NATO-operated International Security Assistance Force (ISAF). The mission generated an image unfamiliar to generations of Canadians: their soldiers engaged in bloody firefights with enemies who cursed them as infidel, imperial aggressors. And then there was the succession of flag-draped coffins bringing back the fallen from a distant front. As UNEF had in the 1950s, this brutal conflict began to reframe the way Canadians perceived their role in the world.

Academics, commentators, and government and defence officials encouraged the shift in self-perception, arguing that in the harsher post-9/11 world of failed states and globalized terrorism, traditional peacekeeping had been rendered obsolete. They sought to persuade the country that the troops in Afghanistan were returning to an honourable warrior tradition that had seen Canadians liberate Europe from tyranny in the Second World War, push back Communist invaders from South Korea, and help stare down the Soviet threat during the Cold War. This revision to some degree succeeded, so that more and more Canadians no longer thought of themselves automatically and solely as neutral peace-keepers; but neither had they forsaken it. In fact, more of a balance had been achieved. This revision inevitably inspired the next pendulum swing, which countered that Canada's peaceable legacy and duty had been tarnished and abandoned by warmongers. No doubt, another wave of counter-argument will take shape, as it should and must, for this is a debate almost as old as the country.[52]

Aside from sharing the commitment to NATO, and understanding the need to rebuild a neglected military, Prime Minister Stephen Harper's response to the Pearsonian legacy can be summed up in many ways by one of the toxically partisan gestures so beloved of his regime. Upon being appointed minister of foreign affairs, John Baird took the time and attention necessary to have Pearson's name removed from his business card, almost as if to say that although he worked in the Lester Pearson building, he didn't want the world to know it. True to the snub, the Harper government invariably practised a diplomacy that bore little resemblance to that of the master diplomat: unbalanced, amateurish, and all too often, marked by hollow gestures intended to win votes at home. Small wonder that Harper's Canada failed to secure a seat on the Security Council during the 2010 election, the first such failure for Canada in some five decades. Contempt works both ways.

***

> The brilliance of [Pearson's] performance on that occasion must not obscure the
> fact that it was a one-night stand, an exceptional turn in circumstances unlikely
> to recur.... One cannot trade on a single achievement, even of this magnitude,
> for ever; and our prestige is on the wane, if it has not yet disappeared.
> — James Eayrs, 1961[53]

At least one person was never mesmerized by what came to be dismissed as "the peacekeeping myth," and that was the architect himself. "Pearson," Robert Bothwell observes, "had the irreverence that comes with being a creator."[54] That irreverence, coupled with his experience and insight, prevented him from believing that he had devised an all-purpose mechanism for settling conflicts or that Canadians should genuflect to this alone.

Even in the midst of trying to make his force proposal a reality, he cautioned the General Assembly, essentially, not to lose sight of the true goal — a political settlement in the Middle East. Without that, Pearson declared, their work remained uncompleted.[55] The 1957 election removed him from the diplomatic arena, so he could not play any part in shaping the unfolding experiment, but from time to time, he voiced his thoughts from the sidelines.

In April 1959, as the leader of the opposition, he delivered a major speech on what he called the UN's "heartening and hopeful experiment in peace preserving." Two and a half years after its conception and implementation, he argued that a force like UNEF could be "effective in securing an armistice, in pacifying a disturbed border, in helping to prevent brush fires spreading." Yet even as the country assumed its new role as peacekeeper, Pearson went on to underline the limitations of what he had helped to launch.[56]

Pearson conceded that, stationed as a buffer, with no authority to intervene, allowed to use weapons only in self-defence, "UNEF could do nothing to prevent a direct and naked aggression by a big or even a middle power which was determined to move. It probably would not be able to operate even in the territory of a small power, if that power objected, unless the great powers were in agreement to exert the necessary pressure." He worried out loud that this "first experiment of a genuine United Nations international peace force ... will have no permanent effect; that its value will be dissipated and lost" unless the UN established the necessary administrative infrastructure to operate future forces. Pointing to an earlier precedent when individual nations rallied to make up for paralysis in the UN, he invoked the NATO model and suggested that interested middle-power nations could establish their own peacekeeping infrastructure and earmark their own forces for UN duty.[57] Pearson also envisioned taking peacekeeping to another level of engagement.

Mirroring his campaign to have NATO establish a social and political component, he mused during a debate on the 1960 Congo crisis about expanding the original force concept from the strictly military to incorporate "technical, economic, and administrative assistance." He suggested that the UN consider creating, in effect, civilian peacekeepers, "a corps of administrative experts which would be available for new states at the beginning of their existence."[58]

He also wanted commitments to come with parameters. Speaking to Parliament in August 1960, he supported the government's intention to contribute troops to the Congo but argued against writing blank cheques. "What are we taking on? Indeed, what is the United Nations taking on?" he asked. "A few weeks' or a few years' assignment? A temporary job in helping to restore order?" Or, he continued, would this become a much longer and difficult task to help rebuild a potentially failing state caught in civil war?[59] Despite the lack of answers, as leader of the opposition he nonetheless accepted the intervention with imprecise parameters, but his long-term goal remained to see the UN secretariat establish some kind of permanent office to bring an essential dose of clarity and efficiency to future missions.

When it came time for Pearson as prime minister to consider sending troops to Cyprus, he remained faithful to a very Canadian foreign policy trinity: caution, skepticism, and pragmatism. In February 1964, he told the House of Commons that no decision would be reached until the UN secretariat had clarified the force's composition and terms of reference. He had no desire to make an indefinite commitment. As always, in his view, stationing the blue berets in the middle of a civil war was never an end in itself but one of multiple means to facilitate a political settlement. Ultimately, Pearson felt compelled to ignore his own advice.[60] Canadians served in United Nations Force in Cyprus (UNFICYP) until 1993, leaving behind a militarily pacified but politically unresolved conflict, just as he had feared.

In May 1967, another of his original concerns proved prescient when Cairo abruptly demanded that UNEF's roughly 3,400 personnel leave the country. This dismissal came without warning, let alone any formal reference to the General Assembly or Security Council. Secretary-General U Thant and member states issued appeals and protests, all in vain. After nearly eleven years of effective service, the Canadian contingent withdrew by the end of May and the remainder of the force by the middle of June.

Looking back to 1956, Brian Urquhart remembered Pearson's attempts in the advisory meetings to strengthen the mission's staying power. "He had always been extremely uneasy about the basis on which UNEF was deployed, which was the basis of Egyptian consent," Urquhart said. "Pearson had warned about this right from the beginning. He had always realized this was a situation based on good faith and therefore, to some extent, a rather weak arrangement. He was very realistic." But Pearson was equally realistic in accepting that the UN could only secure Egyptian consent by acknowledging the primacy of Egyptian sovereignty. A decade later, however galling for some, those sovereign rights were respected, marking an inglorious and troubling conclusion to the Canadian contribution. "Peacekeeping seemed to be discredited," UNEF's first commander, General E.L.M. Burns, lamented, "and there were many voices in Canada calling for abandonment of our efforts in this field." Paul Martin Sr. wrote: "The whole affair made the UN look irrelevant."[61]

The originator did not feel this way, or if he did, he refused to say so in public. Speaking in the Commons in May 1967, Pearson acknowledged the setback but went on to argue that this was no reason to abandon the experiment. "Peace keeping itself becomes even more important than ever in the light of what has happened," he declared. Ignoring the handwringing and disillusionment, he stressed, "What we have to do now is not weaken in our pursuit of peace keeping under the United Nations but…try and keep that blue flag flying between possible combatants." He made the same case two weeks later in June as war raged between Israeli and Arab armies. "This does not mean that the United Nations emergency force was a failure," he insisted. "On the contrary, it was successful in maintaining the peace in that area for ten and a half years. Surely the conclusion to be drawn from this experience is that it is a time not for banishing United Nations forces but for stronger United Nations forces."[62]

Other government officials, academics, and commentators would reach the opposite conclusion, reinforced by the peacekeeping failures to come. Still, if Pearson had seen the slaughter in Rwanda and Yugoslavia, it is highly unlikely he would allow himself to become permanently disillusioned or distracted by momentary episodes, however appalling. Nor would he point the finger at the obviously flawed organization in charge.

In a CBC television interview broadcast in UNEF's first months of existence, Pearson made a fine and essential distinction. "The UN," he said, "reflects the world situation more often than it creates it. And the reflection isn't always a very pleasant one [but] it's not fair to blame the UN for the reflection." Echoing what he wrote about the League of Nations in the 1930s, he reminded his audience: "Some people get very impatient and wonder why the UN doesn't do more. They forget the UN can do just as much or will do just as little as the government members of the UN will permit it to do." If there were flaws in the way peacekeeping missions were conducted or not conducted, he knew competing national interests defined the limits of the possible, not the instrument of that collective will.[63] The man who had unintentionally helped to establish a kind of national religion would in an age of disbelief have remained agnostic, or rather, open minded.

He was blessed after all with a deep acceptance of flux and a wise detachment from blinding orthodoxy, his view captured in one of the most revealing passages from his memoirs: "A sense of the ambivalence and transitory character of political triumph can help the politician to avoid both arrogance and extremism. They can also arm him against disappointment and disillusion."[64] Perhaps he had first gleaned this from the British Empire's greatest man of letters, fellow Nobel laureate Rudyard Kipling. In seeking to illuminate his father's diplomacy, Geoffrey Pearson noted, "I've often referred to Kipling's poem 'If,' which is a cliché in a way but he grew up with Kipling. Kipling was what he read when he was young. It was Kipling who said, You're a man, my son, if you can treat those two imposters Triumph and Disaster just the same. He believed that, and he acted that way."[65]

By the UNEF expulsion episode in 1967, a seventy-year-old Pearson had seen his beloved British Empire fade, the American and Russian empires emerge, two vast wars engulf continents, countless smaller conflicts darken the horizon, the birth and collapse of the League of Nations, and the construction of the United Nations. His country had evolved through profound paradigm shifts from muted extension of an imperial constellation, to a more sovereign state that wished only to turn away from the world, into a respected middle power that understood and accepted there was nowhere to hide. His country and the way it chose to act in the world would inexorably continue to evolve, consciously and not, through triumph and disaster. Lester Pearson had learned to see through both impostors.

Notes

One: WHERE IS HERE?

1 Phillip Buckner, "Introduction," in *Canada and the British Empire*, ed. Phillip Buckner (Oxford: Oxford University Press 2008), 6.

2 Wm. Roger Louis, "Introduction," in *The Oxford History of the British Empire* Volume 4, eds. Wm. Roger Louis and Judith M. Brown (Oxford: Oxford University Press, 1999), 6-7.

3 CBC TV interview, February 3, 1970, film roll 4, p. 15 of transcript, Library and Archives Canada (hereafter LAC).

4 Lester Pearson, *Mike: The Memoirs of the Rt. Hon. Lester Pearson*, vol. 1 (Toronto: University of Toronto Press, 1972) 6; CBC TV interview, February 4, 1970, film roll 8, pp. 4-5 of transcript.

5 Pearson, *Mike* vol. 1, 10.

6 CBC TV interview, February 3, 1970, film roll 1, p. 5 of transcript.

7 John Holmes, *The Shaping of Peace: Canada and the Search for World Order, 1943–1957*, vol. 2, (Toronto: University of Toronto Press, 1982), 359.

8 Pearson, *Mike* vol. 1, 9.

9 Ibid.

10 A.D.P. Heeney diary, September 24-25, 1955, Heeney papers, MG30 E144, vol. 2, LAC; Tom Kent, interview with author, 1993; John B. de Payne, interview with author, 1996.

11 Geoffrey Pearson, interview with author, 1993.

12 Wilfrid Laurier quoted in "Laurier Predicts His Majority Will Increase," *Toronto Daily Star*, August 25, 1911, 17.

13 *House of Commons Debates,* 22nd Parliament, 4th session, vol. 1, November 27, 1956, 55.

14 CBC TV interview February 3, 1970, film rolls 1 and 2, p. 12 of transcript. Information about the pilot engine comes from F. Douglas Reville, *History of the County of Brant* (Brantford, ON: Brant Historical Society, 1920), 197.

15 Simon-Napoleon Parent quoted in "Heir to Britain's Throne Now Guest of Canada" *The Globe* (Toronto), September 17, 1901, 2.

16 Agnes Scott writing for *Saturday Night* magazine as "Amaryllis" quoted in Sandra Gwyn, *The Private Capital* (Toronto: McClelland & Stewart 1984), 327. For anglophone responses to the Boer war, see Carman Miller, *Canada's Little War: Fighting for the British Empire in Southern Africa 1899–1902* (Toronto: James Lorimer 2003), 12-13, and Carman Miller, *Painting the Map Red: Canada and the South African War 1899 - 1902* (Ottawa: Canadian War Museum, 1998), 19.

17 "Calm Words on the War," *Christian Guardian,* January 10, 1900, 1; "French Canadian Loyalty," *Christian Guardian,* January 2, 1900, 9; "The War in South Africa," *Christian Guardian,* January 17, 1900, 1.

18 Sara Jeannette Duncan, *The Imperialist,* Thomas E. Tausky, ed. (Ottawa: Tecumseh Press, 1996), 48-49. In urging the Royal tour, the British Cabinet minister Arthur Balfour sensed the same limitation: "The citizens of this empire know little and care little for British Ministries and British party politics. But they know, and care for, the Empire of which they are members and for the Sovereign who rules it." Arthur Balfour quoted in Phillip Buckner, "Casting Daylight Upon Magic: Deconstructing the Royal Tour of 1901 to Canada," *Journal of Imperial and Commonwealth History* 31, no. 2 (2003), 162.

19 Duncan, *The Imperialist,* 48-49.

20 *House of Commons Debates,* 8th Parliament, 5th session, vol. 1, February 5, 1900, pp. 64-65; John W. Dafoe, *Laurier: A Study in Canadian Politics* (Toronto: Thomas Allen, 1922), 64.

21 Wilfrid Laurier quoted in O.D. Skelton, *Life and Letters of Wilfrid Laurier,* vol. 2 (Oxford: Oxford University Press, 1921), 322.

22 Robert Bothwell, *The Penguin History of Canada* (Toronto: Penguin, 2006), 247.

23 *La Presse* quoted in Skelton, *Life and Letters of Wilfrid Laurier,* vol. 2, 96.

24 CBC TV interview February 3, 1970, film roll 3, p. 3 of transcript. Pearson preferred to cloak his Methodist inheritance in humour. During the 1960s, future senator David P. Smith, then in his twenties and also the son and grandson of a minister, performed various roles in the Liberal party and met Prime Minister Pearson on several occasions at 24 Sussex Drive. Smith recalled: "Somehow, Pearson knew I was a preacher's kid and he would frequently put his arm around me and say, 'We P.K.'s have to stick together' and he would chuckle. Sometime after his initial P.K. reference, he said 'Well you know there are quite a few P.K.'s around but there aren't too many double P.K.'s. I didn't know what he meant and I said 'What's a double P.K.?' Pearson replied 'Father and grandfather.' I said, 'That's me too' and he replied, 'I know, and that's why we *really* have to stick together!'" Senator Smith added that years later while preparing for the 1997 federal election, he told then Prime Minister Jean Chrétien the P.K. anecdote and mentioned the number of times he met with Pearson. Chrétien, who had served under Pearson, "listened closely and then said, 'Pearson didn't have you over that often because you were national youth director... It was because you were a P.K.' I replied, 'I didn't realize that then, but I do know that now.'" Letter to author, 2009.

25 John Wesley, *The Works of the Reverend John Wesley,* vol. 3 (New York: T. Mason and G. Lane, 1840), 74 and 126.

26 "formidable empire of the spirit": David Hempton, *Methodism: Empire of the Spirit* (New Haven: Yale University Press, 2005), 2; Methodism statistics from Neil Semple, *The Lord's Dominion: The History of Canadian Methodism* (Montreal: McGill–Queen's University Press, 1996), 182.

27 Richard P. Bowles, "The Tipperary Bowles," 1993.043V, TR, Richard Pinch Bowles fonds, Victoria University Archives, 31-33.

28 Pearson, *Mike* vol. 1, 9-10.

29 Patricia (Pearson) Hannah and Geoffrey Pearson, interviews with author, 1993.

30 CBC TV interview, March 15, 1971, film roll 215, p. 1 of transcript.

31 I am indebted to Ramsay Cook for these insights on Methodism. Ramsay Cook, interview with author, 2001. See also Cook's *The Regenerators: Social Criticism in Late-Victorian English Canada* (Toronto: University of Toronto Press, 1985).

32 John English, interview with author, 1993; Lester Pearson, *Mike: The Memoirs of the Rt. Hon. Lester B. Pearson,* vol. 2, John A. Munro and Alex I. Inglis, eds. (Toronto: University of Toronto Press, 1973), 32.

33 Pearson, *Mike* vol. 2, 123.

34 Ibid., 35.

35 Hempton, *Methodism: Empire of the Spirit,* 206; Pearson, *Mike* vol. 2, 31.

36 CBC TV interview, April 21, 1970, film roll 72, p. 3 of transcript.

Two: GROWING UP CANADIAN

1 G.A. Henty, *With Kitchener in the Soudan: A Story of Atbara and Omdurman* (London: Blackie & Son, 1903), 23-24.

2 CBC TV interview, February 3, 1970, film rolls 3 and 4, p. 15 of transcript; *Mike, Vol. 1,* 15.

3 CBC TV interview, February 3, 1970, film roll 5, p. 2 of transcript. For someone so devoid of pomposity, Pearson's attraction to regalia is interesting. As a child, he visited the Ontario legislature. "All I can remember about it," he said, "is the pages with the white collars and I thought, 'Gee, if only I could be one of those.'" CBC TV interview, February 10, 1970, film roll 18, p. 5 of transcript.

4 CBC TV interview, February 3, 1970, film roll 7, p. 6 of transcript.

5 CBC TV interview, February 3, 1970, film roll 6, p. 2 of transcript, and film roll 7, p. 5 of transcript; *Mike* vol. 1, 16.

6 CBC TV Interview, February 3, 1970, film roll 7, p. 4 of transcript; Pearson war memoir, undated, 3. Pearson kept a handwritten diary during the war. After the war, he used his letters home as the basis for a more fulsome memoir of his war experience. Lester Pearson fonds, MG26 N8, vol. 1, file 1, LAC. Andrew Cohen has conjured up the Henty-inspired titles that may have flitted through the eighteen-year-old's imagination: *With Pearson in Passchendaele! Under Pearson's Command!* Andrew Cohen, *Lester B. Pearson* (Toronto: Penguin, 2008), 15-16.

7 Pearson war memoir, 6.

8 Ibid., 10 and 28.

9 Pearson, *Mike* vol. 1, 21.

10 Pearson war memoir, 26.

11 Ibid., 26 and 21.

12 Lord Palmerston, letter to Lord Cowley, November 25, 1859, quoted in Evelyn Ashley, *The Life and Correspondence of Henry John Temple, Viscount Palmerston* (London: Richard Bentley and Son, 1879), 337-38.

13 Robert Kubicek, "British Expansion, Empire and Technological Change," in *The Oxford History of the British Empire, Vol. 3: The Nineteenth Century,* ed. Andrew Porter (Oxford: Oxford University Press, 1999), table 12.1, 254.

14 Benjamin Disraeli quoted in Robert Blake, *Disraeli* (London: Eyre & Spottiswoode, 1966), 584.

15 Hugh Cairns to Disraeli, quoted in Blake, *Disraeli,* 581.

16 Robin J. Moore, "Imperial India 1858—1914" in *The Oxford History of the British Empire,* vol. 3, ed. Andrew Porter, 427. Moore writes that in the 1850s, "the forces had included three

distinct structures: the East India Company's 'native army' in Bengal, Madras, and Bombay, which numbered almost a quarter of a million troops, commanded exclusively by cadres of British commissioned officers; the Company's European army, of some 21,000 officers and men, who enlisted for a lifetime's local service; and the regiments of the Queen's Army of the Line, whose number rose during the Mutiny from 24,000."

17 George Nathaniel Curzon, *Speeches on India* (London: John Murray, 1904), 5-6.

18 Lord Curzon to A.J. Balfour, March 31, 1901, quoted in David Dilks, *Curzon in India* (New York: Taplinger, 1970), 113.

19 Pearson war memoir, 49.

20 Ibid. 55-56.

21 *Parliamentary Debates,* Commons, 5th series, vol. 98, October 29, 1917, col. 1247.

22 John H. Morrow Jr., *The Great War in the Air: Military Aviation from 1909 to 1921* (Washington: Smithsonian Institute Press, 1993), 365; James P. Harrison, *Mastering the Sky: A History of Aviation from Ancient Times to the Present* (New York: Sarpedon, 2000), 91; Morrow, *The Great War in the Air*, 238.

23 CBC TV interview, February 4, 1970, film roll 13, p. 3 of transcript; Pearson, *Mike* vol. 1, x. His Christian name might have been chosen because it was the maiden name of his maternal grandmother, Jane Lester. His middle name, Bowles, was taken from his mother's maiden name.

24 Lester Pearson, undated, handwritten diary.

25 Ibid.; CBC TV interview, February 4, 1970, film roll 11, p. 4 of transcript; Morrow, *The Great War in the Air*, 239.

26 Lester Pearson, December 4, 1917, letters to parents, 1917-1918, MG26 N8 vols. 1-2, LAC.

27 Election statistics from J.L. Granatstein and Desmond Morton, *Marching to Armageddon: Canadians and the Great War 1914–1919* (Toronto: Lester and Orpen Dennys, 1989), 173; Lester Pearson, December 24, 1917, letter to parents.

28 CBC TV interview, February 4, 1970, film roll 11, pp. 4 and 7 of transcript.

29 CBC TV interview, February 4, 1970, film roll 11, p. 5 of transcript.

30 Ibid, p. 7 of transcript; Pearson quoted in John R. Beal, *The Pearson Phenomenon* (Toronto: Longmans, 1964), 30.

31 Pearson, January 6, 1918, letter to parents.

32 Pearson, *Mike* vol. 1, 36.

33 Robert Borden to George Perley, January 4, 1916, *Documents on Canada's External Relations* [hereafter *DCER*], vol. 1, 104.

34 Robert Borden to Laura Borden, January 18, 1919, Robert Borden fonds, MC 184, box 5, Thomas Fisher Rare Book Library, University of Toronto (photocopies of the original material at LAC); Robert Craig Brown, *Robert Laird Borden: A Biography, Volume 2: 1914–1937* (Toronto: Macmillan, 1980), 82.

35 CBC TV interview, February 4, 1970, film roll 12, p. 7 of transcript, LAC. Pearson said he tried to sign up for service in Siberia, "so I must still have had a spark in me of crazy adventure.... But the doctor wouldn't pass me fit for that." For the newspaper item, see *Guelph Mercury*, April 8, 1918. Pearson biographer John English discovered this item in the course of his own research. "I was taken aback," Professor English told me in an interview, "because, of course, that wasn't the story that appeared in his memoirs." English was the first scholar to examine

Pearson's military medical records and nervous breakdown. See his chapter "Renewal" in *Shadow of Heaven*. John English, interview with author, 1993.

36 CBC TV interview, February 4, 1970, film roll 12, p. 7 of transcript; Pearson, *Mike* vol. 2, 39.

37 Pearson, *Mike* vol. 1, 36-37. Clifford Hames is buried in Dover, England.

38 CBC TV interview, February 4, 1970, film roll 13, p. 6 of transcript; English, *Shadow of Heaven*, 56.

39 CBC TV interview, February 4, 1970, film roll 13, p. 6 of transcript.

40 April 1919 medical report, Lester B. Pearson file, RG150 1992-93/166, box 7688, LAC.

41 Patricia (Pearson) Hannah, John English, and Geoffrey Pearson interviews with author, 1993.

42 CBC TV interview, February 4, 1970, film roll 13, p. 7 of transcript.

Three: SOVEREIGNTY AND ASSOCIATION

1 *House of Commons Debates*, 18th Parliament, 1st session, vol. 1, March 2, 1936, 680.

2 CBC TV interview, February 10, 1970, film roll 20, pp. 4-5 of transcript.

3 Pearson, *Mike* vol. 1, 41-42.

4 Ibid., 43.

5 Pearson, *Mike* vol. 1, 50. For more on Pearson at the University of Toronto, see chapter six, "Academic Interlude," in English, *Shadow of Heaven*.

6 Patricia (Pearson) Hannah, Geoffrey Pearson, Keith Davey, interviews with author, 1993.

7 Maryon Pearson quoted in Heather Robertson, *More Than a Rose: Prime Ministers, Wives and Other Women* (Toronto: Seal Books, 1991), 273.

8 CBC TV interview, February 12, 1970, film roll 23, p. 2 of transcript.

9 W.L.M. King, *DCER* vol. 3, 248-49.

10 Bruce Hutchison, *Mr. Prime Minister, 1867–1964* (Toronto: Longmans, 1964), 202.

11 King diary, September 16-19, 1922, http://www.bac-lac.go.oa/cng/discover/politics-government/prime-ministers/william-lyon-mackenzie-king/Pages/diaries-william-lyon-mackenzie-king.aspx; Arthur Meighen quoted in *Daily Mail and Empire* (Toronto), September 23, 1922, quoted in Robert MacGregor Dawson, *William Lyon Mackenzie King: A Political Biography, 1874–1923* (Toronto: University of Toronto Press, 1958), 414.

12 King diary, September 26, 1922.

13 King, October 8, 1923, *DCER* vol. 3, 248.

14 Lester Pearson, "The Germany of To-Day," *Christian Guardian*, October 4, 1922, 4.

15 King, October 8, 1923, *DCER* vol. 3, 236-37.

16 Austen Chamberlain quoted in Charles Petrie, *The Life and Letters of Sir Austen Chamberlain*, vol. 2 (London: Cassell, 1939), 251.

17 Peter Larkin to W.L.M. King, November 20, 1924, *DCER* vol. 3, 369-70.

18 King diary, November 23, 1924.

19 Ibid., December 1, 1924.

20 *Parliamentary Debates*, Commons, 5th series, vol. 179, December 15, 1924, col. 667.

21 Norman Hillmer, "The Balfour Report" in *The Canadian Encyclopedia* vol. 1, ed. James Marsh (Edmonton: Hurtig Publishers, 1988), 167; J.L. Granatstein and Norman Hillmer, *Empire to Umpire: Canada and the World to the 1990s* (Toronto: Copp Clark Longman, 1994), 115.

22 CBC TV interview, February 10, 1970, film roll 18, p. 6 of transcript, and film roll 19, p. 4 of transcript.

23 Lester Pearson lecture notes, MG26 N3 vol. 15, pp. 2-4, LAC. The first six pages are numbered and typewritten; over one hundred unnumbered handwritten pages follow.

24 Pearson lecture notes, unnumbered pages.

25 Vincent Massey, *What's Past Is Prologue* (Toronto: Macmillan, 1963), 110.

26 *House of Commons Debates*, 16th Parliament, 1st session, vol. 2, April 13, 1927, 2472.

27 CBC TV interview, February 10, 1970, film roll 18, p. 3 of transcript, LAC; W.P.M. Kennedy letter to O.D. Skelton, January 30, 1927, and May 7, 1928, RG32 vol. 536, LAC.

28 Pearson, *Mike* vol. 1, 59; English, *Shadow of Heaven*, 140.

29 Vincent Massey to O.D. Skelton, July 25, 1928; O.D. Skelton to Vincent Massey, July 27, 1928; W.P.M. Kennedy to O.D. Skelton, May 7, 1928.

30 Charles Ritchie quoted in Peter Stursberg, *Lester Pearson and the American Dilemma* (Toronto: Doubleday, 1980), 9.

31 CBC TV interview, February 10, 1970, film roll 21, p. 6 of transcript.

32 English, *Shadow of Heaven*, 147. See also John Hilliker, *Canada's Department of External Affairs, Volume 1: The Early Years, 1909–1946* (Montreal: McGill-Queen's University Press, 1990), 125; CBC interview, February 10, 1970, film roll 21, p. 4; Hilliker, *Canada's Department of External Affairs*, vol. 1, 127.

33 J.L. Granatstein, interview with author, 1993. For an excellent history of Pearson's contemporaries see Granatstein's *The Ottawa Men: The Civil Service Mandarins 1935–1957* (Toronto: Oxford University Press, 1982).

34 Lester Pearson diary, February 1, 1930, MG26 N8, vol. 1, file 2, LAC.

35 Ibid., January 19, 1930.

36 Ibid., January 27, 1930; March 23-24, 1930.

37 Ibid., March 15, 1930.

38 Ibid., May 1, 1930.

39 Commissioners to R.B. Bennett, April 15, 1935, quoted in Granatstein *"The Ottawa Men,"* 81; *House of Commons Debates*, 17th Parliament, 6th session, vol. 4, July 3, 1935, 4206. Writing to O.D. Skelton years later about a heavy workload, Pearson gently mocked Bennett's hyperbole: "If I were only back in the East Block as of yore, I could let R.B. see me in the corridor looking wan and haggard, convince him that I was on 'the verge of a nervous breakdown' and be sent off to London to a Jubilee or something." March 24, 1939, MG26 series N1, vol. 14, file Skelton, O.D.—Canada—External Affairs, 1939-1940, LAC.

40 Pearson, *Mike* vol. 1, 78.

Four: A SENSE OF PROPORTION

1 CBC TV interview, February 16, 1970, film roll 32, p. 1 of transcript.

2 *House of Commons Debates*, 18th Parliament, 4th session, vol. 3, March 30, 1939, 2419.

3 Pearson diary, January 1, 1936.

4 Lester Pearson writing as Scrutator, "The Political Aspects of the Disarmament Conference," *Canadian Defence Quarterly* 9, no. 2 (January 1932), 168-84.

5 Memorandum, June 20, 1933 for the Department of External Affairs, "The Problems of Security and Sanctions in the Light of Recent Developments at Geneva," R.J. Manion papers, MG 27-111B7, volume 87, misc. subject files—General-League of Nations—Agenda, etc., 1931–1934, LAC.

6 Transcript of proceedings, December 8, 1920, in *The League of Nations Official Journal: Resolutions Adopted by the Assembly November 15th to December 18th 1920,* 328; F.P. Walters, *A History of the League of Nations, Volume 1* (New York: Oxford University Press, 1952), 259.

7 Pearson diary, January 1, 1936.

8 Samuel Hoare, *Nine Troubled Years* (London: Collins, 1954), 170; CBC TV interview, February 16, 1970, film roll 30, p. 1 of transcript. In the interview, Pearson incorrectly remembers Hoare giving this speech during a later vote to condemn Italy.

9 Ernest Lapointe quoted in "Give Labour Voice in CNR Mackenzie King's Promise," *Toronto Daily Star,* September 9, 1935. The speech took place September 7.

10 W.L.M. King quoted in ibid.

11 CBC TV interview, February 16, 1970, film roll 32, p. 2 of transcript.

12 O.D. Skelton, August 23, 1935, *DCER* vol. 5, 379.

13 CBC TV interview, February 16, 1970, film roll 29, p. 7 of transcript.

14 Pearson diary, January 1, 1936.

15 CBC TV interview, February 16, 1970, film roll 29, p. 9, and film roll 30, p. 1 of transcript.

16 Robert Bothwell and John English, "Dirty Work at the Crossroads: New Perspectives on the Riddell Incident," *Canadian Historical Association Historical Papers* 7, no. 1 (1972): 263-85. See also Brock Millman, "Canada, Sanctions and the Abyssinian Crisis of 1935," *The Historical Journal* 40, no. 1 (March 1997), 143-68.

17 King diary, November 2, 1935.

18 CBC TV interview, February 12, 1970, film roll 23, p. 2 of transcript; Pearson to O.D. Skelton, November 22, 1935, MG26 N1, vol. 14, file Skelton, O.D.—Canada—External Affairs 1935–1938, LAC.

19 Only the *Winnipeg Free Press* supported sanctions. See John Herd Thompson with Allen Seager, *Canada 1922–1939: Decades of Discord* (Toronto: McClelland and Stewart, 1985), 310.

20 Pearson to O.D. Skelton, November 22, 1935, MG26 N1, vol. 14, file Skelton, O.D.—Canada—External Affairs 1935–1938; Pearson memorandum, November 1935, RG25 Series G1, vol. 1719, file 927, part 4, pp. 14-15.

21 Ernest Lapointe quoted in "Canada is Not Pressing Sanctions," *The Globe* (Toronto), December 2, 1935.

22 Foreign Office officials quoted in Bothwell and English, "Dirty Work at the Crossroads," 280; Pearson diary, January 1, 1936, 11–12; Bruce Hutchison, *The Incredible Canadian: A Candid Portrait of Mackenzie King* (Toronto: Longmans Green, 1953), 208.

23 CBC TV interview, February 16, 1970, film roll 32, p. 4 of transcript.

24 Pearson diary, January 1, 1936, 5-6.

25 Ibid., 13.

26 Ibid., 15; CBC TV interview, February 16, 1970, film roll 31, p. 3 of transcript.

27 Pearson quoted in Granatstein, *The Ottawa Men*, 86.

28 Rhodes lecture reprinted in Robert Borden, *Canada in the Commonwealth: From Conflict to Co-operation* (Toronto: Oxford University Press, 1929), 128.

29 Pearson, *Mike* vol. 1, 69.

30 Pearson to O.D. Skelton, November 4, 1938, quoted in *Mike* vol. 1, 130. The original letter can be found in MG26 N1 Vol. 14, Skelton, O.D.—Canada—External Affairs 1939–1940 file.

31 Pearson, *Mike* vol. 1, 152; diary entry quoted on p. 176.

32 George Ignatieff, *The Memoirs of George Ignatieff: The Making of a Peacemonger* (Toronto: University of Toronto Press, 1985), 73.

33 Pearson, *Mike* vol. 1, 106; May 15, 1941 speech reprinted in *Words and Occasions* (Toronto: University of Toronto Press, 1970), 37.

34 Pearson, March 18, 1943, *DCER* vol. 9, 1142; CBC TV interview March 12, 1970, film roll 49, pp. 5-6 of transcript.

35 Pearson diary April 12, 1945 and January 6, 1943.

36 "Armed Forces" in www.the canadianencyclopedia.com.

37 The functional principle, or functionalism, mirrored Borden's declaration during the Treaty of Versailles debate: "Upon each nation is imposed a responsibility commensurate with its power and influence. Unless that responsibility is accepted and fulfilled, the peace of the world cannot be maintained." *House of Commons Debates,* 13th Parliament, 3rd session, vol. 1, September 2, 1919, 17. In a similar vein, during the 1930s, King spoke of "a sense of proportion in international affairs," albeit largely to keep his modest and divided country free from any commitments. *House of Commons Debates,* 18th Parliament, 1st session, vol. 1, February 11, 1936, 97.

38 Lester Pearson, July 23, 1942, "Canada and the Combined Boards" in *DCER* vol. 9, 190 and 193.

39 Pearson, *Mike* vol. 1, 251.

40 Memorandum of conversation with Mr. Lester B. Pearson, counselor-minister of the Canadian legation in Washington, Ottawa, July 28, 1942, RG 84 entry 2195a, 350–51–09–03, Canada Ottawa embassy general records, 1936–1947, National Archives and Records Administration [hereafter NARA].

41 Norman Robertson to Lester Pearson, March 4, 1943, *DCER* vol. 9, 785; Pearson diary, March 4, 1943.

42 Pearson diary, March 22-27, March 26-April 1, and March 31, 1943. The minutes of the meeting do not include Pearson's remarks, but he might have asked that they not be recorded. Minutes of the War Committee of the Cabinet, March 31, 1943, RG2 7C, vol. 12, microfilm C4875, LAC.

43 Anthony Eden quoted in King diary April 7, 1943; Pearson diary April 8, 1943.

44 Pearson, *Mike* vol. 1, 248.

45 King diary, November 4, 1943; Holmes, *Shaping of Peace*, 50.

46   Pearson to Lt. Gen. Harry Crerar March 24, 1944, MG26 N1, vol. 3, Crerar file, LAC; CBC TV interview, March 12, 1970, film roll 53, p. 8 of transcript.

47   Pearson to Crerar, March 24, 1944.

48   CBC interview, film roll 54, p. 1. Pearson's memory failed him here, because Crerar's refusal was polite and correct. In June 1944, Pearson wrote to Vincent Massey, still pining for adventure, "I live in hopes of getting across sometime this summer. I am more determined than ever now that the liberation has begun. Washington seems so far away from it all." Pearson to Massey, June 6, 1944, Massey papers, B1987-0082/385(30), University of Toronto archives; King diary, September 29, 1944.

49   Lionel Gelber, "Canada's New Stature," *Foreign Affairs* 24, no. 2 (January 1946), 277 and 280; Granatstein and Hillmer, *From Empire to Umpire,* 178.

50   For more on the friction between Pearson, Wrong, and Robertson see J.L. Granatstein, *A Man of Influence: Norman A. Robertson and Canadian Statecraft 1929-68* (Ottawa: Deneau, 1981) and Adam Chapnick, *The Middle Power Project: Canada and the Founding of the United Nations* (Vancouver: UBC Press, 2005). Escott Reid, *On Duty: A Canadian at the Making of the United Nations, 1945-1946* (Toronto: McClelland and Stewart, 1983), 29. While the professional tensions between Pearson, Wrong, and Robertson were genuine, it is important to note that they also chose to be buried in the same small cemetery outside of Ottawa.

51   English, *Shadow of Heaven,* 287; *Vancouver Sun* quoted in Lester Pearson diary, May 21, 1945.

52   Pearson diary, May 11, 1945.

53   Pearson diary, May 26, 1945; "Evatt Acclaimed for Parley Work," *New York Times,* June 27, 1945; for Pearson's personal impressions of Herbert Evatt, see diary entry quoted in *Mike* vol. 1, 273, and also page 277; Pearson diary, June 11, 1945.

54   CBC TV interview, March 12, 1970, film roll 54, p. 4 of transcript; diary entry quoted in *Mike* vol. 1, 277.

55   Adam Chapnick writes that the Canadian delegates "virtually rewrote the proposed chapter on the Economic and Social Council," and "took a leadership role in ensuring that the great powers did not manipulate the selection of the secretary and deputy secretary general." Chapnick, *The Middle Power Project,* 129 and 134.

56   Jack Hickerson to Ray Atherton, US ambassador, August 4, 1945, John D. Hickerson correspondence, AG, 193447, records of the Department of State, microfilm publication M1244. MHF, NARA; John English, "'A Fine Romance': Canada and the United Nations, 1943-1957" in *Canada and the Early Cold War, 1943-1957,* Greg Donaghy, ed. (Ottawa: Department of Foreign Affairs and International Trade, 1998), 83.

57   Lester Pearson, "Peace Through the United Nations," January 26, 1948, reprinted in *Statements and Speeches 48/2.*

58   Ibid.

59   Lester Pearson, "To the Staff at UNRRA," November 5, 1944, reprinted in *Words and Occasions,* 59.

60   Winston Churchill quoted in "Churchill Seek US Pact to Stem Soviet Expansion," *Globe and Mail* (Toronto), March 6, 1946.

61   Lester Pearson to W.L.M. King, March 11, 1946, *DCER* vol. 12, 2046.

62   CBC TV interview, April 7, 1970, film roll 65, p. 2 of transcript.

63   CBC TV interview, March 13, 1970, film roll 57, pp. 3-4.

Five: HERE I AM IN THE MIDDLE

1   Pearson lecture notes, MG26 N8, vol. 2, file 4, LAC.

2   Pearson, *Mike* vol. 1, 276.

3   King diary, March 20, 1944.

4   King quoted in John Matheson, *Canada's Flag: A Search for a Country* (Boston: G.K. Hall, 1980), 42.

5   Peter Hennessy, *Having It So Good: Britain in the Fifties* (London: Allen Lane, 2006), 9.

6   Lester Pearson to I.M. Gringorten, May 14, 1947, MG26 N1 vol. 64, UN Palestine 1947–1950 file, LAC.

7   Bruce Hutchison, *Mr. Prime Minister*, 288.

8   CBC TV interview, April 7, 1970, film roll 66, pp. 1 and 3 of transcript. Pearson's grasp of Palestine's geography mirrors David Lloyd George's recollection after the First World War that he knew far more about the kings of ancient Israel than he did about the kings of England and Wales.

9   Wm. Roger Louis, *The British Empire in the Middle East, 1945–1951: Arab Nationalism, the United States, and Postwar Imperialism* (Oxford: Clarendon Press, 1984), 467. For British atrocities in the Mandate of Palestine, see Matthew Hughes, "The Banality of Brutality: British Armed Forces and the Repression of the Arab Revolt in Palestine, 1936–39," *English Historical Review* 124, no. 507 (April 2009), 315-54.

10 David McCullough, *Truman* (New York: Simon and Schuster, 1992), 596; Harry Truman quoted on page 599.

11 Harry S. Truman, *Years of Trial and Hope* (New York: Doubleday, 1956), 136.

12 Memorandum to Cabinet, February 13, 1947, CAB/129/17, National Archives (UK) [hereafter NA].

13 Pearson to King, November 15, 1946, statement by Mr. Samuel J. Zacks, president of the Zionist Organization of Canada, King papers, MG26 J4, vol. 310, memoranda and notes, 1940–1950, LAC; Irving Abella and Harold Troper, "'The line must be drawn somewhere': Canada and Jewish Refugees, 1933–1939," *Canadian Historical Review* 60, no. 2 (1979), 181. The authors note that another two thousand Jews may have come into Canada from the UK and the US. According to the *Canadian Encyclopedia*, "Canada took in proportionately fewer Jews than any western country. At the same time, 17 000 Jewish Canadians responded to the call to arms in WWII and served in the armed forces." See "Jews" by Stuart Schoenfeld in the on-line edition. The poll is cited in David Bercuson, *Canada and the Birth of Israel: A Study in Canadian Foreign Policy* (Toronto: University of Toronto Press, 1985), 41.

14 John English e-mail to author, September 2012; transcript of BBC Radio interview, "Cards on the Table," July 12-13, 1938, MG26 N1, vol. 58, pp. 9-11, LAC. I first saw this material in English's *Shadow of Heaven*, 206-206. Pearson, it must be acknowledged, did not go so far as to repudiate his country's restrictive immigrations policies that placed a priority on "agriculturalists" and dutifully defended the prevailing economic arguments made to keep out not just Jews but everyone else during the Depression.

15 Lester Pearson to Annie Pearson and Vaughan Pearson, March 17, 1939, quoted in English, *Shadow of Heaven,* 206; Lester Pearson speech, "Israel's Answer to Racial Persecution," June 1, 1952, reprinted in *Statements and Speeches* 52/ 20, 5-6.

16 *House of Commons Debates,* 20th Parliament, 3rd session, vol. 3, April 14, 1947, 1999.

17 Lester Pearson to Louis St. Laurent, April 19, 1947, *DCER* vol. 13, 914-16.

18 Memorandum, April 24, 1947, *DCER* vol. 13, 916.

19 Foreign Office to UK Mission to the UN, April 24, 1947, FO 371/67585 UN 2649, NA.

20 CBC TV interview, April 7, 1970, film roll 66, p. 4 of transcript.

21 Pearson, *Mike* vol. 2, 214.

22 United Nations, 46th plenary meeting, May 6, 1947, United Nations Archives [hereafter UNA]. Lester Pearson quoted in "Threats are Aired by Palestine Sides," *New York Times*, May 13, 1947.

23 Memorandum of phone call between R.G. Riddell and Lester Pearson, May 3, 1947, RG 25 series G2, vol. 36945475-CD-2–40C, p. 196; Lester Pearson to Louis St. Laurent, May 15, 1947, quoted in Anne Trowell Hillmer, "Canadian Policy on the Partition of Palestine 1947," unpublished MA thesis, Carleton University, 1981, 65.

24 United Nations, 79th plenary meeting, May 15, 1947, A/2/PV.79, UNA; R. H. Hadow to P. Gore-Booth, May 17, 1947, FO 371/67587/ UN 3164, NA; "Palestine Solution in Fall is Predicted by Aranha," *New York Times*, May 17, 1947, 4.

25 King diary, September 19 and 22, 1947.

26 Cabinet conclusions, September 11, 1947, RG2, Privy Council Office, series A-5-a, vol. 2640.

27 Lester Pearson, "Some Principles of Canadian Foreign Policy," *Words and Occasions* (Toronto: University of Toronto Press, 1970), 71.

28 Elizabeth MacCallum's comments recorded in telegram 1319, October 13, 1947, RG25 series A-3-B, vol. 4745, p. 17; memorandum, December 27, 1947, *DCER* vol. 13, 942; Gerry Riddell, "The Plan of Partition for Palestine," November 21, 1947, RG25 series A-3-B, vol. 4745, p. 69.

29 Ignatieff, *Memoirs,* 110-11.

30 Pearson, *Mike* vol. 2, 214.

31 J.L. Ilsley, October 14, 1947, *DCER* vol. 13, 933-34.

32 Bruce Hutchison, memorandum from New York, November 15, 1947, pp. 6-7, Bruce Hutchison fonds, box 1, file 8, MsC 22, University of Calgary Special Collections; CBC TV interview, April 7, 1970, film roll 65, pp. 3-4 of transcript.

33 CBC TV interview, April 7, 1970, film roll 65, pp. 3-4 of transcript. At least one member of the Canadian delegation, Elizabeth MacCallum, believed that Pearson "engineered Ilsley's temporary recall to Ottawa." See Anne Trowell Hillmer, "Here I Am in the Middle: Lester Pearson and the Origins of Canada's Diplomatic Involvement in the Middle East," in *Domestic Battleground: Canada and the Arab-Israeli Conflict,* David Taras and David H. Goldberg, eds. (Montreal: McGill-Queen's University Press, 1989), 130.

34 For Pearson's remarks to the subcommittee, see United Nations and Palestine—correspondence and memoranda, 1947-1948 file in the Walter Harris fonds, MG32 series B50 vol. 4.

35 Lester Pearson to Vincent Massey, November 16, 1947, MG26 N1, vol. 10.

36 Lester Pearson to Louis St. Laurent, telegram 1566, November 6, 1947, RG25 series G2, vol. 3694, 5475-CD-2–40C, pp. 188-90.

37 Bruce Hutchison, memorandum from New York, November 15, 1947, 2, Bruce Hutchison fonds, box 1, file 8, MsC 22, University of Calgary Special Collections.

38 Lester Pearson to Norman Robertson, December 30, 1947, *DCER* vol. 13, 949-50.

39 "US Soviet Accord on Palestine Asks British Go by May 1," *New York Times*, November 11, 1947, 1.

40 Lester Pearson to Louis St. Laurent, telegram 1599, November 10, 1947, RG25 series G2, vol. 3694, 5475-CD-2-40C, p. 155.

41 CBC TV interview, April 7, 1970, film roll 65, p. 4 of transcript.

42 Lester Pearson, November 22, 1947, "Canadian Statement on the Partition Plan for Palestine," quoted in Hillmer, "Canadian Policy on the Partition of Palestine," 155.

43 Norman Robertson quoted the *Manchester Guardian* in a telegram to External Affairs. See telegram 1731, November 19, 1947, RG25 series G2, vol. 3694, 5475-CD-2-40C, p. 69.

44 Colleague Arnold Smith remembers Pearson joking about the divergent viewpoints within the Canadian delegation to the UN, "As he put it, 'We have balanced Canadian representation. We've got Sheik [Andy] McNaughton and Rabbi Pearson.' Those were Mike's words." Arnold Smith interview, April 25, 1978, Peter Stursberg fonds, MG31 D78 vol. 32 file 3, p. 24 of transcript. Pearson made the same quip to the interviewer for his TV memoirs, "They used to make fun of us down there, some of the people used to say: 'There were two Canadian delegates down there, Sheik McNaughton and Rabbi Pearson.'" CBC TV interview April 7, 1970, film roll 65, p. 5 of transcript.

45 Holmes, *The Shaping of Peace,* 63; Bercuson, *Canada and the Birth of Israel,* 132-33; Eliezer Tauber, *Personal Policy Making: Canada's Role in the Adoption of the Palestine Partition Resolution* (Westport, CT: Greenwood Press 2002), 118.

46 Bruce Hutchison, undated memorandum from 1947, p. 3, Bruce Hutchison fonds, box 1, file 8, MsC 22, University of Calgary Special Collections.

47 See Louis, *The British Empire in the Middle East,* 486-87.

48 *Parliamentary Debates,* Commons, 5th series, vol. 445, December 11, 1947, cols. 1219, 1209, and 1211.

49 King diary, December 6, 1947.

50 King diary, December 18, 1947.

51 Brooke Claxton quoted in David Bercuson, *True Patriot: The Life of Brooke Claxton, 1898–1960* (Toronto: University of Toronto Press, 1993), 191.

52 King diary, December 18, 1947.

53 Lester Pearson, memorandum dated January 11, 1948, *DCER* vol. 14, 141; King diary, January 4, 1948.

54 Lester Pearson, "Peace through the United Nations," January 26, 1948, reprinted in *Statements and Speeches 48/2,* 6.

55 Hume Wrong to Louis St. Laurent, February 4, 1948, *DCER* vol. 14, 249-51.

56 Lester Pearson, memorandum, February 17, 1948, *DCER* vol. 14, 254-57.

57 Lester Pearson to Louis St. Laurent, March 1, 1948, *DCER* vol. 14, 259.

58 Secretary of defense to secretary of state, April 19, 1948, *FRUS* vol. 5, 832; CIA report dated February 28, 1948, quoted in Louis, *The British Empire in the Middle East,* 504.

59 Clement Attlee to W.L.M. King, January 14, 1948, *DCER* vol. 14, 400.

60 Statistics on Jewish and Arab populations in Palestine from the *Encyclopedia Britannica Online Library Edition,* "Israel" and "Palestine." Jewish and Arab population figures for 1948 are a highly contentious issue because of incomplete records and unrecorded, unrecognized immigration. See Fred M. Gottheil, "The Smoking Gun: Arab Immigration into Palestine, 1922-1931," *Middle East Quarterly* 10, no. 1 (Winter 2003), 53-64; Lester Pearson to Norman

Robertson, April 24, 1948, UN Palestine 1947–1950 file, MG26 N1, vol. 64. Also found in *DCER* vol. 14, 292.

61 Benny Morris, *1948: A History of the First Arab-Israeli War* (New Haven: Yale University Press, 2008), 78.

62 Lester Pearson to Hume Wrong, May 18, 1948, *DCER* vol. 14, 302, and quoted in *Mike* vol. 2, 216.

63 King diary, May 17, 1948; Bercuson, *Canada and the Birth of Israel*, 182.

64 Trygve Lie to Lester Pearson, May 18, 1948, *DCER* vol. 14, 303-304.

65 Lester Pearson to Trygve Lie, May 27, 1948, *DCER* vol. 14, 308.

66 For Arab figures, see Benny Morris, *Israel's Border Wars 1949–1956: Arab Infiltration, Israeli Retaliation, and the Countdown to the Suez War* (Oxford: Clarendon Press, 1993), 4-5; for Jewish figures, see "International relations" in *Encyclopedia Britannica Online Library Edition*.

67 Louis, *The British Empire in the Middle East*, 561.

68 Lester Pearson quoted in Ralph Maybank diary, November 9, 1948, Maybank papers, MG14 B35, Manitoba Archives. "The Canadian delegation is well formed," Maybank noted. "It comprehends both Sheik McNaughton and Rabbi Pearson."

69 Lester Pearson, November 22 speech, reprinted in *Canadian Foreign Policy 1945–1954: Selected Speeches and Documents*, R.A. Mackay, ed. (Toronto: McClelland and Stewart, 1971), 142-43.

70 Zachary Lockman, *Comrades and Enemies: Arab and Jewish Workers in Palestine, 1906–1948* (Berkeley: University of California Press, 1996), 358.

71 Pearson quoted by E.L.M. Burns, transcript of interview with Peter Stursberg, May 16, 1978, MG31 D78 vol. 28, file 6, p. 11.

72 E.L.M. Burns interview, May 16, 1978, pp. 13-14; Saudi Arabian delegate's remark reported in J. M. Boyer, memorandum, March 27, 1948, MG26 N1, vol. 64, file UN Palestine 1947–1950; Lester Pearson speech, May 16, 1949, MG26 N9, vol. 2, p. 5. Pearson waxed even more lyrically about Israel in "Israel's Answer to Racial Persecution," June 1, 1952, in *Statements and Speeches 52/20*; Pearson, *Mike* vol. 2, 215; CBC TV interview, April 7, 1970, film roll 65, p. 7 of transcript; *House of Commons Debates 22nd Parliament, 3rd session, vol. 1, February 1, 1956, 773.

Six: SAME OLD, SAME OLD

1 CBC TV interview, April 21, 1970, film roll 68, pp. 2-3 of transcript.

2 Pearson first approached Mackenzie King to discuss a political future in January 1946, when Pearson was a contender to become the UN's first secretary-general. He told King he would fill the UN position for five years before returning to Canada. See King diary, January 11, 1946.

3 Grant Dexter, letter to George Ferguson, November 12, 1937, file 007, series S01 correspondence, subseries SS03, Grant Dexter collection, Queen's University Archives. Pearson may not have intended to leave External Affairs. J.L. Granatstein argues that Pearson used the offer from the CBC to secure a raise and promotion at External Affairs. See *The Ottawa Men*, 82-84.

4 Lester Pearson to Norman Robertson quoted in Granatstein, *A Man of Influence*, 200-201. Robertson arguably felt Pearson's qualms more deeply. Upon hearing of King's death, Robertson said, "I never saw a touch of greatness in him." Quoted in ibid., 206.

5   Lester Pearson to W.L.M. King, January 20, 1948 *DCER* vol. 14, 236.

6   Lester Pearson to Louis St. Laurent, June 29, 1948, *DCER* vol. 14, 788.

7   *Evening Standard* headline reported by Norman Robertson to Lester Pearson, June 30, 1948, *DCER* vol. 14, 789.

8   Ibid.

9   Ibid. and Lester Pearson to Louis St. Laurent, June 30, 1948, *DCER* vol. 14, 790.

10 For Cabinet decision, see *DCER* vol. 14, 791-92.

11 CBC TV interview, April 7, 1970, film roll 67, pp. 5-6 of transcript.

12 Arthur Andrew, *The Rise and Fall of a Middle Power: Canadian Diplomacy from King to Mulroney* (Toronto: James A. Lorimer, 1993), 45; Brooke Claxton thought he had a strong shot at being appointed foreign minister. On August 21, 1948 he wrote to a friend, "People generally assume that I will go to External Affairs when Mr. St. Laurent becomes Prime Minister." Quoted in David Bercuson, *True Patriot: The Life of Brooke Claxton 1898–1960* (Toronto: University of Toronto Press, 1993) 200; Pearson, *Mike* vol. 1, 296.

13 Pearson, *Mike* vol. 2, p. 7

14 "Pearson Majority Proves He Can Get Votes—Ottawa," October 26, 1948, *Toronto Daily Star.*

15 Lester Pearson to Brooke Claxton, January 18, 1949, RG25 5475-CX-2-40, vol. 6214, file part 1.1, 9 December 1948–9 September 1949, p. 256, LAC; for other reasons for the mission, see Sean M. Maloney, *Canada and UN Peacekeeping: Cold War By Other Means 1945–1970* (St. Catherines, ON: Vanwell Publishing, 2002), 23-29.

16 Cabinet conclusions, January 13, 1949, RG2, series A-5-a, vol. 2643; memorandum to Lester Pearson, January 15, 1949, RG25 5475-CX- 2-40, vol. 6214, file part 1.1, 9 December 1948—9 September 1949, p. 265.

17 The absence of press attention and the later lack of historical interest by key officials regarding UNMOGIP was noted by Sean M. Maloney, *Canada and UN Peacekeeping,* p. 26.

18 CBC TV interview, February 12, 1970, film roll 23, p. 2 of transcript; Pearson, *Mike* vol. 1, 294; Greg Donaghy, "Coming off the Gold Standard: Reassessing the 'Golden Age' of Canadian Diplomacy"(lecture, Johnson Shoyama Graduate School of Public Policy, University of Regina, Regina, SK, October 2005).

19 Louis St. Laurent quoted in Leigh E. Sarty, "The Limits of Internationalism: Canada and the Soviet Blockade of Berlin, 1948–1949" in *Nearly Neighbours: Canada and the Soviet Union from Cold War to Détente and Beyond,* J.L. Black and Norman Hillmer, eds. (Kingston, ON: Ronald P. Frye, 1989), 69.

20 *House of Commons Debates,* 18th Parliament, 1st session, vol. 1, February 11, 1936, 97. For a concise history of the notion of a Golden Age, see Adam Chapnick, "The Golden Age: A Canadian Foreign Policy Paradox," *International Journal* 64, no. 1, 205-21.

21 Speech, "Some Principles of Canadian Foreign Policy," January 1948, reprinted in *Words and Occasions,* 68; Pearson, *Mike* vol. 2, 35.

22 John A. Macdonald to Charles Tupper, March 12, 1885 in *Correspondence of Sir John Macdonald,* Joseph Pope, ed. (Toronto: Doubleday, Page, 1921), 338.

23 Anthony Eden memorandum to Cabinet, April 13, 1945, CAB 66/65/6, NA.

24 Ernest Bevin memorandum to Cabinet, August 25, 1949, CAB 129/36, NA.

25 Emanuel Shinwell memorandum to chiefs of staff, May 23, 1951, quoted in Louis, *The British Empire in the Middle East,* 673-74.

26 *House of Commons Debates* 21st Parliament, 4th session, vol. 4, May 14, 1951, 3002; "Grand Larceny by Iran," *Globe and Mail* (Toronto), June 21, 1951.

27 Cabinet minutes, September 27, 1951, CAB/128/20, NA.

28 Anthony Eden quoted in "Tale of Error: Mr. Eden on Threat to Policy in Asia," *The Times* (London), October 6, 1951, 4. Gamal Abdel Nasser quoted in Sir Roy Welensky to Sarah Millin, February 15, 1964, quoted in Peter J. Beck, "Britain and the Suez Crisis: The Abadan Dimension" in *Reassessing Suez 1956: New Perspectives on the Crisis and its Aftermath,* Simon C. Smith, ed. (Aldershot: Ashgate, 2008) 57. Some scholars use the more phonetically accurate Jamal Abd al-Nasir, but I have chosen to retain the older, more familiar spelling. Pearson himself saw a potential connection between the two crises: "The Iranian and Egyptian disputes have many elements in common; and indeed there is reason to believe that one is the emotional and possibly the political consequence of the other." *House of Commons Debates* 21st Parliament, 5th session, vol. 1, October 22, 1951, 253.

29 Elizabeth Monroe, *Britain's Moment in the Middle East, 1914–1956* (Baltimore: Johns Hopkins Press, 1963), 194.

30 Patrick Gordon-Walker to the High Commissions of the United Kingdom (Canada, Australia, New Zealand, South Africa), October 13, 1951.

31 Arnold Heeney to Lester Pearson, October 16, 1951, *DCER* vol. 17, 1716-20.

32 *House of Commons Debates,* 21st Parliament, 5th session, vol. 1, October 16, 1951, 69.

33 Arnold Heeney to Lester Pearson, October 17, 1951, *DCER* vol. 17, 1720-21.

34 *House of Commons Debates,* 21st Parliament, 5th session, vol. 1, October 22, 1951, 253; October 23, 1951, 320; October 22, 1951, 253.

35 Cabinet conclusions, October 17, 1951, *DCER* vol. 17, 1722; draft statement on Egypt, October 17, 1951 ibid., 1723.

36 Memorandum from Heeney to Pearson, October 17, 1951 *DCER* vol. 17, 1723-24.

37 Cabinet conclusions, October 18, 1951, *DCER* vol. 17, 1724.

38 *House of Commons Debates,* 21st Parliament, 5th session, vol. 1, October 18, 1951, 191.

39 Ibid., October 19, 1951, 196-97.

40 Lester Pearson to A.J. Pick, October 26, 1951, *DCER* vol. 17, 1724-26

41 Ibid.

42 Peter Hennessy, *Never Again: Britain 1945–1951* (New York: Pantheon Books 1993), 454.

43 Memorandum to Cabinet, June 18, 1952, CAB 129/53, NA.

44 Ibid.

Seven: ONE STRONG YOUNG FIGURE

1   Memorandum, February 16, 1953, CAB 129/59, NA.

2   Lester Pearson diary, January 1, 1936.

3   Anthony Eden, *Facing the Dictators: The Memoirs of Anthony Eden* (Boston: Houghton Mifflin, 1962), 4.

4   Alexander Cadogan, *The Diaries of Sir Alexander Cadogan*, David Dilks, ed. (London: Cassell, 1971), 345; Pearson diary, January 19, 1937.

5   Meeting minutes, December 12, 1951, FRUS vol. 5 (1951), 435-37.

6   Charles Mott-Radclyffe memorandum, May 4, 1954, quoted in D.R. Thorpe, *Eden: The Life and Times of Anthony Eden, First Earl of Avon, 1897–1977* (London: Pimlico, 2003), 424.

7   Burton Y. Berry, December 12, 1951, FRUS vol. 5 (1951), 436.

8   Kyle, Suez, 41; Michael T. Thornhill, Road to Suez: The Battle of the Canal Zone (n.p.: Sutton, 2006), 62.

9   Anthony Eden to Winston Churchill, March 10, 1952, FO 371/96985 JE1202/2, NA.

10 Radio address quoted in Jean Lacouture and Simonne Lacouture, *Egypt in Transition* (New York: Criterion Books, 1958), 150-51.

11 Anwar Sadat, *In Search of Identity: An Autobiography* (New York: Harper and Row, 1978), 107-108; Lacouture and Lacouture, *Egypt in Transition*, 152.

12 Tom Little, *Egypt* (New York: Frederick A. Praeger, 1958), 227.

13 For links between US intelligence and the Free Officers, see Miles Copeland, *Games of Nations: The Amorality of Power Politics* (London: Weidenfeld & Nicolson, 1969), Jon B. Alterman *Egypt and American Foreign Policy Assistance: 1952–1956: Hopes Dashed* (New York: Palgrave Macmillan 2002), and Laura M. James, *Nasser at War: Arab Images of the Enemy* (New York: Palgrave Macmillan, 2006). James writes (p. 2), "Although the CIA took pains to keep itself informed on a friendly basis, it played a minimal active role in the conspiracy and was surprised by its timing."

14 Michael Creswell to Foreign Office, July 23, 1952, quoted in Thornhill, *Road to Suez*, 88; State Department to embassies in London and Cairo, July 23, 1952, RG 59, Box 4015, 774.00/7-2352, NARA.

15 Cabinet minutes, July 24, 1953, CAB 195/10, C.C. 73(52), NA.

16 Winston Churchill's personal minutes, August 26, 1952, quoted in Kyle, *Suez*, 42.

17 John de Courcy Hamilton to Michael Creswell, March 9, 1953, quoted in Kyle, *Suez*, 48.

18 Winston Churchill quoted in Dean Acheson, *Present at the Creation: My Years in the State Department* (New York: W.W. Norton, 1969), 599 and Evelyn Shuckburgh, *Descent to Suez: Foreign Office Diaries 1951–1956* (New York: W.W. Norton, 1986), 75 and 76; Michael T. Thornhill, "Eden, Churchill and the Battle of Canal Zone, 1951–1954," in *Reassessing Suez*, Simon C. Smith, ed., 43 and 42.

19 Anthony Eden memorandum, February 16, 1953, CAB 129/59, NA.

20 James, *Nasser at War*, 176. Nasser's "favourite dinner consisted of chicken rice prepared in the Egyptian style. (Indeed, he served little else in his home—to the deep distress of those of his revolutionary colleagues who had learned to appreciate finer fare.)"

21 Robert Stephens, *Nasser: A Political Biography* (London: Allen Lane, 1971), 566.

22 Anthony Nutting, *Nasser* (London: Constable, 1972), 71-72.

23 Nasser's speech quoted in Said K. Aburish, *Nasser: The Last Arab* (New York: Thomas Dunne, 2004), 54.

24 *Parliamentary Debates*, Commons, 5th series, vol. 531, July 29, 1954, cols. 818 and 819.

25 Anthony Eden, *Full Circle: The Memoirs of Sir Anthony Eden* (London: Cassell, 1960), 224-25.

26   Lord Hankey to Winston Churchill, February 7, 1953, quoted in Kyle, Suez, 43.

27   Gamal Abdul Nasser, *Egypt's Liberation: the Philosophy of the Revolution* (Washington: Public Affairs Press, 1955), 65; Anthony Eden diary, November 22, 1925, quoted in Thorpe, *Eden*, 83; Eden, *Facing the Dictators*, 439; Nasser, *Egypt's Liberation*, 50; Anthony Eden to Miles Lampson, February 5, 1942, telegram no. 621, FO 371/31567, NA; Gamal Abdul Nasser quoted in Anwar Sadat, *Revolt on the Nile* (London: Allan Wingate, 1957), 40.

28   Nasser and Eden quoted in Mohamed H. Heikal, *Cutting the Lion's Tail: Suez Through Egyptian Eyes* (Arbor House 1987), 61-65. The meeting is also discussed in Thorpe, *Eden*, 426, David Dutton, *Anthony Eden: A Life and Reputation* (London: Arnold, 1997), 366, Robert Rhodes James, *Eden* (London: Weidenfeld and Nicolson, 1986), 397, and Eden, *Full Circle*, 221.

29   Nasser quotations from an interview on February 17, 1966, in which he recounted the meeting, quoted in Kennett Love, *Suez: The Twice-Fought War* (Toronto: McGraw Hill, 1969), 199; Anthony Eden's report of his exchange with Nasser to Winston Churchill, February 21, 1955, quoted in *Egypt and the Defence of the Middle East, Part 3: 1953-1956*, John Kent, ed. (London: The Stationery Office, 1998), 372.

30   State Department to NATO allies, March 8, 1955, FRUS vol. 12 (1955-1957), 29; Lester Pearson telegram, March 17, 1955, and Lester Pearson reporting to External Affairs, May 11, 1955, DCER vol. 21, 1245-46 and 358.

31   Ibid.

32   Morris, *Israel's Border Wars*, 412.

33   E.L.M Burns, *Between Arab and Israeli* (Toronto: Clarke Irwin, 1962), 18.

34   Nasser, *Egypt's Liberation*, 21; Michael B. Oren has detailed the exchanges between Egypt and Israel, which "were either indirect—messages passed through foreign embassies or by neutral mediators—or direct, involving discussions between Egyptians and Israelis." Nasser even sent "a short, unsigned, note...the first and only of its kind" to Prime Minister Moshe Sharett, thanking him "for recognizing Egypt's interest in peace and expressing the hope that Israel shared that commitment." Michael B. Oren "Secret Egypt-Israel Peace Initiatives Prior to the Suez Campaign" *Middle Eastern Studies* 26, no. 3 (July 1990), 352 and 356.

35   Anthony Eden quoted by John Foster Dulles to the State Department, February 24, 1955, FRUS vol. 14 (1955-1957), 70; Little, Egypt, 269.

36   Gamal Abdel Nasser quoted in Heikal, *Cutting the Lion's Tail*, 67.

37   John Foster Dulles and Harold Macmillan quoted in memorandum of conversation, September 26, 1955, FRUS vol. 15 (1955-1957), 518.

38   Lester Pearson memorandum, July 1, 1955, DCER vol. 21, 1234-36.

39   Lester Pearson memorandum, November 11, 1955, DCER vol. 21, 1239-40.

40   Burns, *Between Arab and Israeli*, 98; E.L.M. Burns diary, November 4, 5, 10, and 11, 1955, E.L.M. Burns fonds, MG31 G6, vol. 7, LAC.

41   John English, *The Worldly Years: The Life of Lester Pearson, Vol. 2: 1949-1972* (Toronto: Alfred A. Knopf, 1992), 93.

42   John Graham to Guy Millard, November 29, 1955, VE 1073/270, and Guy Millard to Anthony Eden, November 29, 1955, PREM 11/947, NA. I am indebted to Keith Kyle for providing these references. No Canadian records exist to document this talk.

43   Ibid.

44   Ibid.

45 Moshe Sharett quoted by Lester Pearson in memorandum dated December 5, 1955, DCER vol. 21, 1241-42. Sharett's visit took place from December 1 to 2.

46 Ibid.

Eight: ALL GOOD REASONS

1 Eden, *Full Circle*, 431.

2 Anthony Eden quoted in Rhodes James, *Eden*, 430.

3 Harold Macmillan, *The Macmillan Diaries: The Cabinet Years, 1950–1957,* Peter Caterall, ed. (London: Macmillan, 2003), 525.

4 Macmillan, *The Macmillan Diaries*, July 27, 1956, 57; Selwyn Lloyd, *Suez 1956: A Personal Account* (London: Jonathan Cape, 1978) 246; *Parliamentary Debates*, Commons, 5th series, vol. 557, August 2, 1956, col. 1613.

5 Winston Churchill, *The Gathering Storm* (Boston: Houghton Mifflin, 1948), 257-58.

6 *House of Commons Debates,* 22nd Parliament, 3rd session, vol. 1, January 11, 1956, 9, and January 18, 1956, 183; Harvey Hickey, "15 Harvards going to Egypt; not war planes: Pearson," *Globe and Mail*, January 18, 1956, 1.

7 *House of Commons Debates* 22nd Parliament, 3rd Session, vol. 1, January 24, 1856, 464-468; quotation about "playing the communist game" appears on 468.

8 Ibid., 467 and 468.

9 Harold Macmillan quoted in Alistair Horne, *Macmillan 1891–1956* (London: Macmillan, 1988), 371–372; D.R. Thorpe, *Selwyn Lloyd* (London: Jonathan Cape, 1989), 192.

10 *Parliamentary Debates*, Commons, 5th series, vol. 548, January 24, 1956, cols. 158-59. Lloyd couldn't remember exactly when he first suggested a UN force to Dag Hammarskjöld. He thought he might have first raised the idea eighteen months earlier. Neither the Foreign Office nor the UK delegation at the UN could find a record of the earlier conversation. See FO 371/121713, VR 1072/6. NA.

11 Anthony Eden quoted in memorandum of conversation, January 30, 1956, *FRUS* vol. 22 (1955–1957), 243-44.

12 See "US Attitude Cool to UN Policing," *Globe and Mail*, February 1, 1956, "Eden, Eisenhower Weigh UN Force on Israel Border," *New York Times*, February 1, 1956, and "The Eisenhower-Eden Statement and Declaration" *New York Times*, February 2, 1956.

13 *House of Commons Debates,* 22nd Parliament, 3rd session, vol. 1, February 1, 1956, 777-78.

14 Record of talk, February 3, 1956, *DCER* vol. 22, 3-4.

15 *House of Commons Debates,* 22nd Parliament, 3rd session, vol. 1, February 6, 1956, 881; Anthony Eden quoted in "Visit of Prime Minister Eden to Ottawa," *External Affairs* vol. 8, nos. 2 and 3 (February–March 1956), 47.

16 Selwyn Lloyd quoted in memorandum, February 9, 1956, *DCER* vol. 22, 1302-1304 (British records are found in "Visit of the Prime Minister and the Foreign Secretary to Ottawa," PREM 11/1334, NA); "Proposal for a United Nations Police Force in Palestine," FO 371/121713, VR 1072/18, NA.

17 Anthony Eden and Selwyn Lloyd quoted in "Press Conference Excerpts," *External Affairs* vol. 8, nos. 2 and 3 (February–March 1956), 49-51.

18 Lester Pearson to T.W.L MacDermot, March 3, 1956, MG26 N1 vol. 8.

19 Shuckburgh, *Descent to Suez*, 340.

20 Ibid., 342.

21 John Bagot Glubb quoted in ibid., 342; Eden, *Full Circle*, 353.

22 *Parliamentary Debates*, Commons, 5th series, vol. 549, March 7, 1956, cols. 2228, 2229, and 2233; Ian Waller's warning about "silent devastated ranks" quoted in Love, *Suez*, 214; Evelyn Shuckburgh diary, March 7, 1956, quoted in *Descent to Suez*, 345.

23 *House of Commons Debates*, 22nd Parliament, 3rd Session, vol. 2, March 8, 1956, 1963.

24 Anthony Eden quoted in Kyle, *Suez*, 70.

25 Anthony Eden and Anthony Nutting's conversation recounted in Anthony Nutting, *No End of a Lesson: The Story of Suez* (London: Constable, 1967), 33-35. Thirty years after this conversation, Nutting told Keith Kyle that Eden used the word "murdered." See Kyle, *Suez*, 99.

26 Cabinet meeting minutes, March 21, 1956, CAB 195/14, C.M. 24(56), NA.

27 Ibid. The cleaned up conclusions are found in CAB 128/ 30 NA.

28 Stephen Dorril, *MI6: Inside the Covert World of Her Majesty's Secret Intelligence Service* (New York: Simon and Schuster, 2000) 633; Peter Wright, *Spy Catcher: The Candid Autobiography of a Senior Intelligence Officer* (Toronto: Stoddart, 1987), 160-62.

29 For the role of the British embassy in destabilizing Nasser, see Dorril, *MI6*, Wright, *Spycatcher*, Michael T. Thornhill, "Alternatives to Nasser: Humphrey Trevelyan, Ambassador to Egypt" in *Whitehall and the Suez Crisis*, Saul Kelly and Anthony Gorst, eds. (London: Frank Cass, 2000), 11-28; Anthony Eden quoted in Shuckburgh, *Descent to Suez*, 346.

30 Dwight D. Eisenhower quoted by J.H.A. Watson in telegram to Humphrey Trevelyan, April 6, 1956, "B" FO 371/118862, JE 1053/20G, NA.

31 Memorandum of conversation between John Foster Dulles and Lester Pearson, March 27, 1956, *FRUS* vol. 27 (1955–1957), 863; Timothy Eden, *The Tribulations of a Baronet* (London: Macmillan, 1933), 22; William Clark diary quoted in Kyle, *Suez*, 68; unidentified Foreign Office official quoted in W. Scott Lucas, *Divided We Stand: Britain, the US and the Suez Crisis* (London: Hodder and Stoughton, 1991), 53.

32 Memorandum of conversation between John Foster Dulles and Lester Pearson, March 28, 1956, *FRUS* vol. 25 (1955–1957), 426.

33 Cabinet conclusions, March 15 and April 5, 1956, RG2, Privy Council Office, series A-5-a, vol. 5775.

34 Arnold Heeney to Lester Pearson, April 7, 1956, *DCER* vol. 22, 66.

35 Memorandum of meeting between Lester Pearson and John Foster Dulles, May 10, 1956, *DCER* vol. 22, 69-70.

36 Lester Pearson memo to Louis St. Laurent, May 9, 1956, MG26 series L, vol. 220; Anthony Eden referred to a report in *The Times* (London) that Pearson was a likely candidate for secretary general of NATO in note to Selwyn Lloyd, May 3, 1956, PREM 11/ 1347 NATO, NA.

37 CBC TV interview, May 6, 1970, film roll 86, p. 2 of transcript.

38 Memorandum, May 14, 1956, *DCER* vol. 22, 76-78.

39 Memorandum, May 21, 1956, *DCER* vol. 22, 79-81.

40 Memorandum, June 11, 1956, *DCER* vol. 22, 86.

41 Memorandum, July 11, 1956, *DCER* vol. 22, 96; State Department to US embassy in Ottawa, July 18, 1956, *FRUS* vol. 15 *(1955–1957)*, 859.

42 US embassy in Ottawa to State Department, July 19, 1956, ibid., 874-75.

43 Anthony Eden quoted in David Carlton, *Britain and the Suez Crisis* (London: Basil Blackwell, 1988), 33.

44 Memorandum, July 19, 1956, *FRUS* vol. 15 *(1955–1957)*, 866.

45 Maurice Couve de Murville quoted in Kyle, *Suez*, 130.

Nine: EGYPT FOR EGYPTIANS

1 Newspaper estimate of crowd reported by Nicholas S. Lakas to State Department, despatch 1, July 28, 1956, RG 59, CDF, 774–11/7–2856, NARA.

2 Nasser's speech reprinted in "Appendix A: Egypt," *BBC Summary of World Broadcasts, Part 4: The Arab World, Israel, Greece, Turkey, Persia,* daily series no. 5, pp. 1, 5, and 6; Nicholas S. Lakas to State Department, despatch 1, July 28, 1956, RG 59, CDF, 774–11/7–2856, NARA; Jean Lacouture and Simone Lacouture, "The Night Nasser Nationalised the Suez Canal," *Le Monde Diplomatique*, www.mondediplo.com/2002/07/12canal (subscription required). Originally published in a different version in *Egypt in Transition*, 471.

3 Nasser quoted in *BBC Summary of World Broadcasts, Part 4*, 21.

4 Lacouture and Lacouture, *Egypt in Transition*, 472.

5 Nicholas S. Lakas to State Department, despatch 1, July 28, 1956, RG 59, CDF, 774–11/7–2856, NARA.

6 *Parliamentary Debates*, Commons, 5th series, vol. 233, December 23, 1929, col. 2048.

7 Eden, *Full Circle*, 422.

8 William Clark, *From Three Worlds,* p. 166.

9 Selwyn Lloyd quoted by Hugh Gaitskell, *The Diary of Hugh Gaitskell, 1945–1956,* Philip M. Williams, ed. (London: Jonathan Cape, 1983), 552-53.

10 Nuri al-Said "overheard by one present in Downing Street" and quoted in Thorpe, *Eden*, 493.

11 US embassy in London to State Department, July 27, 1956, *FRUS* vol. 26 (1955–1957), 4–5; Gerald Templer's warning about holding Cairo quoted in Anthony Verrier, *Through the Looking Glass: British Foreign Policy in an Age of Illusions* (New York: W.W. Norton, 1983), 138; William Clark's diary quoted in Clark, *From Three Worlds,* 166.

12 Richard Gardiner Casey, *Australian Foreign Minister: The Diaries of R.G. Casey 1951–60*, T. B. Millar, ed. (London: Collins, 1972), 56.

13 *House of Commons Debates*, 22nd Parliament, 3rd session, Vol. 4, July 26, 1956, 6463-66.

14 Pearson diary, February 3, 1953.

15 Hutchison, *Mr. Prime Minister,* 287 and 297.

16 Jack Pickersgill, *My Years with Louis St. Laurent: A Political Memoir* (Toronto: University of Toronto Press, 1975), 159.

17 Canadian Gallup poll, No. 212, August 1951. A clear majority of respondents, sixty percent, supported the idea of a Canadian-born governor general; fourteen percent wanted to abolish the position.

18 Louis St. Laurent quoted in "St. Laurent Rejects Idea Canadian Not Good Enough For Post," *Toronto Daily Star,* January 25, 1952, and "St. Laurent's Viewpoint: Defends Continued Use of Dominion," *Globe and Mail,* January 26, 1952.

19 Phillip Buckner, "Canada and the End of Empire, 1939–1982" in *Canada and the British Empire,* Phillip Buckner, ed. (Oxford: Oxford University Press, 2008), 114-15. Canadian Gallup poll no. 227, May 1953; Pearson diary, January 14, 1953.

20 *Canada Year Book 1957–58* (Dominion Bureau of Statistics), p. 177.

21 John Hilliker and Greg Donaghy, "Canadian Relations with the United Kingdom at the End of Empire 1956–73" in *Canada and the British Empire,* ed. Phillip Buckner (Oxford: Oxford University Press, 2008), 25.

22 Lester Pearson to Arthur Irwin, April 25, 1956, MG26 N1, Pre-1958 series, vol. 2, file 7.

23 *Parliamentary Debates,* Commons, 5th series, vol. 557, July 27, 1956, cols. 777-80.

24 Ibid.; Rhodes James, *Anthony Eden,* 455 and 456.

25 Cabinet conclusions, July 27, 1956 CAB/128/30, NA.

26 Ibid.

27 Anthony Eden letter to Dwight D. Eisenhower, *FRUS* vol. 16 (1955–1957), 12.

28 Lester Pearson writing as "T," "Canada and the Far East," *Foreign Affairs* 13, no. 3 (April 1935), 393.

29 Montreal *Gazette, Toronto Daily Star,* and *Globe and Mail* led with the *Andrea Doria* disaster. The *Calgary Herald* ran a photo of Communist weapons purchased by Cairo along with a prominent story on the nationalization, but pride of place above the fold went to stories about con men and horse racing scandals. The *Winnipeg Free Press, Ottawa Citizen,* and *Halifax Chronicle Herald* made Suez the lead headline.

30 Cabinet conclusions, July 27, 1956, RG2, Privy Council Office, series A-5-a, vol. 5775.

31 Norman Robertson to Lester Pearson, July 27, 1956, *DCER* vol. 22, 131.

32 State Department press release reprinted in *FRUS* vol. 16 (1955-1957), 7; Lester Pearson quoted in "Ottawa Concerned," *Globe and Mail,* July 28, 1956, 2, and "Ottawa Concerned," *Winnipeg Free Press,* July 28, 1956, 4.

33 "Canada Plans No Move on Suez Canal," *Ottawa Journal,* July 27, 1956, 2.

Ten: SEEN BUT NOT HEARD

1 Speech reprinted in *DCER* vol. 2, 243.

2 Memorandum of meeting, July 28, 1956, *DCER* vol. 22, 100-101.

3 *House of Commons Debates,* 22nd Parliament, 3rd session, vol. 7, July 28, 1956, 6607.

4 Ibid., 6607-608.

5 University professor's remarks and *Toronto Daily Star* item reported in telegram 735, July 30, 1956, DO35/6317 FILE ME 190/4, NA; Anthony Eden minute on telegram 734, July 30, 1956, DO35/6317 FILE ME 190/4, NA.

6 See Terence Robertson, *Crisis: The Inside Story of the Suez Conspiracy* (Toronto: McClelland and Stewart, 1964), 74; Anthony Eden to Commonwealth prime ministers, July 28, 1956, *DCER* vol. 22, 132.

7   Granatstein, *A Man of Influence,* 299.

8   Lester Pearson to Norman Robertson, July 28, 1956, *DCER* vol. 22, 133.

9   Egypt committee memorandum, July 30, 1956, quoted in Kyle, *Suez,* 148; Lester Pearson to Norman Robertson, July 28, 1956, *DCER* vol. 22, 133; Lester Pearson's phone call to Robert Menzies reported by Menzies to Australian External Affairs, Canberra, July 29, 1956, "Inward Cables Ottawa Post 1956," A6364-OT1956/01, Australian National Archives.

10   Holmes, *The Shaping of Peace,* 353; Denis Stairs, interview with the author, 1996.

11   Lester Pearson to N.A.M. MacKenzie, January 17, 1957, Seize the Day: Research, Suez Ch. 9 file, GAHP-009, Geoffrey Pearson fonds, Carleton University Archives.

12   Lester Pearson to Norman Robertson, July 28, 1956, *DCER* vol. 22, 135.

13   Lester Pearson to Norman Robertson, July 30, 1956, *DCER* vol. 22, 137. Regarding Robertson showing the draft telegram to Norman Brook, see footnote on page 138.

14   R.G. Casey, July 29, 1956, statement in *The Commonwealth and Suez: A Documentary Survey,* ed. James Eayrs (Oxford: Oxford University Press, 1964), 52; Robert Menzies quoted in W.J. Hudson, *Blind Loyalty: Australia and the Suez Crisis, 1956* (Melbourne: Melbourne University Press, 1989), 51; UK embassy in Washington to Foreign Office, July 31, 1956, telegram 1624, DO 35/6317.

15   Sidney Holland speaking in NZ House of Representatives, August 7, 1956, in Eayrs, ed., *The Commonwealth and Suez: A Documentary Survey,* 60; statements by Johannes Strijdom and Eric Louw, July 27 and 31, 1956, in ibid., 62; Eric Louw quoted in "Synopsis of views of Commonwealth governments and of press comment," July 31, 1956, DO 35/6317, NA.

16   S.W.R.D. Bandaranaike statement, August 6, 1956, in Eayrs, ed. *The Commonwealth and Suez,* 74-75; Hamidul Haq Chowdhry quoted in "Synopsis of views of Commonwealth Governments and of press comment," July 31, 1956, DO 35/6317, NA.

17   Robertson, *Crisis,* xiii.

18   John Foster Dulles quoted in memorandum, August 1, 1956, *FRUS* vol. 16 (1955–1957), 95.

19   Anthony Eden quoted by John Foster Dulles in memorandum, August 1, 1956, ibid, 98.

20   Macmillan, August 1, 1956, *The Macmillan Diaries,* 580.

21   This section on military planning relies heavily on Kyle, *Suez,* 161-72.

22   Love, *Suez,* 364.

23   *House of Commons Debates,* 22nd Parliament, 3rd session, vol. 7, August 1, 1956, 6787, 6793, and 6831.

24   Lester Pearson quoted by Archibald Nye in memo to Commonwealth Relations Office, August 1, 1956, DO 35/6317 NA. The Canadian notes of this meeting can be found in *DCER* vol. 22, 138.

25   *Parliamentary Debates,* Commons, 5th series, vol. 557, August 2, 1956, col. 1606.

26   Royal proclamation reported in "Ships Requisitioned: Queen Proclaims Emergency," *Globe and Mail* (Toronto), August 4, 1956. Lester Pearson to Norman Robertson, August 3, 1956, copy in "Commonwealth reactions to the tripartite statement and the invitation to the conference," DO 35/6317 NA. The "soothing reply" is in telegram 1061, August 8, 1956, RG25 vol. 6107, file 50372-40, part 2, p. 224 of PDF.

27   Charles Foulkes to John Watkins, August 3, 1956, ibid., p. 115 of PDF.

28 Anthony Eden to Louis St. Laurent, undated, in "Commonwealth reaction to the tripartite statement and the invitation to the conference," August 4, 1956, DO 35/6317 NA.

29 CBC TV interview, May 19, 1970, film roll 97, p. 4 of transcript; Dwight Eisenhower and John Foster Dulles reported in "Eisenhower's Remarks and Dulles' Report on Suez: By Secretary Dulles," *New York Times,* August 4, 1956.

30 Arnold Heeney to Lester Pearson, telegram 1427, August 4, 1956, RG25, vol. 6107, file 50372-40, part 1.3 pp. 42-46 of PDF.

31 Arnold Heeney to Lester Pearson, telegram 1451, August 7, 1956, ibid., 280-82; Anthony Eden to Archibald Nye, August 1, 1956, DO 35/6317 NA.

32 *House of Commons Debates,* 22nd Parliament, 3rd session, vol. 2, August 6, 1956, 7047-48.

33 Cabinet conclusions, August 7, 1956, RG2, Privy Council Office, series A-5-a, vol. 5775.

34 Lester Pearson to Norman Robertson, August 7, 1956, *DCER* vol. 22, 141-42; for the British response to Pearson's suggestion, see memorandum, August 10, 1956, DO 35/6314, NA.

35 Transcribed from Anthony Eden's August 8, 1956 TV address, tape from BBC News archive.

36 Lester Pearson to Norman Robertson, August 9, 1956, *DCER* vol. 22, 144; Robertson quoted by Alec Douglas Home to Anthony Eden, August 17, 1956, DO 35/6315, NA.

37 Anthony Eden minute in memorandum from Philip de Zulueta to J. Ward, August 17, 1956; Eden minute in memorandum, August 19, 1956, DO 35/6314 NA. Macmillan, *The Macmillan Diaries,* 588.

38 Clark, *From Three Worlds,* 170; Oliver Pool quoted in Kyle, *Suez,* 226; ibid., 203; Clark, *From Three Worlds,* 173.

39 Cabinet conclusions, August 29, 1956, RG2, Privy Council Office, series A-5-a, vol. 5775.

40 Lester Pearson quoted in "Canada Backs 18 Powers for Suez Canal Control," *Globe and Mail* (Toronto), August 31, 1956.

41 Lester Pearson to Louis St. Laurent, September 3, 1956, *DCER* vol. 22, 153.

42 Ibid., 154.

43 Lester Pearson's NATO speech reported by Pearson in telegram, September 5, 1956, *DCER* vol. 22, 156; Eisenhower press conference reported in "Text of President Eisenhower's News Conference on Foreign and Domestic Affairs," *New York Times,* September 6, 1956.

44 John Foster Dulles quoted by Arnold Heeney in telegram to Lester Pearson, September 12, 1956, *DCER* vol. 22, 158.

45 *Parliamentary Debates,* Commons, 5th series, vol. 558, September 12, 1956, col. 10.

46 John Foster Dulles quoted in "Transcript of the Remarks by Secretary of State Dulles at His News Conference," *New York Times,* September 14, 1956.

47 Lester Pearson telegram, September 14, 1956, *DCER* vol. 22, 162-63.

48 Lester Pearson telegram, September 17, 1956, ibid., 163-64. Pearson's antipathy to the proposal perhaps arose from his view that Dulles, a lawyer, liked to reduce complex diplomatic issues to legal cases needing the proper contract. External Affairs officer Geoff Murray recalled Pearson telling him: "You have to remember that Foster Dulles is only a corporation lawyer, and everything he does has to do with a bundle of papers, that he carries in his bag, agreements that he tries to get people to sign. The other thing about Foster is that he can only handle one case at a time." Murray added with a smile, "I think Mr. Pearson was not very

fond of lawyers. I, as a lawyer, had sort of an instinctive feeling about that." Interview with the author, 1995.

· 49 Selwyn Lloyd quoted in Kyle, *Suez*, 207.

50 Robert MacKay to Lester Pearson, September 24, 956, *DCER* vol. 22, 166; Ibid., September 25, 1956, 168-69.

51 T.R.D. Belgrave to T.W. Keeble, September 27, 1956, DO 35/6314, NA.

Eleven: IN SORROW AND ANGER

1 Macmillan, *The Macmillan Diaries*, 587.

2 Unidentified British official quoted in Love, *Suez*, 363.

3 Norman Robertson to Lester Pearson, September 28, 1956, *DCER* vol. 22, 174-75; Pearson, *Mike* vol. 2, 236.

4 Kyle, *Suez*, 288.

5 Robert MacKay to Lester Pearson, telegram 897, October 13, 1956, RG 25 vol. 6109, file 50372–40, part 8.2, p. 124 of PDF; Cabinet conclusions, October 18, 1956, RG 2 Privy Council Office, series A-5-a, vol. 5775.

6 High Commission official's prediction about Hammarskjöld reported by Lester Pearson to Robert MacKay, October 26, 1956, RG25 vol. 6109, file 50372-40, part 8.2, pp. 42-43 of PDF file.

7 Jules Léger to Norman Robertson, October 29, 1956, *DCER* vol. 22, 178.

8 Moshe Dayan, *Diary of the Sinai Campaign* (London: Weidenfeld and Nicolson, 1965), 77 and 79; Heikal, *Cutting the Lion's Tail*, 177-78.

9 CBC TV interview, May 19, 1970, film roll 98, p. 3 of transcript; "Canada Will Review Sale of Jets to Israel," *Globe and Mail* (Toronto), October 30, 1956.

10 Anthony Eden to Dwight Eisenhower, September 6, 1956, *FRUS* vol. 16 (1955–1957), 403.

11 Robertson learned from the Commonwealth Relations Office that Eden would be making a statement and told them that he would be in attendance. If he did see Eden announce the ultimatum, Robertson could have rushed back to Canada House in Trafalgar Square and phoned Pearson within minutes of the announcement. Norman Robertson meeting with CRO, "Note for Record," October 31, 1956, DO 35/6334, NA.

12 Lester Pearson to Arnold Heeney, October 30, 1956, *DCER* vol. 22, 179; Lester Pearson to Jean Désy, telegram 2-5074, October 30, 1956, Geoffrey Pearson fonds, GAHP-009, Seize the Day: Research, Suez Ch. 9 file, Carleton University Archives and Research Collections.

13 Anthony Eden quoted in Thorpe, *Eden,* 513.

14 Anthony Nutting, *No End of a Lesson: The Story of Suez* (London: Constable, 1967), 18.

15 Thorpe, *Eden*, 385 and 387; Shuckburgh, *Descent to Suez*, 14.

16 David Owen, *In Sickness and In Power: Illness in Heads of Government During the Last 100 Years* (London: Methuen, 2008), 138; Alec Douglas-Home, Richard Powell, and William Dickson quoted in Owen, 120 and 128.

17 Norman Robertson to Lester Pearson regarding a report by Arnold Smith, November 1, 1956, MG26 N5, vol. 5; Pearson, *Mike* vol. 2, 241.

18 David Dutton, *Anthony Eden: A Life and Reputation* (London: Arnold 1997), 424.

19 Shuckburgh, *Descent to Suez,* 29 and 127; Kyle, *Suez,* 85; Macmillan, *The Macmillan Diaries,* 583; Kyle, *Suez,* 259 and 262; Robertson, Crisis, 136.

20 Thorpe, *Eden,* 515; for Israeli views of Selwyn Lloyd's discomfort, see Kyle, *Suez,* 319.

21 *Parliamentary Debates,* Commons, 5th series, vol. 562, December 20, 1956, cols. 1458 and 1518.

22 David Ben-Gurion quoted in Kyle, *Suez,* 264.

23 Lester Pearson phone call with John Foster Dulles, October 30, 1956, *FRUS* vol. 16 (1955–1957), 865; Lester Pearson to Norman Robertson, October 30, 1956, *DCER* vol. 22, 180.

24 Pearson, *Mike* vol. 2, 238.

25 Anthony Eden to Louis St. Laurent, October 30, 1956, DO 65/6334, NA. Reprinted in *DCER* vol. 22, 182; Robertson, *Crisis,* 182; CBC TV interview, May 19, 1970, film roll 98, p. 5, and film roll 99, p. 2 of transcript.

26 Ibid., film roll 99, p. 3 of transcript.

27 Ibid.; Lester Pearson quoted by Livingston Merchant in memorandum to State Department, October 31, 1956, Canada–Ottawa Embassy–Classified General Records, 1956–1958, box 26, RG 84 NND 959142.

28 Douglas Hurd, *Memoirs* (London: Abacus, 2003), 152.

29 Peter Ramsbotham, interview with the author, 1998.

30 "Canada Not Backing U.K.," *Vancouver Sun,* October 31, 1956, and "Canada stands with the United Nations, not Britain," *Calgary Herald,* October 31, 1956.

31 Lester Pearson quoted in "Canada stands with the United Nations, not Britain," *Calgary Herald,* October 31, 1956. See also "1956 Ottawa Notes," R11207-0-0-E, Victor Mackie fonds, LAC.

32 Lester Pearson quoted in "British US Split in UN Deplorable Need Unity—Pearson," *Toronto Daily Star,* October 31, 1956. The Vancouver *Province, Calgary Herald,* and *Globe and Mail* also covered his appearance on *Press Conference.*

33 *Parliamentary Debates,* Commons, 5th series, vol. 558, October 31, 1956, cols. 1447 and 1448.

34 Ibid., cols. 1455 and 1569.

35 Arnold Heeney to Lester Pearson, October 3, 1956, *DCER* vol. 22, 183-184.

36 Louis St. Laurent quoted in Dale Thomson, *Louis St. Laurent: Canadian* (Toronto: Macmillan, 1967), 470, and "Cabinet Ends Meeting Without A Decision," *Winnipeg Free Press,* November 1, 1956.

37 Cabinet conclusions, October 31, 1956, RG2, PCO, series A-5-a, vol. 5775.

38 Thomson, *Louis St. Laurent,* 466. Although Thomson reports this meeting occurred on October 30, the Cabinet did not meet that day.

39 Hutchison, *Mr. Prime Minister,* 308.

40 Commonwealth Relations Office to High Commission in Ottawa, telegram Z no. 84, October 31, 1956, and High Commission in Ottawa to Commonwealth Relations Office, telegram 1037, October 31, 1956, DO 65/6334, NA.

41 Lester Pearson quoted in Ibid., telegram 1037.

42 Ibid.

43 Amikam Nachmani, *International Intervention in the Greek Civil War: The United Nations Special Committee on the Balkans 1947–1952* (New York: Praeger, 1990), 42.

44 John Allphin Moore Jr. and Jerry Pubantz, eds. *Encyclopedia of the United Nations* (New York: Facts on File, 2002), 313; Nachmani, *International Intervention in the Greek Civil War,* 156.

45 Robertson, *Crisis,* 184. No documents in the External Affairs archives record Pearson's request to Norman Robertson and Arnold Heeney to circulate the UN police force idea informally. However, journalist Terence Robertson (no relation to Norman) interviewed Pearson and various senior officials, who then read his manuscript, so presumably his account is correct.

Twelve: EYE OF THE STORM

1 Anthony Evelyn M. Ashley, *The Life and Correspondence of Henry John Temple, Viscount Palmerston,* vol. 2 (London: Richard Bentley and Son, 1879), 338.

2 Extract from a letter forwarded in another letter dated January 1930 in miscellaneous papers, ADM 116/2717, NA.

3 Unidentified Foreign Office official quoted by Norman Robertson to Lester Pearson, November 1, 1956, memoirs vol. 2, November 1956–December 1957, MG26 N5 vol. 41.

4 Lloyd, *Suez, 1956,* 200.

5 Clark, *From Three Worlds,* 202-203.

6 Lloyd, *Suez, 1956,* 200. Lloyd's private discussion with Eden regarding the UN taking over Britain's so-called police action was apparently not documented; transcript of William Clark interview with BBC, October 1978, MS ENG c. 4811, Bodleian Library, Oxford University, 28.

7 Eden, *Full Circle,* 536.

8 Guy Millard, interview with author, 2011; Donald Logan, interview with author, 2006.

9 Kyle, *Suez,* 564-65.

10 CBC TV interview, May 6, 1970, film roll 82, p.3 of transcript.

11 George Bain, "Minding Your Business," *Globe and Mail* (Toronto), November 1, 1956; "The Shameful Day That Canada Ran Out," *Calgary Herald,* November 1, 1956.

12 For analysis of Canadian press coverage of Suez, see James Eayrs, *Canada in World Affairs: October 1955 to June 1957* (Oxford: Oxford University Press, 1959), 182-93 and José E. Igartua, "'Ready, Aye, Ready' No More? Canada, Britain, and the Suez Crisis in the Canadian Press" in *Canada and the End of Empire,* Phillip Buckner, ed. (Vancouver: UBC Press, 2005), 47-65.

13 Roland Michener and Charles Ritchie quoted in Peter Stursberg, *Lester Pearson and the Dream of Unity* (Toronto: Doubleday, 1978), 21 and 52.

14 Hume Wrong quoted in Ignatieff, *Memoirs,* 80.

15 Transcript of John Holmes interview with Peter Stursberg, MG31, D78, vol. 29, container 32, file 4, Peter Stursberg fonds, pp. 46 and 48, LAC.

16 Ibid., 42. Holmes categorically rejected the claim that he was the true author of the peace-keeping proposal, and he wasn't just being modest. Yet the idea persists. Adam Chapnick has written, "Colleagues recall how it was largely Holmes' mediatory and diplomatic abilities, along with his drafting skills, that made Pearson's ultimate success possible." However, he does not identify these colleagues. His footnote refers to a UN oral history interview with External Affairs' Geoff Murray, but Murray did not make the claim in that interview, nor did

he when I interviewed him twice. To date, I have found nothing in the historical record that supports this claim about Holmes, who was unquestionably a valuable and valued member of Pearson's team. See Adam Chapnick, *Canada's Voice: The Public Life of John Wendell Holmes* (Vancouver: UBC Press, 2009), 89.

17 Norman Robertson to Lester Pearson, November 1, 1956, *DCER* vol. 22, 189. As noted earlier, Terence Robertson wrote that Pearson suggested the police force idea on the night of October 31. See endnote 46, chapter 11.

18 Thomson, *Louis St. Laurent,* 465-66. Pearson's line about "changes to make the tone somewhat softer" comes from his comment on a draft chapter of Thomson's book, which Thomson incorporated as written into his text. For the draft of the official reply, see MG26 N4 vol. 273, file 914.25.

19 Louis St. Laurent to Anthony Eden, October 31, 1956, *DCER* vol. 22, 187.

20 Ibid.

21 Cabinet conclusions, November 1, 1956, RG2 Privy Council Office, series A-5-a, vol. 5775.

22 Norman Robertson to Lester Pearson, November 1, 1956, *DCER* vol. 22, 191.

23 Cabinet conclusions, November 1, 1956, RG2 Privy Council Office, series A-5-a, vol. 5775.

24 John Holmes to Geoffrey Pearson, February 4, 1969, memoirs vol. 2 file, MG26 N5, vol. 40.

25 *Parliamentary Debates,* Commons, 5th series, vol. 558, November 1, 1956, col. 1620; *Times* editor Iverach McDonald quoted in Kyle, *Suez,* 388-89.

26 *Parliamentary Debates,* Commons, 5th series, vol. 558, November 1, 1956, cols. 1641 and 1650.

27 Geoff Murray, interviews with the author, 1994 and 1995.

28 Ibid.

29 Transcript of John Holmes interview, p. 42; Geoff Murray, interviews with the author, 1994 and 1995.

30 United Nations, 561st plenary meeting, first emergency special session, November 1, pp. 3 and 5-6.

31 Pierson Dixon, *Double Diploma: The Life of Sir Pierson Dixon, Don and Diplomat* (London: Hutchinson, 1968), 277-78; Peter Ramsbotham, interview with the author, 1998; John Holmes to Michael G. Fry, January 13, 1988, box 51, file 2, part 2, F2260, John Holmes fonds, Trinity College Archives, University of Toronto.

32 Peter Ramsbotham, interview with the author, 1998.

33 United Nations, 561st plenary meeting, first emergency special session, November 1, 1956, 8.

34 Peter Ramsbotham, interview with the author, 1998; CBC TV interview, May 19, 1970, film roll 99, p. 10 of transcript; Peter Ramsbotham, interview with author, 1998.

35 Geoff Murray, interviews with the author, 1994 and 1995.

36 Pearson, *Mike* vol. 1, 217.

37 Pearson, *Mike* vol. 2, 245; Grant Dexter, draft of undated, untitled article, file External Affairs 1956–1958 typescript memos, folder 45, box 17 series 3, Grant Dexter fonds, Queen's University Archives. Dexter did not attribute these words directly to Pearson, but he was a trusted confidant and would have heard this from either Pearson or a senior official at External Affairs.

38 United Nations, 561st plenary meeting, first emergency special session, November 1, pp. 10 and 12.

39 Transcript of Geoff Murray interview, United Nations Oral History Project, folder 117, box 7, MS 1703, p. 8, UNA; Pearson diary, February 14-15, 1953, and March 7, 1953.

40 Permanent Representative to United Nations to External Affairs, November 2, 1956, *DCER* vol. 22, 194-95.

41 Geoff Murray, interviews with the author, 1994 and 1995; Krishna Menon quoted in Michael Brecher, *India and World Politics: Krishna Menon's View of the World* (Oxford: Oxford University Press, 1968), 40 and 107-108.

42 Geoff Murray, interviews with author, 1994 and 1995.

43 Peter Ramsbotham letter to the author, August 28, 1997, and interview with the author, 1998. In a letter to Geoffrey Pearson, Holmes noted, "When I saw Peter Ramsbotham for the first time in ten years last year in Cologne he said that he thought he and I had been responsible for the UNEF idea because of our collusion to match the Canadian proposal to what Eden had said." Holmes disagreed and concluded, "This collaboration with the British helped shape the idea...but it certainly didn't give birth to it." John Holmes to Geoffrey Pearson, February 4, 1969, memoirs vol. 2 file, MG26 N5, vol. 40. During my interview with Peter Ramsbotham, I showed him the letter, and he concurred about the effect of his entreaties, "I think it helped, to use John Holmes's words, to shape the presentation by Lester Pearson of this proposal."

44 CBC TV interview, May 19, 1970, film roll 101, p. 2, and film roll 99, pp. 13-14 of transcript.

45 Geoff Murray, "Glimpses of Suez," *International Journal* 29, no. 1, 55-56; transcript of Geoff Murray interview with Munroe Scott, box 21, Munroe Scott fonds, Trent University Archives.

46 CBC TV interview, May 19, 1970, film roll 100, p. 14 of transcript.

47 United Nations, 562nd plenary meeting, first emergency special session, Nov. 2, 1956, 35-36.

48 Ibid.

49 United Nations, 562nd plenary meeting, first emergency special session, November 2, 1956, 39.

50 Gabriella Rosner, *The United Nations Emergency Force* (New York: Columbia University Press, 1963), 216.

51 Despite the obvious historical links, Gabriella Rosner notes that there was "no reference to the Saar Force in any of the Secretary-General's reports or in the Assembly debates on the United Nations Emergency Force." Ibid., 217.

52 CBC TV interview, April 27, 1970, film roll 76, pp. 5-6 of transcript.

53 Mohammed Mir Khan quoted in Robertson, *Crisis,* 197.

54 Selwyn Lloyd quoted by Norman Robertson to Lester Pearson, November 2, 1956, *DCER* vol. 22, 196- 197.

55 Memorandum, November 2, 1956, FO 371/ 118904, NA.

56 Douglas Hurd, *Memoirs* (London: Abacus, 2003), 154-55; Paul Gore-Booth, *With Great Truth and Respect* (London: Constable, 1974), 229 and 230.

57 Geoff Murray, "Glimpses of Suez," 50.

58 Pearson, *Mike* vol. 2, 247; Brian Urquhart, interview with the author, September 1996.

59 Pearson, *Mike* vol. 2, 248; Pierson Dixon to Foreign Office, telegram 1009, November 2, 1956, FO 371/ 121747, NA.

60 Ibid., telegram 1020; Geoff Murray interview with Munroe Scott.

61 Arnold Heeney to Lester Pearson, November 2, 1956, *DCER* vol. 22, 124, and State Department memorandum, *FRUS* vol. 16 (1955–1957), 941-42.

62 Ibid.

63 "Cabinet Meets Today on Peace Force," *Ottawa Evening Journal,* November 3, 1956, and "News on Suez 'Encouraging' to St. Laurent," *Toronto Daily Star,* November 3, 1956.

Thirteen: OFF THE HOOK

1 Lester Pearson to James Ralston, disarmament correspondence 1929–1931, vol. 6, MG27, J.L. Ralston fonds, LAC.

2 Palmerston quoted in Ronald Hyam, *Britain's Imperial Century 1815–1914: A Study of Empire and Expansion* (London: B. T. Batsford, 1976), 64.

3 *Parliamentary Debates,* Commons, vol. 558, November 3, 1956, cols. 1857-58, 1865-66, and 1868.

4 High Commission in Ottawa to Commonwealth Relations Office, telegram 1057, November 3, 1956, DO 65/6334, NA.

5 C. Burke Elbrick quoted in memorandum, November 3, 1956, Department of State files, 684A.86/ 11 – 356, SS-S9, Box 2697, NARA. The Canadian record of this meeting can be found in November 3, 1956, *DCER* vol. 22, 205-207. This critical document, infinitely more informative about the November 3 Cabinet discussion than the official minutes, was used heavily but not cited in Volume 2 of Pearson's memoirs.

6 Ibid; Jawaharlal Nehru to R.K. Nehru, November 3, 1956, *Selected Works of Jawaharlal Nehru,* 2nd series, vol. 35 (New Delhi: Jawaharlal Nehru Memorial Fund, 2005), 435.

7 Memorandum, November 3, 1956, *DCER* vol. 22, 207.

8 Anthony Eden, TV and radio broadcast, November 3, 1956, transcribed from tape, BBC News archive.

9 Norman Smith, "Pearson, people, and press," *International Journal* 29, no. 1, 21; CBC TV interview, May 19, 1970, film roll 101, p. 3 of transcript.

10 Memoranda, November 3, 1956, *DCER* vol. 22, 206, and *FRUS* vol. 16 (1955–1957), 953-54.

11 Memorandum, November 3, 1956, *FRUS* vol. 16 (1955–1957), 956–57. The editors were unable to find a copy of this draft resolution in the U.S. archives, but it is contained in a memo in *DCER* vol. 22, 213.

12 For Lodge's faulty grasp of the discussion with Pearson at the UN emergency session, see Stursberg, *Lester Pearson and the American Dilemma,* 146-47 and Henry Cabot Lodge, *The Storm Has Many Eyes: A Personal Narrative* (New York: W.W. Norton, 1973), 132-33.

13 See transcript of interview with Joseph Sisco, October 18, 1990, UN Oral History Project, 10.

14 Jules Léger to Lester Pearson, November 3, 1956, *DCER* vol. 22, 207-208.

15 Geoff Murray, interview with author, 1995.

16 Memorandum, November 4, 1956, *DCER* vol. 22, 213; Pearson, *Mike* vol. 2, 251.

17 Gooff Murray, interview with the author, 1994 and 1995.

18 Ibid.

19　Ibid.

20　Dag Hammarskjöld quoted by Geoff Murray, interview with author, 1995.

21　Michael Wilson, interview with the author, 2007.

22　John Holmes, "Geneva: 1954," *International Journal* 22, no. 3, 458.

23　Like Pearson and other diplomats, Arthur Lall had seen Eden's offer to hand over military operations to the UN as "a way out of the situation." He discussed this with Henry Cabot Lodge and Egyptian ambassador Omar Loutfi, who spoke with Cairo and reported back Nasser's initial tentative acceptance. John Holmes to Lester Pearson, December 6, 1956, *DCER* vol. 22, 301; memorandum, November 5, 1956, ibid., 214.

24　Robert Menzies to Anthony Eden quoted in Hudson, *Blind Loyalty,* 118; Leslie Munro, November 2, 1956, in Eayrs, ed., *The Commonwealth and Suez,* 243.

25　Michael Wilson and Malcolm Templeton, interviews with the author, 2007. New Zealand's deputy minister of external affairs, Alister McIntosh, lamented his government's complete support for Britain and wrote in private, "I think Mike Pearson has been magnificent and I do envy the Canadians in being able to follow the line they did," quoted in Malcolm Templeton, *Ties of Blood and Empire: New Zealand's Involvement in Middle East Defence and the Suez Crisis 1947–57* (Auckland: Auckland University Press/NZ Institute of International Affairs, 1994), 185.

26　John Holmes to Joe Lash, July 31, 1961, file 5, box 63, F2260, John Holmes fonds, Trinity College Archives, University of Toronto.

27　Geoff Murray, "Glimpses of Suez," 53.

28　Geoff Murray, interview with the author, 1994.

29　United Nations, 563rd plenary meeting, first emergency special session, November 3-4, 1956, 55.

30　Ibid., 70.

31　Ibid., 71.

32　Pierson Dixon to Foreign Office, telegram 1033, November 3, 1956, and telegram 1048, November 4, 1956, PREM 11/1105 NA.

33　Harold Macmillan quoted by Brendan Bracken to Lord Beaverbrook, quoted in Kyle, *Suez,* 257; Macmillan's lament about oil sanctions quoted in Lloyd, *Suez, 1956,* 206.

34　Cabinet minutes, November 4, 1956, CAB/128/30 NA; R.A. Butler, *The Art of the Possible* (London: Hamish Hamilton, 1971), 193; Anthony Eden diary entry quoted in David Dutton, *Anthony Eden: A Life and Reputation* (London: Arnold, 1997), 440.

35　Clarissa Eden, diary entry, quoted in Rhodes James, *Anthony Eden*, 567.

36　Peter Ramsbotham, interview with author, 1998.

37　Robert Menzies speech in House of Representatives, November 3, 1956, ed. Eayrs, *The Commonwealth and Suez,* 346; Holland's statement found in External Affairs (New Zealand) to UN permanent mission, telegram 211, November 4, 1956, and NZ External Affairs support is in telegram 210, November 3, 1956, PM 217/1/11 NZ National Archives.

38　Douglas Hurd, *Memoirs* (London: Abacus, 2003), 158.

39　Arthur Lall quoted in summary of meeting November 4, 1956, *DCER* vol. 22, 210.

40　Ibid., 212.

41 Lester Pearson quoted in Robertson, *Crisis,* 287.

42 Abba Eban quoted in telegram from Canadian Mission in NY to External Affairs, November 5, 1956, *DCER* vol. 22, 215-16; report on UN emergency session, November 5, 1956, ibid., 219-20.

43 Louis St. Laurent, November 4, 1956, *Statements and Speeches* no. 56/24.

44 United Nations, 565th plenary meeting, first emergency special session, November 4, 1956, 79 and 82-83.

45 Hans Engen quoted in Robertson, *Crisis,* 242.

46 Anthony Eden to Louis St. Laurent, November 5, 1956, *DCER* vol. 22, 214-15.

47 Neil Pritchard to Commonwealth Relations Office, telegram 1065, November 5, 1956, FO 371/121796, NA.

48 Neil Pritchard to Gilbert Laithwaite, November 5, 1956, FO 371/121796, NA.

49 Robertson, *Crisis,* 238.

50 Louis St. Laurent to Anthony Eden, November 5, 1956, *DCER* vol. 22, 221; Henry Cabot Lodge to State Department November 5, 1956, *FRUS* vol. 16 (1955–1957), 982.

51 External Affairs report of General Assembly proceedings, November 5, 1956, *DCER* vol. 22, 220; resolutions adopted by the General Assembly, UN official records, first emergency special session, supplement no. 1 (A/3354).

52 John Holmes interview notes, January 30, 1975, John Holmes fonds, 002–0001/033(15), Trinity College Archives, University of Toronto; "Duties of UN Force Being Defined," November 6, 1956, *Globe and Mail,* 25.

53 Quoted in Kyle, *Suez,* 448.

54 Brian Urquhart, interview with the author, 1996.

55 See Robertson, *Crisis,* 248.

56 Lester Pearson's report to External Affairs, November 6, 1956, *DCER* vol. 22, 223.

57 Ibid.

58 For the French paratrooper's recollection and the British doctor's report see Love, *Suez,* 619-20; the description of the sea landings relies heavily on Kyle, *Suez,* 461-64.

59 Harold Macmillan quoted in Kyle, *Suez,* 258.

60 Diane B. Kunz, *The Economic Diplomacy of the Suez Crisis* (Chapel Hill, NC: University of North Carolina Press, 1991), 193; unidentified Cabinet minister quoted in Iverach McDonald, *Man of the Times: Talks and Travels in a Disrupted World* (London: Hamish Hamilton, 1976), 153.

61 Eden, *Full Circle,* 558.

62 Anthony Eden quoted by Norman Robertson in telegram to External Affairs, November 6, 1956, *DCER* vol. 22, 224.

63 Rhodes James, *Anthony Eden,* 575-76.

64 Pearson's report to Ottawa, November 6, 1956, *DCER* vol. 22, 224.

65 Memorandum of meeting, November 6, 1956, *DCER* vol. 22, 220 31, 55 See Robertson, *Crisis,* 248.

Fourteen: TRIUMPH AND DISASTER

1 *House of Commons Debates*, 24th Parliament, 3rd session, vol. 7, August 1, 1960, 7334.

2 "Mike Is Hero of Hour," *Telegram,* November 9, 1956, 6.

3 "Canada's Lead," *Halifax Chronicle Herald,* November 5, 1956; "Mr. Pearson Speaks for Canada," *Winnipeg Free Press,* November 2, 1956; "The Shameful Day That Canada Ran Out," *Calgary Herald,* November 1, 1956; for *Fredericton Daily Gleaner, Saint John Telegraph-Journal, Telegram, Globe and Mail,* and *Toronto Daily Star,* see James Eayrs, *Canada in World Affairs,* 187; "Advice from Meighen: Stand by the British," *Globe and Mail,* November 5, 1956, 5; James Eayrs, *Canada in World Affairs,* 182-83.

4 United Nations, 567th plenary meeting, November 7, 1956, 125; memorandum, November 7, 1956, *DCER* vol. 22, 234-35.

5 "'Ridiculous' Says Premier Of Report He Sent Eden 'Blistering' Wire On Suez," November 8, 1956, *Toronto Daily Star*; High Commission official quoted in memorandum to undersecretary of state, November 2, 1956, *DCER* vol. 22, 197-98.

6 Pearson, *Mike* vol. 2, 261-62.

7 Lester Pearson quoted in "Not Out of Woods Yet is Pearson's Warning," *Toronto Daily Star,* November 9, 1956; "Bulganin Warning to UK Threat to Peace—Pearson," *Toronto Daily Star,* November 10, 1956; Pearson's joke quoted by Brian Urquhart, interview with the author, 1996.

8 Summary of Pearson's meeting with Ambassador Loutfi November 12, 1956, *DCER* vol. 22, 245, 246.

9 Ibid.

10 Memorandum, November 12, 1956, *DCER* vol. 22, 242-46, and memorandum, November 12, 1956, *DCER* vol. 22, 247; Jawaharlal Nehru, November 15, 1956, *Selected Works of Jawaharlal Nehru* vol. 35, 445.

11 Meeting minutes, November 14, 1956, Brian Urquhart personal files, background papers for Hammarskjöld manuscript, 1949–1971, box 331, file 2583, DAG–1/2.3.18.7.0, NA.

12 Brian Urquhart, interview with the author, 1996.

13 Lester Pearson, "A New Kind of Peace Force," *Maclean's,* May 2, 1964.

14 Howard Graham, *Citizen and Soldier: The Memoirs of Lt. Gen. Howard Graham* (Toronto: McClelland and Stewart, 1987), 233.

15 Burns, *Between Arab and Israeli,* 215.

16 Harold Greer, "Picking Queen's Own for UN Police Said Mistake of Century" and "Canada Limited to 'Typewriter' Army by Egypt," *Toronto Daily Star,* November 19, 1956, 1 and 2.

17 Michael K. Carroll, *Pearson's Peacekeepers: Canada and the United Nations Emergency Force, 1956–67* (Vancouver: UBC Press, 2009), 42-43.

18 Lester Pearson told J.L. Granatstein that the Suez Crisis was a key factor in his decision to bring in the Maple Leaf flag. J.L. Granatstein, interview with author, 1993.

19 *House of Commons Debates,* 22nd Parliament, 4th session, vol. 1, November 26, 1956, 18 and 20.

20 Raymond Daniell, "Pearson Declares Canada Pursues Independent Line," *New York Times,* November 28, 1956, 1; *House of Commons Debates,* 22nd Parliament, 4th session, vol. 1, November 27, 1956, 49 and 51.

21 *House of Commons Debates,* 22nd Parliament, 4th session, vol. 1, November 27, 1956, 51; Bruce Hutchison, "St. Laurent Wins Confidence Vote on Suez Policy," *Christian Science Monitor,* December 5, 1956, 23; Grant Dexter, "Mr. Pearson Defines His Policy," *Winnipeg Free Press,* November 28, 1956.

22 *House of Commons Debates,* 22nd Parliament, 4th session, vol. 1, November 27, 1956, p. 57; Hutchison, "St. Laurent Wins Confidence Vote on Suez Policy," 23. Moving beyond the bounds of even journalistic hyperbole, Hutchison wrote of Pearson's warning that the Commonwealth almost split apart: "probably no more shattering statement has ever been made in the Canadian Parliament. Its effect throughout the nation was electric."

23 Pearson, *Mike* vol. 2, 218.

24 Dexter, "Mr. Pearson Defines His Policy," *Winnipeg Free Press;* Clark Davey, "Special Session Ended," *Globe and Mail,* November 30, 1956; "Parliament Hears a Pathetic Story," *Calgary Herald,* November 28, 1956.

25 Lester Pearson to Louis St. Laurent, December 18, 1956, *DCER* vol. 22, p. 320 and 321.

26 Ibid., 322.

27 Anthony Eden quoted in Kyle, *Suez,* 532.

28 Eden, *Full Circle,* 541; transcript of Anthony Eden interview, December 10, 1959, *Close-Up,* CBC TV, Middle East 1958–1964 file, MG26 N2, vol. 88.

29 Anthony Eden quoted in "Pearson Whole World's Loss—Eden," *Toronto Daily Star,* December 29, 1972; Anthony Eden to Maryon Pearson, January 7, 1973, condolences file, MG26 N5, vol. 63.

30 Selwyn Lloyd quoted in Ignatieff, *Memoirs,* 124; William Clark interview, MG31 D78, container 28, file 12; Harold Macmillan, *Riding the Storm* (London: Macmillan, 1971), 162-63.

31 Lester Pearson to Norman Robertson, January 11, 1957, *DCER* vol. 22, 346.

32 CBC TV interview, October 8, 1970, film roll 128, pp. 1 and 6 of transcript.

33 Quoted in Peter C. Newman, *Renegade in Power: The Diefenbaker Years* (Toronto: McClelland and Stewart, 1963), 34.

34 "In the tradition of this party," quoted in John Meisel, *The Canadian General Election of 1957* (Toronto: University of Toronto Press, 1962), 57-58; "Do you agree" and "Why did you" quoted in J. H. Aitchison, "Canadian Foreign Policy in the House and on the Hustings," *International Journal,* 12 no. 4, 285-86; "found itself allied" and "our good friends the Israelis" quoted in Eayrs, *Canada in World Affairs,* 191.

35 "The Election and Democracy," *Maclean's,* June 27, 1956, 4.

36 Meisel, *The Canadian General Election of 1957,* 273. The UK High Commissioner Joseph Garner reported from Ottawa, "nothing was made of the Suez issue during the campaign" but went on to add that in his tours through the Maritimes and Ontario, "it has been brought home to me again and again that a large majority of those of British origin…bitterly resented the fact that the Canadian government did not support Britain at a time of crisis." High Commission to Commonwealth Relations Office, July 8, 1957, DO 35/5184, NA.

37 "An Unstuffy Diplomat: Lester Bowles Pearson," *New York Times,* October 15, 1957, 14; "Canada's Deadlock," *Manchester Guardian,* June 12, 1957.

38 Margaret K. Welers, interview with the author, 2013; Brian Urquhart, interview with the author, 1996; Hans Hansen quoted in transcript of H.F. Feaver, interview with Peter Stursberg, June 1978, MG31 D78, vol. 29, file 1, p. 40.

39 Pearson, *Mike* vol. 2, 275.

40 *House of Commons Debates,* 23rd Parliament, 1st session, vol. 1, October 15, 1957, 12.

41 Harvey Hickey, "Sydney Smith: Was Too Much Expected of Him in Ottawa?" *Globe and Mail,* May 10, 1958.

42 Blair Fraser, *The Search for Identity: Canada 1945–1967* (Toronto: Doubleday, 1967) p. 60; Diefenbaker at Tory gathering quoted by Pearson in *House of Commons Debates,* 24th Parliament, 3rd session, vol. 1, January 18, 1960, 43-44; John Diefenbaker quoted by Stewart MacLeod in Charles Lynch, *A Funny Way to Run a Country: Further Memoirs of a Political Voyeur* (Edmonton: Hurtig Publishers, 1986), 86-87. MacLeod tells the anecdote slightly differently in Denis Smith, *Rogue Tory: The Life and Legend of John G. Diefenbaker* (Toronto: MacFarlane Walter and Ross, 1995), 567.

43 Robert Fulford, interview with author, 1993.

44 Maryon Pearson, quoted by Lester Pearson, CBC TV interview, June 8, 1970, film roll 109, p. 8 of transcript.

45 *House of Commons Debates,* 22nd Parliament, 4th session, vol. 1, November 27, 1956, 54.

46 Malcolm MacDonald, "Canada, a New Moral Force in the World," *International Journal* 1, no. 2, 161, 160, and 163; A.R.M. Lower, "Canada, the Second Great War, and the Future" Ibid., 109-10.

47 Grant Dexter, "Mr. Pearson's Objective Achieved," *Winnipeg Free Press,* November 26, 1956; "Commonwealth," *Manchester Guardian Weekly,* November 8, 1956; Maxwell Cohen, "A New Responsibility in Foreign Policy," *Saturday Night,* January 19, 1957, 5; *Parliamentary Proceedings,* 5th series, vol. 566, March 14, 1957; "Canada's New Minister," *Globe and Mail,* September 14, 1957, 6 , reprinted from *New York Times*; Robert Bothwell, *Alliance and Illusion, Canada and the World, 1945–1984* (Vancouver: UBC Press, 2007), 390.

48 "Pearson Won Prize with PC Plan, Hees Tells Lakehead Audience," *Globe and Mail,* February 21, 1958, 3; Smith Rogue Tory, 454,

49 Alan James, "Reluctant Heroes: Assembling the United Nations Cyprus Force, 1964," *International Journal* 53, no. 4, 743.

50 Manon Tessier and Michel Fortmann, "The Conservative Approach to International Peacekeeping" in *Diplomatic Departures: The Conservative Era in Canadian Foreign Policy, 1984–93,* Kim Nossal and Nelson Michaud, eds. (Vancouver: UBC Press, 2001), 114, 121, and 113.

51 David Pugliese, "Nobel Fever," *Saturday Night,* May 1997, 56.

52 For a critique of how Ottawa abandoned its peacekeeping legacy, see Noah Richler, *What We Talk about When We Talk about War* (Fredericton: Goose Lane Editions, 2012). See also Ian McKay and Jamie Swift, Warrior Nation: *Rebranding Canada in an Age of Anxiety* (Toronto: Between the Lines, 2012).

53 James Eayrs, *Northern Approaches Canada and the Search for Peace* (Toronto: Macmillan, 1961), 173-74.

54 Robert Bothwell, interview with author, 1996.

55 United Nations, 566th plenary meeting, November 7, 1956, 93-94.

56 Lester Pearson speech, April 27, 1959, peacekeeping statements 1959–1966 file, MG26 N6, vol. 9. He evidently considered this speech a fairly fundamental expression of his thinking, because as prime minister in 1964 he submitted virtually the same text for publication. See "A New Kind of Peace Force," *Maclean's,* May 2, 1964.

57 Ibid.

58 *House of Commons Debates*, 24th Parliament, 3rd session, vol. 6, July 14, 1960, 6273.

59 *House of Commons Debates*, 24th Parliament, 3rd session, vol. 7, August 1, 1960, 7332.

60 *House of Commons Debates*, 26th Parliament, 2nd session, vol. 1, February 19, 1964, 6.

61 Brian Urquhart, interview with the author, 1996; Paul Martin quoted in Maloney, *Canada and UN Peacekeeping*, 235.

62 *House of Commons Debates*, 27th Parliament, 2nd session, vol. 1, May 24, 1967, 534, and vol. 2, June 8, 1967, 1290.

63 March 3, 1957, CBC TV News Library, no. 41, consultation copy V1 8303-0124, ISN 106486, CBC fonds, LAC.

64 Pearson, *Mike: The Memoirs of the Rt. Hon. Lester B. Pearson*, Vol. 3: 1967–1968, John A. Munro and Alex I. Inglis, eds. (Toronto: University of Toronto Press, 1975), 186.

65 Geoffrey Pearson, interview with the author, 1993.

Bibliography

PRIMARY SOURCES

Library and Archives Canada

Canadian Broadcasting Corporation, Television: CBOT Film Library.

From February 1970 to March 1971, Lester Pearson sat for a long series of interviews with the CBC which used them for his television memoirs, "First Person Singular," and a documentary series on his time as Liberal leader facing John Diefenbaker, "The Tenth Decade." I went back to the original interview transcripts because while Pearson wrote the first volume of his memoirs, he was only able, while dying from cancer, to prepare drafts of certain chapters, including the one on Suez, for the next two volumes. These interview transcripts contain many gems, and indeed his editors incorporated portions of them into the final volumes. The transcripts are held in the CBC fonds. See finding aid for accession 1985-0298.

Eedson Louis Millard Burns fonds

Walter Harris fonds

Arnold Danford Patrick Heeney fonds

William Lyon Mackenzie King fonds

Victor Mackie fonds

Peter Stursberg fonds

Personal Papers and Interviews

UN Oral History Project, United Nations Archives

James Barco

Abba Eban

Arthur Lall

Geoff Murray

Joseph Sisco

Brian Urquhart

Personal Papers

Lord Avon, University of Birmingham

Richard P. Bowles, Victoria University

John Holmes, Trinity College

Bruce Hutchison, University Of Calgary

Selwyn Lloyd, Cambridge University

Kennett Love, Princeton

Geoffrey Pearson, Carleton University

Terence Robertson, McMaster University

Dale Thompson, McGill University

Munroe Scott, Trent University

Author Interviews

Robert Bothwell, Ramsay Cook, John English, Robert Fulford, Jack Granatstein, Patricia (Pearson) Hannah, Lord Douglas Hurd, Pierre Hutton, James Ingram, Tom Kent, Keith Kyle, Sir Donald Logan, Sir Guy Millard, Geoff Murray, John B. de Payne, Geoffrey Pearson, Sir Peter Ramsbotham, Denis Stairs, Malcolm Templeton, Sir Brian Urquhart, Margaret K. Weiers, Michael Wilson.

Published Government Documents

Documents on Canada's External Relations (Government of Canada): vols. 2, 3, 5, 9, 12, 13, 14, 17, and 22.

Foreign Relations of the United States (US Government Printing Office): 1948 vol. v, part 2; 1951 vol. v; 1955–1957 vols. 12, 14, 25, 26 and 27.

Statements and Speeches (Government of Canada)

Parliamentary Proceedings

House of Commons Debates (Canada)

Parliamentary Debates, Commons (United Kingdom)

SECONDARY SOURCES

Abella, Irving and Harold Troper. "'The line must be drawn somewhere': Canada and Jewish Refugees, 1933–1939." *Canadian Historical Review* 60, no. 2 (1979): 178-209.

Aburish, Said K. *Nasser: The Last Arab.* New York: Thomas Dunne, 2004.

Acheson, Dean. *Present at the Creation: My Years in the State Department.* New York: W.W. Norton, 1969.

Aitchison, J.H. "Canadian Foreign Policy in the House and on the Hustings." *International Journal* 12, no. 4 (Autumn 1957): 273-287.

Andrew, Arthur. *The Rise and Fall of a Middle Power: Canadian Diplomacy from King to Mulroney.* Toronto: James A. Lorimer, 1993.

Ashley, Anthony Evelyn M. *The Life and Correspondence of Henry John Temple, Viscount Palmerston*, vol. 2. London: Richard Bentley and Son, 1879.

Balfour-Paul, Glen. "Britain's Informal Empire in the Middle East." In *The Oxford History of the British Empire, Vol. 4: The Twentieth Century* edited by Judith M. Brown and Wm. Roger Louis, 490-514. Oxford: Oxford University Press, 1999.

Beal, John R. *The Pearson Phenomenon.* Toronto: Longmans Canada, 1964.

Beatty, Charles. *De Lesseps of Suez: The Man and His Times.* New York: Harper & Brothers, 1956.

Bennett, Paul W. *Years of Promise, 1896–1911.* Toronto: Grolier, 1986.

Bercuson, David. *Canada and the Birth of Israel: A Study in Canadian Foreign Policy.* Toronto: University of Toronto Press, 1985.

——. *True Patriot: The Life of Brooke Claxton 1898–1960.* Toronto: University of Toronto Press, 1993.

Berger, Carl. *The Sense of Power: Studies in the Ideas of Canadian Imperialism, 1867–1914.* Toronto: University of Toronto Press, 1970.

Black, J.L. and Norman Hillmer, eds. *Nearly Neighbours: Canada and the Soviet Union from Cold War to Détente and Beyond* (Kingston, ON: Ronald P. Frye, 1989).

Blake, Robert. *Disraeli.* London: Eyre & Spottiswoode, 1966.

Bliss, Michael. *Pearson: His Life and World.* Toronto: McGraw-Hill Ryerson, 1978.

——. *The Penguin History of Canada.* Toronto: Penguin Canada, 2006.

——. *Right Honourable Gentlemen: The Descent of Canadian Politics from Macdonald to Mulroney.* Toronto: Harper Collins, 1994.

Bothwell, Robert. *Alliance and Illusion, Canada and the World, 1945–1984.* Vancouver: UBC Press, 2007.

——. *Pearson: His Life and World.* Toronto: McGraw-Hill Ryerson, 1978.

——. *The Penguin History of Canada.* Toronto: Penguin Canada, 2006.

Bothwell, Robert and John English. "Dirty Work at the Crossroads: New Perspectives on the Riddell Incident." *Canadian Historical Association Historical Papers 1972*: 263–285.

Bourne, Kenneth. *The Foreign Policy of Victorian England.* London: Clarendon Press, 1970.

Brecher, Michael. *India and World Politics: Krishna Menon's View of the World.* London: Oxford University Press, 1968.

Brendon, Piers. *The Decline and Fall of the British Empire 1781–1997.* London: Jonathan Cape, 2007.

Brown, Robert Craig. *Robert Laird Borden: A Biography, Volume 2, 1914–1937.* Toronto: Macmillan, 1980.

Buckner, Phillip, ed. *Canada and the British Empire.* Oxford: Oxford University Press, 2008.

——. *Canada and the End of Empire.* Vancouver: UBC Press, 2005.

Buckner, Phillip. "Casting Daylight Upon Magic: Deconstructing the Royal Tour of 1901 to Canada." *Journal of Imperial and Commonwealth History* 31, no. 2 (2003): 158–189

Burns, E.L.M. *Between Arab and Israeli.* Toronto: Clarke, Irwin, 1962.

Butler, R.A. *The Art of the Possible: the Memoirs of Lord Butler.* London: Hamish Hamilton, 1971.

Carlton, David. *Anthony Eden: A Biography.* London: Allen Lane, 1981.

——. *Britain and the Suez Crisis.* London: Basil Blackwell, 1988

Carroll, Michael K. *Pearson's Peacekeepers: Canada and the United Nations Emergency Force, 1956–67.* Vancouver: UBC Press, 2009.

Champion, C.P. *The Strange Demise of British Canada: The Liberals and Canadian Nationalism, 1964–1968.* Montreal: McGill Queen's University Press, 2010.

Chapnick, Adam. *Canada's Voice: The Public Life of John Wendell Holmes.* Vancouver: UBC Press, 2009.

——. "The Golden Age: A Canadian Foreign Policy Paradox." *International Journal* 64, no. 1 (Winter 2008/2009): 205-221.

——. *The Middle Power Project: Canada and the Founding of the United Nations*. Vancouver: UBC Press, 2005.

Churchill, Winston. *The Gathering Storm*. Boston: Houghton Mifflin, 1948.

Clark, William. *From Three Worlds* London: Sidgwick & Jackson, 1986.

Clarke, Peter. *The Last Thousand Days of the British Empire*. London: Allen Lane, 2007.

Cohen, Andrew. *Lester B. Pearson*. Toronto: Penguin Canada, 2008.

Cohen, Maxwell. "A New Responsibility in Foreign Policy." *Saturday Night,* January 19, 1957.

Cook, Ramsay. "A Canadian Account of the 1926 Imperial Conference." *Journal of Commonwealth Studies* 3 (1965): 50-63.

——. *The Regenerators: Social Criticism in Late-Victorian English Canada*. Toronto: University of Toronto Press, 1985.

Crane, John O. and Sylvia E. Crane. *Czechoslovakia: Anvil of the Cold War*. Princeton: Praeger, 1991.

Curzon, George Nathaniel. *Speeches on India*. London: John Murray, 1904.

Dafoe, John W. *Laurier: A Study in Canadian Politics*. Toronto: Thomas Allen, 1922.

Dawson, Robert MacGregor. *William Lyon Mackenzie King*. Toronto: University of Toronto Press, 1958.

Dayan, Moshe. *Diary of the Sinai Campaign*. London: Weidenfeld and Nicolson, 1965.

Dilks, David. *Curzon in India*. New York: Taplinger, 1970.

Dixon, Piers. *Double Diploma: The Life of Sir Pierson Dixon: Don and Diplomat*. London: Hutchinson, 1968.

Donaghy, Greg, ed. *Canada and the Early Cold War, 1943-1957*. Ottawa: DFAIT, 1998.

Dorril, Stephen. *MI6: Inside the Covert World of Her Majesty's Secret Intelligence Service*. New York: Simon & Schuster, 2000.

Duncan, Sara Jeannette. *The Imperialist*. Thomas E. Tausky, ed. Toronto: Tecumseh Press, 1996. First published 1904 by Copp Clark.

Dutton, David. *Anthony Eden: A Life and Reputation*. London: Arnold, 1997.

Eayrs, James. *Canada in World Affairs: October 1955 to June 1957*. London: Oxford University Press, 1959.

——. *The Commonwealth and Suez: A Documentary Survey*. Toronto: Oxford University Press, 1964.

——. *In Defence of Canada: Growing Up Allied*. Toronto: University of Toronto Press. 1980.

——. *Northern Approaches: Canada and the Search for Peace*. Toronto: Macmillan, 1961.

Eden, Anthony. *Facing the Dictators: The Memoirs of Anthony Eden*. Boston: Houghton Mifflin, 1962.

——. *Full Circle: The Memoirs of Sir Anthony Eden*. London: Cassell, 1960.

Eden, Timothy. *The Tribulations of a Baronet*. London: Macmillan, 1933.

English, John. *Shadow of Heaven: The Life of Lester Pearson, Volume One: 1897-1948*. Toronto: Lester & Orpen Dennys, 1989.

——. *The Worldly Years: The Life of Lester Pearson, Volume Two: 1949-1972*. Toronto: Alfred A. Knopf, 1992.

Fraser, Blair. *The Search for Identity: Canada 1945-1967*. Toronto: Doubleday Canada, 1967.

Frye, William R. *A United Nations Peace Force*. New York: Oceana, 1957.

Garciá-Granados, Jorge. *The Birth of Israel: The Drama As I Saw It*. New York: Alfred A. Knopf, 1948.

Gelber, Lionel. "Canada's New Stature." *Foreign Affairs* 24, no. 2 (January 1946): 277-289.

Gore-Booth, Paul. *Great Truth and Respect*. London: Constable, 1974.

Gottheil, Fred M. "The Smoking Gun: Arab Immigration into Palestine, 1922–1931." *Middle East Quarterly Winter* 10, no. 1 (2003): 53-64.

Graham, Howard. *Citizen and Soldier: The Memoirs of Lt. Gen. Howard Graham*. Toronto: McClelland and Stewart, 1987.

Granatstein, J.L. *Canada's Army: Waging War and Keeping the Peace*. Toronto: University of Toronto Press, 2002.

——. *A Man of Influence: Norman A. Robertson and Canadian Statecraft 1929–68*. Ottawa: Deneau, 1981.

——. *The Ottawa Men: The Civil Service Mandarins 1935–1957*. Toronto: Oxford University Press, 1982.

Granatstein, J.L. and Norman Hillmer. *Empire to Umpire: Canada and the World to the 1990s*. Toronto: Copp Clark Longman, 1994.

Granatstein, J.L. and Desmond Morton. *Marching to Armageddon: Canadians and the Great War 1914–1919*. Toronto: Lester & Orpen Dennys, 1989.

Gwyn, Sandra. *The Private Capital*. Toronto: McClelland and Stewart, 1984.

Harrison, James P. *Mastering the Sky: A History of Aviation from Ancient Times to the Present*. New York: Sarpedon Publishers, 2000.

Hattersley, Roy. *A Brand From the Burning: The Life of John Wesley*. London: Little, Brown, 2002.

Hecht, Ben. *A Child of the Century*. New York: Simon and Schuster, 1954.

Heikal, Mohamed H. *Cutting the Lion's Tail: Suez Through Egyptian Eyes*. New York: Arbor House, 1987.

Hempton, David. *Methodism: Empire of the Spirit*. New Haven: Yale University Press, 2005.

Hennessy, Peter. *Having It So Good: Britain in the Fifties*. London: Allen Lane, 2006.

——. *Never Again: Britain 1945–1951*. New York: Pantheon Books, 1993.

Henty, G.A. *With Kitchener in the Soudan: A Story of Atbara and Omdurman*. London: Blackie & Son, 1903.

Hilliker, John. *Canada's Department of External Affairs: Volume 1, The Early Years, 1909–1946*. Montreal: McGill-Queen's University Press, 1990.

Hillmer, Anne Trowell. "Canadian Policy on the Partition of Palestine 1947." MA thesis, Carleton University, 1981.

——. "Here I Am in the Middle: Lester Pearson and the Origins of Canada's Diplomatic Involvement in the Middle East." In *Domestic Battleground: Canada and the Arab-Israeli Conflict*, edited by David Taras and David H. Goldberg, 125-143. Montreal: McGill-Queen's University Press, 1989.

Hillmer, Norman, ed. *Pearson: The Unlikely Gladiator*. Montreal: McGill-Queen's University Press, 1999.

Hoare, Samuel. *Nine Troubled Years*. London: Collins, 1954.

Holmes, John. "Geneva: 1954." *International Journal* Volume 22, no. 3 (1966–67): 457-483.

———. *The Shaping of Peace: Canada and the Search for World Order, 1943–1957, Volume 2.* Toronto: University of Toronto Press, 1982.

Horne, Alistair. *Macmillan 1891–1956.* London: Macmillan, 1988.

Hudson, W.J. *Blind Loyalty: Australia and the Suez Crisis, 1956.* Melbourne: Melbourne University Press, 1989.

Hughes, Matthew. "The Banality of Brutality: British Armed Forces and the Repression of the Arab Revolt in Palestine, 1936–39." *English Historical Review* 124, no. 507 (April 2009): 315-54.

Hurd, Douglas. *Memoirs.* London: Abacus, 2003.

Hutchison, Bruce. *The Incredible Canadian: A Candid Portrait of Mackenzie King.* Toronto: Longmans Green, 1953.

———. *Mr. Prime Minister 1867–1964.* Toronto: Longmans Canada, 1964.

Hyam, Ronald. *Britain's Imperial Century, 1815–1914: A Study of Empire and Expansion.* London: B. T. Batsford, 1976.

Igartua, Jose E. *The Other Quiet Revolution: National Identities in English Canada, 1945–71.* Vancouver: UBC Press, 2006.

Ignatieff, George. *The Memoirs of George Ignatieff: The Making of a Peacemonger.* Toronto: University of Toronto Press, 1985.

James, Alan "Reluctant Heroes: Assembling the United Nations Cyprus Force, 1964." *International Journal* 53, no. 4 (Autumn 1998): 733-52.

James, Laura M. *Nasser at War: Arab Images of the Enemy.* New York: Palgrave Macmillan, 2006.

Jenkins, Roy. *Gladstone.* London: Macmillan, 1995.

Karabell, Zachary. *Parting the Desert: the Creation of the Suez Canal.* London: John Murray, 2003.

Kelly, Saul and Anthony Gorst. *Whitehall and the Suez Crisis.* London: Frank Cass, 2000.

Kinross, Patrick Balfour. *Between Two Seas: The Creation of the Suez Canal.* New York: William Morrow, 1969.

Kubicek, Robert. "British Expansion, Empire and Technological Change." In *The Oxford History of the British Empire, Vol. 3: The Nineteenth Century,* edited by Andrew Porter, 247-69. Oxford: Oxford University Press, 1999.

Kunz, Diane B. *The Economic Diplomacy of the Suez Crisis.* Chapel Hill, North Carolina: University of North Carolina Press, 1991.

Kyle, Keith. *Suez: Britain's End of Empire in the Middle East.* London: I.B. Tauris, 2003.

Lacouture, Jean and Simonne Lacouture. *Egypt in Transition.* New York: Criterion Books, 1958.

Lesseps, Ferdinand de. *Recollections of Forty Years, Volumes 1 and 2.* London: Chapman and Hall, 1887.

Little, Tom. *Egypt.* New York: Frederick A. Praeger, 1958.

Lloyd, Selwyn. *Suez 1956: A Personal Account.* London: Jonathan Cape, 1978.

Lloyd, Trevor. *Canada in World Affairs 1957–1959.* Toronto: Oxford University Press, 1968.

Lockman, Zachary. *Comrades and Enemies: Arab and Jewish Workers in Palestine, 1906–1948.* Berkeley: University of California Press, 1996.

Lodge, Henry Cabot. *The Storm Has Many Eyes: A Personal Narrative.* New York: W.W. Norton, 1973.

Londey, Peter. *Other People's Wars: A History of Australian Peacekeeping*. Sydney: Allen & Unwin, 2004.

Louis, Wm. Roger. *The British Empire in the Middle East, 1945-1951: Arab Nationalism, the United States, and Postwar Imperialism*. Oxford: Clarendon Press, 1984.

Louis, Wm. Roger and Judith M. Brown, eds. *The Oxford History of the British Empire, Volume 4: The Twentieth Century*. Oxford: Oxford University Press, 1999.

Louis, Wm. Roger and Roger Owen, eds. *Suez 1956: The Crisis and Its Consequences*. Oxford: Clarendon Press, 1989.

Love, Kennett. *Suez: The Twice-Fought War*. Toronto: McGraw Hill, 1969.

Lower, A.R.M. "Canada, the Second Great War, and the Future." *International Journal* 1, no. 2, (April 1946): 97-111.

Lucas, W. Scott. *Divided We Stand: Britain, the US and the Suez Crisis*. London: Hodder and Stoughton, 1991.

Lynch, Charles. *A Funny Way to Run a Country: Further Memoirs of a Political Voyeur*. Edmonton: Hurtig Publishers, 1986.

MacDonald, Malcolm. "Canada, a New Moral Force in the World." *International Journal* 1, no. 2, (April 1946): 159-63.

Mackay, R.A., ed. *Canadian Foreign Policy 1945-1954: Selected Speeches and Documents*. Toronto: McClelland and Stewart, 1971.

Macmillan, Harold. *The Macmillan Diaries: The Cabinet Years 1950-1957*. Edited by Peter Caterall. London: Macmillan, 2003.

———. *Riding the Storm*. London: Macmillan, 1971.

MacMillan, Margaret. *Paris 1919: Six Months that Changed the World*. Toronto: Random House, 2001.

Maloney, Sean M. *Canada and UN Peacekeeping: Cold War By Other Means, 1945-1970*. St. Catherines, ON: Vanwell Publishing, 2002.

Massey, Vincent. *What's Past Is Prologue*. Toronto: Macmillan, 1963.

Matheson, John. *Canada's Flag: A Search for a Country*. Boston: G.K. Hall, 1980.

McCullough, David. *Truman*. New York: Simon & Schuster, 1992.

McDonald, Iverach. *Man of the Times: Talks and Travels in a Disrupted World*. London: Hamish Hamilton 1976.

McKay, Ian and Jamie Swift. *Warrior Nation: Rebranding Canada in an Age of Anxiety*. Toronto: Between the Lines, 2012.

McNaught, Kenneth. *The Penguin History of Canada*. London: Penguin Books 1988.

Meisel, John. *The Canadian General Election of 1957*. Toronto: University of Toronto Press, 1962.

Melady, John. *Pearson's Prize: Canada and the Suez Crisis*. Toronto: Dundurn, 2006.

Millar, T.B., ed. *Australian Foreign Minister: The Diaries of R.G. Casey, 1951-60*. London: Collins, 1972.

Miller, Carman. *Canada's Little War: Fighting for the British Empire in Southern Africa 1899-1902*. Toronto: James Lorimer, 2003.

———. *Painting the Map Red: Canada and the South African War 1899-1902*. Montreal: McGill-Queen's Press, 1998.

Millman, Brock. "Canada, Sanctions and the Abyssinian Crisis of 1935." *The Historical Journal* 40, no. 1, March 1997: 143-68.

Monroe, Elizabeth. *Britain's Moment in the Middle East, 1914–1956*. Baltimore: Johns Hopkins University Press, 1963.

Moore, John Allpin Jr. and Jerry Pubantz. *Encyclopedia of the United Nations*. New York: Facts on File, 2002.

Morris, Benny. *1948: A History of the First Arab-Israeli War*. New Haven: Yale University Press, 2008.

———. *Israel's Border Wars 1949–1956: Arab Infiltration, Israeli Retaliation, and the Countdown to the Suez War*. London: Clarendon Press, 1993.

Morrow, John H. Jr. *The Great War in the Air: Military Aviation from 1909 to 1921*. Washington,: Smithsonian Institute Press, 1993.

Murray, Geoff. "Glimpses of Suez." *International Journal* 29, no. 1 (1973–74): 46-66.

Nachmani, Amikam. *International Intervention in the Greek Civil War: The United Nations Special Committee on the Balkans 1947–1952*. New York: Praeger, 1990.

Nasser, Gamal Abdel. *Egypt's Liberation: The Philosophy of the Revolution*. Washington: Public Affairs Press, 1955.

Neatby, H. Blair. *William Lyon Mackenzie King, 1924–1932: The Lonely Heights*. Toronto: University of Toronto, 1963.

Nehru, Jawaharlal. *Selected Works of Jawaharlal Nehru*. 2nd series, vol. 35. New Delhi: Jawaharlal Nehru Memorial Fund, 2005.

Newman, Peter C. *Renegade in Power: The Diefenbaker Years*. Toronto: McClelland and Stewart, 1963.

Nossal, Kim. *The Politics of Canadian Foreign Policy*. Scarborough, ON: Prentice-Hall Canada, 1989.

Nossal, Kim and Nelson Michaud, eds. *Diplomatic Departures: The Conservative Era in Canadian Foreign Policy, 1984–93*. Vancouver: UBC Press, 2001.

Nutting, Anthony. *Nasser*. London: Constable, 1972.

———. *No End of a Lesson: The Story of Suez*. London: Constable, 1967.

Oren, Michael B. "Ambivalent Adversaries: David Ben-Gurion and Israel vs. the United Nations and Dag Hammarskjold, 1956–57." *Journal of Contemporary History* 27, no. 1 (January 1992): 89-127.

———. "Secret Egypt-Israel Peace Initiatives Prior to the Suez Campaign." *Middle Eastern Studies* 26, no. 3 (July 1990): 351-70.

Owen, David. *In Sickness and In Power: Illness in Heads of Government During the Last 100 Years*. London: Methuen, 2008.

Paris, Timothy J. *Britain, the Hashemites, and Arab Rule, 1920–1925: The Sherifian Solution*. London: Frank Cass, 2003.

Pearce, Malcolm and Geoffrey Stewart. *British Political History: 1867–1990*. London: Routledge, 1992.

Pearson, Geoffrey. *Seize the Day: Lester B. Pearson and Crisis Diplomacy*. Ottawa: Carleton University Press, 1993.

Pearson, Lester. "A New Kind of Peace Force." *Maclean's* May 2, 1964.

———. *Mike: The Memoirs of the Rt. Hon. Lester B. Pearson, Volume 1, 1897–1948*. Toronto: University of Toronto Press, 1972.

———. *Mike: The Memoirs of the Rt. Hon. Lester B. Pearson, Volume 2, 1948–1957*. John A. Munro and Alex I. Inglis, eds. Toronto: University of Toronto Press, 1973.

——. *Mike: The Memoirs of the Rt. Hon. Lester B. Pearson, Volume 3, 1957–1968*. John A. Munro and Alex I. Inglis, eds. Toronto: University of Toronto Press, 1975.

——. [as "Scrutator"]. "The Political Aspects of the Disarmament Conference." *Canadian Defence Quarterly* 9, no. 2. (January 1932): 153-84.

——. *Words and Occasions*. Toronto: University of Toronto Press, 1970.

Peres, Shimon. "The Road to Sevres: Franco-Israeli Strategic Cooperation." In *The Suez-Sinai Crisis: Retrospective and Reappraisal*, edited by Selwyn Ilan Troen and Moshe Shemesh, 140-149. London: Frank Cass, 1990.

Petrie, Charles. *The Life and Letters of Sir Austen Chamberlain, Volume 2*. London: Cassell, 1939.

Pickersgill, Jack. *My Years with Louis St. Laurent: A Political Memoir*. Toronto: University of Toronto Press, 1975.

Pope, Joseph, ed. *Correspondence of Sir John Macdonald*. Toronto: Doubleday, Page, 1921.

Porter, Andrew, ed. *The Oxford History of the British Empire, Volume 3: The Nineteenth Century*. Oxford: Oxford University Press, 1999.

Porter, Bernard. *The Lion's Share: A Short History of British Imperialism 1850–2004*. New York: Longman, 2004.

Pugliese, David. "Nobel Fever." *Saturday Night*. May 1997.

Reid, Escott. *On Duty: A Canadian at the Making of the United Nations, 1945–1946*. Toronto: McClelland and Stewart, 1983.

——. *Time of Fear and Hope: The Making of the North Atlantic Treaty 1947–1949*. Toronto: McClelland and Stewart, 1977.

Reville, Douglas F. *History of the County of Brant*. Brantford, ON: Brant Historical Society, 1920.

Rhodes James, Robert. *Eden*. London: Weidenfeld and Nicolson, 1986.

Richler, Noah. *What We Talk About When We Talk About War*. Fredericton, NB: Goose Lane Editions, 2012.

Robertson, Heather. *More Than a Rose: Prime Ministers, Wives and Other Women*. Toronto: Seal Books, 1991.

Robertson, Terence. *Crisis: The Inside Story of the Suez Conspiracy*. Toronto: McClelland and Stewart, 1964.

Rosner, Gabriella. *The United Nations Emergency Force*. New York: Columbia University Press, 1963.

Sadat, Anwar. *In Search of Identity: An Autobiography*. New York: Harper & Row, 1978.

——. *Revolt on the Nile*. London: Allan Wingate, 1957.

Sarty, Leigh E. "The Limits of Internationalism: Canada and the Soviet Blockade of Berlin, 1948–1949." In *Nearly Neighbours: Canada and the Soviet Union from Cold War to Détente and Beyond*, edited by J.L. Black and Norman Hillmer, 56-73. Kingston, ON: Ronald P. Frye & Co., 1989.

Schlesinger, Stephen. *Act of Creation: The Founding of the United* Nations. Cambridge, MA: Westview Press, 2003.

Semple, Neil. *The Lord's Dominion: The History of Canadian Methodism*. Montreal: McGill-Queen's University Press, 1996.

Shuckburgh, Evelyn. *Descent to Suez: Foreign Office Diaries 1951–1956*. London: W.W. Norton, 1986.

Skelton, Oscar Douglas. *Life and Letters of Wilfrid Laurier, Volume 2.* Toronto: Oxford University Press, 1921.

Smith, Charles D. *Palestine and the Arab-Israeli Conflict.* Boston: Bedford-St. Martin's, 2010.

Smith, Denis. *Rogue Tory: The Life and Legend of John G. Diefenbaker.* Toronto: MacFarlane Walter and Ross, 1995.

Smith, Norman. "Pearson, People, and Press." *International Journal* 29, No. 1 (Winter 1973-74): 5-23.

Smith, Simon C., ed. *Reassessing Suez 1956: New Perspectives on the Crisis and Its Aftermath.* Aldershot: Ashgate, 2008.

Spry, Graham. "Canada, the United Nations Emergency Force, and the Commonwealth." *International Affairs* 33, no. 3 (July 1957): 289-300.

Stairs, Denis. *The Diplomacy of Constraint: Canada, the Korean War and the United States.* Toronto: University of Toronto Press, 1974.

Stein, Leonard. *The Balfour Declaration.* New York: Simon and Schuster, 1961.

Stephens, Robert. *Nasser: A Political Biography.* London: Allen Lane 1971.

Stursberg, Peter. *Lester Pearson and the American Dilemma.* Toronto: Doubleday, 1980.

Tauber, Eliezer. *Personal Policy Making: Canada's Role in the Adoption of the Palestine Partition Resolution.* Westport, CT: Greenwood Press, 2002.

Thompson, John Herd with Allen Seager. *Canada 1922-1939: Decades of Discord.* Toronto: McClelland and Stewart, 1985.

Thomson, Dale C. *Louis St. Laurent: Canadian.* Toronto: Macmillan, 1967.

Thornhill, Michael T. *Road to Suez: The Battle of the Canal Zone.* N.P.: Sutton, 2006.

Thorpe, D.R. *Eden: The Life and Times of Anthony Eden, First Earl of Avon, 1897-1977.* London: Pimlico, 2003.

——. *Selwyn Lloyd.* London: Jonathan Cape, 1989.

Truman, Harry S. *Years of Trial and Hope.* Garden City, NY: Doubleday & Co., 1956.

Veatch, Richard. *Canada and the League of Nations.* Toronto: University of Toronto Press, 1975.

Verrier, Anthony. *Through the Looking Glass: British Foreign Policy in an Age of Illusions.* New York: W.W. Norton, 1983.

Walters, F.P. *A History of the League of Nations.* Oxford: Oxford University Press, 1952.

Wesley, John. *The Works of the Reverend John Wesley,* Vol. 3. London: T. Mason & G. Lane, 1840.

Wigley, Philip G. *Canada and the Transition to Commonwealth: British-Canadian Relations 1917-1926.* Cambridge: Cambridge University Press, 1977.

Williams, Philip M., ed. *The Diary of Hugh Gaitskell 1945-1956.* London: Jonathan Cape, 1983.

Wilson, A.N. *Our Times.* London: Hutchison, 2008.

Wright, Peter. *Spy Catcher: The Candid Autobiography of a Senior Intelligence Officer.* Toronto: Stoddart, 1987.

Index